FIFTY YEARS OF TELEVISION

TV GUIDE

FIFTY YE

TELEV

INTRODUCTION by MARY TYLER MOORE

PREFACE BY STEVEN REDDICLIFFE

 A MELCHER MEDIA BOOK

ARS
OF
ISION

AFTERWORD by WILLIAM SHATNER

TEXT BY MARK LASSWELL

 CROWN PUBLISHERS NEW YORK

LOCAL PROGRAM LISTINGS • Week of March 26–April 1

MLA

TV GUIDE

®

15¢

Gleason: TV's No. 1 Good Time Charlie

TOOTS

COVER:
BY WILLIAM KAHN,
MARCH 26, 1954

Imagine a perfect week of television, seven days and nights of your all-time favorite shows. Cartoons and subversive silliness on sleepy Saturday mornings, hopping dance shows on idle weekend afternoons, surprising variety on Sunday nights, indelible dramas and endlessly clever comedies—every night a celebration of creativity, every hour a treasure.

And that's what this book is all about—out of 50 years of television, one ideal week of nothing but shows America loved, the lineup of all lineups.

As Jimmie Dodd used to say on *Mickey Mouse Club*: Roll call! Bugs and Elmer. Rocky and Bullwinkle. Bart and Homer. Ed and the Beatles. Mulder and Scully. Dave and Hugh and Barbara and Tom and Jane and Bryant and Katie and Matt. Winfrey and Springer. (Together? Never!) Oscar and Felix. Andy and Opie. 86 and 99. Rob and Laura. Ralph and Alice. Tony and Carmela. Ozzie and…Ozzy(!). Johnny, then Dave.

For 50 years, the TV GUIDE week—the TV week for millions of us—has started with Saturday. And it does here: Pee-wee and Howdy Doody cut up while one Wile E. Coyote plotted against an even wilier Road Runner. Hours later, Paladin and Dillon took on the wild West, and *All in the Family* and *The Mary Tyler Moore Show* took on modern life. *Your Show of Shows* and *Saturday Night Live* took on just about everything—and won.

On Sunday, we started with the stopwatch on *60 Minutes*, and we met the Beatles. Bart Simpson reminded all of us not to have a cow (man). *The X-Files* looked for an elusive truth, and Alfred Hitchcock told us nothing was what it seemed.

And then it was off to work (but not before turning on *Today*) or school (but not before checking in with *Romper Room*) or the living room, where kids spent smart sessions on *Sesame Street* and in *Mister Rogers' Neighborhood*. The rest of us devoted stolen hours to watching the world turn in serial style (*General Hospital*, *All My Children*) or smart-person-with-a-microphone mode (*Donahue*, *Oprah*).

In times of national tragedy (the assassination of President John F. Kennedy), television explained and comforted. In times of national triumph (a man on the Moon!), television gave us a chance to see it live and celebrate. A nation saw *Roots*, and we thought about our country—and ourselves—in an entirely different way.

And on countless other occasions, in prime time, television had us laughing with Bill Cosby and Carol Burnett and Carrie Bradshaw, singing with Elvis and wanting to be a millionaire. We had to know who shot J.R., who killed Laura Palmer, who Danno was gonna book, who was gonna win Game 7. We had to see who'd be voted off the island. We had to see if Buffy survived. We had to know if anyone could survive Tony Soprano.

Here's Johnny. Here's Lucy. Here's Jerry never getting to eat in the Chinese restaurant (not that there's anything wrong with that).

And here, as Rod Serling said so memorably in a different time and a different zone, is a dimension of imagination.

—STEVEN REDDICLIFFE,
EDITOR-IN-CHIEF, TV GUIDE

TABLE OF CONTENTS

8 INTRODUCTION
by MARY TYLER MOORE

10 WEEKENDS

56 DAYTIME

66 COVERS OF THE '50S

74 "WHAT WE ALL CAN DO TO CHANGE TV"
by OPRAH WINFREY

90 EVENINGS

98 "A FORCE THAT HAS CHANGED
THE POLITICAL SCENE"
by JOHN F. KENNEDY

100 PRIME TIME

128 COVERS OF THE '60S

138 "ROOTS REMEMBERED"
by ALEX HALEY

178 COVERS OF THE '70S

196 "M*A*S*H WAS ONE OF A KIND"
by ALISTAIR COOKE

198 COVERS OF THE '80S

206 "WHY I CONSIDER CAGNEY & LACEY THE BEST SHOW ON TELEVISION"
by GLORIA STEINEM

218 COVERS OF THE '90S

236 "IS SEINFELD THE BEST COMEDY EVER?"
by JAY McINERNEY

240 LATE NIGHT

252 AFTERWORD
by WILLIAM SHATNER

254 THE BEST OF TELEVISION ACCORDING TO TV GUIDE

256 INDEX OF COVERS

When Carl Reiner, the very funny creator of *The Dick Van Dyke Show*, decided to put my character, Laura Petrie, in capri pants in 1961 and give her the words for a real spat or two with her sexy husband, it was considered shocking. Today on MTV, the Osbournes go 12 rounds with gloves off every (*bleep*ing) week, and they're considered the Ozzie and Harriet of a new generation.

Things certainly have changed.

But one thing hasn't. TV still holds a very special place in our lives. Since its earliest days, television's strength has been the richness and breadth of its storytelling. Getting those stories out there hasn't always been easy, however. David Sarnoff's notion to use broadcasting for entertainment purposes was waved off; Bill Paley's concept for his broadcast network was folly; Michael Fuchs's premium pay-television channel, HBO, was sure to fail; Ted Turner's CNN was ridiculed as the "Chicken Noodle Network."

But the naysayers didn't stop these pioneers. People of vision, passion and talent, they had the confidence to face down the critics and persevere. We owe television to them and to other groundbreakers like *Sesame Street*'s Joan Ganz Cooney, MTV's Bob Pittman, Nickelodeon and Nick at Nite's Geraldine Laybourne, TV newsmen Fred Friendly and Don Hewitt, Fox's Barry Diller and, I must say, Grant Tinker, who co-founded with me MTM Enterprises as a writers' company in 1970. These risk takers were willing to go the distance in the service of their "big idea." They really thought "outside the box."

Television isn't simply about those of us in front of the camera fortunate enough to have found our way into the hearts of the viewing public. TV is about myriad contributors—engineers, businesspeople, laborers, producers, writers, directors and crews—who come together to make magic happen, at least sometimes.

The thing that is so fascinating and frustrating and wonderful about TV is that nobody really knows when that magic will strike. ABC passed on a family comedy, *The Cosby Show*, in 1984 but green-lighted a police musical called *Cop Rock* in 1990. Both were from highly regarded creators (Bill Cosby and Steven Bochco, respectively), and both were considered risky at the time. Unfortunately for ABC, the comedy made our hearts sing for eight seasons (on NBC), while the musical went silent in 12 weeks. No one recognizes the next big thing, except in hindsight.

Journalist Edward R. Murrow once said that television "will broadcast filth or inspiration with equal facility and will speak the truth as loudly as the falsehood. It is, in sum, no more or less than the people who use it." Those of us who have spent our lives making television have the responsibility of finding a balance—balance that respects our diverse sensibilities, that shows awareness of our audiences and that helps viewers find their way to truth. People often ask me why I think *The Mary Tyler Moore Show* is so evergreen. I think it's because we found that sweet spot.

TV GUIDE has walked beside us on most of TV's 50-plus-year journey of creative, business and technical exploration. Along the way, we have witnessed as viewers things that have engaged, enlightened and enraged us. Sharing our stories on that screen, we have seen our strengths, our flaws and our hopes for a better world. We have shed some tears and had some wonderful laughs. Altogether, that's not too shabby.

Over the last half century, television has been both a wake-up call and a comfort to audiences. It has challenged us to be the best we can be, and, like a certain young career woman I knew years ago, it has let us know that we just might make it after all.

—MARY TYLER MOORE

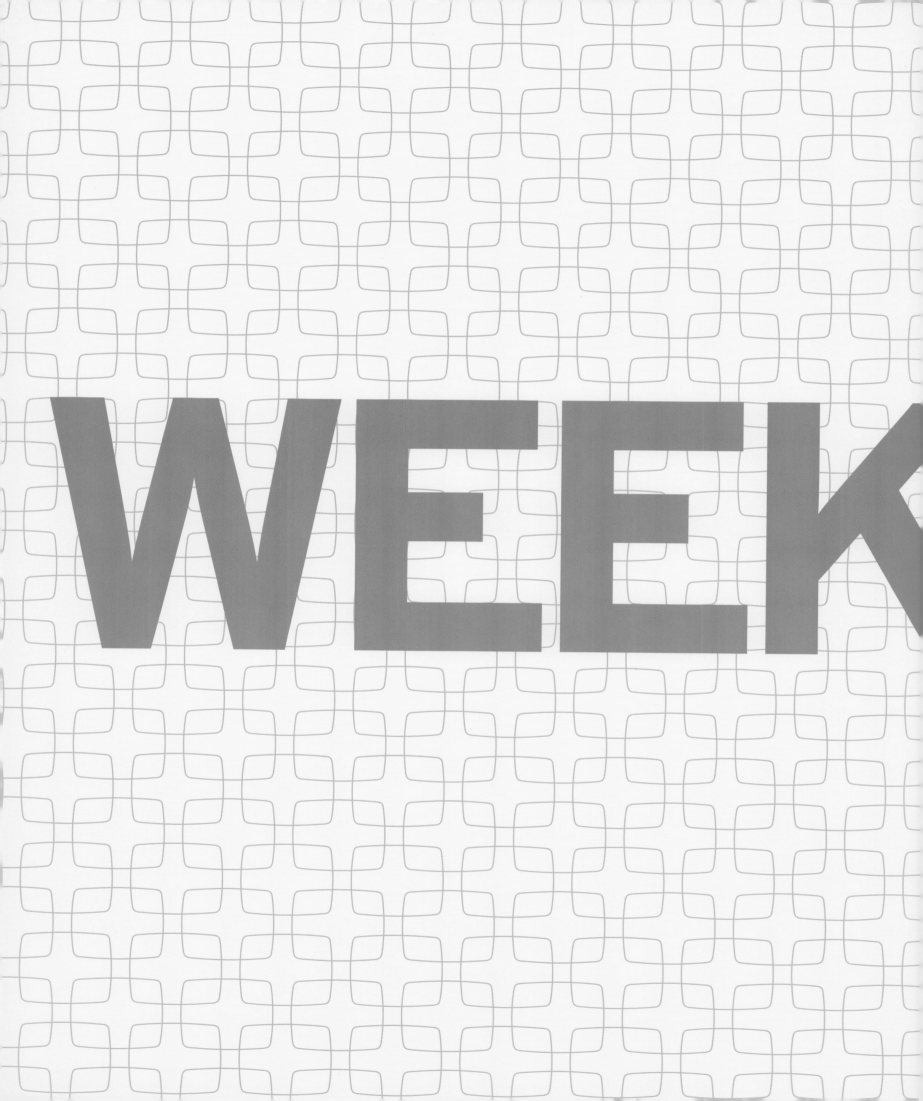

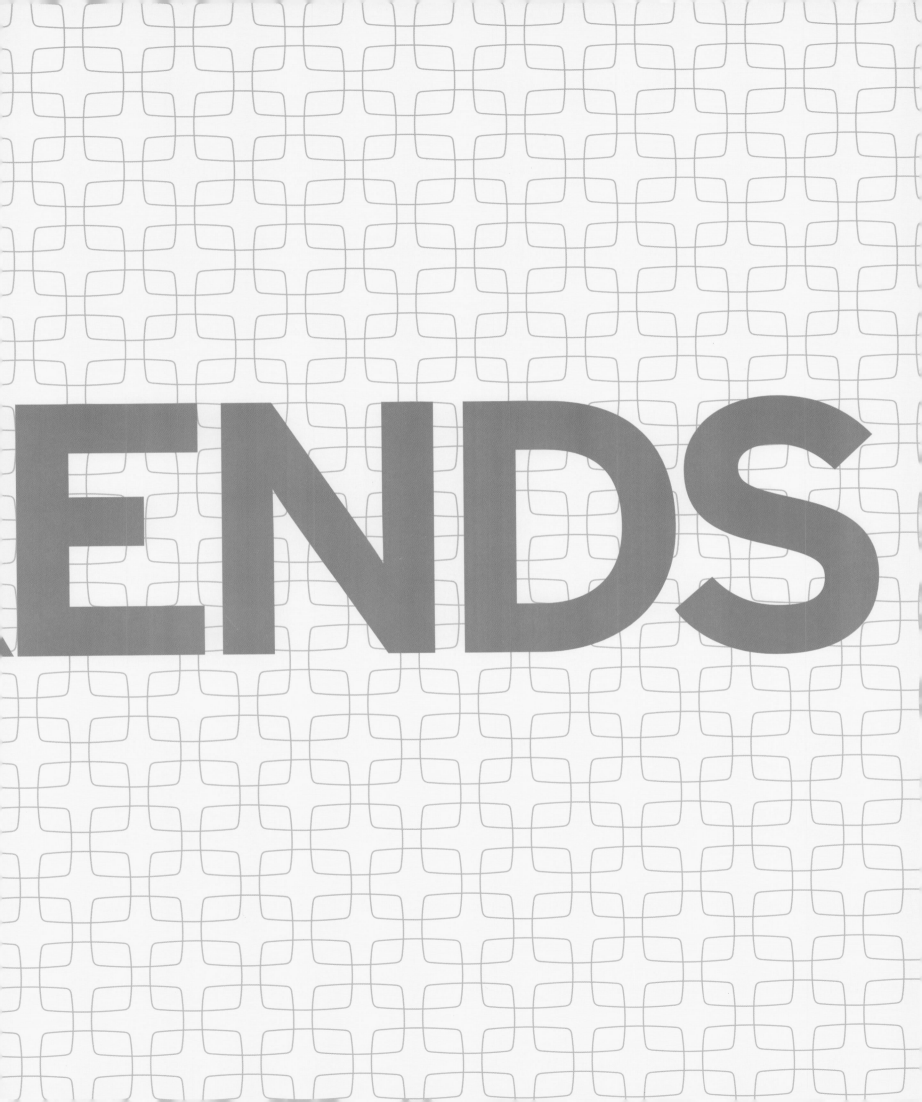

WARNER BROS. CARTOONS
Bugs Bunny, Elmer Fudd; Wile E. Coyote, Road Runner.
ABC, 1960–68, 1971–75 and 1985–2000; CBS, 1966–73
and 1975–85; NBC, 1978–82; Nickelodeon, 1988–99;
Fox, 1992–94; WB, 1995–98; Cartoon Network, 2000–

Though they got their start in the 1930s as movie-matinee fodder, Warner Bros. cartoons—flying under the *Looney Tunes* and *Merrie Melodies* banners—will be forever cherished as giddy Saturday-morning TV treats for anyone who happened to be in the room when Bugs Bunny, Daffy Duck, Road Runner and Co. romped into view. The cartoons were the "world's greatest single source of animated dementia," said TV GUIDE in 1985, on the occasion of a Warner Bros. animation exhibition at the Museum of Modern Art in New York City, "fast and eternally disrespectful of authority and privilege. They are about chase, pursuit and retribution—about perennial forms of passion, in short, from the helpless romanticism of Pepé Le Pew to the voracious vainglory of the eternally thwarted Coyote." Towering over the crowd of characters, not only because of his long ears, was Bugs, whom director Chuck Jones once said he imagined as "a sort of male Dorothy Parkerish D'Artagnan." Bugs starred, along with the indefatigable Elmer Fudd, in the opera send-up "What's Opera, Doc?" (1957), considered by many to be the ultimate Warner Bros. achievement, though a strong contender for that title was Daffy's epic battle with his animators in "Duck Amuck" (1953). Jones directed both, but plenty of credit for the Warner oeuvre also went to the murderers' row of animation stalwarts who brought the creations to life: Tex Avery, Friz Freleng, Bob Clampett and Bob McKimson. And where would any of them have been without the miraculous vocal talents of Mel Blanc? Thanks to the Warner Bros. creative pool, TV GUIDE said, "these cartoons are as funny, and as enduring, as the film comedy of Chaplin and Keaton, Capra and Sturges."

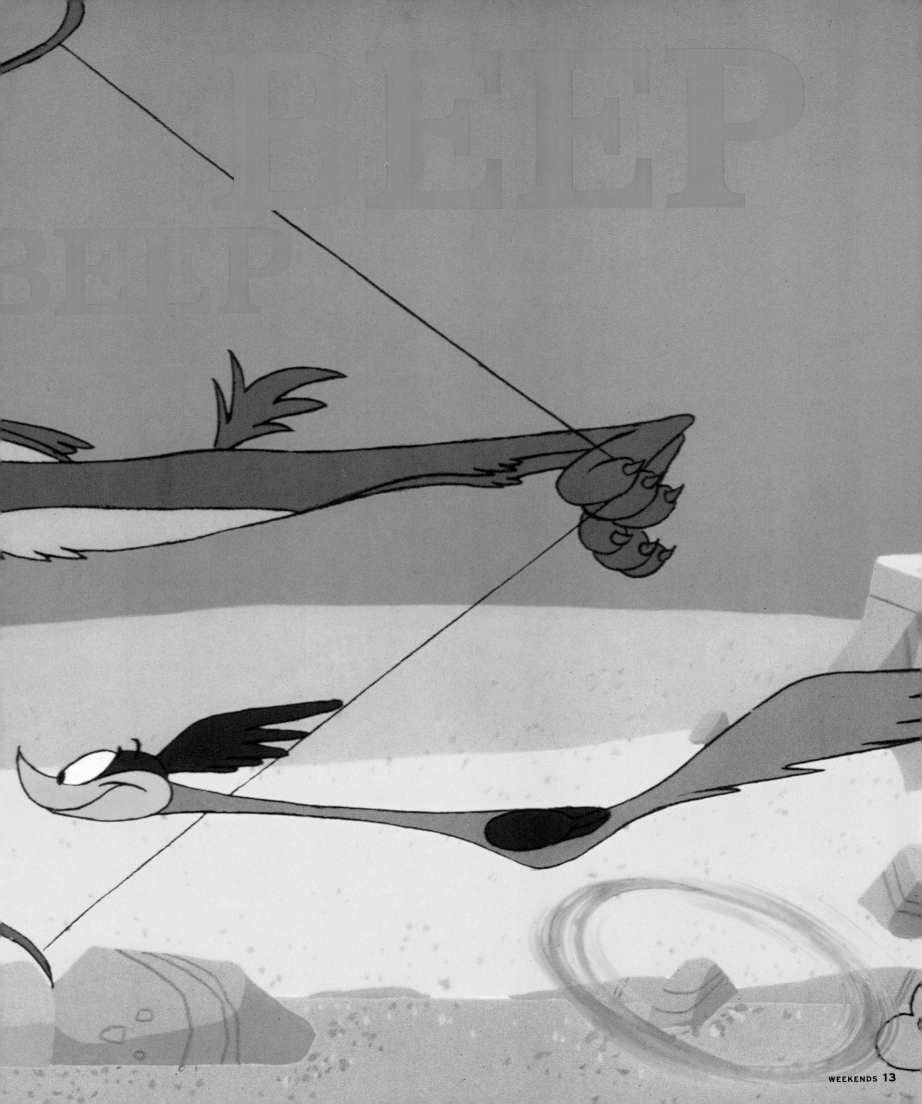

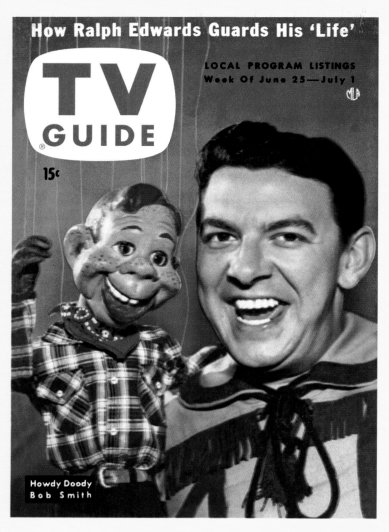

HOWDY DOODY
NBC, 1947–60
COVER: **PHOTOGRAPHER UNKNOWN, JUNE 25, 1954**

TV journalist and pop-culture aficionado Jeff Greenfield advanced this theory in TV GUIDE in 1983: "*Howdy Doody* represents one of the most authentically subversive TV shows in American history." It sowed the seeds of '60s rebellion, he said, with kids and fanciful characters playing the insurgent heroes of Doodyville, and grown-ups either the establishment bad guys (Mayor Phineas T. Bluster) or the butts of practical jokes (host Buffalo Bob). Seltzer-spraying Clarabell the Clown, Greenfield wrote, was "the very first yippie." All this would have been news to Buffalo Bob, aka Bob Smith. During the show's prime, he was busy defending himself against charges of excessive silliness. "We're entertainers," Smith told TV GUIDE in 1954. "And have *you* ever watched a 3-year-old play?"

Pee-wee Herman (Paul Reubens). CBS, 1986–91

One of the most perverse outcomes of Paul Reubens's 1991 arrest for indecent exposure
was the way it tainted memories of his deliriously creative *Pee-wee's Playhouse*. In the show,
which won 22 Emmys and at its peak drew almost a third of its 9.3 million viewers from
adults over 18, the sweet-natured devil Pee-wee Herman manically presided over a surreal
romper room populated by talking objects (Globey! Chairry!) and endearingly off-kilter
characters, such as Cowboy Curtis (future movie star Laurence Fishburne). As TV GUIDE
recalled in 1996, "Pee-wee managed to make a rare peace with the wild side of childhood."

DENNIS THE MENACE
**Dennis Mitchell (Jay North).
CBS, 1959–63**
COVER: BY RICHARD R. HEWETT,
OCTOBER 24, 1959

Jay North is "sweet, with electricity," cartoonist
Hank Ketcham told TV GUIDE in 1959, describing
the kid starring in the TV version of his comic-
strip creation. Dennis was a menace, of course,
only to grown-ups. The well-intentioned boy had
a special knack for exasperating them—
especially finicky next-door neighbor Mr. Wilson.
(Joseph Kearns, who died during the third
season's filming, was replaced by Gale Gordon.)
But kids loved Dennis, and the show became a
Sunday-night staple on CBS for four years,
making good on TV GUIDE's prediction in 1960
that children would commandeer television sets
to watch it. The magazine also had a warning for
adults: "Be prepared to like the show yourself."

LASSIE
Timmy (Jon Provost), Lassie. CBS, 1954–71; syndication, 1971–74
COVER: BY GARRETT-HOWARD, JULY 7, 1956

"With a boy and his dog," executive producer Sherman Harris told TV GUIDE in 1959, "*how* can you miss?" Indeed, the kid-plus-canine formula was such a fail-safe Sunday-night hit after its debut in 1954 that viewers weren't fazed three years later when the original boy (Jeff, played by Tommy Rettig) was jettisoned along with his whole family because Rettig got too old. Lassie found a new best friend in Timmy (Jon Provost). Audiences tuned in, after all, to see Lassie fight crime, prevent disasters and nurse the injured. The premise prospered until 1974, when *Lassie* rolled over and played dead (and she *was* only playing: *The New Lassie* premiered in 1989).

Text inside the magazine cover image:
$150 A Week May Be Awaiting You
— See Page 23
TV GUIDE
LOCAL PROGRAM LISTINGS WEEK OF JULY 7–13
15c
Lassie

ALL IN THE FAMILY

Edith Bunker (Jean Stapleton), Archie Bunker (Carroll O'Connor). CBS, 1971–79

COVER: BY GENE TRINDL, MAY 29, 1971

Producer Norman Lear's comedy had been on the air for a month, and, struggling in the ratings, its future did not appear bright. Certainly, the show looked unexceptional: *All in the Family*'s simple set and small cast would have seemed right at home in a '50s TV lineup. It was what Archie (Carroll O'Connor), Edith (Jean Stapleton), Gloria (Sally Struthers) and Mike "Meathead" Stivic (Rob Reiner) were *saying* that blew the doors off conventional comedy. As TV GUIDE recognized in 1971, "*All in the Family* is...a complete breakthrough—one that opens up a whole new world for television and has already made the old world seem so dated that we very much doubt that any new program, from here on in, will ever be quite the same again." It wasn't just that, for the first time, racism, abortion, homosexuality, birth control and other hot-button issues were made ripe for one-liners. What established a riveting new level of reality in the format were the hilarious, often poignant struggles of four people grappling with their feelings about one another and the tumultuous world outside the Bunker living room at 704 Hauser Street in Queens, New York. The characters were types, certainly—the blue-collar bigot versus the idealistic liberal—but types never seen on TV, and never invested with the imagination that O'Connor and Reiner brought to them. Edith's foggy optimism and Gloria's caught-in-the-middle confusion were vital elements, but it was the firefighting between Archie, low on intellectual ammunition but immovable, and the implacable Meathead that permanently altered television and the way it measured creative achievement.

"WHEN I FIRST SAW THE SCRIPT FOR ALL IN THE FAMILY,

I thought, 'Well, this is certainly beyond anything that anybody's ever done in television.' I mean, not just in subject matter and how controversial and edgy it was, but in the quality of the writing, which was so far superior to anything that I had seen anywhere. But never in my wildest dreams did I think it was going to go past 13 weeks because it was, as we say in the parlance of stand-up comics, too hip for the room. And that was fine, too, because we just wanted to be part of something special and different and groundbreaking.

"There wasn't one guiding person for the show, but Norman Lear and Carroll O'Connor set a tone that allowed all of the cast members to contribute creatively. We were asked to be part of the process, and we contributed a tremendous amount to the scripts and on our feet and in rehearsal. Norman liked to stir things up and force us to dig deeper and try harder, and Carroll wanted to be as realistic and honest as possible. So you had two very, very strong-willed men fighting to make the show better, and a lot of times I was caught between them. I had respect and admiration and love for both of them, and it was tough for me at times, but it always was to make a better show—it was never a personal thing. It wasn't an easy process, but it was a great creative experience.

"I don't think *All in the Family* changed public opinion on any issues, but I think it certainly stimulated the dialogue. When you think about where we've come as a country, in terms of race relations, we've come a long, long way. Obviously, the civil-rights movement, Martin Luther King Jr., Bobby Kennedy and people like that did the heavy lifting, but we certainly played a role in shining a light on bigotry and allowing a discussion to happen.

"The last episode was my favorite. It wasn't the funniest or the best or anything like that, but it was just so emotional, and it was one of those moments where your life and your character converge. When I said goodbye to Archie, I was saying goodbye to Carroll, and I didn't have to act. It was just very, very emotional, and all the feelings were right there.... The one scene that I remember—a goofy, nutty scene that wasn't a meaningful scene in any way—was when Archie lectures me on how to put on socks and shoes. Everybody talks to me about that scene. Everybody says that they now think about how they put on their socks and shoes because of that scene."

—ROB REINER

THE MARY TYLER MOORE SHOW
Clockwise from above: Rhoda Morgenstern (Valerie Harper), Mary Richards (Moore); Ted Baxter (Ted Knight), Lou Grant (Ed Asner); Baxter, Georgette Franklin (Georgia Engel), Richards, Sue Ann Nivens (Betty White), Grant, Murray Slaughter (Gavin MacLeod). CBS, 1970–77
COVER: BY PETER KREDENSER, MARCH 19, 1977

"You know what? You've got spunk," TV news producer Lou Grant tells his beaming new associate producer, Mary Richards. "I hate spunk." It was a priceless moment—occurring in the first season of *The Mary Tyler Moore Show*—but it was hardly the last. The show was a benchmark for what could be achieved in the genre. With its two distinct comedy platforms, Mary's apartment and her office, *MTM* was an apt metaphor for the internal battle that many young women in the '70s faced as they entered the workforce. At home, where the adorably single and striving Mary's neighbors were forever dropping in (Valerie Harper and Cloris Leachman landed their own shows as a result of their work here), cooking and entertaining were sure to end badly. In one episode, Mary managed to get Johnny Carson to show up for a party only to have the power go out. Meanwhile, at work the good-hearted Mary fought to keep her innate niceness from sabotaging her ambition. Of course, that was all much harder when surrounded by male coworkers like cranky-affectionate Mr. Grant (Ed Asner), sensible yet smoldering newswriter Murray Slaughter (Gavin MacLeod) and preening fathead anchorman Ted Baxter (Ted Knight). However, like the line from the theme song, "Love Is All Around," we always knew that lovable Mary was "going to make it after all." TV GUIDE championed the show a few months into its first season, lauding the supporting actors but adding: "The show is still Miss Moore's. We admit to a slight prejudice. We think she's wonderful." So did America, and for seven years—until the whole gang shuffled off stage in its famous group hug—love was indeed all around.

"MY MANAGER SAID TO ME, 'WOULD YOU LIKE TO DO TELEVISION?'

I said, 'Yeah, I think so.' I was married and had kids and I wanted to be home, not on the road. So he put me together with a couple of writers from *The Mary Tyler Moore Show*, and we kicked around some ideas. They said, 'Bob—he's like a listener, you know? He listens to people. He reacts to people. Let's try to find a profession where somebody listens. What about a psychiatrist?'

"I had two stipulations: One was I didn't want to be a psychiatrist—I wanted to be a psychologist. I felt that psychiatrists dealt with more deeply disturbed people, and I didn't want to be making fun of schizophrenics or the John Nashes of the world. And the other one was that I didn't want to have kids. They asked, 'Why not?' And I said, 'Because I don't like those shows where Daddy is a dolt and keeps getting in trouble and the precocious kids and the wife get him out of it. "Look at the fix Daddy's gotten himself into." ' I said, 'That really isn't the kind of show I want to do.' And when I saw the first script, it felt very comfortable. I thought, 'I can play that guy because I know him.' That's the main reason, I think, that shows with former stand-ups work. The performer knows himself better than anybody else does.

"But we weren't completely sure about whether a psychologist was a viable occupation for a comedy. There was still a kind of feeling in this country that, as Samuel Goldwyn said, 'Anybody who goes to see a psychiatrist ought to have his head examined.' There was still a sentiment that you don't go to someone and spill out all your problems. You just work them out yourself. So we didn't know if it was going to work.

"[Fans] confused the role with me. Sometimes I would come into a city, and there'd be a message from someone saying they're having a problem and would I please return their call. And I had to explain to them that it was just a role I played on television. I wasn't qualified to solve their problems. [Today when people come up to me,] the men think that they were in the service with me, and the women think I was their first husband."

—BOB NEWHART

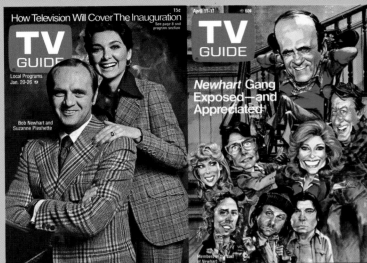

THE BOB NEWHART SHOW
Mr. Stevens (Neil Flanagan), Bob Hartley (Newhart). CBS, 1972–78
COVERS: BY SHERMAN WEISBURD, JANUARY 20, 1973. BY BRUCE STARK, APRIL 11, 1987

A gloomy Bob Newhart told TV GUIDE in 1962, at the end of what turned out to be only one season of a variety series called *The Bob Newhart Show*, that even if he stayed in television, he'd never have the ratings of, say, a Bob Hope. But at least he'd made the attempt: "If you're a pitcher," he said, "you'd better pitch in the major leagues." A decade later, he resurfaced. The show had the same name, but this time it was an inspired comedy that had the bright idea to cast the low-key performer as a psychologist. Bob Hartley did a fine job counseling his wacko clientele (though real progress was tough with that epic paranoid Elliot Carlin, memorably played by Jack Riley). But back home in his Chicago high-rise apartment, it was his wife, Emily (Suzanne Pleshette), who held the tighter grip on reality and sometimes seemed to think Bob was certifiable. The show was a hit throughout much of the '70s. Then the comedian amazed the television industry by launching *Newhart*, about an inn owner in Vermont, which became a hit of the '80s. Two series, two home runs: Those are big-league, hall-of-fame numbers anyone can appreciate.

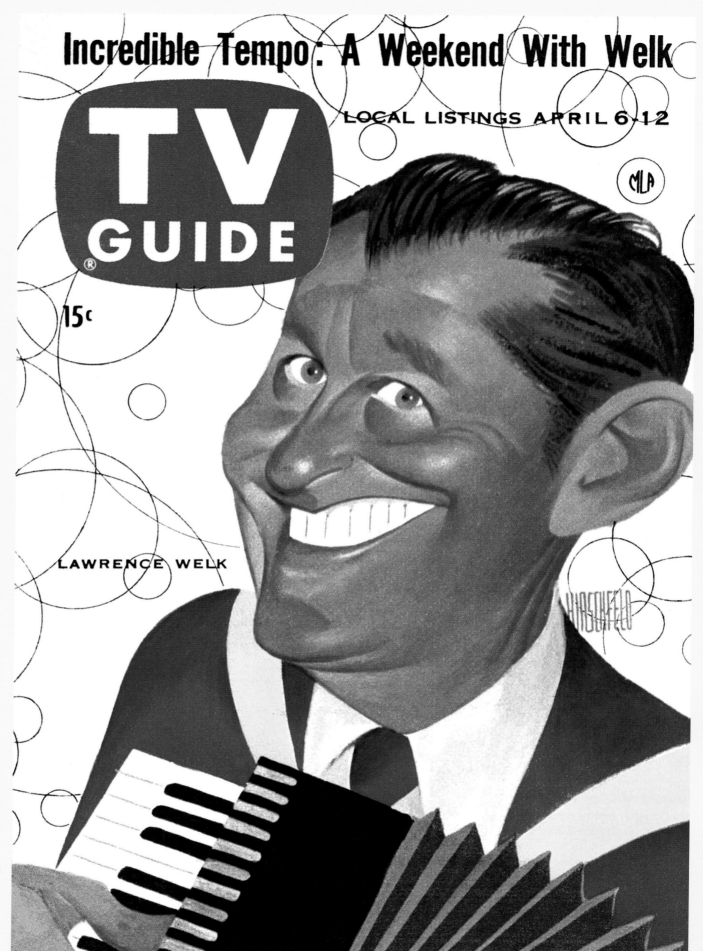

THE LAWRENCE WELK SHOW
ABC, 1955–71;
syndication, 1971–82
COVER: BY AL HIRSCHFELD,
APRIL 6, 1957

Could you blame TV GUIDE for missing the boat on *The Lawrence Welk Show*? When the program surfaced as a summer replacement series in 1955, the magazine called the accordion-playing bandleader with the heavy German accent "rather stiff and ill at ease"—which was true. It also said the show lacked "sparkle and verve"—true again. Finally, the magazine declared that it was nothing more than "a pleasant and relaxed hour of viewing"—right again, and more than enough, apparently, for America, or at least rockphobic America, who adored Welk's "champagne music." For nearly three decades, you could find Welk and his well-scrubbed musicians performing traditional popular fare, to the accompaniment of a gently puffing bubble machine. A-one, and a-two...

AMERICAN BANDSTAND
Dick Clark. ABC, 1957–87; syndication, 1987–88
COVER: BY ROBERT GIUSTI, DECEMBER 30, 1978

The World's Oldest Living Teenager, Dick Clark, explained the secret of the world's longest-running sock hop, *American Bandstand*, to TV GUIDE in 1970: "People-watching! You just can't beat it! It's been going on since folks just sat in the railroad station. All it needs is a personality to head it up who will subjugate himself to the audience, and that's me." Certainly, one attraction was the astonishing array of music stars lip-synching their latest hit—everyone from the Doors, Buddy Holly and Stevie Wonder to Public Image Ltd., Blondie and the Beastie Boys performed on the show. But it was teenagers' insatiable urge to study one another's personal style with an anthropological intensity—while the benign chaperon Clark looked on—that made *Bandstand* classic viewing for more than 30 years.

How Fame Affected Berle, Gleason, Caesar
—See Page 28

TV GUIDE

LOCAL PROGRAM LISTINGS
WEEK OF NOVEMBER 10-16

15¢

Loretta Young

THE LORETTA YOUNG SHOW
NBC, 1953–61
COVER: **BY ELMER HOLLOWAY, NOVEMBER 10, 1956**

In the early 1950s, actress Loretta Young broke ranks with the movie industry and plunged right in to the nascent medium of television, producing and starring in her own dramatic anthology series. Rather than committing the career suicide predicted for her, Young flourished. She swept in to introduce each show dressed in a sumptuous designer dress (available in stores the following week for a not-inexpensive $200 to $600) and starred in more than half of the show's 300 inspiring stories, portraying a housewife one night, perhaps, and a queen the next. A devout Catholic, Young concluded the evening by summing up the episode's message with a poem or Bible passage. "I don't miss movies one bit," she said in a 1958 TV GUIDE cover story (one of 11 featuring her). Having grown up in the Hollywood studio system, she was delighted to be in charge of her own show, reaping its profits, supervising the scripts and exercising the sort of career control that her movie peers could only dream of.

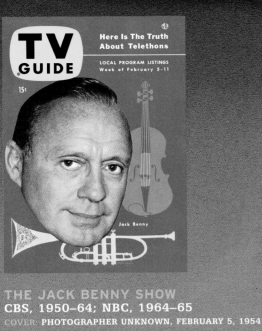

THE JACK BENNY SHOW
CBS, 1950–64; NBC, 1964–65
COVER: PHOTOGRAPHER UNKNOWN, FEBRUARY 5, 1954

Jack Benny was such a familiar and popular comedian after 18 years on the radio that when he moved to the new medium of television in 1950, he didn't need a specific format—or even a regular weekly schedule—to immediately claim a prominent place in the ratings. All that was required was his well-loved persona as a violin-mangling, perennial 39-year-old with easily bruised feelings ("Well!") and a less easily opened wallet. Airing sporadically, and later biweekly, on Sundays through-out the '50s, *The Jack Benny Show* was a bona fide variety show on some nights (the remarkable guest list included Frank Sinatra, Marilyn Monroe and Humphrey Bogart) and a single-sketch, quasi-situation comedy on others. That sort of flexibility "could cement his career in TV another 20 years," TV GUIDE said in 1954, "so long as the old master of the dou-ble take and perfect comedy timing retains that 39-year-old youthfulness." As it happened, he would stay on the air another 11 years, finally going weekly in 1960. Benny was in reality an adept violinist, but he didn't need to reveal that as a performer—his music was in his comedy.

YOUR SHOW OF SHOWS

Sid Caesar, Imogene Coca. NBC, 1950–54
COVERS: BY PHILIPPE HALSMAN, JANUARY 25, 1958, AND FEBRUARY 19, 1955

Of all the ambitious endeavors undertaken when television was broadcast live with no margin for error, *Your Show of Shows* was perhaps the most breathtaking of all. For 90 minutes every Saturday night, extravagantly gifted comedians Sid Caesar and Imogene Coca led a small army of actors, singers, dancers and guest stars into action—supported by such comedy writers as Woody Allen, Mel Brooks, Larry Gelbart and Neil Simon. The array of entertainment offered was daunting. In a nod to highbrow culture, *Your Show of Shows* would feature grand opera, ballet and Broadway-worthy production numbers. But the centerpiece, and what *Your Show of Shows* would be remembered for, was its comedy—particularly Caesar's staggering repertoire of double-talking foreigners, bogus authorities on any subject, henpecked husbands and almost any other characters the writers dreamed up. Caesar was perhaps the only entertainer in the world who could perform mime without making you want to strangle him. *Your Show* burned brightly for four years, but the frenetic pace was brutal. The strain began to show, and viewership sagged. "By its very nature...the show is beginning to pall," TV GUIDE said in 1954 as the ratings declined. "But even as it stands, it is well worth the effort to catch Caesar and Coca in one of their frequent flights into sheer comic greatness." Even though the two could hilariously, effortlessly send up the famous roll-in-the-surf scene in *From Here to Eternity*, the show couldn't go on forever. Caesar and Coca would later return to television, but they never quite recaptured the magic of those madcap early years.

"THE NETWORKS HATED LIVE COMEDY, BECAUSE THEY COULDN'T CONTROL IT.

For all intents and purposes, there was nobody editing me. There was nobody saying, 'Cut this out, cut that out.' You were your own editor, and it was much more personal because it was from you to the audience. You couldn't depend on tricks and technology.

"I allowed no cue cards, and there wasn't anything such as a Tele-PrompTer. If something happened, you just kept on going, and a lot of times a laugh came where you didn't expect it. A lot of times you'd expect a laugh and it didn't come, and you still had to make your timing. You had to think fast because you couldn't stop and say, 'Hold it, hold it, hold it. Let's back it up.' And the audience knew it.

"I didn't do anything political because you couldn't. We could do a generic politician, but you couldn't zero in on one guy. The comedy was 'Look at me, look how crazy I am!' But I never went with jokes. I never said, 'Where's the joke?' I said, 'What's the situation?' And we always played up the situation because that's what made it funny, not the joke."

—SID CAESAR

FANTASY ISLAND
Top left: Mr. Roarke (Ricardo Montalban), Tattoo (Herve Villechaize). ABC, 1978–84
COVER: BY AL HIRSCHFELD, MARCH 1, 1980

THE LOVE BOAT
Top right: Julie McCoy (Lauren Tewes), Burl "Gopher" Smith (Fred Grandy), Capt. Merrill Stubing (Gavin MacLeod), Isaac Washington (Ted Lange), Dr. Adam Bricker (Bernie Kopell). ABC, 1977–86
COVER: BY BRUCE STARK, DECEMBER 24, 1983

Talk about offshore assets: From the late '70s to the mid-'80s, ABC owned Saturday night with its back-to-back escapist hours, *The Love Boat* and *Fantasy Island* (both produced by mass-appeal wizard Aaron Spelling). *Fantasy Island* posited a tropical outpost where regular Joes could live out their dreams. "All the elements were there," Ricardo Montalban, who played the island's suave host, told TV GUIDE in 1980. "*Fantasy Island* is every book ever written." It was also, as the magazine noted in '78, every moral ever mouthed: "Ordinary folks shouldn't yearn for wealth, glamour and power because the best things in life are free and there's no place like home and so forth." The unspoken proverb aboard *The Love Boat*, meanwhile, was "love conquers all." Each episode introduced three romantic story lines (strangers meet, a quarreling couple reunites, etc.) that were enacted, over the years, by a battalion of old-time movie stars and B-grade TV personalities, all under the command of Gavin MacLeod as Capt. Merrill Stubing. Viewers got to see characters whose lives "change for the better," MacLeod told TV GUIDE in '82, plus "opulent surroundings, sumptuous food and beautiful, scantily dressed bodies." Bon voyage!

SATURDAY NIGHT LIVE

Clockwise from below, right: Patrick Swayze (guest host), Chris Farley; Mike Myers, Dana Carvey; Will Ferrell, Cheri Oteri; Joe Piscopo, Eddie Murphy; John Belushi. NBC, 1975–
COVER: BY JACK DAVIS, JULY 29, 1978

"It's so *weird*," John Belushi told TV GUIDE in the spring of 1976, "to go on TV and do what you want." That exhilarating sense of freedom was palpable both to the performers of *Saturday Night Live* and to its almost disbelieving audience during the show's first season. Television in the mid-'70s wasn't that far removed from its censorious roots, and here was a gang of smart, funny young players with a rock and roll sensibility who were wantonly making barely disguised references to sex, drugs and unholy acts. "The traditional variety show needed to be redefined," Lorne Michaels, *SNL*'s creator and longtime producer, told the magazine in 1999 for its 25th-anniversary tribute. Over the course of that quarter century, *SNL* was declared dead many times, but no matter how stale certain seasons seemed, something fresh and funny always emerged as the show continued to reinvent itself with new ideas and cast members. It was a lesson Michaels learned early, after the first season, when breakout star Chevy Chase left and Belushi and Gilda Radner stepped in to pick up the slack. In subsequent years, an amazing roster of comics and their characters rose to the occasion: Bill Murray's lounge singer, Eddie Murphy's Gumby, Mike Myers and Dana Carvey's suburban basement rockers Wayne and Garth. The list goes on (and *on*: Is there any other show in history with a longer all-star reel?). In 2002, the series' drive to innovate even achieved the impossible: Tina Fey and Jimmy Fallon's "Weekend Update" segments acquired a buzz they hadn't had since the days of Chevy Chase. There is no rational explanation for *SNL*'s amazing, never-ending rebirth. Could it be...Satan?

"SATURDAY NIGHT LIVE CHANGED THE FACE OF COMEDY-VARIETY ON TELEVISION.

Everything that came before it had been taped and sweetened. The *Sonny and Cher* show. The *Smothers Brothers* show, which I had worked for. These shows were too pat. There were no surprises. *SNL* has always had surprises.

"The first year of the show was the only year that I was there, and I became very famous very fast. But the ratings really only started coming up in the second year, after I left. Most of the time that first year, we thought, 'We're just this late-night, top-of-the-minors show, so this is a chance to do what we love to do,' which was heavy satire, political stuff and parody. I thought we might be kicked off the air for that matter. I didn't know.

"At the time, there was another show called *Saturday Night Live with Howard Cosell*—which meant we couldn't name the show *Saturday Night Live*. This is the whole reason—and the only reason—I came out and started the show by saying, 'Live from New York, it's *Saturday Night*!' We couldn't use the word 'live.' But when Cosell's show went off the air, we got the rights to call it *Saturday Night Live*.

"We were able to do political satire that could actually affect the nation. Gerald Ford wrote in a book that my imitation of him—I made no attempt to do an actual impression of him, but instead just this clumsy guy—really did influence the 1976 election. And we were also doing things nobody had done before us, like parodies of TV commercials. I wanted the show to be about television. I wanted to puncture the traditions of TV and do some taboo things. That was my concept as a head writer back then. I think it changed the way we look at commercials and made commercials themselves become more self-conscious and aware of how to be funny. The 'Weekend Update' news segment became the precursor for things like *The Daily Show*. But it wasn't the first of its kind. There had been shows like *That Was the Week That Was* even earlier.

"There used to be this idea that if people can see you for free on television, they're not going to pay to see you in a theater. But

I obviously broke through to film. It took me about 20 movies to learn how to act. And 60 to learn how to behave. For guys who had talent—like Eddie Murphy and Mike Myers—the show became a kind of show-case, a launching pad. John Belushi was kind of upset that I became the star; he rightfully thought he should have been the big star. But I told John, 'I say my name every week—I say, "I'm Chevy Chase and you're not"—and nobody can even pro-nounce your name, much less sell it.' These are just empirical things that have nothing to do with talent. And eventually John did become a big movie star.

"If there is any reason that the first cast of *SNL* was the best cast, it's because we had nothing on the line. None of us expected we were going to go anywhere. I was recently watching one of the first-year shows with my daughter, and I started laughing out loud. Dan Aykroyd and John and I were up there doing something, and I saw a real looseness there, a complete devil-may-care attitude. 'Who cares if we get the lines right? Let's just be as funny as we can, because we don't know if we'll be on next week.'

"I always take offense when I hear people say, 'No one can compare to the first cast,' because it's not fair to the casts that came after us. But I must admit, we were damn good. We were very funny."

—CHEVY CHASE

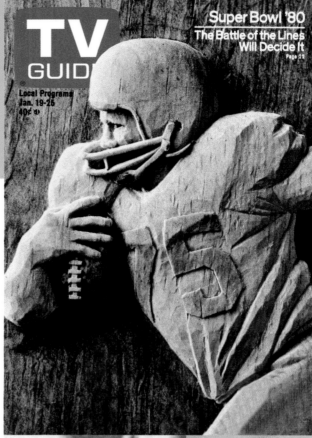

Super Bowl '80
The Battle of the Lines
Will Decide It
Page 22

TV GUIDE
Local Programs
Jan. 19-25
40¢

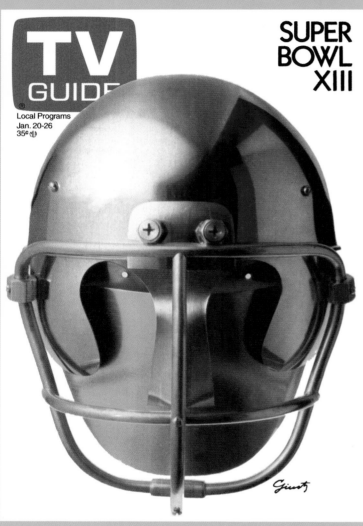

TV GUIDE
Local Programs
Jan. 20-26
35¢

SUPER
BOWL
XIII

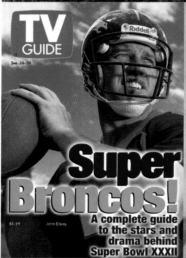

TV GUIDE
Jan. 24-30

Super
Broncos!
A complete guide
to the stars and
drama behind
Super Bowl XXXII

$1.19   John Elway

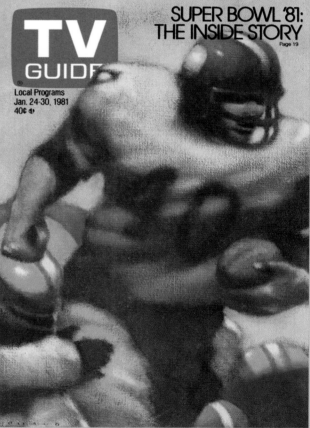

TV GUIDE
Local Programs
Jan. 24-30, 1981
40¢

SUPER BOWL '81:
THE INSIDE STORY
Page 19

NFL AND THE SUPER BOWL
Joe Namath, January 12, 1969
COVERS (CLOCKWISE FROM ABOVE): BY GEORGE GIUSTI, JANUARY 20, 1979. BY NICK FASCIANO, JANUARY 19, 1980.
BY BRAD HOLLAND, JANUARY 24, 1981. BY JEFFREY LOWE, JANUARY 24, 1998

In 1989, author David Halberstam chose six momentous events for an article in TV GUIDE called "TV That Changed Our Lives." One of them was the 1958 National Football League championship between the New York Giants and the Baltimore Colts, won by Johnny Unitas and the Colts in overtime. "The game marked many things," Halberstam wrote. "The ascent of pro football to a level enjoyed in the past only by baseball; the explosion of sports as a crucial ingredient in...a new television-driven, entertainment-oriented society; and, perhaps most importantly, it marked the ability of television to find an event that it favored (that is, something it could cover well) and virtually reinvent it, taking it from something ordinary to something that was part of the national fabric." If TV favored football, then it was positively smitten with the Super Bowl. Joe Namath making good on his boast that the underdog New York Jets would beat the Colts in 1969's Super Bowl III helped turn the affair into an unprecedented summit of social, athletic and corporate interests. After all, the games themselves were often less than memorable: Only because of a last-minute Joe Montana-engineered comeback victory for the San Francisco 49ers over the Cincinnati Bengals in '89 did the game make it into TV GUIDE's "50 Greatest TV Sports Moments of All Time" (1998). Yet thanks to Apple Computer's bravura Orwell-inspired commercial in 1984, advertisers turned the TV showcase into their own Super Bowl of creativity; even if the game was a lemon, viewers knew the day wasn't a total loss if the *ads* were good. That's the thing about the Super Bowl—and, on a lesser scale, the NFL's regular-season games—as a national gathering: Just like any family get-together, what happens at the event isn't as important as the fact of the gathering itself.

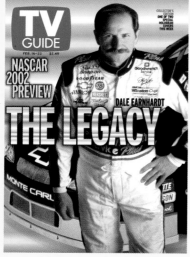

NASCAR

Final practice for EA Sports 500, Talladega Superspeedway, Talladega, Alabama, October 20, 2001; Tony Stewart at Sharpie 500, Bristol Motor Speedway, Bristol, Tennessee, August 25, 2001

COVER: BY CIA STOCK PHOTOGRAPHY, FEBRUARY 16, 2002

Until the advent of cable television, stock-car racing was a TV afterthought: The Daytona 500—the sport's Super Bowl—didn't even air live until 1979. But with cable's embrace, the National Association for Stock Car Auto Racing flourished, and by '96 it could even make a credible case as "the hottest sport of the '90s," as TV GUIDE put it. The year 2001 was momentous: NASCAR drew more TV viewers than ever, an impressive start to its six-year, $2.4 billion contract with Fox, FX, NBC and Turner Sports. But the sport also tragically lost elite driver Dale Earnhardt in a crash at Daytona. The overwhelming outpouring of grief that erupted across the nation demonstrated not only the sport's triumphant popularity, but also the special kinship between NASCAR's fearless competitors and their millions of fans.

ABC's Wide World of Sports reveled in the "thrill of victory and the agony of defeat," as the famous opening line from longtime host Jim McKay goes, for 36 years. "Our original idea," Roone Arledge, executive producer for four years and later vice president of ABC Sports, told TV GUIDE in 1966, "was to give viewers the kind of human picture story they couldn't find in their sports sections." An early, misbegotten attempt to depict the "soul" of the Le Mans Grand Prix road race cured Arledge of that vision: "Today, we leave the art to Fellini and Kazan. We stick to action. This is what our viewers want." The action might come from anywhere: figure skating; Irish hurling; the Tour de France; rattlesnake hunting; the Olympics; the '72 Fischer–Spassky chess match in Reykjavik, Iceland; the Indy 500; Evel Knievel's abortive Snake River Canyon motorcycle jump; the Kentucky Derby; or Howard Cosell verbally sparring with Muhammad Ali. It should have been enough to make even sports junkies sprint into rehab, but instead ABC proved that America's fascination with the baseball-football-basketball trinity could easily be expanded to accommodate virtually any form of athletic drama. (That was Yugoslavian ski jumper Vinko Bogataj epitomizing the agony of you-know-what when he turned himself into a human yard sale at the 1970 International Ski Flying Championships in Oberstdorf, Germany.) In an era of X Games and multiple ESPN channels, the concept hardly seems groundbreaking, but in the 1960s and '70s there was something utterly exotic about watching, say, Acapulco cliff divers plummet 87 feet into the perilous waters of the Pacific. As early as 1969, however, TV GUIDE was feeling sated—if you've "seen too many sports you don't like, move over. We're with you"—but nonetheless acknowledged the show as "a truly staggering undertaking—easily the most remarkable program in its field."

THE THRILL OF VICTORY...

"I CAN REMEMBER WATCHING CRONKITE AND REALIZING THAT WALTER WAS NOT AN ANCHOR WHO WAS CHAINED TO THE DESK.

He went out and did other things. When Walter was covering the space program, he would go through some of that training, and you would see him in a space suit dealing with gravity issues. And I would just say, 'Man, that's a great job.' I didn't know anyone else who was doing anything like that.

"*60 Minutes* has succeeded because we do good work. And I think that we don't talk down to our audience. We go out every week, and we say, 'Hey, here are three stories we think you should be interested in. You might not like it, you might not agree with the points of view expressed by the people in those stories, but we think you should know about this.'

"Unfortunately, I would say that people who live in other countries, in many European countries, know more about us than we know about them. I think the biggest change in network news is probably the dramatic decrease in the amount of foreign coverage. When I'm overseas on assignment and I look at a local program in London or in Paris, there's always something on it about the United States. But there's not always something about Paris or London on our broadcasts. We are the economic giant of the world, the only military superpower. We are the most important country in the world. But we are a stronger country when we know more about what's going on in the rest of the world. We are a better, more informed population when we know and understand the concerns of other people."

—ED BRADLEY

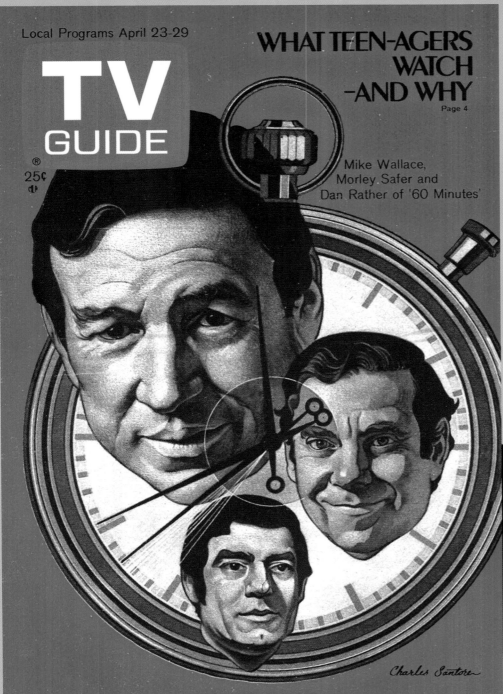

Local Programs April 23-29

TV GUIDE

®

25¢

WHAT TEEN-AGERS WATCH –AND WHY

Page 4

Mike Wallace, Morley Safer and Dan Rather of '60 Minutes'

Charles Santore

COVERS (CLOCKWISE FROM ABOVE):
BY CHARLES SANTORE, APRIL 23, 1977
BY DARRYL ESTRINE, APRIL 27, 1996
BY ROBERT PHILLIPS, FEBRUARY 25, 1984

60 MINUTES
CBS, 1968–

Tick-tick-tick-tick-tick... For decades, that sound has set the Sunday-night rhythm in millions of households as football- and dinner-sated Americans settled in to root for a show that turned investigative journalism into dramatic entertainment. *60 Minutes* has offered many pleasures over the years—Morley Safer's intriguing exploration of the paradisiacal Maldive Islands, Harry Reasoner's tribute to the movie *Casablanca*—but the real draw is watching correspondents such as Mike Wallace knock some ne'er-do-well heads together. When it first went on the air in 1968, the show seemed an unlikely candidate to become not only a TV institution but also a staggering network profit center and inspiration for a legion of imitators (including its own legitimate off-spring, *60 Minutes II*). At the time, documentary-style television was considered a prestige operation, not a lure for viewers or advertisers. In fact, it wasn't until the mid-'70s that a few adjustments to the show—adding correspondent Dan Rather to the team and moving to its now-customary Sunday-night slot—turned it into the news and ratings juggernaut it became. Over the years, executive producer Don Hewitt's crew covered thousands of stories, from Rather's trek into Afghanistan during the Soviet invasion to Ed Bradley's interview with Oklahoma City bomber Timothy McVeigh. One of the great joys of watching the show is seeing "something that does not appear often in nonfiction television," TV GUIDE said in 1984: "the process of watching the correspondents discover the story at the same time that we do." Or, as Wallace described it to the magazine: "What we were able to do is bring the technique of live reportage to the documentary." Although some things on *60 Minutes* have changed over the years—remember the righty-lefty "Point-Counterpoint" spats of James Kilpatrick and Shana Alexander?—the show now feels like an American landmark. It is hard to imagine that these 60 minutes won't go on...forever. *Tick-tick-tick-tick-tick...*

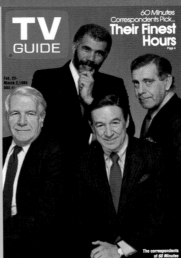

TV GUIDE

60 Minutes
Correspondents Pick...
Their Finest Hours
Page 4

Feb. 25–
March 2, 1984
50¢

The correspondents
of 60 Minutes

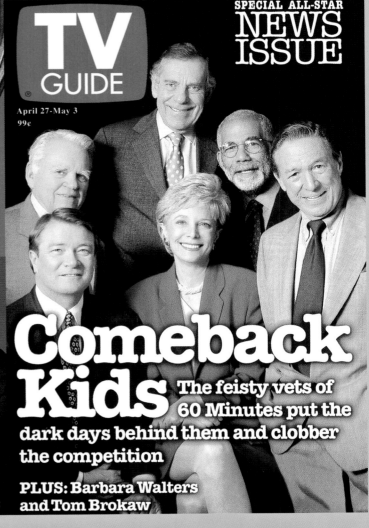

SPECIAL ALL-STAR
NEWS ISSUE

TV GUIDE

April 27-May 3
99¢

Comeback Kids

The feisty vets of 60 Minutes put the dark days behind them and clobber the competition

PLUS: Barbara Walters and Tom Brokaw

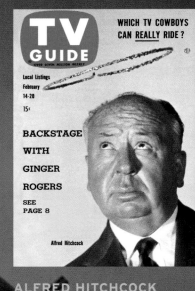

ALFRED HITCHCOCK PRESENTS
CBS, 1955–60; NBC, 1960–62
COVER: BY MAX YAVNO,
FEBRUARY 14, 1959

"The more outrageous a subject can get, the better I like it," Hitchcock told TV GUIDE in 1959. "I am no different from a child who gloats over the horrific." The master filmmaker found plenty to gloat over during his decade as the host and occasional director of *Alfred Hitchcock Presents*, an anthology of "situation tragedies," as he once described these tales of murder, mystery and surprise. The show's "best feature," TV GUIDE said, was Hitch himself, "a sly grin on his cherubic face" as he introduced the ultimate horror: the next commercial break.

THE X-FILES
Fox, 1993–2002
COVERS: BY DAVID LAVY, DECEMBER 21, 1996

Though there is only one *X* in *The X-Files*, for fans this show was a sexy triple-*X* feature: sci-fi action, nefarious plots and horror-story creatures—all wrapped in a lushly produced package. When the series debuted in 1993, it tapped into the conspiracy-theorist gene lurking in millions of otherwise rational viewers, transfixing them with tales of FBI cases considered too bizarre for the bureau to solve—until it put agents Fox Mulder and Dana Scully on the job. David Duchovny played the romantic dreamer with an Oliver Stone-like paranoia to Gillian Anderson's rational pragmatist. The matchup provided the ingredients for a classic romantic pas de deux, except the couple stubbornly remained nothing more than coworkers and friends. The sexual tension between Mulder and Scully crackled for an amazing seven years without consummation (frustrated fans should have demanded an FBI investigation into *that*) before Duchovny left in 2000, announcing that he was tired of the grind. Creator Chris Carter's brainchild continued for two more years, still looking ravishing at $4 million per episode but unable to make up for Duchovny's departure. And perhaps the X-files themselves had become exhausted. After all, over the years Mulder and Scully tracked down everything from evil clones and a human-size parasite feasting in a New Jersey sewer system to a cocooning monster that emerged every 30 years to kill. Bidding goodbye to the show as its end in spring 2002 approached, TV GUIDE said: "Nothing on TV lasts forever, not even a landmark like Fox's marvelously inventive *X-Files*, with its dense and dark explorations of paranoia, government conspiracy and otherworldly menace—and the resilient humanity of its charismatic leads."

"SCIENCE-FICTION SHOWS CAN BE HOKEY BUT GRITTY AT THE SAME TIME.

They lend themselves to a certain kind of moralizing. You can be moralistic and allegorical and get away with it. You can tell a poignant story, teach lessons and still make it fun. This is a harder thing to do when you're dealing with a show that takes place in the real, everyday world.

"When I was a kid, I liked the message of *Star Trek*—you know, the hokey moral of the day. The same thing with *The Twilight Zone*.

The cool thing about these shows was picking up on these messages, these little ironic tags—whether it was 'be kind to strangers' or 'don't prejudge people.' You kind of felt smart when you got what they were talking about.

"Incidentally, my mom loved Captain Kirk. She thought he had a good build. She liked the way he filled out his Starfleet uniform."

—DAVID DUCHOVNY

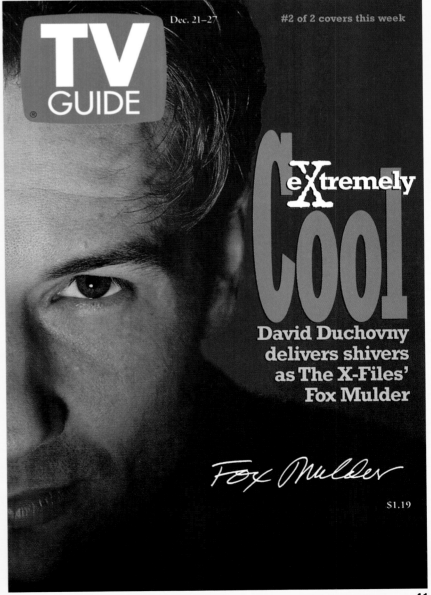

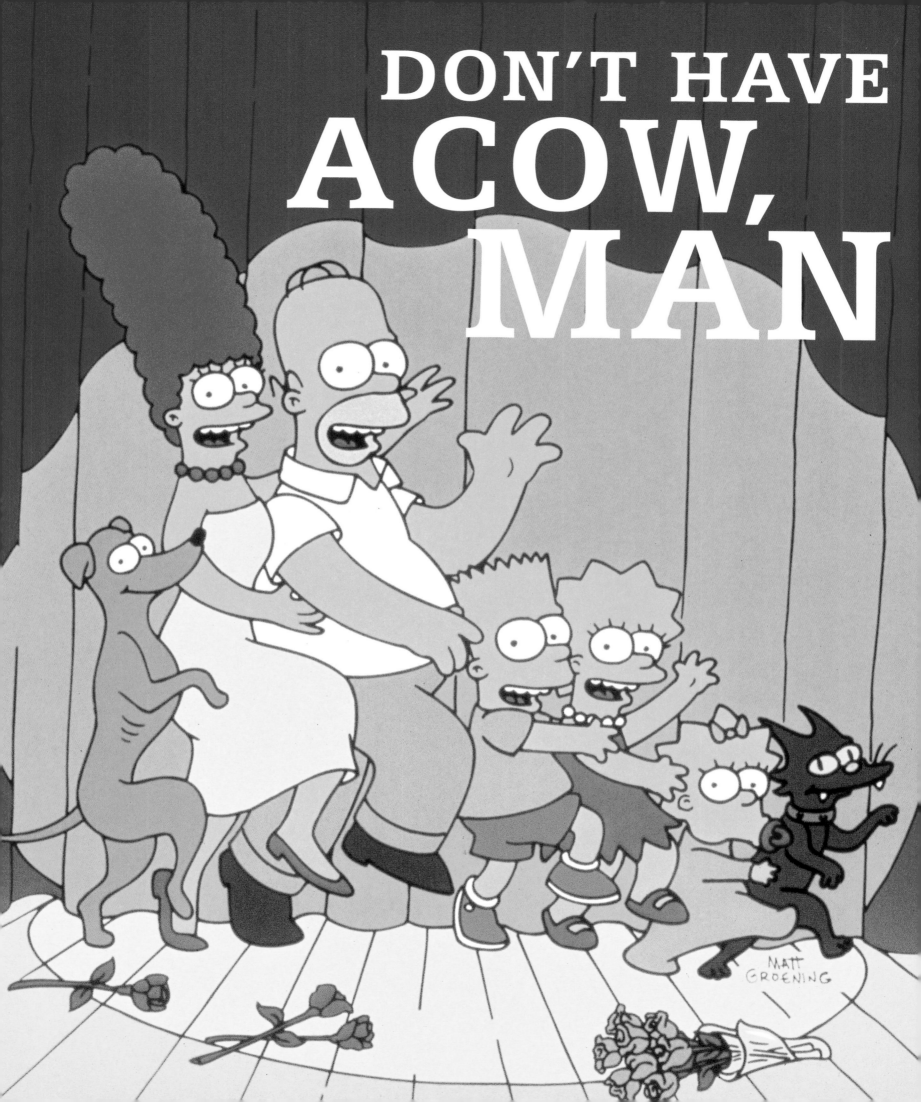

THE SIMPSONS

Santa's Little Helper, Marge Simpson, Homer Simpson, Bart Simpson, Lisa Simpson, Maggie Simpson, Snowball. Fox, 1989–
COVERS: OCTOBER 21, 2000 (THE SIMPSONS™ AND ©2000 TWENTIETH CENTURY FOX FILM CORP. ALL RIGHTS RESERVED)

It was the Christmas season, 1989, a time when TV is blanketed with counterfeit sentiment and saccharine fables. Then the pilot episode of *The Simpsons* elbowed its way onto the air: "Simpsons Roasting on an Open Fire" introduced viewers—those who had missed creator Matt Groening's short segments of the cartoon family on *The Tracey Ullman Show*—to what would become the most exhilaratingly subversive, reliably hilarious series on television. In fact, the popularity of *The Simpsons* burned so hot at first that the show seemed destined for the life span of a fad—in the early '90s, every other person you saw seemed to be wearing a Bart Simpson T-shirt emblazoned with one of the lovable, underachieving fourth-grader's catchphrases ("Ay caramba," "Don't have a cow, man"). It soon became apparent that the show wasn't just a brilliant cartoon; it was one of the best comedies on television, period, with enough complexity and emotional nuance to last a very long time. Nine years

later, TV GUIDE would declare that "America's funniest family is more irreverent—and irresistible—than ever," praising the show's "textual density" and characters that had more "heft than the flesh-and-blood characters of other sitcoms." The Simpson family itself—led by Homer, the tenderly negligent dad, and Marge, the practical mom with the impractical hair—was captivating, but so was the supporting cast of Springfield residents ("Worthy of a Preston Sturges movie," said TV GUIDE, which also found them worthy of 24 covers in one week). Celebrities gladly lent their voices to the show, and over the years we heard everyone from Buzz Aldrin and Johnny Carson to Hugh Hefner and Barry White. But the voice that will always conjure *The Simpsons*, the spoken *syllable* that instantly evokes the show's appreciation for life's unexpected turns and our futile attempts to anticipate them, is Homer's utterly eloquent *d'oh!*

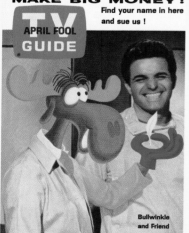

Bullwinkle and Friend

THE BULLWINKLE SHOW
Bullwinkle Moose, Rocket J. Squirrel. ABC, 1959–61; NBC, 1961–64; ABC, 1964–73
SPECIAL INSERT COVER: PHOTOGRAPHER UNKNOWN, MARCH 30, 1963

Jay Ward might have been a graduate of the Harvard School of Business Administration and a real-estate dealer in Berkeley, California, but he loved cartooning a lot more than calculating square footage. And it didn't pay too badly, either. In 1959, after his success with *Crusader Rabbit*—a series of five-minute animated TV segments for kids—Ward dreamed up Rocket J. Squirrel (aka Rocky the Flying Squirrel) and a moose called Bullwinkle. They first appeared on ABC in *Rocky and His Friends*, then moved to NBC, where—in recognition of the dim-witted moose's popularity—the billing changed to *The Bullwinkle Show*. As it jumped around from evening to afternoon to morning slots on two networks over the course of 12 years, *The Bullwinkle Show* became a classic that was fun for kids, who loved the goofy characters, and irresistible to adults, who dug the sophisticated puns and clever satire. The "irreverent, outrageous humor...made Bullwinkle the best-known moose in television," TV GUIDE said in '62. Rocky and Bullwinkle, natives of Frostbite Falls, Minnesota, were forever fending off the hapless spies Boris and Natasha. There were also plenty of other deeply amusing segments, including the "Fractured Fairy Tales" parodies (wonderfully narrated by Edward Everett Horton), "Peabody's Improbable History" (the wealthy dog-genius Mister Peabody and his adopted boy, Sherman, tramped through history using the Way-Back Machine) and, of course, the gripping adventures of Dudley Do-Right, the Canadian Mountie who felt almost as tenderly toward the beautiful Nell as he did toward his horse. Anyone who doesn't have a tender spot of his own for the *Bullwinkle* gang—seen in omnipresent reruns over the years—must be a descendant of Snidely Whiplash.

WALT DISNEY
ABC, 1954–61, 1986–89 and 1997–; NBC, 1961–81 and 1989–90; CBS, 1981–83
COVER: BY WALT DISNEY PRODS., OCTOBER 23, 1954

In its early days, television was anathema to Hollywood movie studios, which generally shunned it for siphoning off filmgoers and turning out inferior entertainment. "Of all the moguls, only Walt Disney sensed opportunity rather than disaster in the new medium," TV GUIDE said in 1978, in anticipation of the 25th anniversary of Disney's historic 1954 leap onto the airwaves. His immediate success with *Disneyland* (it went through eight different names, including *Walt Disney's Wonderful World of Color* and *The Wonderful World of Disney*) opened the floodgates for Hollywood's rush into television production. But the show, divided into segments called "Adventureland," "Frontierland," "Fantasyland" and "Tomorrowland," also instigated a change in the way the TV industry thought about programming. For one thing, it provided a fresh outlet for Disney's animated movies, and it popularized the nature documentary, sending flocks of imitators into the field. The art of cross promotion, meanwhile, was practically invented by the show, which featured insider looks at the building of the Disneyland theme park and previews of forthcoming Disney theatrical releases. Finally, the continuing saga of *Davy Crockett*, starring Fess Parker, presaged the TV miniseries. (It also touched off one of the great fads of the 1950s, making the coonskin cap a must-have childhood accessory.) "I'm really having fun with television," Disney told TV GUIDE in 1957. "I haven't had so much fun since my early days in the business when I had the latitude to experiment. With TV, it's like a cage has been opened—and I can fly again." And again and again: *Disney*'s status as a beloved TV institution has prompted repeated reinventions—most recently on ABC, the show's original home and a network now owned by—who else?—the Walt Disney Company.

"I, Claudius was just an incredible production for television. The level of writing, the production values, the acting—it was really TV at its best. There wasn't one false note in it. We always think the British do everything better, and maybe

it's just empire envy. But if you think about it, the acting of Derek Jacobi as Claudius and Siân Phillips as Livia—in a way, she was really the paradigm for Tony Soprano's mother, Livia."

—Larry Gelbart, creator of M*A*S*H

MASTERPIECE THEATRE
Alistair Cooke; Livia (Siân Phillips), Augustus (Brian Blessed) of *I, Claudius* (1977–78); Queen Elizabeth I (Glenda Jackson), Davison (John Graham) of *Elizabeth R* (1972); Rose (Jean Marsh), Mrs. Bridges (Angela Baddeley) of *Upstairs, Downstairs* (1974–77). PBS, 1971–

In more than 30 years, not much has changed about *Masterpiece Theatre*. Sure, host Alistair Cooke, the British journalist who struck just the right note of informed hospitality with his introductions, retired in 1993 and gave way to American journalist Russell Baker. And the original sponsor, Mobil Oil, merged with Exxon in 1999, so that viewers now settle in to watch the ungainly *ExxonMobil Masterpiece Theatre*. But the stately signature music by Jean-Joseph Mouret remains, as does the anthology series' mission: to make a home for original works and adaptations—usually British, usually multipart—that are too classy for American commercial networks. Of course, that doesn't preclude their being hugely entertaining: *Upstairs, Downstairs* was itself a masterpiece of storytelling, about the sea change in British culture after World War I, as seen through the lives of the moneyed Bellamy family upstairs and the servants quartered downstairs. The year *Upstairs* ended, *I, Claudius* began, with Derek Jacobi as the Roman emperor brilliantly stuttering and stumbling his way through poet Robert Graves's comic horror tale of Rome's decline. Not every *Masterpiece* offering lived up to its billing, but as TV GUIDE noted in 1978, "that's the price paid for excellence." What was admirable about British TV, the magazine said, was its "chanciness—the occasional attempt to bring off something difficult and hazardous," reminding American audiences that "we could do with fewer mediocre successes and more grand failures." On the series' 15th anniversary, Cooke wrote a piece for TV GUIDE downplaying his role in its success. The producers, he said, chose the menu, while "I was, at this end, simply the headwaiter."

HAVE GUN, WILL TRAVEL
Paladin (Richard Boone). CBS, 1957–63
COVER: BY PHILIPPE HALSMAN, MAY 10, 1958

When Westerns ruled television, the triumvirate atop the ratings for three consecutive years (1958-61) was *Gunsmoke, Wagon Train* and *Have Gun, Will Travel*, in that order. Of the three, *Have Gun* was the most intriguing: A dandified hired gun named Paladin lived in vaguely decadent opulence at a San Francisco hotel, but observed a code of honor so strict that he'd turn on his employer if that's where the ethical needle pointed. In an unusual twist, this Western hero dressed in black when he was on the job, and star Richard Boone was hardly a rock-jawed cowboy prototype—he looked, TV GUIDE said in a three-part profile in 1961, like he had been "recently stung by hunting wasps, for the face is pocked and puffy and, in Boone's words, more 'interesting' than handsome." Paladin solicited work with a wonderful marketing tool (and one of the coolest talismans of that television era), a business card that bore the image of a chess-piece knight. Alas, Paladin didn't survive the endgame: The popularity of Westerns waned, and *Have Gun* traveled off the air in '63.

GUNSMOKE
Kitty Russell (Amanda Blake), Marshal Matt Dillon (James Arness). CBS, 1955–75
COVER: BY GARRETT-HOWARD, MAY 11, 1957

"Good evening. My name's Wayne"—as in *John* Wayne, who was dressed in full cowboy gear as he introduced the first episode of *Gunsmoke* on September 10, 1955. "Some of you may have seen me before," Wayne said. "I hope so. I've been kicking around Hollywood a long time. I've made a lot of pictures out here. All kinds. Some of them have been Westerns. That's what I'm here to tell you about tonight—a Western. A new television show called *Gunsmoke*. No, I'm not in it. I wish I were, though, because I think it's the best thing of its kind to come along. And I hope you'll agree with me. It's honest, it's adult, it's realistic." Wayne was right: *Gunsmoke* was like no other TV Western before it. And with the oater icon's imprimatur—and his friend James Arness as Matt Dillon—it began what turned out to be a historic run. Twenty years later, when the doors of the Long Branch Saloon

finally quit swinging, *Gunsmoke* owned the record—and still does—as the longest-running prime-time series featuring continuing characters. Audiences accustomed to the impossibly courageous leading men on kid-oriented Westerns like *The Lone Ranger* loved the bracing stories of a hero who wasn't particularly popular with anyone but his immediate friends, such as saloon owner Miss Kitty (Amanda Blake) and Doc Adams (Milburn Stone). Dillon was a hero who could be wounded in gunfights and beaten up by bad guys, a hero who didn't talk to his horse. Arness also rarely spoke to the press, but in 1987 he talked to TV GUIDE about the success of the series. "What made the difference was they didn't try to do an entertainment fiction-alized Western," Arness said. "They really tried like hell to make it hot and dry and dusty, and people were ready for it."

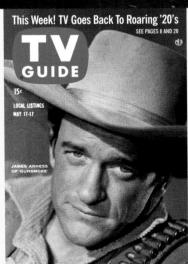

This Week! TV Goes Back To Roaring '20's
SEE PAGES 8 AND 20

TV GUIDE

15¢
LOCAL LISTINGS
MAY 11-17

JAMES ARNESS
OF 'GUNSMOKE'

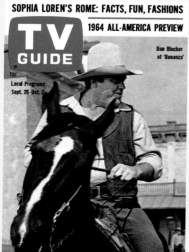
BONANZA

Eric "Hoss" Cartwright (Dan Blocker), Ben Cartwright (Lorne Greene), Adam Cartwright (Pernell Roberts), Little Joe Cartwright (Michael Landon). NBC, 1959–73

COVER: BY CARL FRITH, SEPTEMBER 26, 1964

Bonanza occupies such a familiar place in TV history that it's easy to overlook how atypical it seemed when it first began airing. In an era of *Shane*-inspired heroes who were rootless loners, here was a TV Western—the first in color—that still featured gunplay and pounding hooves, but centered on a family. Even in that respect, though, it broke the mold: This family consisted of four men—thrice-widowed Ben Cartwright and the grown sons he had from each marriage. Although watching *Bonanza* became a Sunday-night tradition for millions of households throughout the 1960s, creator David Dortort was just as averse to TV-family conventions as he was to Old West clichés. "We do not have any moms built into our show.... We don't have any little brats who talk like Leonard Bernstein," Dortort told TV GUIDE in 1960. "We deal with a love affair between four strong men and, even more

importantly, with the land and with roots." The strongest of the quartet working the sprawling Ponderosa ranch near Virginia City, Nevada, was the 300-pound "Hoss," memorably played by Dan Blocker as not the brightest bull in the herd, but the biggest-hearted one. He was a gentle foil to Michael Landon's hotheaded Little Joe, and a humorous counterweight to the reserved, cerebral eldest brother, Adam, who was written out of the series in 1965 when actor Pernell Roberts tired of the role. "I think the show is popular basically because of the four characters, not because of the stories—which are sometimes terrible," Blocker told TV GUIDE. *Bonanza* easily coped with Roberts's departure, but Blocker's death in 1972, coupled with a switch to Tuesday nights after 11 years in its Sunday slot, was more than the remaining two strong men could handle.

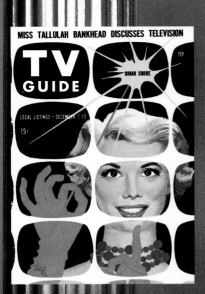

TV GUIDE

DINAH SHORE

LOCAL LISTINGS · DECEMBER 7-13
15¢

THE DINAH SHORE CHEVY SHOW
NBC, 1956–63
COVER: BY AL PARKER,
DECEMBER 7, 1957

Singer Dinah Shore's gracious,
friendly style helped turn *The Dinah
Shore Chevy Show* into a TV fixture.
The variety series had plenty of
guest stars (Ginger Rogers, Jimmy
Durante, Ella Fitzgerald), but
Shore—singing "See the U.S.A. in
your Chevrolet" and giving a big
show-ending kiss to the audience—
was the real draw. "The show is like
a party," Shore told TV GUIDE in
1959. "I like people to have a good
time at my parties." Cowboy star
Roy Rogers told the magazine
in '57 that he liked being a guest
because "you just don't have the
tension" of other programs. The
reason? "That girl knows what she's
doin', that's why."

THE ED SULLIVAN SHOW

Clockwise from above: Elvis Presley; Sullivan with the Beatles; Diana Ross; plate spinner; Liza Minnelli and Judy Garland. CBS, 1948–71

COVER: **BY PHILIPPE HALSMAN, JUNE 17, 1967**

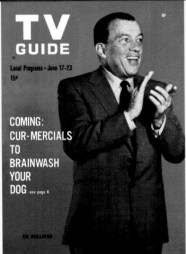

From our vantage point more than a half century later, it's easy to blame the infancy of television for the fact that someone like Ed Sullivan could get on the air as the host of his own variety show. After all, the guy looked like the runner-up in a Bogart-imitates-Nixon contest. But even back then, Sullivan's mug raised eyebrows. "In 1948, television writers laughed at his appearance," TV GUIDE recalled 20 years later. He didn't just look stiff; the introducer also suffered from the chronic inability to actually make introductions. Sullivan heralded Massachusetts-born singer Robert Goulet as a Canadian. He turned clarinetist Benny Goodman into a "trumpeter," columnist Walter Winchell into a "sports star" and a visiting group of New Zealand natives into "the fierce Maori tribe from New England." That list of blunders, though, also provides a glimpse of the tremendous range of guests who appeared on *The Ed Sullivan*

Show (it was called *Toast of the Town* from 1948 to '55). What Sullivan lacked in on-air skills he made up for with his reporter's instincts to jump on timely subjects and a willingness to fly anywhere in the world to check out an act. The list of stars who made their first television appearance on his show includes the Beatles, Dinah Shore, Lena Horne, Eddie Fisher and the comedy team of Dean Martin and Jerry Lewis. Despite all these high-octane acts, Sullivan singled out the unplanned speech of a less well-known guest as his most memorable moment: In 1953, playwright, producer and director Josh Logan (*South Pacific*) touchingly addressed the country about his own experience with mental illness and the need to de-stigmatize it. "As far as I'm concerned," Sullivan told TV GUIDE in 1968, three years before his epic run ended, "it was the all-time big moment on the show."

"Although it's somewhat politically incorrect, The Sopranos seems to mirror more closely the world we really live in, the world my friends and I know. It's shocking and upsetting, but so is what really happens in our lives."
—Edie Falco

THE SOPRANOS

A.J. Soprano (Robert Iler), Carmela Soprano (Edie Falco), Tony Soprano (James Gandolfini), Meadow Soprano (Jamie-Lynn Sigler); Paulie Walnuts (Tony Sirico), Silvio Dante (Steven Van Zandt), Tony Soprano, Christopher Moltisanti (Michael Imperioli). HBO, 1999–

COVER: BY FRANK W. OCKENFELS 3, JANUARY 8, 2000

In 1999, the broadcast networks, already bloodied by a long turf war with the cable channels, were kneecapped by a deadly new foe: *The Sopranos*. The HBO series, unfettered by network censors or squeamish advertisers, capitalized on America's abiding fascination with the Italian Mafia, asking the question: What would happen if a shrewd but depressed mobster, struggling to operate a RICO-diminished business while living the wealthy suburban life, suffered an is-that-all-there-is midlife crisis? The answer proved to be one of the most riveting, funny and appalling series ever on television. Suffering panic attacks, Tony Soprano (James Gandolfini) sought the help of therapist Dr. Jennifer Melfi (Lorraine Bracco) and started to plumb his relationship with his poisonous mother, Livia (the brilliant Nancy Marchand, who died after the second season). Shuttling between his meat-market Mafia clubhouse, the Bada Bing! strip club and his Jersey Luxe house, Tony managed to avoid prison, kill his rivals, deal with his children's problems at school and almost convince his wife, Carmela (Edie Falco), that despite his incorrigible cheating, he really loved her. But while this tale of a mobster on Prozac might easily have been played just for laughs—the feature film *Analyze This* was released the same year—instead creator David Chase and the superlative cast managed to achieve a moral and artistic complexity that went far beyond the usual sex, violence and *braciole*. As TV GUIDE critic Matt Roush observed: "Carmela once told her husband, 'You're like an alien life force among us,' and she's partly right. James Gandolfini as Tony Soprano truly is out of this world."

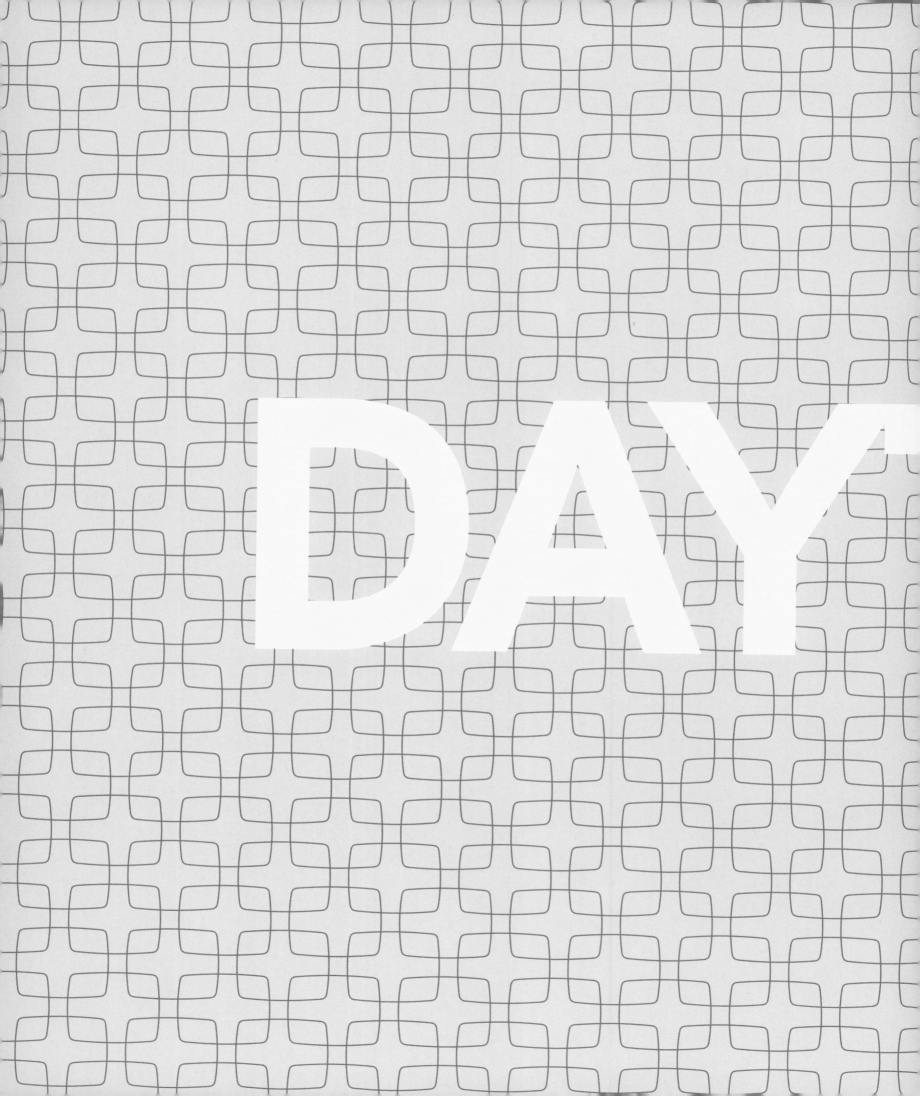

TODAY

Clockwise from top: Al Roker; Willard Scott, Jane Pauley; Matt Lauer, Katie Couric, Jenny Larou, Jeff Scott; J. Fred Muggs, Dave Garroway; Rudolph Giuliani, Couric, Bryant Gumbel, Mario Cuomo. NBC, 1952–

COVERS: BY SHELDON SECUNDA, AUGUST 5, 1967. BY DANIEL KRAMER, MAY 14, 1977

"Good morning to you," said bow-tied host Dave Garroway, announcing the debut broadcast of *Today* on January 14, 1952, "the very first good morning of what I hope and suspect will be a great many good mornings between you and I." Critics weren't so sure—they panned the experiment in morning news, information and entertainment that viewers were supposed to dip in and out of as they got ready for their day. Ratings stayed as soft as a soggy Cheerio for the first year. But then someone had the inspiration to bring in the loose cannon J. Fred Muggs, a chimpanzee that had kids begging their parents to tune in. The ratings soared, and soon *Today* became a habit for millions. "As television and society changed and matured," TV GUIDE said in January 2002, marking the show's 50th anniversary, "so did *Today*—never more noticeably than in its presentation of women." The program that for years had featured a comely new "Today Girl" every day shook up the industry in 1974 by anointing Barbara Walters as a bona fide cohost. Almost 30 years later, the show set another record, signing cohost Katie Couric to a five-year deal reportedly worth $65 million, making her the highest-paid television journalist in history. Couric and cohost Matt Lauer were just the latest in a long line of stars who made *Today* so memorable: Hugh Downs, John Chancellor, Tom Brokaw, Jane Pauley, Bryant Gumbel, Al Roker, Ann Curry and many others. "It's been on all these years without me and Hugh, and it will go on after Katie and Matt," Walters told TV GUIDE in 2001. "Our grandchildren will probably still be watching it." Watching it, and waiting to hear the weather report from someone who might be sending birthday greetings to Willard Scott on *his* 100th.

TV—Powerful Weapon for D.A.s

TV GUIDE

Local Programs Aug. 6-12
25¢

Behind
the Muppet
Empire

15¢ Local Programs July 10-16

TV GUIDE

'SESAME STREET':
How well has it
worked? What
have they learned?
What next?
Page 20

The Cookie Monster

TV GUIDE

SPECIAL PARENTS'
GUIDE

Oct. 30-Nov. 5 89¢

TV THAT'S
GOOD
FOR
YOUR
KIDS
SURPRISE!
THERE ARE
SMART
SITCOMS,
TOONS,
AND GAME SHOWS

Ernie (top) and Bert
of PBS's Sesame Street

TV GUIDE

Nov. 13-19
89¢

MARIAH CAREY
Up close with the
sweet-voiced
singer in
her first
TV special

**First
Lady
Meets
First
Bird!**
Sesame Street's
Birthday Bash
By Judy Blume

PLUS:
Video Game Guide
Return to
Lonesome Dove

Hillary Rodham
Clinton and Friend

SESAME STREET
PBS, 1969–

COVERS (CLOCKWISE FROM ABOVE): BY JACK DAVIS, JULY 10, 1971. BY KEN REGAN, AUGUST 6, 1977.
BY MARC BRYAN-BROWN, NOVEMBER 13, 1993, AND OCTOBER 30, 1993

In 1967, documentary producer Joan Ganz Cooney launched a company called the Children's Television Workshop. CTW was formed with the backing of federal and foundation dollars, and its intention was to create educational programming to help inner-city children do better in school. What Cooney and her crew came up with, as TV GUIDE raved in 1970, was "far and away the greatest children's program that has ever been on the air." Three decades later, it's easy to forget just how startling the world of Bert, Ernie, Cookie Monster and Kermit the Frog really was. The quick-cut stream of cartoons, savvy Muppets, grown-up characters and catchy songs were by themselves a groundbreaking approach to children's programming, but then to marshal all those forces for the purpose of teaching preschoolers the alphabet and numbers—well, that was simply astonishing. *Sesame Street* never lost its city-street setting or multicultural mind-set, yet right from the start, children of every social and economic background clustered around the TV to watch it. By the mid-'70s, some critics had begun to doubt its value, but TV GUIDE concluded that the show "has kept its basic promise—to be imaginative, to use television to teach as well as amuse young children." Besides, what's not to love about a program that, in its early days, showed Burt Lancaster doing push-ups while counting to 10, and much later morphed the Fine Young Cannibals' "She Drives Me Crazy" into "C Drives Me Crazy"?

MISTER ROGERS' NEIGHBORHOOD
Fred Rogers. PBS, 1968–75 and 1979–2001

After a staggering 33 years, Mister Rogers finally hung up his cardigan and put away his comfy shoes for the last time in 2001. Although children's television had evolved radically over the course of his three decades in residence, the changes never seemed to touch Fred Rogers's neighborhood, where he reigned as a gentle, avuncular presence for countless millions of preschoolers. Using songs, puppets and simple chats directed to the camera, he helped kids understand their feelings while showing them a good time. What was the appeal? "It is, simply, that he doesn't either play up to children or talk down to them," said TV GUIDE in 1970. "And above all, he doesn't put them down."

ROMPER ROOM
Miss Connie with students. Syndication, 1954–94

"The world's largest kindergarten," as TV GUIDE described *Romper Room* in 1956, had gotten its start in Baltimore two years earlier but spread faster than chicken pox through a playground via syndication and locally produced versions. The format: A pleasant woman (often a teacher) tried gamely to organize preschoolers into finger painting, sing-alongs and other toddler-targeted activities. Highlights dimly recalled by nearly every baby boomer alive included the Do Bee report card ("Prayer sayer," "Truth teller," "Turn taker," etc.) and the Magic Mirror, when "Miss" whoever gazed through an empty mirror frame and named all the children she could see in TV land—while millions of kids listened raptly each day to find out if they would be called.

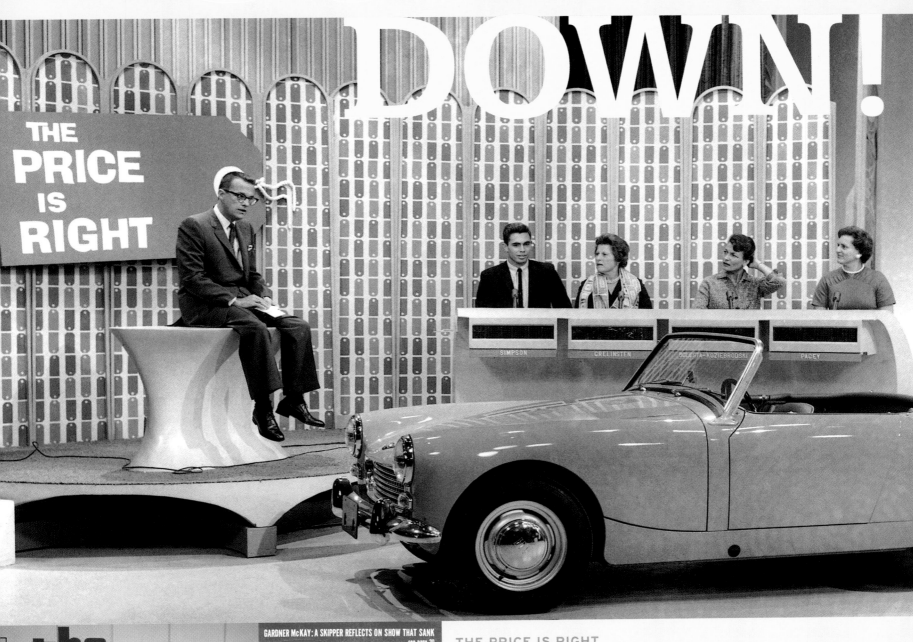

COME ON DOWN!

THE PRICE IS RIGHT

THE PRICE IS RIGHT

From top: Bill Cullen with contestants; Bob Barker. NBC, 1956–63; ABC, 1963–65; syndication, 1972–74, 1985 and 1994; CBS, 1972–
COVER: BY CURT GUNTHER, JULY 28, 1962

Whether hosted by Bill Cullen, Dennis James or Bob Barker, everything always seemed to ultimately go right for *The Price is Right*. In 1976, two decades after the debut of the guess-the-cost-of-the-merchandise game show, TV GUIDE said that four-year host Barker "looks as if he will be around a lot longer." A whopping 26 years later, there he was—on CBS, as the only host of a daytime network game show.

JEOPARDY!
Alex Trebek. NBC, 1964–75 and 1978–79; syndication, 1974 and 1984–
COVER: BY ULI ROSE, JANUARY 27, 2001

Back in 2000, when *Who Wants to Be a Millionaire* was bigfooting the ratings, the usually unruffled Alex Trebek was feeling decidedly perturbed when he spoke to journalism students at the University of Georgia. As TV GUIDE reported, the *Jeopardy!* host dissed the competition for asking no-brainer questions like "What's the usual color of Post-Its?" Trebek's irritation was understandable. For nearly 40 years, *Jeopardy!* had been TV's fortress of knowledge. Outside the gates, in the game-show wilderness, you might find contestants wearing funny hats, models caressing dining-room sets and hosts doubling as cheerleaders. But once you were inside the *Jeopardy!* compound with your thumb poised over the button, the rule was strictly "May the smartest person win." The show has moved around from networks to syndication since its launch in 1964, but the format has always remained the same: Contestants, after selecting from a category, are given an "answer" (e.g., "The Greek god of shepherds") and must supply the correct "question" ("Who is Pan?"). Created by Merv Griffin, who also hit the jackpot with *Wheel of Fortune*, *Jeopardy!* was originally hosted by the genial Art Fleming, who remained the face of the show for 15 years in daytime. After a few years off the air, *Jeopardy!* returned in 1984 with bigger dollar amounts and Trebek as host. That's when the show entered what has to be regarded as its classic era. Trebek seemed perfectly suited to the job: polite, efficient, commiserating, but ever so slightly condescending toward losers and winners alike. He always gave the faint impression that he could run the table if someone would just give him the chance. TV GUIDE in 1987 called *Jeopardy!* "the truest, purest test of general knowledge on the air today"—and that remained true well after the ratings reign of Regis Philbin's *Millionaire* began to wane.

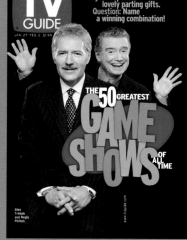

Answer: Beloved hosts, big money and lovely parting gifts. Question: Name a winning combination!

THE 50 GREATEST GAME SHOWS OF ALL TIME

Alex Trebek and Regis Philbin

"I THINK GAME SHOWS HAVE LASTED SO LONG BECAUSE THEY ARE BASICALLY FEEL-GOOD TELEVISION.

You're not dealing with the problems of the world. The viewers are watching ordinary people having, in some cases, spectacularly rewarding moments on national television. They're watching their peers do well. I used to liken game shows to the Great American Dream. Anybody can be president, anybody can do well, anybody can be rich. And game shows provide people with that opportunity. They make America feel better. A lot of the talk shows in recent years have gone into confrontational situations. They deal with problems, emotional distress, physical abuse, but game shows are just the opposite. You say, 'Well, isn't this nice, look at that. This little girl here lost her job, and now she just won $32,000 and a brand-new car.' We've got a lot of stories like that. One of our contestants had come to California and was on his last legs—he had no money and couldn't pay the rent. All of a sudden, he made it on *Jeopardy!* and won a lot of dough, and that enabled him to stay in California. His appearance on our show got him noticed, and he wound up being a radio commentator.

"On game shows, people have a chance to win big and demonstrate some measure of skill, whether it's coming up with a correct estimate of how much something costs in a supermarket or, as in the case on *Jeopardy!* and some of the other quiz shows in the past, coming up with very esoteric correct responses to difficult questions.

"But game shows have changed dramatically in terms of presentation. If you look at *Jeopardy!* today and compare it to the 1964 edition that aired on NBC, it's night and day. We have electronics; we have our clue crew of four young people who travel around the country and videotape clues to insert into the program; we even have celebrities doing clues for us. If you look at *Who Wants to Be a Millionaire* and *Weakest Link*, the presentation is very slick. They've almost got a rock-concert feel with the bank of lights above that switch and move. And there are sound effects and heightened drama. The presentation is head and shoulders above what used to be the case. If you think back, the early television game and quiz shows evolved from radio quiz shows. They were very static and not particularly eye-pleasing. But then again, in the 1950s a lot of television was like that. Television has evolved in the past 50 years by leaps and bounds."

—ALEX TREBEK

THE '50s

May 29, 1953
Photographer unknown
Queen Elizabeth II

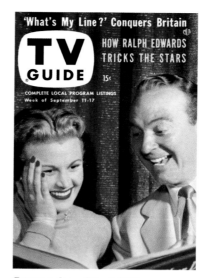

September 11, 1953
Photographer unknown
Joan Caulfield and Ralph Edwards
of *This Is Your Life*

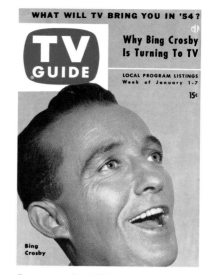

January 1, 1954
Photographer unknown
Bing Crosby

January 1, 1955
By Elmer Holloway
Loretta Young of *The Loretta
Young Show*

July 2, 1955
By Graphic House
Tommy Rettig of *Lassie* and Aaker Lee of
The Adventures of Rin Tin Tin

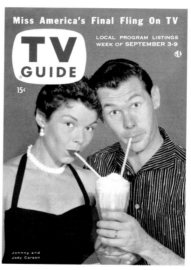

September 3, 1955
By Gaby Rona
Jody Carson and Johnny Carson of
The Johnny Carson Show

November 26, 1955
By Phillipe Halsman
Martha Raye of *The Martha Raye Show*

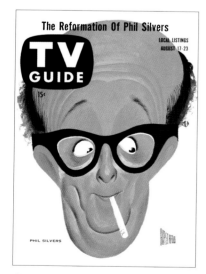

August 17, 1957
By Al Hirschfeld
Phil Silvers of *The Phil Silvers Show*

August 31, 1957
By Warner Bros.
Clint Walker of *Cheyenne*

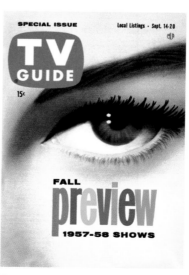

September 14, 1957
By Arthur Williams
Fall Preview

November 2, 1957
By Al Hirschfeld
Lucille Ball of *I Love Lucy*

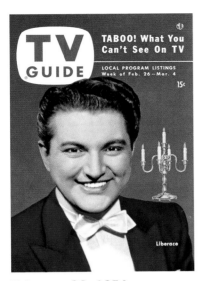

February 26, 1954
Photographer unknown
Liberace of *The Liberace Show*

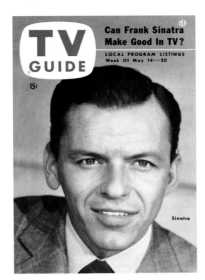

May 14, 1954
Photographer unknown
Frank Sinatra

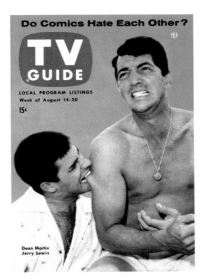

August 14, 1954
Photographer unknown
Jerry Lewis and Dean Martin

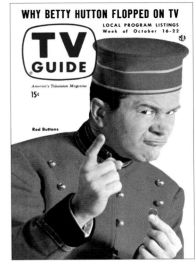

October 16, 1954
Photographer unknown
Red Buttons of *The Red Buttons Show*

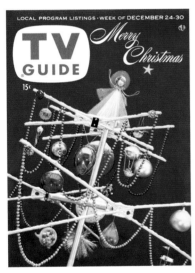

December 24, 1955
By Larry Fritz
Christmas

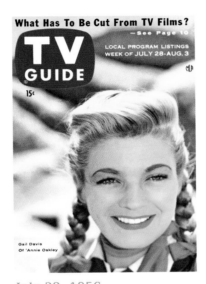

July 28, 1956
By Garrett-Howard
Gail Davis of *Annie Oakley*

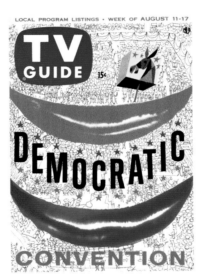

August 11, 1956
By KMLG-Barron
Democratic Convention

August 18, 1956
By Kramer, Miller, Lomden, Glassman
GOP Convention

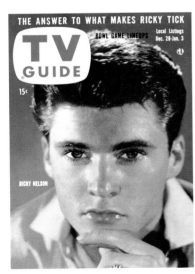

December 28, 1957
By John Engstead
Ricky Nelson of *The Adventures of Ozzie & Harriet*

March 22, 1958
By Al Hirschfeld
Perry Como of *The Perry Como Show*

April 26, 1958
By Dave Preston
Guy Williams of *Zorro*

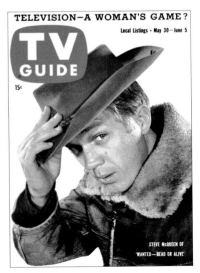

May 30, 1959
By Gene Trindl
Steve McQueen of *Wanted—Dead or Alive*

THE FRENCH CHEF
Julia Child. NET and PBS, 1963–73

"Part of cooking," Julia Child told her TV audience in 1964, "is in recovering one's mistakes. A cook's motto should be 'Never Despair.'" It was a message that millions of American cooks—so intimidated by French cuisine that they despaired of even attempting it—needed desperately to hear. And Child, a cooking instructor and author, was the perfect person to deliver it: With a fascinating blend of absolute focus and a *c'est la vie* offhandedness, she delightfully demystified Cordon Bleu cooking for a country stuck in a swamp of meat loaf, ketchup and SpaghettiOs. "Julia Child is not just a natural, she is without doubt the most natural performer television has yet uncovered," TV GUIDE said in '68. "She is so completely oblivious to the camera that she seems to come right through to us without any camera at all." Throughout her long public-TV career, Child was famous for slamming pots around and slopping mixtures onto the countertop ("Oh, bother!") in her enthusiasm for the task at hand. "It's an absolute *tragedy* if you don't have something that's really your life's purpose," she told the magazine in 1970. Never has missionary zeal provided such a tasty TV dinner.

TH

IT'S A GOOD THING

MARTHA STEWART LIVING
Syndication, 1993–

Martha Stewart's empire of domestic perfection wouldn't be complete without conquering the republic of television. So she launched a typically surgical strike: the syndicated *Martha Stewart Living*, which invited viewers to assiduously take notes on activities like cooking elaborate chocolate-filled puff pastries–or to daydream about living a life where such an undertaking was even conceivable. "I hope it's an interlude for people," Stewart said in TV GUIDE, "and a place to turn to get a sense of the lovely, the delicious and the elegant."

TABLOID TV
Security guard and guests on *The Jerry Springer Show*, **1998**
COVER: BY GARY HANNABARGER (2), MARC BRYAN-BROWN AND STEVE HILL, APRIL 1, 1995

Alan Burke and Joe Pyne pioneered what the latter called "fist-in-the-mouth" television in the 1960s. But they, and Morton Downey Jr. in the late '80s, largely relied on vitriol spewing back and forth between a repellent guest and a disgusted host. It took the trash TV, tabloid talk-show epidemic of the 1990s to discover the ratings gold mine of pitting guest against guest under the sleaziest possible pretext—and rabid studio audiences roared in delight at the obscenity-bleeped, hair-pulling punchfests that resulted. Jenny Jones, Ricki Lake, Geraldo Rivera and Jerry Springer ("the emcee of our darker side," TV GUIDE called him in '98) flourished by turning afternoons into an exploitation circus. When guests of Jones and Springer were later murdered in what seemed to be emotional fallout from the shows, both hosts claimed only a remote connection to the actual content of the productions and their guests. "I show up and I do the show. I have no idea who they are," he told TV GUIDE in 2000. But Springer had a pretty good idea of who he was. When he was beating *The Oprah Winfrey Show* consistently in the ratings in 1998, he told the magazine: "It's not fair to Oprah to put me in the same conversation as her. She's made a positive imprint on the medium."

THE GONG SHOW
Chuck Barris. NBC, 1976–78; syndication, 1976–80

The dislocated, post-'60s pop culture of the mid-'70s never looked more merrily bizarre than during *The Gong Show*'s day and night half hours. Here, an endless stream of the talentless but indefatigable—a dentist playing "Stars and Stripes Forever" with his drill, for instance—was rated by a panel of B-list celebrities. (Jaye P. Morgan, Jamie Farr and Phyllis Diller were regulars.) The truly bad got gonged, the winners pelted with confetti by a midget. "People always like to see other people fed to the lions," frenetic host and producer Chuck Barris told TV GUIDE in 1978. "To get out there and be tormented, that takes guts." Guts: required. Talent: optional.

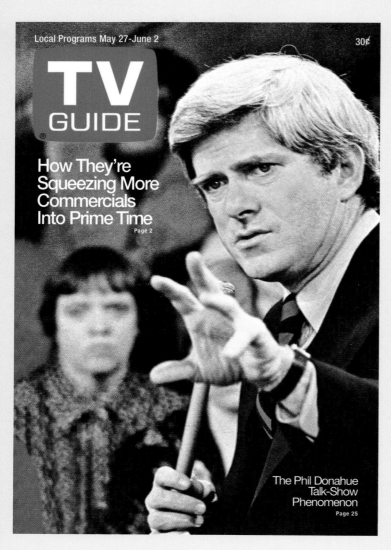

DONAHUE
Syndication, 1970–96
COVER: **BY ARNOLD ZANN, MAY 27, 1978**

Before Oprah Winfrey, Sally Jessy Raphaël and all the rest of the microphone-clutching, guest-prodding, audience-challenging daytime talk-show hosts, there was Phil Donahue. Those TV heirs "are all my illegitimate children, and I love them all equally," Donahue told TV GUIDE in 1992, 25 years after the daddy of all audience-participation talk shows started out in Dayton, Ohio, with *The Phil Donahue Show*. Though he certainly did his share of non-sensational shows–presidential candidate Bill Clinton was a guest in '92–Donahue cheerfully admitted that "sometimes you have to tap-dance a little faster to draw a crowd…. We got here by being outrageous. We've televised an abortion and the birth of a baby. I've wrestled women, belly danced and was thrown out of a Roller Derby ring. I've been body wrapped, acupunctured. We are tabloid–I'm happy to wear the label." He was also happy to wear a skirt for a transvestite fashion show in 1988, though Donahue told the magazine that his wife, actress Marlo Thomas–whom he met as a guest on his show–wasn't so thrilled. She "felt that this would give critics a big opportunity to take potshots." But the only potential critics Donahue himself worried about were his millions of largely female fans, who were represented by his studio audience ("Wait a minute," he'd say, interrupting guests and looking out into the crowd, "there's a lot of wisdom out here"). "The secret of it all," TV GUIDE said in 1978, "is that Donahue has one quality that is almost nonexistent" among TV interviewers: "He still cares. He still thinks that somehow, some way, it all matters." *Donahue* closed down in 1996, and its silver-haired host seemed to retire from television. But he apparently got bored being on the other side of the TV screen: In 2002, at age 66, he signed up to host a new talk show on cable-news channel MSNBC.

THE OPRAH WINFREY SHOW
Clockwise from left: Winfrey with Toni Morrison; Nelson Mandela; Tina Turner. Syndication, 1986–
COVERS (FROM TOP): **BY PAUL ELLEDGE, JANUARY 7, 1995, AND MAY 16, 1992**

There was a specific moment when it became clear that Oprah Winfrey was going to become an unprecedented hit on television. Early in 1984, the Baltimore talk-show cohost took on the thankless task of turning around a bottom-dwelling morning chat show in Chicago, home base of Phil Donahue. Two months later, Winfrey was beating Donahue on his own turf. If she could do that, she obviously could do anything—as Winfrey quickly demonstrated, becoming within a few years the unrivaled ruler of the daytime television landscape. Witness the power of "Oprah's Book Club," which turned unknown authors into household names. Appraising the Oprah phenomenon on a more personal level, TV GUIDE said, "She is a one-woman mission hell-bent on lifting other women out of their self-image as helpless victims." One advantage was that her own life had been an *Oprah*-worthy nightmare: a childhood spent shuttling from one care-giver to another, troubled teenage years, an adulthood with an emotionally traumatic romance and a lifelong struggle with her weight. The drama on her show came from guests and audience members, who spoke unguardedly in her presence knowing that if they cried, she would be there to cry with them, offer a hug and, in one case, confess that she, too, had been sexually abused as a child. "People like me because they see themselves in me," Winfrey told TV GUIDE. "That's how it is on TV. It's either, 'I want to be like that,' or 'I *am* like that.' " Winfrey offered both options: She had struggled and suffered, but at the same time she was now a daily advertisement for the power of personal responsibility. She had become, after all, one of the richest entertainers—one of the richest *people*—in America. "My feet are still planted firmly on the ground," she told the magazine in '88, after syndication of *The Oprah Winfrey Show* had made her a millionaire. "They're just wearing more expensive shoes."

WHAT WE ALL CAN DO TO
CHANGE TV

It was a night that changed my life forever. Sunday night, December 27, 1964. The Supremes were on *The Ed Sullivan Show*. It was the first time I had seen a black woman on television with such beauty and grace. I was a 10-year-old girl sitting on a cold linoleum floor in Milwaukee. I was inspired by the possibilities of what I would be. That, to me, is one of television's greatest functions: to inspire us, to give us hope and to help us improve our lives.

I always felt better after watching *The Andy Griffith Show*. Life was so simple—the characters all really cared for one another, and the biggest scandal was whether those were really Aunt Bee's pickles in the pickle contest. Even though I never saw a black person in Mayberry, I always thought that if one of us dropped in, Andy and Aunt Bee would give us a slice of pie and make us feel right at home.

Another one of my favorites was *The Mary Tyler Moore Show*. Mar' showed every young woman that independence was worth obtaining—she showed us the possibilities. Watching the show made me feel good about being a single woman with a career in the '70s. I wanted an *O* on my wall, because Mar' had an *M* on hers. I mourned the day *The Mary Tyler Moore Show* went off the air. It left a void. Television was never the same for me.

Since then, I rarely watch TV—not even my own show.... And for years, I made it a point never to watch other talk shows—I didn't want to be accused of imitation. But because there's been so much criticism of the genre, I began

looking around recently to see what all the fuss was about.

Picture me at home, flipping through the channels to see what I can find.

Aha—here's a talk show. The host is telling us that not even he knows which of his guests is telling the truth. We can call a 900 number and decide if a guy who looks like a Barry White wannabe is really the father of this teenager's baby. Is he lying? Is she? The call will cost 75 cents. *Click!*

Another talk show, this one with a kissing contest. I imagine there is an audience for this, judging by the reaction of the kiss-cheering supporters. *Click!*

The next day, I catch another talk show, and the issue is "Men Who Are Dogs." I can't believe it. The men are discussing the number of babies they have fathered and the number of women they have had—and they have the audacity to boast about it.

All this is in my mind a few weeks later when I am deciding whether to keep my own show going—or quit. I wonder, is this a sign that my time in TV has come and gone? I believe life gives you subtle and sometimes not-so-subtle messages that can guide you to the right answers. Should I just get out of the business and let the "Kissing Contest," "Men Who Are Dogs" and "Big-Butt Contest" rule? Another host did that show, with Nipsey Russell as one of the judges. Yes, Nipsey Russell of *To Tell the*

Truth is now rating the size of women's behinds on national television. Why?

I understand that the push for ratings causes programmers to air what's popular, and that's not going to change. I am embarrassed by how far over the line the topics have gone, but I also recognize my own contribution to this phenomenon.

Ten years ago, when my show was first syndicated, we started doing what we called "confrontational TV"—adult incest survivors confronting their abusers, children of alcoholics confronting their parents and victims of crime confronting the people who attacked them.

I believe it was important to introduce these issues and face the truth of who we were. We grew up in a society that for years denied dysfunction. TV brought some of that to the surface, but the problem, as I see it now, is that it didn't evolve from there. We needed to be solving these problems. Instead, TV got stuck *thriving* on them, and for the worst possible reasons—exploitation, voyeurism and entertainment.

This became very clear during my most humiliating moment on television. A man came on the show with his wife and mistress. Both women had given birth to children—his children—in the same time period. Neither woman knew it, and they found out on my show. The audience gasped. I was speechless. It's irrelevant that neither I nor the producers knew this bombshell was coming—because the pain on their faces remains a memory seared in my brain. People should not be surprised and humiliated on national television for the purpose of entertainment. I was ashamed of myself for creating the opportunity that allowed it to happen.

For many days afterward, I thought about them. What happened in the grocery store? Did the checkout clerk say, "Aren't you the woman whose husband was cheating?" How did their coworkers react? Were their mothers embarrassed?

Well, that was five years ago. As my friend and mentor Maya Angelou always says, "You did then what you knew how to do. When you knew better, you did better."

Since then, I've done a thousand more shows, shook 200,000 more hands and come to understand the power of this great medium a lot more. When I began my talk show, I was so thrilled to have the opportunity that I never thought much about the tremendous influence TV could have. Now I feel both the power and the enormous responsibility that come with it.

Thirty-seven years ago, Edward R. Murrow said of television, "This instrument can teach, it can illuminate—yes, and it can even inspire. But it can do so only to the extent that humans are determined to use it to those ends. Otherwise, it is merely wires and lights in a box." He continued, "There is a great and decisive battle to be fought against ignorance, intolerance and indifference. This weapon of television could be useful."

I believe we can use television for incredible changes, but only to the extent that people demand it. We all must ask for more shows that are positive and uplifting, that give messages of hope and possibility. I think of the 10-year-old girls sitting on the floor watching TV today, and wonder if there are shows on the air that will inspire them as I was inspired. We need shows with images of life as we would like it to be. We need to ask programmers for positive role models for ourselves and our children, for television that will strengthen the human spirit.

Television, like life, provides choices. By controlling the choices you make, you change what TV offers. It's only when viewers decide that they've had enough of violence, sensationalism and trash that it will end. Television is a reflection of who we are and who we say we want to be. It's time to offer new choices, new possibilities. It's time to elevate our potential.

—OPRAH WINFREY, EXCERPT FROM TV GUIDE, NOVEMBER 11, 1995

MTV

Carson Daly of *Total Request Live* with fans

COVER: BY LORRAINE DAY, AUGUST 3, 1991

As every trivia buff knows, the cable music-video network MTV launched in 1981 with the Buggles' "Video Killed the Radio Star," and as the rest of the world knows, almost nothing involving visual art has ever been the same. The music business was transformed by the network's star-making ability, of course (hello, Cyndi Lauper, Madonna, Duran Duran, et al.), but television, movies, advertising, fashion...you name the creative endeavor, and MTV's DNA is probably in there somewhere. Over time, the network began playing fewer and fewer videos as their visual-shorthand novelty wore off (even Michael Jackson's innovative "Thriller" video got old after the 73rd viewing) and found new success in other areas of programming, from the diabolical genius of the *Beavis and Butt-head* cartoon and *Celebrity Deathmatch* claymation to the trendsetting inspiration of *The Real World* (a reality-TV forerunner) and the network's biggest hit yet, *The Osbournes*. But MTV hasn't totally abandoned its music-video roots—just listen to the fan frenzy surrounding the countdown show *Total Request Live*. As Aerosmith lead singer Steven Tyler told TV GUIDE on the network's 20 anniversary, "MTV is like a stake in the tent of the rock and roll circus. It's really that integral." Thanks to the onetime upstart cable channel, the tent is now pitched daily in 350 million households worldwide, in 140 countries.

MICKEY MOUSE CLUB
Walt Disney with Mouseketeers. ABC, 1955–59
COVER: BY WALT DISNEY PRODS., OCTOBER 1, 1955

A year after the show's 1955 debut, *Mickey Mouse Club* director Sidney Miller—himself a former child actor—told TV GUIDE what a relief it was to be working with "normal kids," most of whom just "happened to take dancing or singing lessons when they were younger," compared with the showbiz brats he'd grown up beside. The normalcy of the Mouseketeers, along with a five-times-a-week afterschool time slot, might help explain the show's devoted following and, decades later, the warm memories many have of the M-I-C-K-E-Y theme song. The two dozen Mouseketeers introduced cartoons, acted in filmed serials, danced, sang and formed the audience for visitors (Tuesday was "Guest Star Day" and Friday was "Talent Roundup Day," when young performers were made honorary Mouseketeers). Oddly, only one breakout star emerged during the show's four years on the air. It was the girl, said a perplexed TV GUIDE, whose "singing is just adequate and whose dancing is only fair...neither brilliant nor dull, neither stagestruck, lazy nor ambitious." Still, those limitations didn't stop Annette Funicello from going on to beach-blanket immortality in the 1960s—helped along, no doubt, by legions of adolescent former *Mickey Mouse Club* fans.

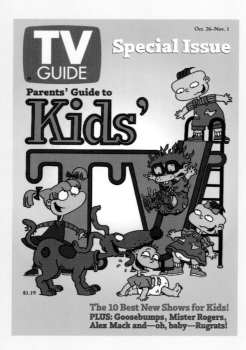

RUGRATS
Nickelodeon, 1991–
COVER: BY NICKELODEON, OCTOBER 26, 1996

"Animated" was the last word you'd apply to the kids' cartoon genre in the 1980s—the moribund format hadn't seen a spark of invention since Bullwinkle last tried to pull a rabbit out of his hat in the 1960s. But then, in 1991, *Rugrats* toddled onto the Nickelodeon schedule, helping to ignite a new era of creativity fostered by kid-oriented cable channels hungry for programming. Even a decade later, with the airwaves brimming with fresh cartoons like *The Powerpuff Girls* and *SpongeBob SquarePants*, *Rugrats* remains a major player,

presenting its tyke's-eye view of the world long after good-hearted Tommy and his best pal, the fearful Chuckie, should have been in junior high. Instead, they carry on in a universe where the fridge can be scary and potty training a nightmare. Gabor Csupo, cocreator of the show, told TV GUIDE in 1998: "You have to watch it to realize it's not just for babies. We write on two levels: for kids and adults." Which helps explain why parents, instead of groaning when the *Rugrats* theme song sounds, often sink into the sofa to watch, too.

"WHEN YOU'RE MAKING ANIMATED TELEVISION FOR CHILDREN,

you should never talk down to them and you should give them a lot of credit. They're smart, and they want to see something new or fresh or funny so they can talk about it. You can't hit them over the head with educational stuff because they can smell that from a mile away. And kids want to be entertained. If you can entertain and sneak in some cool information, that's the best way to do it. And if the cartoons are funny and they're telling a good story with great characters, it doesn't matter if they're stick figures or beautifully rendered three-dimensional computer animation. If it holds your attention and it's engaging, then it can be anything."

—GABOR CSUPO, COCREATOR OF *RUGRATS*, *THE WILD THORNBERRYS* AND *ROCKET POWER*

ABC AFTERSCHOOL SPECIALS
Sharon Lee (Jodie Foster) of "Rookie of the Year" (1973).
ABC, 1972–96

ABC Afterschool Specials didn't have a unifying theme, other than trying to put something more substantial than *Brady Bunch* reruns in front of school-age kids. The specials ran the programming gamut and included documentaries, interviews, cartoons (like Hanna-Barbera's eco-minded "Last of the Curlews," 1972), dramas (such as 1980's "Schoolboy Father," starring Rob Lowe) and discussions (the Oprah Winfrey-moderated program "Shades of a Single Protein," 1993, about race). The shows themselves were not always as memorable as some of their amusingly direct titles—"Me and My Hormones," "Can a Guy Say No?" and "Please Don't Hit Me, Mom." Nevertheless, the term "afterschool special" lives on—as a loose synonym for any mild entertainment with a worthy message.

GENERAL HOSPITAL

Laura Spencer (Genie Francis), Luke Spencer (Anthony Geary). ABC, 1963–

COVERS (FROM TOP): BY PETER KREDENSER, AUGUST 23, 1980. BY MARIO CASILLI, JULY 17, 1982

General Hospital premiered on April Fools' Day in 1963, and more than once over the course of the next four decades, the soap opera appeared to be pulling the audience's leg—a villain's diabolical plot to freeze the entire city of Port Charles, the hospital's hometown, comes to mind. But as TV GUIDE said in 1972, "if you'll promise not to breathe a word of it to a living soul, we just love this show. It's really so awful that it is, in its awful way, wonderful." The wonderful awfulness reached a sort of peak in 1981 when the wedding of Luke and Laura drew the biggest audience ever for a daytime drama. Your heart had to go out to the bride after all she'd been through: While still a teen, Laura had killed a boyfriend who was sleeping with her mother, joined a commune and married her childhood sweetheart before falling for a shady character who, despite raping her in a deserted disco, still held a claim on her affection. Oh, the troubles Laura had known! Not that her fellow characters couldn't empathize: Life in Port Charles often seemed to be just one long string of car wrecks, murders, disappearances, amnesia attacks, nervous breakdowns and Byzantine romantic entanglements. It was the top-rated soap for much of the 1980s, with much of the credit going to producer Gloria Monty, who kept those story lines rattling. (Having pop star Rick Springfield in the cast didn't hurt, either.) In 1996, the death of actor John Beradino, who played General Hospital's director of medicine, Steve Hardy, marked the passing of the show's last original cast member. But *General Hospital* itself would not die. It finished the decade with respectable ratings, steaming toward 2003 and its 40th anniversary as one of TV's greatest successes.

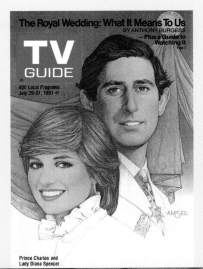

WEDDING OF PRINCE CHARLES AND LADY DIANA
July 29, 1981
COVER: BY RICHARD AMSEL, JULY 25, 1981

Regardless of all that would later transpire, the wedding of Prince Charles and Lady Diana Spencer was a truly enchanting moment. It was a celebration of "the consummation of love and the hope of a posterity," as author Anthony Burgess wrote in *TV Guide* in anticipation of the event, which was seen by a worldwide television audience of 750 million (including many Americans who had to get up as early as 5 A.M. Eastern Time to catch the festivities). "The common man has had too complete a triumph and has dressed us all in gray," Burgess wrote. "It will be a shot in the arm to see gold and scarlet and purple again, and to hear the silver trumpets."

ALL MY CHILDREN

**Bianca Montgomery (Eden Riegel), Erica Kane (Susan Lucci),
Jack Montgomery (Walt Willey). ABC, 1970–**
COVER: BY ROGER PRIGENT, NOVEMBER 10, 1990

Launched during the social tumult of 1970, *All My Children* immediately distinguished itself from the competition by grappling with hot-button topics of the day. Not that the denizens of the fictional New York City suburb of Pine Valley neglected to pursue more customary concerns—many of which revolved around the evil queen of all bitches, Erica Kane, a role that Susan Lucci made "the most famous soap-opera character in the history of daytime TV," as TV GUIDE declared in 1989. *AMC* fans are particularly devoted, even by soap standards: Carol Burnett had already been a three-time guest star when she told the magazine in '89, "I can't get through the day without it."

"I THINK DAYTIME TELEVISION HAS BEEN QUITE GROUNDBREAKING.

And I feel so lucky to have been part of it. This is really [creator] Agnes Nixon's doing. Before I ever came onto the *All My Children* canvas, she was known for addressing important social issues. That's a hallmark of Agnes's work. My character, Erica, had the first legal abortion on daytime television, and recently we did a really innovative and beautifully written two-year story line about the relationship between Erica and her 16-year-old daughter, Bianca, who was coming out about being gay.

"Also, we have the luxury of time. That's what daytime drama has that other mediums don't. Because it's five days a week with no hiatus, you can explore things very realistically and with continuity. There doesn't have to be a cliff-hanger at the end of 13 or 22 weeks. You can continue exploring issues and do so in a lot of detail—which allows someone like Agnes, who has a social conscience as well as a tremendous ability to entertain, to do groundbreaking work. It gives her the perfect forum. This luxury of time also allows you to have better character development and lets the viewers get to know the characters. They grow very attached. Erica has really been naughty over the years, but viewers have also seen all the underpinnings, so they understand her better. She's a complicated character, and they get to love her *and* hate her."

—SUSAN LUCCI

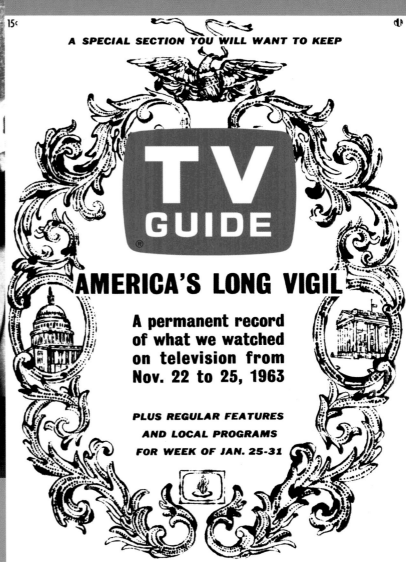

THE ASSASSINATION AND FUNERAL
OF PRESIDENT JOHN F. KENNEDY

**Clockwise from far left: John F. Kennedy Jr.; Lee Harvey Oswald, Jack
Ruby; Lyndon B. Johnson, Jacqueline Kennedy. November 22–25, 1963**
COVER: BY ARTHUR WILLIAMS, JANUARY 25, 1964

It was 1:40 P.M. Eastern Time on Friday, November 22, 1963, when the words CBS BULLETIN
blacked out the live production of *As the World Turns*. "In Dallas, Texas, three shots
were fired at President Kennedy's motorcade," intoned the voice of Walter Cronkite.
"The first reports say the president was seriously wounded...." Over the next four con-
vulsive days, television was transformed. It would no longer be just the most dominant
form of national entertainment. Instead, it found that it could also bear witness for an
entire country, if not the world, and make an "historic contribution," as President
Lyndon B. Johnson wrote in a special section of TV GUIDE two months later.

The section was the magazine's attempt to combat the fleeting nature of the medium
and provide "a permanent reminder" of what the nation had experienced in those four
days of nonstop news coverage. Indeed, the magazine pointed out, certain TV images
remain indelible parts of the national memory: distraught news anchors struggling to
maintain their composure as they confirm Kennedy's death; Jacqueline Kennedy, still in
her blood-spattered pink suit, arriving with the casket and a new president in Washington;
the still unbelievable live coverage of Lee Harvey Oswald being shot by Jack Ruby;
John-John's heartbreaking salute to his father's casket.

But there were many smaller moments, too. Among the anchors who hurried on to the
air and stayed for hours, the magazine said, "it was Cronkite who agonized the most
and controlled it best." NBC took its cameras outside in New York City, capturing grief-
stricken reactions of people gathered on the sidewalk who were hearing the news from
car radios. ABC replayed tape taken earlier that day of the president and first lady,
smiling and bathed in sunlight, arriving at the Dallas airport. Condolence statements
were broadcast from former president Dwight D. Eisenhower, Gen. Douglas MacArthur
and former Illinois governor Adlai Stevenson. That night, viewers saw Oswald led
through the Dallas police station, a scene of bedlam that foretold Sunday's disaster. It
was also on Sunday that about a quarter of a million citizens began filing past Kennedy's body, lying in state in the Capitol rotunda. Viewing that scene, Edward P. Morgan
on ABC said to his colleague, Howard K. Smith: "You keep thinking, Howard, that this is
a dream from which you will awake—but you won't."

On Monday, the entire nation witnessed the stately funeral. "This was," said Charles
Collingwood at CBS, "the day we were restored to sanity." It was also a time of
beginning, TV GUIDE noted, for a new government and a new era in television. The
medium had "gained a new sense of what it could do," a sense that it was "capable of
encompassing not just life's trivia, but the deepest of human experience."

O.J. SIMPSON BRONCO CHASE
June 17, 1994
COVER: BY MARK MALABRIGO,
JULY 30, 1994

TV GUIDE simply called it "O.J.: The News as Miniseries." And that was in July 1994, when the country had only been through the slo-mo Bronco chase (seen by 95 million TV viewers) and pretrial hearings. The bloody glove, DNA evidence and LAPD officer Mark Fuhrman all lay ahead, in the gripping, tedious and appalling criminal trial of O.J. Simpson for the stabbing deaths of his ex-wife, Nicole Brown Simpson, and her visitor, waiter Ronald Goldman. Author Neal Gabler, writing in that issue of the magazine, called the story "the news equivalent of a great beach read"—with a football hero, a gorgeous blond, tempestuous romance, etc.—but he also pondered the overwhelming news coverage of the case. "The media are no longer primarily purveyors of information," Gabler wrote, "they are purveyors of drama." They are also great ones, he said, for turning a trashy melodrama into "a festival of national reflection and self-criticism." Whatever the meaning of Simpson's eventual acquittal on criminal charges and his loss in a subsequent civil trial, Gabler recognized that it all would play out in a "theater called America," where the nation would find "a common subject, if not exactly common ground."

CHALLENGER
January 28, 1986
COVER: BY NASA, FEBRUARY 24, 1990

Throughout the 1960s, space exploration was the repository of the nation's dreams, with families clustering around TV sets to share in the communal pursuit. But by the mid-'80s, rocket launches from Cape Canaveral were barely even noteworthy—that is, until one devastating day in 1986. There was the usual thunderous liftoff, the slow, powerful climb into the Florida sky. Then came the horrible explosion, the smoking debris plummeting for what seemed like an eternity down into the Atlantic. Once again, Americans huddled around their TV sets, only this time it was not to celebrate, but to mourn the stunning loss of seven lives.

"SEPTEMBER 11 WAS SUCH A HUGE TRAGEDY,

but in a terrible way, it brought the television news business back. We'd been doing half-hour news programs, with 10 minutes of news and then [the rest] like a magazine piece: 'You and Your Money.' 'You and Your Health.' 'You and Your Diet.' TV newsmagazines were doing celebrities. We were doing movie stars in trouble. The week before 9/11, I had a 30-minute interview with Anne Heche.

"It was horrific, but for the industry it made a big difference. After 9/11, all of us were mobilized. We were doing reports and special interviews. We were on all the time. On *20/20*, we did almost every program live. One of my colleagues sent me an e-mail: 'What a terrible tragedy. But isn't it amazing that we're now back in the news business?'"

–BARBARA WALTERS

ONE OF FIVE SPECIAL
COVERS TO CELEBRATE
THE AMERICAN SPIRIT
SEE PAGE 3

MAY IT
EVER WAVE
BY AL
HIRSCHFELD

DEC. 22–28 $1.99

SEPTEMBER 11, 2001
Police officers at the World Trade Center, New York City, September 12, 2001
COVER: BY AL HIRSCHFELD, DECEMBER 22, 2001

Television has never seemed more pitiless as an unblinking witness to history than it was on September 11, 2001. The still unbelievable images of jetliners smashing into the World Trade Center towers, and of the buildings' dumbfounding, terrible collapse, will stay with viewers for the rest of their lives. But as TV GUIDE said later that month, the medium's coverage of the aftermath of the terror attacks—in New York City; Washington, D.C.; and Pennsylvania, where United Airlines Flight 93 crashed—also "provided a reassuring reminder that we were all in this together. Our enemies hadn't destroyed our ability to communicate: to share grief, express hope and investigate the truth."

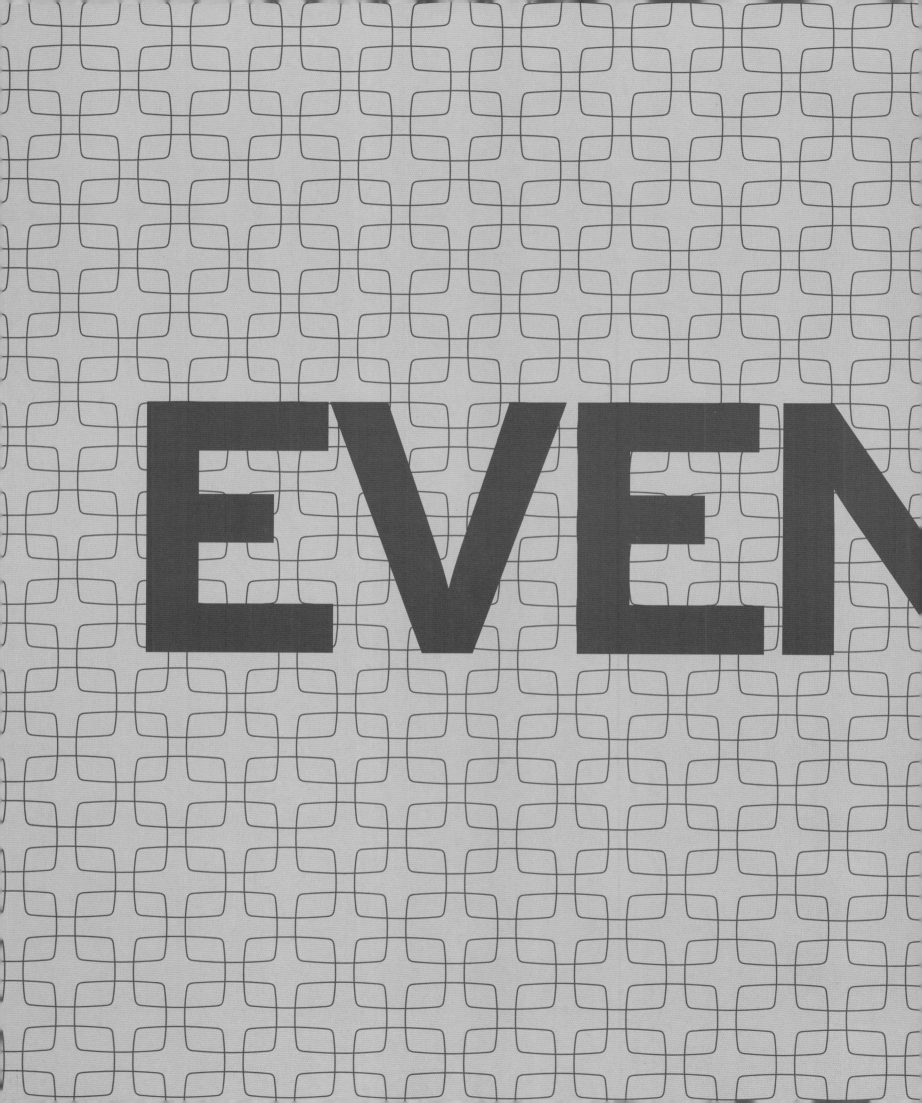

EDWARD R. MURROW
From top: 1959; 1951
COVER: BY AL HIRSCHFELD,
NOVEMBER 3, 1956

"For courage, intelligence and dignity," TV GUIDE said in 1958 of Edward R. Murrow's *See It Now* documentary series, "it has demonstrated an excellence rare in any form of journalism." Murrow tackled civil rights, the smoking/cancer link and, most memorably, Sen. Joseph McCarthy's anti-Communist witch-hunt, setting a standard that reporters have aspired to for generations. As author Theodore H. White wrote in TV GUIDE in '86: "His exploration of television's new range was so powerful in its impact on our dreams and lives that in American journalism only Horace Greeley and Walter Lippmann matched him in shaping our history."

and THAT'S the WAY IT IS

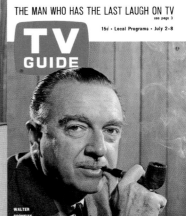

WALTER CRONKITE
From top: 1960; Cronkite with John F. Kennedy, 1960
COVER: BY PHILIPPE HALSMAN, JULY 2, 1966

"I never did have any desire to be a pundit," Walter Cronkite told TV GUIDE in 1966, recalling his days as a reporter before being installed as the *CBS Evening News* anchor in '62, "though I do like to think I have always brought a certain compassion to my coverage." That instinctive sensitivity, along with a comfortable but authoritative manner, helped make Cronkite the definitive network-news anchor for 19 years. Every major event of the '60s and '70s—John F. Kennedy's assassination, the *Apollo* rocket launches, Vietnam, political conventions, Watergate—seemed to have the same narrator: the voice most trusted by America.

CNN AND THE GULF WAR
Antiaircraft fire over
Baghdad, Iraq,
January 18, 1991

"There has never been anything like the way that television has colored, shadowed, illuminated and distorted the war in the Persian Gulf," veteran media analyst Jeff Greenfield wrote in TV GUIDE in 1991, as Operation Desert Storm unfolded. During those riveting days, CNN for a time became our only window into bomb-rocked Baghdad, Iraq, thanks to a special phone line that enabled the cable channel to keep reporting long after the major news networks were knocked off the air. The networks had no choice but to broadcast their rival's coverage, and officials of countless governments tuned in to stay informed. Although CNN had been around for a decade, it was the Gulf War that finally vindicated the concept of a 24-hour news channel.

"Nothing changed news coverage like the advent of CNN. Its impact has enormously affected every aspect of broadcasting. Twenty-four-hour news changed the world." —Larry King

BROADCAST NEWS
COVERS: BY PHILIPPE HALSMAN, JULY 9, 1960. BY RICHARD AMSEL, OCTOBER 26, 1985

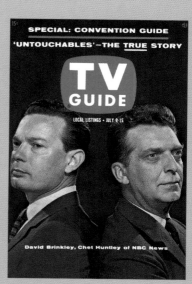

In May 2002, when Tom Brokaw announced his intention to retire as *NBC Nightly News* anchor in two years and the network said it planned to install Brian Williams in his chair, it was only fitting. Brokaw's retirement would mark the end of nearly a half century when network anchors incontestably ruled TV news; Williams would be coming over from MSNBC, one of the 24-hour cable-news operations that had helped make it unlikely we would ever again see network anchors accorded the status they enjoyed for decades. Though television had offered news reports since its infancy, it wasn't until NBC teamed sober, seasoned correspondent Chet Huntley with a young and wryly detached David Brinkley in 1956 that the modern network-news era got under way. *The Huntley-Brinkley Report*'s brisk pace and wide range (for starters, Huntley reported from New York City, Brinkley from Washington, D.C.) made it the dominant news show for most of its 14 years. Meanwhile, a tradition of granite stability developed at CBS, with Douglas Edwards in the 1950s, Walter Cronkite and his fabled tenure in the '60s and '70s, and Dan Rather ("equal parts Will Rogers and Edward R. Murrow," TV GUIDE said in 2002), who took over as anchor in 1981 and began a run of more than two decades. That time included a 1993–95 session of coanchoring with Connie Chung—a chemistry-free arrangement spurred by the rise of the longtime underachiever, ABC's *World News Tonight*, which began thriving after Peter Jennings's arrival in '83. Jennings built a reputation as the "go-to anchor in times of crisis," TV GUIDE said in 2001, an assessment that was prompted by September 11, 2001, and its aftermath. Though the age of the network anchor might be waning, or maybe just changing, that emergency reminded us why the need for a reliable, calm and clear source of news will always remain.

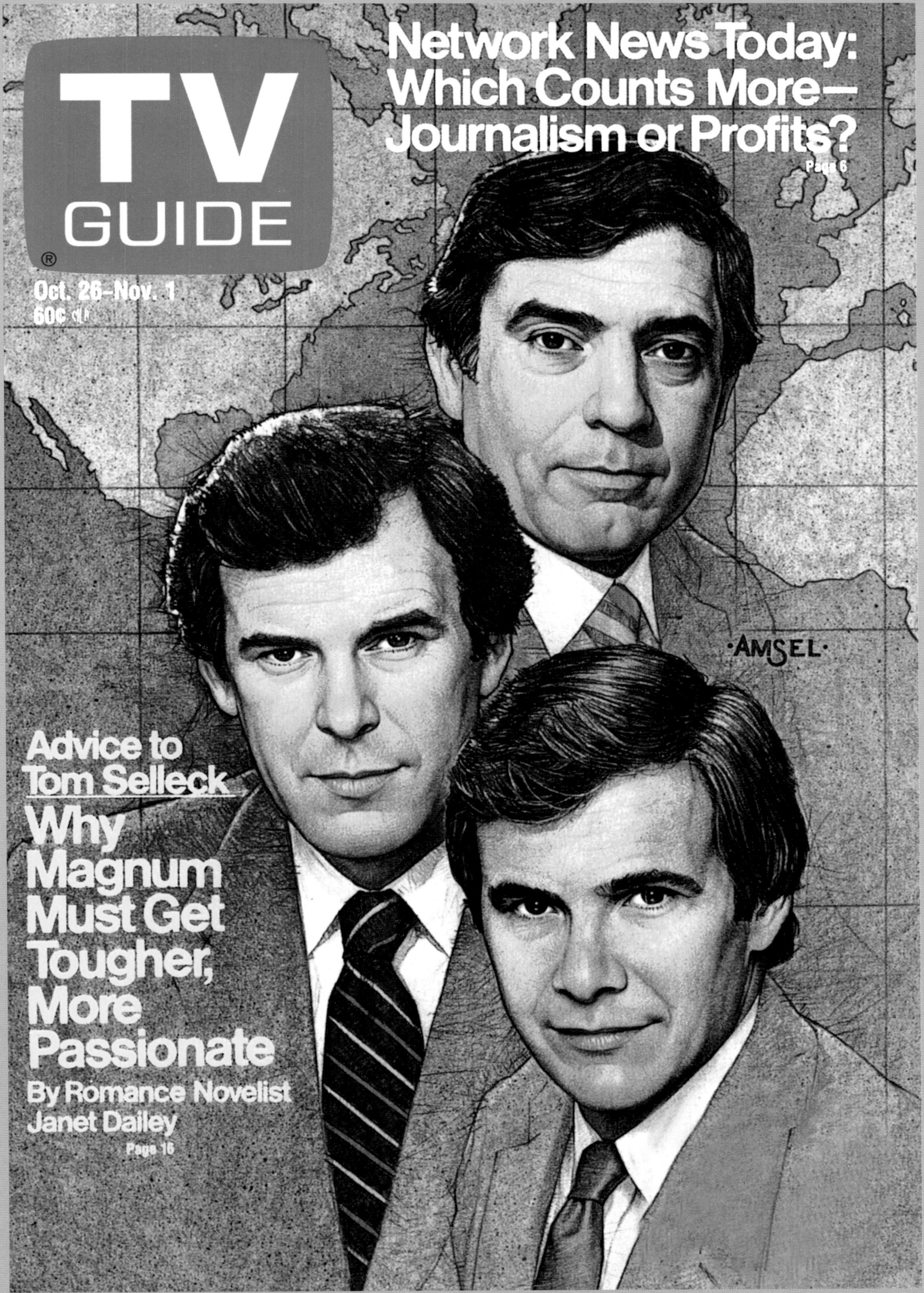

TV GUIDE®

Oct. 26–Nov. 1
60¢

Network News Today: Which Counts More— Journalism or Profits?

Page 6

Advice to <u>Tom Selleck</u>

Why Magnum Must Get Tougher, More Passionate

By Romance Novelist Janet Dailey

Page 16

·AMSEL·

THE VIETNAM WAR

COVER: BY NEIL HICKEY, OCTOBER 1, 1966

In September 1973, eight months after the United States and North Vietnam signed a cease-fire agreement and the Vietnam War started to come to its ragged conclusion, TV GUIDE began publishing a three-part investigation of television's role in reporting more than 10 years of conflict and in shaping public opinion. Even then, the conventional wisdom that prevails three decades later had already begun to form: It was the sight of bloody American soldiers and body bags on the nightly news that turned public opinion against the war. But that assumption was "not warranted," said TV GUIDE, after reviewing a decade's worth of network newscasts. "Television was neither monolithic nor consistent in its coverage and commentaries." Indeed, as the Vietnam War progressed, so did the nature of the televised war—and public opinion with it. In the period between 1962 and 1968, the magazine reported, a time when TV reporters were shuttled around the war zone by military press officers in helicopters, coverage focused on the overwhelming technological advantage of the growing U.S. force. In 1967, a *Newsweek* magazine poll found that 64 percent of Americans said that TV news broadcasts made them *more* supportive of American involvement in Vietnam. Then came the Tet Offensive in 1968, when "the televised picture of gradual progress in the war was abruptly shattered." With Saigon under assault, TV GUIDE reported, "merely by stepping outside their hotels, correspondents found themselves willy-nilly in the midst of bloody fighting." Reporters scrambled to get footage of the chaos and violence, and networks paid for expensive satellite transmissions to rush those dispatches to the air. Even though the Tet Offensive was successfully repulsed and the Vietcong grievously damaged by their losses, they "paradoxically won a decisive psychological victory in America," TV GUIDE said. "The American public was unable to digest the unprecedented violence and gore they saw during Tet." CBS newsman Walter Cronkite was equally stunned; he flew to Vietnam to gauge the situation himself and, upon returning, told his viewers the war was a "bloody stalemate." That appeared to be an assessment almost universal in network newsrooms, and post-Tet coverage reflected it, until peace negotiations began in late '68 and "television gradually changed its focus to the story of the American withdrawal," TV GUIDE said. The magazine's series ended with these words: "It is no doubt true that television was to a large extent responsible for the disillusionment with the war, as those in the media take relish in pointing out. But it is also true that television must take the responsibility for creating—or at least reinforcing—the illusion of American military omnipotence on which much of the early support of the war was based."

KENNEDY-NIXON PRESIDENTIAL DEBATES
Below: Sen. John F. Kennedy, Frank McGee, Vice President Richard M. Nixon. September 26, October 7, October 13, October 21, 1960

The prevailing opinion is that the 1960 presidential election just may have hinged on these unprecedented TV debates, when a sweaty, ill-at-ease Vice President Richard M. Nixon, who had disdained wearing makeup, wilted under Sen. John F. Kennedy's charismatic gleam. While experts are still debating the ultimate impact of "The Great Debates," as they were billed, one point is inarguable: The face-offs revealed television's tremendous power to shape public perceptions of a candidate.

A FORCE THAT HAS CHANGED THE POLITICAL SCENE

The wonders of science and technology have revolutionized the modern American political campaign. Giant electronic brains project results on the basis of carefully conducted polls. Automatic typewriters prepare thousands of personally addressed letters, individually signed by automatic pens. Jet planes make possible a coast-to-coast speaking schedule no observation-car back platform could ever meet. Even wash-and-wear fabrics permit the wilted nonstop candidate to travel lighter, farther and faster.

But nothing compares with the revolutionary impact of television. TV has altered drastically the nature of our political campaigns, conventions, constituents, candidates and costs. Some politicians regard it with suspicion, others with pleasure. Some candidates have been advised to avoid it. To the voter and vote getter alike, TV offers new opportunities, new challenges and new problems.

But for better or worse—and I side with those who feel its net effect can definitely be for the better—the impact of TV on politics is tremendous. Just 40 years ago, Woodrow Wilson exhausted his body and mind in an intensive cross-country tour to plead the cause of the League of Nations. Three weeks of hard travel and 40 speeches brought on a stroke before he had finished "taking his case to the people" in the only way then available. Today, President Dwight D. Eisenhower, taking his case to the people on the labor situation, is able to reach several million in one 15-minute period without ever leaving his office.

Many new political reputations have been made on TV—and many old ones have been broken. The searching eye of the television camera scrutinizes the candidates—and the way they are picked. Party leaders are less willing to run roughshod over the voters' wishes and handpick an unknown, unappealing or unpopular candidate in the traditional "smoke-filled room" when millions of voters are watching, comparing and remembering.

The slick or bombastic orator, pounding the table and ringing the rafters, is not as welcome in the family living room as he was in the town square or party hall. In the old days, many a seasoned politician counted among his most highly developed and useful talents his ability to dodge a reporter's question, evade a "hot" issue and avoid a definite stand. But today a vast viewing public is able to detect such deception and, in my opinion, willing to respect political honesty.

Honesty, vigor, compassion, intelligence—the presence or lack of these and other qualities make up what is called the candidate's "image." While some intellectuals and politicians may scoff at these images—and while they may in fact be based only on a candidate's TV impression, ignoring his record, views and other appearances—my own conviction is that these images or impressions are likely to be uncannily correct. I think, no matter what their defenders or detractors may say, that the television public has a fairly good idea of what Eisenhower is really like—or Jimmy Hoffa or John McClellan or Vice President Nixon or countless others.

This is why a new breed of candidates has sprung up on both the state and national levels. Most of these men are comparatively young. Their youth may still be a handicap in the eyes of older politicians—but it is definitely an asset in creating a television image people like and (most difficult of all) remember.

This is not to say that all the politicians of yesteryear would have been failures in the Age of Television. The rugged vigor of Teddy Roosevelt, the determined sincerity of Woodrow Wilson, the quiet dignity of Abraham Lincoln and the confidence-inspiring calm of Franklin D. Roosevelt—all would have been tremendously effective on television.

Can you imagine the effect of televising FDR's "fireside chats"?

But political success on television is not, unfortunately, limited only to those who deserve it. It is a medium that lends itself to manipulation, exploitation and gimmicks. It can be abused by demagogues, by appeals to emotion and prejudice and ignorance.

Political campaigns can actually be taken over by the public relations experts, who tell the candidate not only how to use TV but what to say, what to stand for and what "kind of person" to be. Political shows, like quiz shows, can be fixed—and sometimes are.

The other great problem TV presents for politics is the item of financial cost. It is no small item. In the 1956 campaign, the Republican National Committee, according to the Gore report, spent over $3 million for television—and the Democratic National Committee, just under $2.8 million on television broadcasting.

If all candidates and parties are to have equal access to this essential and decisive campaign medium, without becoming deeply obligated to the big financial contributors from the worlds of business, labor or other major lobbies, then the time has come when a solution must be found to this problem of TV costs.

This is not the place to discuss alternative remedies. But the basic point is this: Whether TV improves or worsens our political system, whether it serves the purpose of political education or deception, whether it gives us better or poorer candidates, more intelligent or more prejudiced campaigns—the answers to all these questions are up to you, the viewing public.

It is your power to perceive deception, to shut off gimmickry, to reward honesty, to demand legislation where needed. Without your approval, no TV show is worthwhile and no politician can exist.

That is the way it always has been and will continue to be—and that is the way it should be.

—SEN. JOHN F. KENNEDY,
EXCERPT FROM TV GUIDE, NOVEMBER 14, 1959

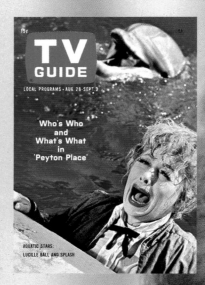

LUCILLE BALL

1957. Opposite page, top: Ethel Mertz (Vivian Vance), Lucy Ricardo (Ball), Ricky Ricardo (Desi Arnaz), Fred Mertz (William Frawley) of *I Love Lucy*
COVER: BY SHEEDY-LONG, AUGUST 28, 1965

Hollywood studio heads took one look at the luminous beauty of Lucille Ball and thought, "Glamour girl." It required the fledgling medium of television—and the roll-the-dice attitude of its pioneers—to see the former model's genius for physical comedy and rescue her from B-movie limbo. *I Love Lucy* made its debut in 1951, a perhaps unlikely candidate for becoming one of the defining shows of TV's classic era—for one thing, Ball insisted on working with her husband, Desi Arnaz, a Cuban bandleader who spoke English with an accent thicker than the Havana phone book. Nevertheless, this domestic comedy about a young couple setting up house instantly hit home with millions of postwar Americans who were doing the same and launching the baby boom. Yes, the carrot-topped, blue-eyed actress made an uncommonly attractive homemaker, but she never put on airs, stuffing her face full of production-line chocolates or pretending to get blotto as the spokeswoman for an alcohol-laced health tonic called Vitameatavegamin ("Do you pop out at parties? Are you un-poop-ular?"). A 1953 episode heralding the arrival of Little Ricky—and mirroring the real-life birth of Desi Jr.—drew a prodigious 72 percent of the TV audience. In 1960, Ball divorced the carousing Arnaz ("I've been humili-ated," she told TV GUIDE 10 days later) but continued to be a power in Hollywood as president of Desilu Productions and star of *The Lucy Show* and *Here's Lucy*. Those series had different casts and premises, but one constant remained: an indomitable comedian who enjoyed a "poop-ularity" achieved by few performers before or since.

VITAMEATAVEGAMIN
FOR HEALTH

HAPPY DAYS

Arthur Fonzarelli (Henry Winkler), Richie Cunningham (Ron Howard), Ralph Malph (Donny Most), Warren "Potsie" Weber (Anson Williams). ABC, 1974–84

COVER: BY GENE TRINDL, DECEMBER 15, 1979

Roiled by the cultural upheaval of the '60s, America started in the early '70s to look back fondly to a simpler era of hot rods, drive-in movies, poodle skirts and teens in search of fun. This nostalgia made hits out of the stage musical *Grease* (1972) and the movie *American Graffiti* (1973), the latter featuring Ronny Howard, ex-Opie of Mayberry, as a nice-guy adolescent. TV producer Garry Marshall, who had been trying unsuccessfully to interest the networks in a '50s-themed show starring Howard, suddenly found himself very popular. But not as popular as *Happy Days* itself would become. Howard starred as Richie Cunningham in the comedy, which was saved from predictability—high school kid from nice family in Milwaukee comes of age—by the presence of a leather-jacketed greaser named Arthur Fonzarelli. "This is a very *little* part," Marshall recalled warning Henry Winkler before he took the role as the Fonz. "Don't start up if you want a bigger part." But Winkler's ability to show a tough guy's vulnerability, especially when he counseled Richie about life, turned him into such a star that audiences soon overruled Marshall. A classic episode that became a holiday tradition found the Fonz, alone on Christmas with just his motorcycle and a shabby sprig of a tree, agreeing to join the Cunningham celebration at their home. *Happy Days* ran until 1984, but the Smithsonian couldn't wait: It enshrined Fonzie's leather jacket in 1980.

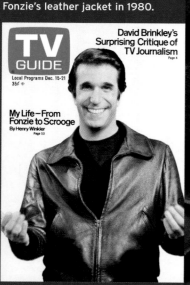

TV GUIDE
Local Programs Dec. 15-21
35¢

David Brinkley's Surprising Critique of TV Journalism
Page 4

My Life—From Fonzie to Scrooge
By Henry Winkler
Page 22

"WHEN I WENT TO PARAMOUNT STUDIOS TO AUDITION FOR HAPPY DAYS,

I only had enough money to stay in California for another month. And at the end of that month, I got the call: Would I like to play Fonzie? I told them that if I could show the other side of him when he takes off his leather jacket, it would be my pleasure. The first time I knew that the role had really taken off was when I went to make a personal appearance in Little Rock, Arkansas, and there were thousands of people waiting for me at the airport at 11:30 at night. It was an unbelievable time. [It was around then] that my wife and I had our first date. When you take a girl out, you're already nervous, and at that particular moment, if you walked into a 7-Eleven, I was on every cover on the newsstand. The entire time we were driving around, I was waving to people. Stacey kept saying to me, 'So, who is that?' and I said, 'I don't have the slightest idea. If they're waving at me, I'm waving back.'

"In this cast, there was a feeling of family—we still have that feeling. And I'm very, very proud that I was a part of *Happy Days*, and proud that the show somehow connected with so many people around the world. [Even today] I'm invited into people's homes for dinner wherever I go. There hasn't been a place that my wife and I have traveled to where people haven't been so warm that they've treated us like a part of their family."

—HENRY WINKLER

THE ANDY GRIFFITH SHOW
Andy Taylor (Griffith), Opie Taylor (Ronny Howard). CBS, 1960–68
COVER: BY RICHARD R. HEWETT, MAY 11, 1963

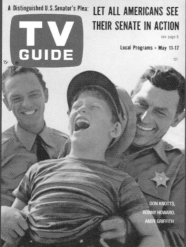

From the first moments of *The Andy Griffith Show*, you knew there was something different about it: The chipper, carefree tune whistled over the opening credits stood out amid the noise and clutter of TV. Griffith, who had used his North Carolina accent to make his name as a comedian in the 1950s, slipped easily into the role of Andy Taylor, sheriff of the mythical small town of Mayberry, North Carolina. At a time when Marshal Matt Dillon was facing down six-shooters on *Gunsmoke* and Eliot Ness was gangbusting on *The Untouchables*, Sheriff Taylor had almost no law enforcing to do—other than letting Otis, the town drunk, occasionally crash for the night in a jail cell. Instead, Andy helped Floyd the barber, gas-pump jockey Gomer Pyle and the rest of Mayberry's denizens sort out their entirely noncriminal troubles— often in spite of the "assistance" from the sheriff's tightly wound,

pop-eyed deputy, Barney Fife, played to jittery perfection by Don Knotts. "It won't be all comedy," Griffith told TV GUIDE a few days before the show's debut in 1960. "We'll be usin' lots of fine character actors. It's sort of easy to get too much of me. I'm stoic. I mean, I just sort of sit there and nothin' much happens." Stoic or not, Sheriff Taylor used his good sense and ingenuity to carry the day on most occasions, whether he was settling a long-standing feud between two mountain families or teaching a life lesson to his son, Opie (little "Ronny" Howard). The formidable Aunt Bee, of course, was also a stalwart presence, always prepared to help out her widower nephew in between pie-making sessions. In 1968, Griffith left the show, which was rechristened *Mayberry R.F.D.*, but the original series continued to run in syndication like a long, lazy river.

THE BRADY BUNCH

Marcia Brady (Maureen McCormick), Peter Brady (Christopher Knight), Cindy Brady (Susan Olsen), Bobby Brady (Mike Lookinland), Jan Brady (Eve Plumb), Greg Brady (Barry Williams). ABC, 1969–74

COVER: BY GENE TRINDL, APRIL 4, 1970

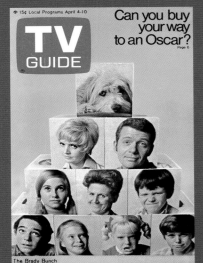

The Brady Bunch

In its 1970 review of *The Brady Bunch*, TV GUIDE virtuously pleaded that the "millions of stepchildren nowadays" deserved "something more than this mish-mush." Perhaps they deserved more, but many of them also apparently yearned for just such an idealized portrait of two partial families blissfully living as one. In the five years of its original run and, perhaps most important to the development of a devoted cult following, in its seemingly permanent status as an after-school TV baby-sitter, the comedy presented a vision of family life where nothing—not even the deaths of mom's first husband and dad's first wife—could dim the happiness of the six children. As married widow and widower Carol and Mike Brady, Florence Henderson and Robert Reed handled the half-dozen kids (she had three girls, he had three boys!) with the help of Alice, the housekeeper-counselor played by Ann B. Davis.

Not that the children presented too many challenges: Plots tended to revolve around such white-knuckle issues as why Jan tied up the phone for so long, what possessed Marcia to enter her stepdad in a Father of the Year contest and whether Peter's class-project volcano would function. "There's nothing really wrong with *The Brady Bunch*," said the magazine. "But nothing is really right, either. Everything is so contrived that you don't believe what goes on any more than you believe sketches in a variety show." Funny that should come up: The cultural power of the show was so strong that *The Brady Bunch* did inspire a variety show, *The Brady Bunch Hour*, in 1977—not to mention a Saturday-morning cartoon, a TV-movie, two prime-time specials, two satirical feature films, a stage production and several books. Just try to find someone who *hasn't* heard this story of a lovely lady and a man named Brady.

THE TRIBE HAS SPOKEN

SURVIVOR
Rudy Boesch, Kelly Wiglesworth, Richard Hatch. CBS, 2000–
COVER: BY DENNIS MARSICO, JULY 8, 2000

"Remember those innocent days," TV GUIDE asked in 2001, "before we took it for granted that people will eat pretty much anything for money, no matter how much it squirms?" The reality-television phenomenon, from *Fear Factor* to *Big Brother*, taught us plenty about the way humans behave under TV's glare, but no series was more instructive than the trendsetting *Survivor*. The debut series in late spring of 2000 was like nothing else on television, a "prime-time cocktail of *Who Wants to Be a Millionaire*, *Gilligan's Island* and *Lord of the Flies*," as TV GUIDE described it at the time. That first season on the tropical island of Pulau Tiga, contestant Richard Hatch ("the naked fat guy," David Letterman liked to call him) proved to the world that secret alliances and greed were a winning combination. With sequels in Australia, Africa and the Marquesas, the show's white-hot popularity began to wane—the genre became more familiar, word spread that the "reality" was rather contrived and contestants seemed all too aware of their possible stardom. But for a while, watching regular folks plot and scheme against one another in an exotic place was a nationwide guilty pleasure.

GILLIGAN'S ISLAND
Skipper (Alan Hale Jr.), Ginger Grant (Tina Louise), Gilligan (Bob Denver). CBS, 1964–67
COVER: BY IVAN NAGY, MAY 8, 1965

The storms that tossed the S.S. *Minnow* were nothing compared to the critical tsunami that greeted this improbable comedy about a charter-boat crew and passengers marooned on what looked more like the site of a Burbank luau than a tropical isle. TV GUIDE was more tolerant than most: Yes, "it's the viewer's intelligence that sometimes gets slapped" by the show's slapstick, the magazine said in 1965, but "the fact remains there are bright touches, too." Viewers made it a hit and a long-running syndication champ, with the kitschy appeal of Gilligan and his fellow castaways even winning a special place in the pantheon of Gen-X heroes.

MR. VAN DOREN

ON THE AIR

YOU BET YOUR LIFE
NBC, 1950–61
COVER: ILLUSTRATOR UNKNOWN,
JULY 24, 1953

You Bet Your Life wasn't so much a quiz show as a Groucho Marx performance with a few questions tacked on. The host teased contestants; a decrepit duck dropped from the ceiling with $100 as a reward for saying the secret word; and if players somehow failed to win anything, they'd get one last chance with a softball final question ("Who's buried in Grant's Tomb?" was a favorite). But the essence of *You Bet Your Life* was just Groucho being Groucho. "I don't insult the people on my show. I spoof them," he told TV GUIDE in 1953. "There's a big difference between kidding and ridicule." Viewers loved it—here was a comedy genius in their living room every week, after all—and made the show one of the great hits of the 1950s.

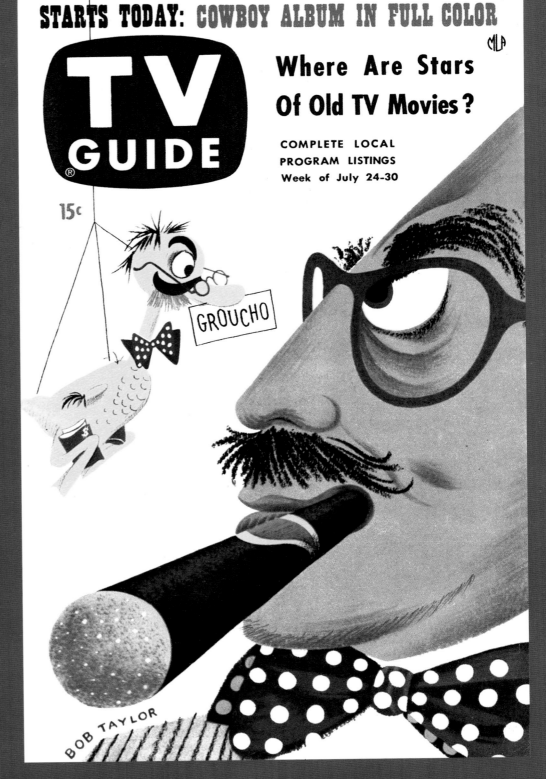

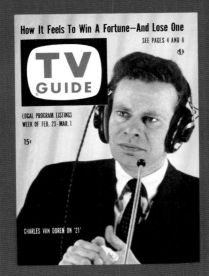

TWENTY ONE
Charles Van Doren. NBC, 1956–58
COVER: BY AL WERTHHEIMER, FEBRUARY 23, 1957

The quiz-show scandals of the 1950s started with revelations about an NBC game called *Dotto*, but the most spectacular disgrace resulted from the network's rigging of *Twenty One*—and the stunning downfall of its most celebrated champion, Charles Van Doren. The affable college professor was so popular after winning a grand total of $129,000 (grand indeed, at the time) that he was rewarded with a job as a cultural commentator on NBC's *Today*. As *Twenty One* host Jack Barry gushed to TV GUIDE a year before the scandals broke, the Van Doren phenomenon basically ensured the game show's success:

Before him, when the less appealing Herb Stempel reigned, producers were unable to even get enough audience members to fill the studio seats. With Van Doren, however, they had to "turn on the fire hose to get them all out of there," Barry told the magazine. "Charlie was just right for our show. No freak with a sponge memory, but a genuinely charming young guy." Of course, as Robert Redford's 1994 movie *Quiz Show* depicted, a fantastic memory wasn't required: Van Doren had already been fed the answers, which made his isolation booth a tad superfluous. In 1958, *Twenty One* was deep-sixed.

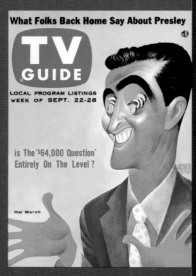

What Folks Back Home Say About Presley

TV GUIDE

LOCAL PROGRAM LISTINGS
WEEK OF SEPT. 22-28

is The '$64,000 Question'
Entirely On The Level?

Hal March

THE $64,000 QUESTION

Bertha Key, Gloria
Lockerman, Hal March.
CBS, 1955–58
COVER: BY AL HIRSCHFELD,
SEPTEMBER 22, 1956

The unanticipated popularity of
The $64,000 Question in the
summer of 1955 touched off an
explosion of game-show mania
that swept the country. The Hal
March–hosted show was a smash
almost instantly, making walking
celebrities out of its regular-folk
contestants as they answered
increasingly arcane trivia questions and the jackpot swelled.
(One winner, psychologist Joyce
Brothers, even parlayed her fame
into a long media career.) Soon,
the airwaves were teeming with
copycats, all hoping to cash in on
the phenomenon. It didn't take
long, however, for the craze to
collapse: Revelations that shows
like *Twenty One* were fixed put
an end to all the fun and games
by 1958. As early as 1956,
TV GUIDE was reporting "nasty
whispers" about *The $64,000
Question*'s being rigged and gave
producer Steve Carlin space to
reply (his answer: "Absolutely
not"). No evidence of cheating
was ever proved against it, but it
was canceled nonetheless.

IS THAT YOUR FINAL ANSWER?

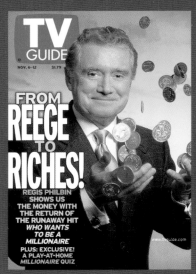

WHO WANTS TO BE A MILLIONAIRE
Lance Bass, Regis Philbin. ABC, 1999–2002
COVER: BY JOSEF ASTOR, NOVEMBER 6, 1999

It was the most extraordinary programming phenomenon in television history: This multiple-choice quiz show was such an instant, rival-slaying hit in 1999 that ABC—apparently regarding *Who Wants to Be a Millionaire* as the "final answer" to any of the network's ratings problems—ran it for an unprecedented 18 nights in a single month. But the carpet-bombing strategy ultimately exploded in its face. By late 2002, the much-copied franchise was downgraded from series to occasional special. Even so, by then host Regis Philbin (who already had a daytime talk-show hit) had once again proved, as TV GUIDE said early in the year, that he was "the most consistently entertaining presence on television."

FAMILY ALBUM

1) **THE ADVENTURES OF OZZIE & HARRIET** *Clockwise from top left:* David Nelson, Ricky Nelson, Harriet Nelson, Ozzie Nelson. ABC, 1952-66

2) **FATHER KNOWS BEST** Kathy "Kitten" Anderson (Lauren Chapin), James "Bud" Anderson Jr. (Billy Gray), Jim Anderson (Robert Young), Margaret Anderson (Jane Wyatt), Betty "Princess" Anderson (Elinor Donahue). CBS, 1954-55; NBC, 1955-60

3) **LEAVE IT TO BEAVER** Ward Cleaver (Hugh Beaumont), Wally Cleaver (Tony Dow), June Cleaver (Barbara Billingsley), Theodore "Beaver" Cleaver (Jerry Mathers). CBS, 1957-58; ABC, 1958-63

4) **THE BEVERLY HILLBILLIES** *Clockwise from top left:* Elly May Clampett (Donna Douglas), Duke, Daisy "Granny" Moses (Irene Ryan), Jethro Bodine (Max Baer Jr.), Jed Clampett (Buddy Ebsen). CBS, 1962-71

5) **THE ADDAMS FAMILY** *Clockwise from top left:* Uncle Fester Frump (Jackie Coogan), Gomez Addams (John Astin), Grandmama Addams (Blossom Rock), Lurch (Ted Cassidy), Pugsley Addams (Ken Weatherwax), Morticia Frump Addams (Carolyn Jones), Wednesday Addams (Lisa Loring). ABC, 1964-66

6) **THE BRADY BUNCH** *Clockwise from top left:* Greg Brady (Barry Williams), Mike Brady (Robert Reed), Carol Brady (Florence Henderson), Alice Nelson (Ann B. Davis), Marcia Brady (Maureen McCormick), Peter Brady (Christopher Knight), Bobby Brady (Mike

Lookinland), Cindy Brady (Susan Olsen), Jan Brady (Eve Plumb). ABC, 1969-74

7) ALL IN THE FAMILY
Edith Bunker (Jean Stapleton), Archie Bunker (Carroll O'Connor), Gloria Bunker Stivic (Sally Struthers), Mike Stivic (Rob Reiner). CBS, 1971-79

8) GOOD TIMES
Clockwise from left:
Michael Evans (Ralph Carter), Thelma Evans (BernNadette Stanis), Willona Woods (Ja'net DuBois), Florida Evans (Esther Rolle), James "J.J." Evans Jr. (Jimmie Walker), James Evans (John Amos). CBS, 1974-79

9) FAMILY TIES
Clockwise from top right:
Steven Keaton (Michael Gross), Mallory Keaton (Justine Bateman), Alex P. Keaton (Michael J. Fox), Jennifer Keaton (Tina Yothers), Elyse Keaton (Meredith Baxter-Birney). NBC, 1982-89

10) THE COSBY SHOW
Denise Huxtable (Lisa Bonet), Vanessa Huxtable (Tempestt Bledsoe), Dr. Heathcliff Huxtable (Bill Cosby), Rudy Huxtable (Keshia Knight Pulliam), Clair Huxtable (Phylicia Rashad), Theodore Huxtable (Malcolm Jamal-Warner). NBC, 1984-92

11) ROSEANNE
Becky Conner (Lecy Goranson), Dan Conner (John Goodman), Roseanne Conner (Roseanne Barr), D.J. Conner (Michael Fishman), Darlene Conner (Sara Gilbert). ABC, 1988-97

12) THE SIMPSONS
Bart Simpson, Lisa Simpson, Maggie Simpson, Marge Simpson, Homer Simpson. FOX, 1989-

THE COSBY SHOW
NBC, 1984–92
COVER: BY MARIO CASILLI, OCTOBER 13, 1984

Just when experts were predicting the demise of the comedy format in the *Dallas*- and *A-Team*-dominated mid-'80s, *The Cosby Show* surfaced on NBC and singlehandedly rescued the genre. It ranked No. 1 for four consecutive years and finished in the Top 20 every year of its run. And yet, can you name a single catchphrase or running gag from the show? Probably not, because one of *The Cosby Show*'s virtues was its aversion to comedy conventions and cheap gimmicks. Bill Cosby's creative control was so complete—his name appeared in the credits as many as six times for a single episode—that the show remained immune to producer meddling and gang-of-writers thinking. Cosby wanted a series about an upper-middle-class couple coping with the pleasures and challenges of raising a large family of kids, and he delivered it—as obstetrician Dr. Heathcliff Huxtable—with the cranky-amiable clown persona audiences already knew and loved. But what viewers were not prepared for, yet quickly embraced, was the show's determination to overturn stereotypes of African-Americans by portraying a financially comfortable black family in a loving household. The decor of the Huxtables' Brooklyn brownstone included antiapartheid posters and pictures of Martin Luther King Jr., but the "blackness" of the show was simply a given, not a battle cry. Speaking to TV GUIDE in 1984, Cosby seemed most concerned about influencing the way people thought about child rearing: "If this show can get to a parent who has never really thought about behaving differently and makes a change that works best for all, I'll be happy."

TV GUIDE
Oct. 13–19
60¢

The Plight of the Excluded
Cold-Shouldered in Hollywood
Page 6

Witness the Humors of Bill Cosby— On Screen and Off
Page 35

Keshia Knight Pulliam and Bill Cosby of *The Cosby Show*

THE FUNNIEST STORIES EVER TOLD ON TV
—SAY THE COMICS; SEE PAGE 22
TV GUIDE
15¢
Local Listings · Aug. 24–30

MARJORIE LORD · DANNY THOMAS

MAKE ROOM FOR DADDY
Rusty Williams (Rusty Hamer), Danny Williams (Danny Thomas).
ABC, 1953–57; CBS, 1957–64
COVER: BY GARRETT-HOWARD, AUGUST 24, 1957

After struggling to make it in television, comedian Danny Thomas famously dismissed the medium as "only for idiots." But then, in 1953, Thomas broke through with *Make Room for Daddy* (retitled *The Danny Thomas Show* after three seasons, with Marjorie Lord joining the cast soon after), about a nightclub entertainer whose absenteeism at home undermines his efforts to remain lord of his castle. "We honest-to-Pete got a hit!" Thomas exulted to TV GUIDE in 1954, before retracting his anti-TV remarks. "So I was an idiot myself," he said. "So I was wrong. That's a crime?" If it was, Thomas got off easy: 11 years' hard time on a successful comedy.

YABBA DABBA DOO!

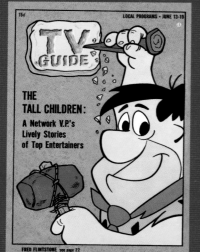

THE FLINTSTONES
Wilma Flintstone, Fred Flintstone, carhop. ABC, 1960–66
COVER: BY HANNA–BARBERA, JUNE 13, 1964

The arrival in 1960 of the first prime-time cartoon—set in the Stone Age and populated by characters who sounded suspiciously like ancestors of Ralph Kramden and *The Honeymooners*—delighted almost everybody, it seems, except critics like TV GUIDE. Tsk-tsking *The Flintstones* for its "flat jokes" and "stale" approach, the magazine lamented that the show was "better than nothing. But only the least bit better." Oh, well, when you're talking about prehistoric times, it's probably advisable to take the long view. *The Flintstones*, which held the record for the longest-running prime-time cartoon until *The Simpsons* stole it in 1997, eventually distinguished itself with a deft hand for using antiquity to parody modernity. Animation kingpins William Hanna and Joe Barbera conceived the cartoon for grown-ups after a survey showed that 65 percent of the audiences watching *Quick Draw McGraw* and *Huckleberry Hound*

were adults. "We wanted to satirize suburbanites for nighttime TV, but nothing we drew in a modern setting was funny," Barbera told TV GUIDE in 1960. "Finally, we put our little man into a convertible with fins fashioned out of tree trunks and a thatched roof for a top. Looking at it, we all broke up." Fred worked as the operator of a dinosaur-powered crane, but most of the action in Bedrock took place back at home, where his dutiful wife, Wilma, vacuumed with a baby mammoth's trunk. Their neighbors, dim bulb Barney Rubble and sensible wife Betty, completed the *Honeymooners* comparisons. But unlike the Kramdens, Fred and Wilma had a baby girl, Pebbles; the Rubbles, keeping up with the 'stoneses, adopted an orphan boy, Bamm Bamm, soon after. *The Flintstones* went off the air in 1966 but earned a place in the morning-cartoon rotation that seemed as permanent as the cave paintings at Lascaux.

EVERYBODY LOVES RAYMOND
Marie Barone (Doris Roberts), Ray Barone (Ray Romano). CBS, 1996–
COVER: BY DARIEN DAVIS, FEBRUARY 20, 1999

"The year's most consistently hilarious comedy," TV GUIDE said in a roundup of critical favorites in 1999, "is also that rarest of shows: a smart family sitcom that lovingly but warily acknowledges the strangling ties that bind parents and children." The premise of *Everybody Loves Raymond* mirrored the life of its star, stand-up comedian Ray Romano: Like his character, sportswriter Ray Barone, Romano had three kids and a police-officer brother who lived with his parents. In the hands of skillful writers and gifted costars, including Doris Roberts and Peter Boyle as Ray's interfering parents, these elements coalesced into a winning comedy. Ray's level-headed wife, Debra (Patricia Heaton), was forever trying to get him to confront his parents, but as TV GUIDE observed in '96, "he inevitably chickens out because he's too nice and they're too nuts." (Ray's mom, for instance,

berates him for signing her up in a fruit-of-the-month club; the relentless arrival of succulent produce makes her shriek, "He's got us in some kind of cult!") The show adroitly evolved over time, finding a fresh supply of material in having Ray's big-lunk brother, Robert (Brad Garrett), finally move out of his parents' place, which added some empty-nest mania to their mom's lunacies and made Ray envy Robert's independence. But the heart of *Raymond* was his devoted relationship with his wife and affectionate guff-love with the kids (using the baby twins as barbells, for instance); they raise the show above the level of the typical, disposable comedy and provide some real tender-funny moments. "Miserable in each other's company," the magazine said of the Barone clan in '99, "they'd be even more so without it. And so would we."

THE ROCKFORD FILES
NBC, 1974–80
COVER: BY GENE TRINDL,
MARCH 6, 1976

If there's such a thing as comfort food, is there comfort TV? That would describe *The Rockford Files* in the mid-'70s, a detective drama featuring the solid, reassuring presence of James Garner as Jim Rockford. The private eye lived in a trailer home on a California beach and was, as TV GUIDE called him in 1974, a "hero sandwich—part hero and part antihero." Creator Stephen J. Cannell told the magazine that he intended "to break every rule about a TV detective" when he devised the character. For one thing, Rockford occasionally enlisted the help of his father, "Rocky" (Noah Beery), a retired trucker—that fact alone set him apart from the Philip Marlowe school of loner detectives. He also hated violence and never let his interest in solving cases overwhelm his interest in making money. So, naturally, Rockford got slugged in almost every episode and was routinely stiffed by his clients. Garner's rendition of the character was "*slow* funny," according to TV GUIDE. "In other words, he grows on you." Keeping the customers amused was in line with Garner's philosophy of acting. "We're the court jesters," he told the magazine in 1975. "That's our function, to entertain people. It's a hell of a lot better than laying carpet." But not less physically taxing, at least for Garner, whose bad back and painful knees—the result of a variety of sports injuries and car wrecks—made working an agony. Garner quit *The Rockford Files* abruptly in the middle of its sixth season, finally opting for his own personal comfort over that of the audience.

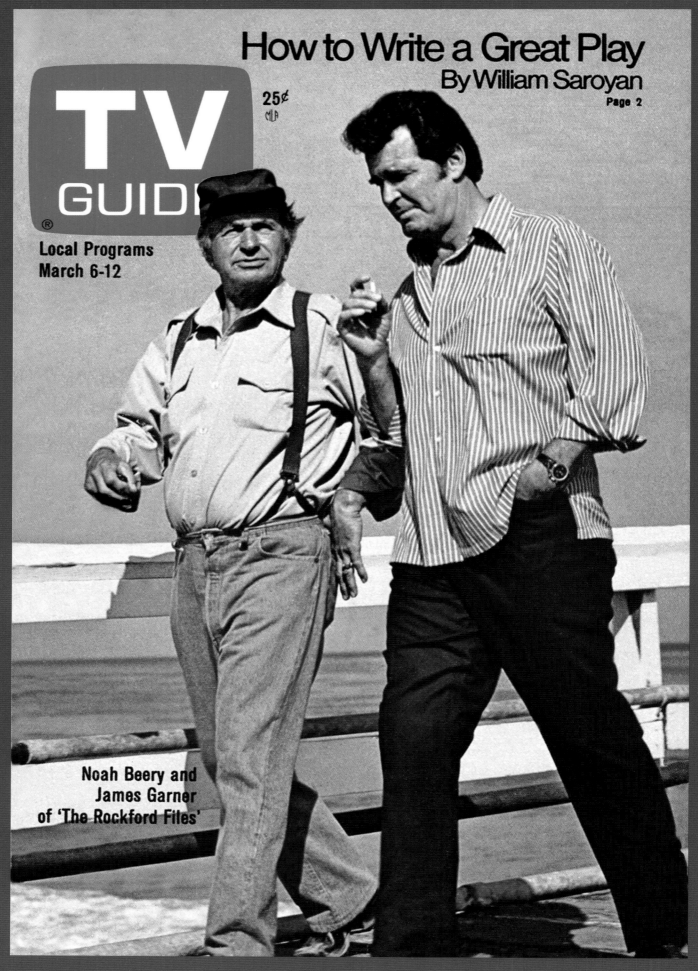

How to Write a Great Play
By William Saroyan
Page 2

25¢

TV GUIDE®

Local Programs
March 6-12

Noah Beery and
James Garner
of 'The Rockford Files'

SANFORD AND SON

Lamont Sanford (Demond Wilson), Fred Sanford (Redd Foxx). NBC, 1972–77
COVER: BY GENE TRINDL, MAY 13, 1972

After shaking up American television by adapting a British series to create *All in the Family*, Norman Lear and Bud Yorkin hit a second home run a year later when they reinvented the U.K. comedy *Steptoe and Son*. The key change wasn't the new title, *Sanford and Son*, but the fact that the junk-dealing main character—and most of the rest of the cast—was African-American. "I've been working for 35 years to get three or four years of steady work in a row," Redd Foxx told TV GUIDE in '72, at the beginning of what would become five years as the star of the smash series. Though he was a stand-up comedy veteran ("Redd was the comedic father of us all," Bill Cosby told TV GUIDE in 1973) with a reputation for doing filthy jokes, Foxx translated seamlessly to television. One of his trademarks in the role as the doddering Fred Sanford was clutching his heart and crying out to his long-gone wife in heaven, "I'm coming, Elizabeth, I'm coming!"— usually when his devoted but impatient son, Lamont (Demond Wilson), seemed on the verge of leaving him. "The amazing thing" about Foxx, TV GUIDE said, is "that it's impossible, despite his outrageous disreputableness, not to love him."

THE DEFENDERS
CBS, 1961–65
COVER: BY CURT GUNTHER,
MARCH 17, 1962

With its first episode, *The Defenders* signaled that it was a complete departure from conventional legal dramas: A doctor went on trial for the mercy killing of a baby born with severe birth defects; after the show presented the arguments for and against a murder conviction, he was found guilty on a lesser charge of manslaughter. It was the sort of case you'd never see Perry Mason handle, TV GUIDE said. At a time when television preferred to skirt controversy, *The Defenders* embraced it, tackling topics from the debut episode's mercy killing to abortion rights for teenagers to the question of whether a pregnant Jehovah's Witness should be able to refuse a blood transfusion that would save her baby's life. (So many obstetrics-related issues came up they could have called the show *The Deliverers*.) "Certain issues in the news become hot copy, and you have to be sensitive to them. That's when I think the show is most effective," actor E.G. Marshall told TV GUIDE in 1964. Marshall starred as Lawrence Preston, the senior lawyer in the father-and-son team of Preston & Preston (Robert Reed played his son, Kenneth). The magazine criticized their intra-office quarrels and reconciliations during the show's initial season as coming "right out of the promptbooks of melodrama," but praised *The Defenders* the following year as "a show with a 'message' and a powerful dramatic technique for communicating it to the public." *The Defenders*, which lasted four seasons, also succeeded in delivering a powerful message to television itself: By '64, the medium had developed an appetite for more controversial fare, and as Marshall noted, "you have to give *The Defenders* at least part of the credit for that."

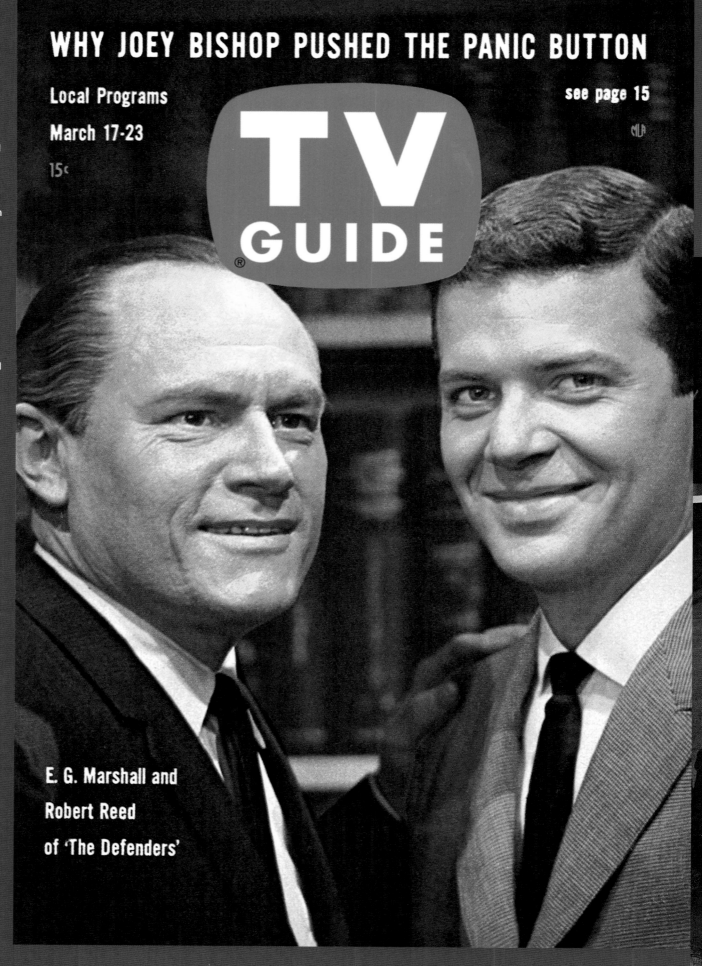

WHY JOEY BISHOP PUSHED THE PANIC BUTTON

Local Programs
March 17-23

15¢

see page 15

TV GUIDE ®

E. G. Marshall and
Robert Reed
of 'The Defenders'

PERRY MASON
Mason (Raymond Burr). CBS, 1957–66
COVER: BY YOUSUF KARSH, MARCH 4, 1961

Perry Mason may be the only lawyer in the world who's spent more time in the public eye than Alan Dershowitz. The character first appeared in the 1930s in the novels of lawyer-writer Erle Stanley Gardner, then moved on to a radio show that ran for 12 years, several TV-movies and two series. But from the moment Raymond Burr first appeared as Mason in 1957, every other incarnation seemed to fade away. The burly actor invested the character with such a sense of purpose in his pursuit of the truth that viewers never seemed to mind *Perry Mason*'s formulaic, eyebrow-raising courtroom scenes (last-minute discoveries of crucial evidence, sobbing witness-stand confessions). In 1958, TV GUIDE praised Burr's "rugged interpretation" of the character and the work of Barbara Hale as his devoted secretary, Della Street. But by 1965, the magazine wanted *Mason* thrown out of court, complaining about the "compulsion to cram into every episode not only a plot and a subplot, but also a sub-subplot," which complicated matters so much that viewers didn't have "a reasonable chance to guess who done it." A year later the magazine got its wish and the show was canceled. Still, Burr inhabited the role with such power that nearly 40 years later, all you have to do is mention the name Perry Mason and we all know who done it.

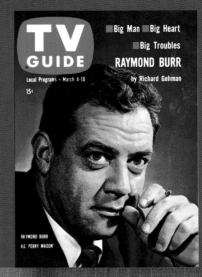

THE FUGITIVE
Dr. Richard Kimble (David Janssen). ABC, 1963–67
COVER: BY RONALD SEARLE, JANUARY 22, 1966

Harrison Ford certainly made an acceptable Richard Kimble in the 1993 feature film *The Fugitive*, but David Janssen defined this role of a doctor wrongly convicted of his wife's murder, roaming the country searching for the one-armed man he'd seen fleeing the scene of the crime. Over the course of four years, Janssen's character was relentlessly chased by a detective, held dozens of odd jobs that allowed the altruistic doc to help others and suffered enough injuries to make an EMT wince—he was blinded by an explosion, hit by a car, stabbed four times, wounded by gunshots eight times and knocked unconscious 10 times. The punishment took its toll: Janssen told TV GUIDE in 1967 that he turned down half a million dollars to return for a fifth year. "I think I would have fallen apart," he said. The series ended with Kimble fighting the one-armed man atop a water tower, until Kimble's detective pursuer saved his life by shooting the bad guy. The finale drew 72 percent of the TV audience, a record not to be topped by any series until *Dallas*'s "Who Shot J.R.?" episode 13 years later.

SEARLE CAPTURES THE FUGITIVE—With a Pencil

SEE PAGE 11

TV GUIDE ®

Local Programs • January 22-28

15¢

DAVID JANSSEN

Ronald Searle

THE PRISONER
No. 6 (Patrick McGoohan). CBS, 1968–69

The Prisoner was a temporary replacement for *The Jackie Gleason Show* during the summer of '68, but it earned a permanent place in television's annals as one of the most fascinating dramatic series ever made. Patrick McGoohan, fresh from the action-adventure series *Secret Agent*, created and starred in this story of a spy who resigned his job and was immediately abducted—either by his own people or the enemy's, he was never sure—and installed in a strangely festive penal colony known as the Village (actually the Welsh seaside resort Portmeirion). In the Village, where the perimeter was patrolled by giant, menacing rubbery balls, everyone was known by a number and the inmates were ex-spies who'd been reduced to cheerful obliviousness by the techniques used to extract their secrets. But No. 6 (McGoohan) was too valuable to be handled so crudely; a succession of wardens known as No. 2 tried wilier ways of making the rebellious (or "unmutual," in Village parlance) prisoner answer the question "Why did you resign?" The show combined good, old-fashioned action/sci-fi with an eerily ambiguous surrealism that left fans and college professors alike debating the show's real significance. The loss of freedom? The dehumanization of society? The absurdity of existence? McGoohan himself told TV GUIDE in 1968 that he thought people were "being imprisoned and engulfed by a scientific and materialistic world," but refused to elaborate on the meaning of the series, which concluded after 17 episodes with No. 6 finally escaping. Or did he? *The Prisoner* left the answer, as usual, deliciously unclear.

MIAMI VICE
NBC, 1984–89
COVER: BY RICHARD AMSEL, JULY 27, 1985

"We're not revolutionary," *Miami Vice* executive producer Michael Mann told TV GUIDE in 1985. "We're just current." *Miami Vice*'s debut the previous fall had certainly made every other cop show on television seem hopelessly antique. From the opening-title sequence—a headlong plunge into a luscious riot of flamingos, race-horses and bikini tops, all to the cool frenzy of Jan Hammer's theme song—you knew that episodic TV was going somewhere new. The still-fresh fast-cut, MTV pace and rock soundtrack gave *Miami Vice* a feel unlike anything else in prime time. And its under-cover detectives, James "Sonny" Crockett (Don Johnson) and Ricardo Tubbs (Philip Michael Thomas), whose work usually dealt with Miami's prodigious drug trade, looked like no one on TV who'd ever carried a badge: Crockett's two-day-old stubble and pastel jackets worn over T-shirts inspired a lamentable trend, and neither guy seemed to own a sock. Having vaulted to ninth in the ratings in its second season, *Miami Vice* was undone in its third as NBC pitted it against CBS's popular *Dallas* and the show inexplicably exchanged its signature palette for a grim color scheme. Viewers fled. "That's the thing about cutting edges," TV GUIDE said in 1987, two years before *Vice* was iced. "They're the first things to get dull."

L.-r.:
Philip Michael Thomas
and Don Johnson
of *Miami Vice*

DRAGNET
Sgt. Joe Friday (Jack Webb), Officer Frank Smith (Ben Alexander). NBC, 1952–59
COVER: PHOTOGRAPHER UNKNOWN, DECEMBER 11, 1953

When *Dragnet* began on radio in 1949, police dramas were improbable shoot-'em-up tales of heroic law enforcement. Creator and star Jack Webb had a novel idea: that simply showing the workaday life of a detective—following leads, interviewing witnesses and solving crimes based on actual cases—could be fascinating. Audiences agreed, making *Dragnet*'s TV version a Top 10 ratings fixture in the mid-'50s. Elements of the show still instantly evoke Eisenhower-era pop culture, from the "dum, da-*dum*-dum" musical signature to LAPD sergeant Joe Friday's buzz cut. But the essence of *Dragnet*—summed up in its show-ending voiceover, "The story you have just seen is true. The names have been changed to protect the innocent"—remains as contem-porary as the latest cop show that makes realism its goal.

THE '60s

February 27, 1960
By Philippe Halsman
Robert Stack of *The Untouchables*

August 6, 1960
By Larry Fried
Esther Williams

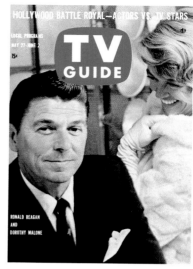

May 27, 1961
By Todd Walker
Ronald Reagan and Dorothy Malone of *General Electric Theater*

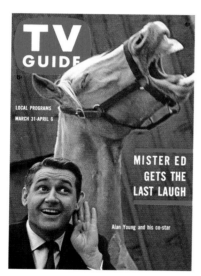

March 31, 1962
By Richard R. Hewett
Alan Young and Mister Ed of *Mister Ed*

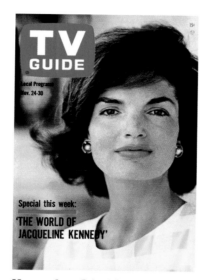

November 24, 1962
By Jacques Lowe
Jacqueline Kennedy

December 8, 1962
By Larry Schiller
Dick Van Dyke of *The Dick Van Dyke Show*

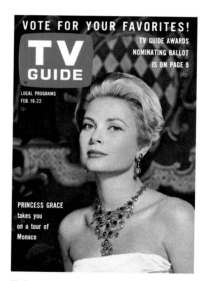

February 16, 1963
By Philippe Halsman
Princess Grace of Monaco

November 27, 1965
By Gene Trindl
Cynthia Lynn and Bob Crane of *Hogan's Heroes*

December 11, 1965
By Sheedy-Long
Cast of *F Troop*

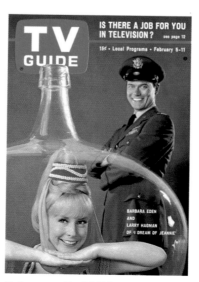

February 5, 1966
By Gene Trindl
Barbara Eden and Larry Hagman of *I Dream of Jeannie*

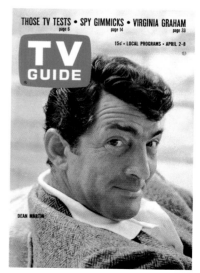

April 2, 1966
By Philippe Halsman
Dean Martin of *The Dean Martin Show*

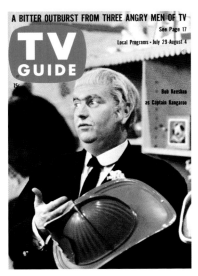

July 29, 1961
By George E. Joseph
Bob Keeshan of *Captain Kangaroo*

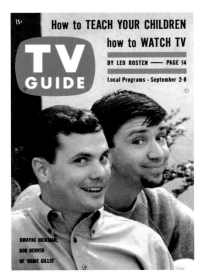

September 2, 1961
By Gene Trindl
Dwayne Hickman and Bob Denver of
The Many Loves of Dobie Gillis

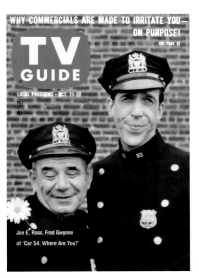

October 21, 1961
By George E. Joseph
Joe E. Ross and Fred Gwynne of
Car 54, Where Are You?

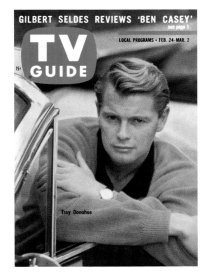

February 24, 1962
By Julian Wasser
Troy Donahue of *Surfside 6*

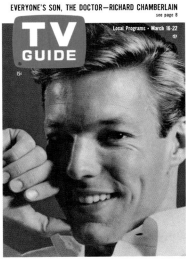

March 16, 1963
By Gene Trindl
Richard Chamberlain of *Dr. Kildare*

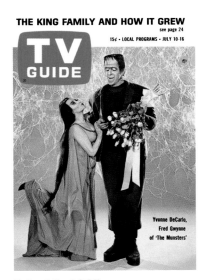

July 10, 1965
By Gene Trindl
Yvonne DeCarlo and Fred Gwynne
of *The Munsters*

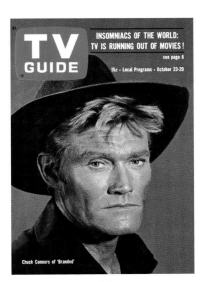

October 23, 1965
By Sheedy-Long
Chuck Conners of *Branded*

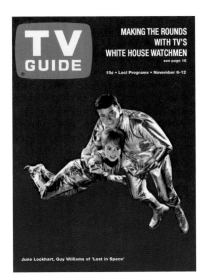

November 6, 1965
By Gene Trindl
June Lockhart and Guy Williams
of *Lost in Space*

May 28, 1966
By Sheedy-Long
Sally Field of *Gidget*

December 30, 1967
By Mario Casilli
Carol Burnett of *The Carol
Burnett Show*

September 7, 1968
By Gene Trindl
Cast of *Family Affair*

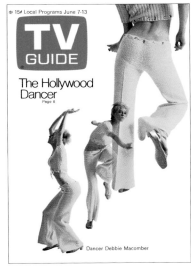

June 7, 1969
By Richard R. Hewett
Debbie Macomber

THE WALTONS
John-Boy Walton (Richard Thomas), Olivia Walton (Michael Learned), John Walton (Ralph Waite). CBS, 1972–81
COVER: BY JACOB KNIGHT, JUNE 25, 1977

Replying to readers who accused the magazine of never liking anything, TV GUIDE pointed out in 1972 that it regarded a new family drama called *The Waltons* as "a wise, warm, wonderful show.... There is, at last, a show about the poor." *The Waltons*, defying TV's custom of addressing only the concerns of the rich and middle class, chronicled the struggles of a family in Virginia's Blue Ridge mountains during the Depression. When we first met the extended clan, we saw them through the eyes of a high schooler, John-Boy Walton, the eldest of John and Olivia Walton's seven children and an aspiring writer (played with affecting intelligence and sensitivity by Richard Thomas). One of the virtues of the popular series was its realistic depiction of the passage of time: By series' end in 1981, John-Boy had gone to college, started his own local paper, sold a novel and become a war correspondent in London. Creator Earl Hamner Jr., a writer who based the show on his own boyhood memories, told TV GUIDE in 1973 that "if *The Waltons* is saying anything important, maybe it is just that ordinary people are capable of more nobility than they know."

LITTLE HOUSE ON THE PRAIRIE
Charles Ingalls (Michael Landon). NBC, 1974–83
COVER: BY SCOTT ENYART,
MAY 29, 1976

When it launched in 1974, *Little House on the Prairie* was considered a flatlander's knockoff of *The Waltons'* tales from the Blue Ridge mountains. But the series about a frontier family's hardscrabble life in 1870s Minnesota had two advantages: generations of viewers familiar with the Laura Ingalls Wilder books that were the inspiration for the series and a vast TV audience with a big thing for Michael Landon, who'd spent 14 years on *Bonanza.* It was his wife and daughter's love of the Wilder titles, though, that convinced Landon to produce, act in and often direct the show. "I thought, 'How wonderful if parents and children can watch this series together—and maybe it would start the kids *reading* the books,' " Landon said to TV GUIDE in '74. " 'Imagine a TV show that would make kids read?' " The following year, the magazine described the series' plots as "pretty quiet" but called Landon "one of our favorites... particularly in the devastating-smile department." His grin got a little bigger over the next few years as *Little House* became a hit, surpassing *The Waltons* in the ratings.

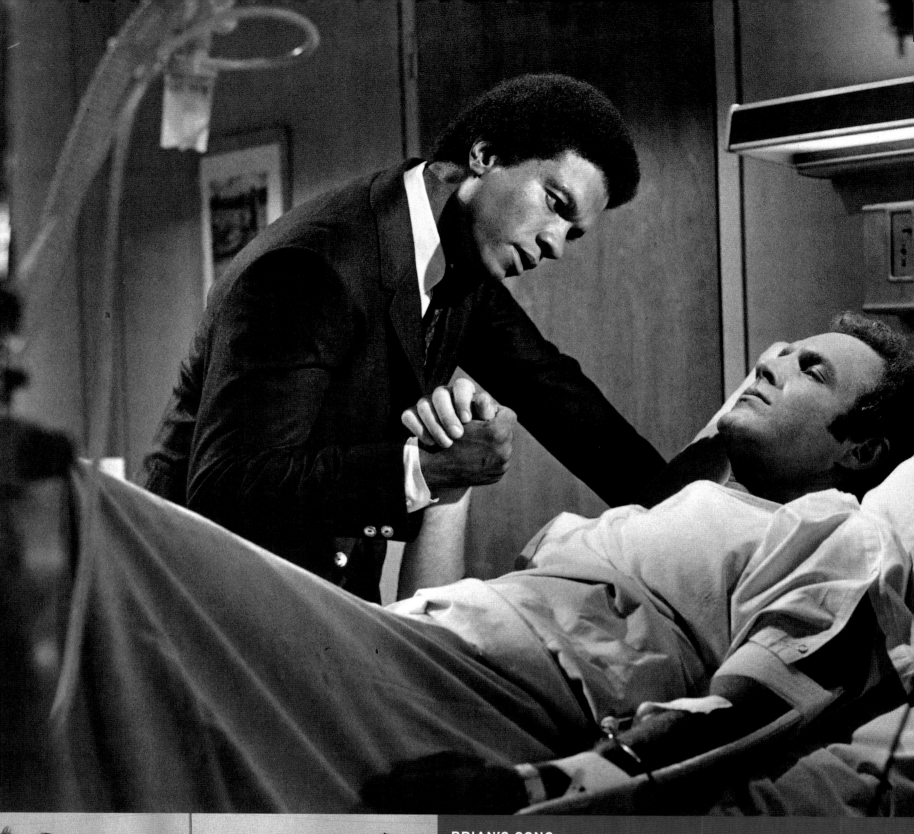

BRIAN'S SONG
Gale Sayers (Billy Dee Williams), Brian Piccolo (James Caan).
ABC, November 30, 1971

In 1971, heartstrings were tugged, and maybe a few minds were opened, with *Brian's Song*, the story of the close friendship between Chicago Bears football teammates Gale Sayers, an African-American, and Brian Piccolo, who was white. The Emmy-winning TV-movie made stars of both Billy Dee Williams and James Caan. On the occasion of a 2001 remake, the real-life Sayers talked to TV Guide about his relationship with Piccolo, who lost his battle against a rare form of cancer at age 26: "People saw that a black and a white could get along together, could have a good time together and maybe be friends. It wasn't a big deal to Brian and me. We didn't think anything of it. We were teammates."

PLAYHOUSE 90
Mountain McClintock (Jack Palance) of "Requiem for a Heavyweight" (1956). CBS, 1956–60

In 1957, producer Martin Manulis told TV Guide that his only goals for this dramatic anthology show were "to bring the greatest variety possible to the series and to strive for excellence.... I feel that *Playhouse 90* should entertain the grown-ups." *Playhouse 90*'s reputation for excellence was established after just its second broadcast, with Jack Palance's performance as a broken-down boxer in "Requiem for a Heavyweight"—the first 90-minute drama written (by Rod Serling) specifically for television and the winner of five Emmy awards. As for variety, *Playhouse 90* presented a head-spinning assortment of productions—including "Judgment at Nuremberg," "The Days of Wine and Roses" and "For Whom the Bell Tolls"—and featured an all-star roster of performers, such as Errol Flynn, Jack Lemmon, Carol Channing, Jeanette MacDonald, Mickey Rooney, Paul Newman and Joanne Woodward. On top of that, many of the weekly performances were presented live. That helped make *Playhouse 90* a pricey proposition, as did paying for top-tier writers, directors and actors. Unfortunately, the show didn't attract enough grown-ups to register the sort of ratings that would support the expense. And even though in retrospect it is regarded as a paragon of the era of live, high-quality, New York City–based programming, the series—a latecomer to the dramatic-anthology genre—was fighting a losing battle as TV production increasingly shifted to the West Coast and to less-expensive formats. Late in *Playhouse 90*'s third season, TV Guide celebrated the show as "a symbol of television at its best—a program with a point of view, a program unafraid of controversy, a program alive with a sense of excitement. Long may it be with us." A few months later in '59, CBS cut the series back to every other week and shut it down completely the following spring.

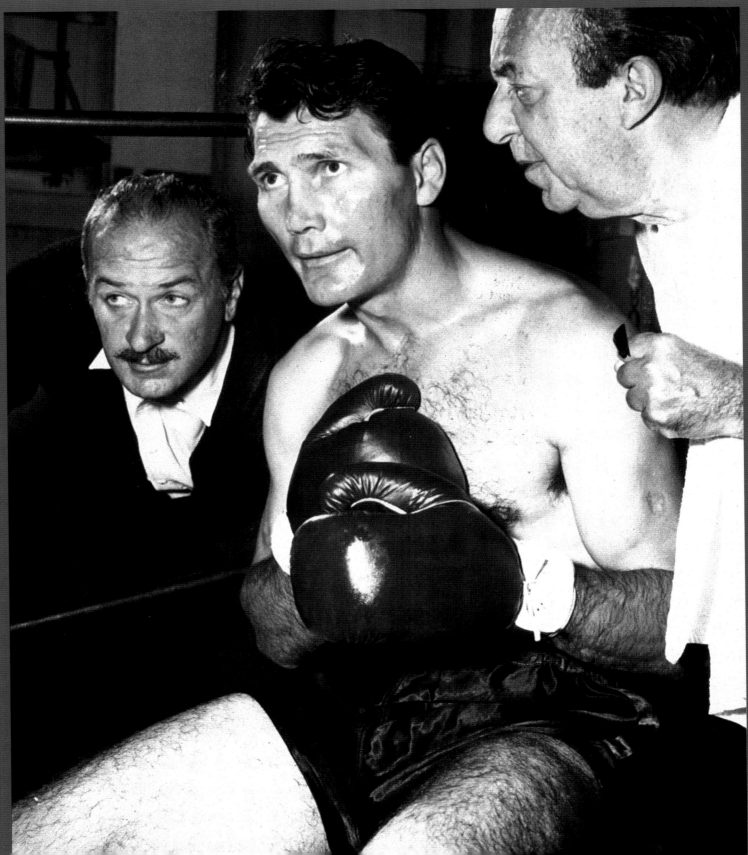

TV GUIDE

March 26–April 1, 1983
50¢

Priests, Sex and 'The Thorn Birds'
By Father Andrew M. Greeley
Page 4

Richard Chamberlain and Rachel Ward in this week's 'The Thorn Birds'

THE THORN BIRDS
ABC, 1983
COVER: BY DENNIS PIEL, MARCH 26, 1983

In the heyday of the miniseries, *The Thorn Birds* virtually ruled the ratings roost: The four-part, 10-hour adaptation of Colleen McCullough's massively popular novel ranks second only to *Roots* as the most-watched miniseries of all time. Set in Australia between 1920 and 1962, the epic drew protests for its depiction of an ambitious Catholic priest (Richard Chamberlain) falling in love with a beautiful woman (Rachel Ward). But the novelist Father Andrew M. Greeley, writing in TV GUIDE, pointed out that ultimately the series wasn't about "an uncontrollably passionate priest" so much as "a passionate God" who loves sinners as well as saints.

BRIDESHEAD REVISITED
Sebastian Flyte (Anthony Andrews), Julia Flyte (Diana Quick), Charles Ryder (Jeremy Irons). PBS, 1982

Great Performances waded into TV's miniseries competition in 1982, bringing the 11-part British production of *Brideshead Revisited* to PBS. The setting was lavish in this faithful adaptation of Evelyn Waugh's between-the-wars novel about friendship, art and religious faith. And the casting was equally sumptuous, from Jeremy Irons's career-making performance (as a young man whose life changes when he meets the family at Brideshead Castle) to John Gielgud and Laurence Olivier in supporting, yet masterful, roles. "In character, pace and acting," TV GUIDE said in 1983, *Brideshead Revisited* "is a television classic: worth watching again—and again."

HALLMARK HALL OF FAME

Jacob Witting (Christopher Walken), Sarah Wheaton (Glenn Close) of "Sarah, Plain and Tall" (1991). NBC, CBS, PBS, ABC and Hallmark Channel, 1952–

"I don't have a philanthropic attitude toward culture," Hallmark greeting-card company founder Joyce Hall told TV GUIDE in 1961, on *Hallmark Hall of Fame*'s 10th anniversary. He added: "The simple truth is that good TV is good business." Early productions relied on classic drama—a two-hour, live "Hamlet" in 1953 was the first full-length Shakespeare play broadcast on TV and, at the time, also the longest dramatic program ever aired. But subsequently, the *Hall of Fame* undertook everything from documentaries and comedies to contemporary drama ("Promise," in 1986, starred James Woods as a schizophrenic whose brother, played by James Garner, reluctantly becomes his caregiver; it won five Emmy awards). In its adventurous programming, "*Hallmark* has always leaped off the cliff," Glenn Close, the star of "Sarah, Plain and Tall," told TV GUIDE on the series' 50th anniversary. "That's why actors go back." Indeed, the *Hall of Fame* is itself a hall of fame—cast members have included George C. Scott, Jason Robards, Dame Judith Anderson and Julie Harris. With talent of this caliber, *Hallmark* has easily upheld the standard that Hall voiced to the magazine in '61: "I want to be able to look people in the eye without cringing the day after a show."

ROOTS
Kunta Kinte (LeVar Burton). ABC, 1977
COVER: BY ROMARE BEARDEN, JANUARY 22, 1977

For eight consecutive nights in January 1977, America was riveted as never before by a single television show: the miniseries *Roots*, a 12-hour dramatization of author Alex Haley's account of his African ancestry. At the time, it was the most-watched program ever made for TV, with the finale drawing more than 80 million viewers, or 71 percent of the entire television audience. The story began in 1750 and depicted the capture of a young African warrior, Kunta Kinte (LeVar Burton), by white slave traders and his transportation to America. Spanning 150 years, the epic followed Kinte (renamed Toby, and played by John Amos as an adult) and his descendants through the tragic story of slavery in the United States, ending with the slaves' emancipation and embrace of the opportunity to start life anew and free. The enormous cast, which included Edward Asner, Vic Morrow and Lloyd Bridges, was dominated by a remarkable gathering of African-American talent, including Cicely Tyson, Leslie Uggams, Louis Gossett Jr. and Ben Vereen (who memorably played Chicken George, a slave sent to England in the 1820s). "Television at its best is not only entertaining, it informs or even enlightens," Burton told TV GUIDE on the miniseries' 25th anniversary. By that time, four plagiarism lawsuits had cast a shadow on Haley's methods. The author won three and settled the other out of court, saying any similarities to another work were inadvertent. But what could never be undone was *Roots'* historic achievement: It took a nation too often riven by racial differences and bound it together with the power of storytelling.

REMEM

In January 1977, my friend Warren Beatty and I caught up with each other in New York City for a long-standing dinner date. As it happened, that night was the premiere of the miniseries *Roots*, and Warren and I watched it together in his suite at the Pierre hotel. Neither of us spoke one word during those two hours. At the end, Warren stood up, looked at me and said, "Your life's changed as of tonight." He was so right.

The next morning, besieged for autographs at JFK airport, I missed my flight home. Within days, my usual weekly handful of mail had grown to three or more canvas bagfuls. And as dubbed versions of the film joined the translated book abroad, letters from afar bore such creative addresses as "Alex Haley, 'Roots,' U.S.A."

Invitations to visit every country imaginable poured in so thick and fast that I felt, metaphorically, as though I were hurtling over Niagara Falls in a barrel—quite a contrast to the beginning of *Roots*, back in my hometown of Henning, Tennessee.

I was a 5-year-old boy when my beloved Grandpa, a lumber dealer named Will Palmer, died. To soothe her grief, my

Grandma Cynthia invited her five sisters to come and spend the summer with us—which they did. Early evenings found us gathered on the front porch, as the sisters, their gray heads bobbing atop their rocking chairs, regaled the family with their reminiscing.

The stories always began with Grandma's strict blacksmith father, Tom Murray, who had "jumped the broom" (married) and raised a family. Next came the clucking and clacking over the "sinfulness" of the sisters' paternal grandfather, who was both the son and the slave of Tom Lea. A master gamecocker, George Lea was known far and wide by his indelible nickname: "Chicken George." Then came his mother, the much-venerated Miz Kizzy, and her mother, Bell.

Throughout that summer, I heard the family stories, in all their detail, until they became glued within my young memory—which is where they remained until some four decades later, when I found myself standing in front of the stately and imposing National Archives Building in Washington, D.C. Compelled by simple curiosity, I entered the Archives and asked to view the 1870 Census of Alamance County, North Carolina, where my grandmother said she'd been

BERED

born and reared. I found there a record of the freed blacksmith Tom Murray and his family.

The chance visit set off nine years of research, an endeavor that took me from the dusty roads of Alamance County—where I found a deeply rusted old horseshoe that just couldn't have been made by anybody but my blacksmith great grandfather (I smuggled it to New York City, wrapped in a sheet of newspaper and stashed inside my shirt)—to a tiny village in Gambia, West Africa: the home of Kunta Kinte.

The end result of that endeavor was a phenomenon that neither I nor my publisher could ever have anticipated. Why did it happen? Reflecting now, I think that, without my intent, the book awakened a worldwide perception that genealogy isn't reserved for royalty. Quite the contrary, the peasant's family line is probably stronger than the prince's.

But more than that, people seemed to recognize that *Roots* symbolized their own ethnic struggles. In Beijing, *Roots* and I were feted by lineage masters who had traced families as far back as 1,000 years. In Tokyo, I was astounded to see my hugely enlarged photo displayed three stories high. The biggest crowd I ever drew was in Morocco, where people formed a human carpet over streets and housetops to meet the man who had dramatized the story of an African-Muslim youth who'd been kidnapped into slavery in the Christian West—and kept his Islamic faith intact until his death.

Just recently, the government of Egypt expressed interest in my writing an Egyptian equivalent to the Kunta Kinte saga. And the continuing classroom usage of *Roots* by West African educators is certainly one of my most gratifying experiences.

So it has been for 15 years now that, again and again, I've told the *Roots* story to hundreds of audiences, and responded to the unabating questions that the subject generates. (I'm always pleased to tell inquirers that my Henning boyhood home is now an official state of Tennessee museum.) I hope to bring forth other works, but my best hope is that *Roots* will find new viewers in future generations.

—ALEX HALEY, EXCERPT FROM TV GUIDE, FEBRUARY 29, 1992

The Plain Truth About Elvis Presley

TV GUIDE

LOCAL PROGRAM LISTINGS
WEEK OF SEPTEMBER 8-14

15¢

Elvis Presley

ELVIS
Elvis Presley.
NBC, December 3, 1968
COVER: BY WERTHEIMER,
SEPTEMBER 8, 1956

By 1968, Elvis Presley's heyday had passed—he was starring in corny movies while pop culture was grooving to the psychedelic era. But then, at 33, Presley returned to the medium that had helped make him a '50s icon, doing what he did best: singing and playing rock and roll. The electrifying "comeback special," as it came to be known among Elvisionados, was simply called *Elvis*, reflecting the stripped-down, raw nature of the performance. In the most memorable segments, Presley, clad entirely in black leather and never looking better, performed both alone and with some of his early band mates, ripping through his classic songs and reminding the world why the appalled curators of popular culture got so rattled when he first strutted onto the American scene. The King, TV GUIDE recalled of the special in 1996, had "reclaimed his throne."

MY NAME IS BARBRA
Barbra Streisand.
CBS, April 28, 1965
COVER: BY FIROOZ ZAHEDI,
JANUARY 22, 2000

In the early 1960s, record buyers knew her as a singer, and theater-goers knew her as the star of the hit Broadway musical *Funny Girl*. But it wasn't until her first television special that a national audience discovered what a potent force of nature Barbra Streisand could really be. In one segment, the quirky-looking Brooklyn waif waltzed through the fashion fortress Bergdorf Goodman, trying on outfits as she stunned viewers with her rendition of "Brother, Can You Spare a Dime?" It was that regal voice that would propel one of show business's most storied careers. *My Name Is Barbra* won five Emmy awards, a feat she repeated 30 years later with another special, HBO's *Barbra Streisand: The Concert.*

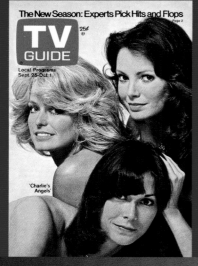

CHARLIE'S ANGELS
Sabrina Duncan (Kate Jackson), Jill Munroe (Farrah Fawcett), Kelly Garrett (Jaclyn Smith). ABC, 1976–81
COVER: BY PETER KREDENSER, SEPTEMBER 25, 1976

"When the show was No. 3, I figured it was our acting," said Farrah Fawcett, discussing the success of *Charlie's Angels* with TV GUIDE at the end of its instant-hit debut season. "When we got to be No. 1, I decided it could only be because none of us wears a bra." Bingo. The previous fall, the magazine had similarly divined the appeal of this show, about a trio of female private detectives who "drive race cars, stack decks, karate-chop 300-pound brutes.... Is any of this believable? Not remotely." Ditto the acting, which ranged "from adequate to preposterous. But with all that skin and hair on display, who notices?" If the series itself was popular, Fawcett was a bona fide phenomenon. "No one ever attained this kind of superstardom so fast," said the magazine. Though other actresses took over as relief Angels during the show's five-year run, the classic threesome was Fawcett, Jaclyn Smith and Kate Jackson. They fearlessly followed the instructions of their unseen boss, Charlie (the voice of John Forsythe), to investi-gate any dirty deed—as long as it also afforded an opportunity to don a bikini or maybe just a towel. Not that there was really much sex on *Charlie's Angels*—the show was all a big tease. Which also helps explain the hair.

BAYWATCH
C.J. Parker (Pamela Anderson). NBC, 1989–90; syndication, 1991–2001
COVER: BY JON RAGEL,
AUGUST 13, 1994

In 1994, when TV GUIDE selected "TV's Top 10 Guilty Pleasures," choosing No. 1 was "no contest," the magazine said. "It's *Baywatch*, the most popular TV show on the planet." That wasn't an exaggeration: Producer and star David Hasselhoff's syndicated series about the trials and titillations of stud-muffin and jiggly-minx lifeguards on Malibu Beach was being seen in 142 countries every week by an audience of more than one billion viewers. "I think there is this mystery about California that everybody in the world is sort of drawn to," costar Pamela Anderson told the magazine—the primary mystery being, of course, how long you would have to wait to see the next female lifeguard jog down the beach in slow-motion splendor.

PRIME TIME **143**

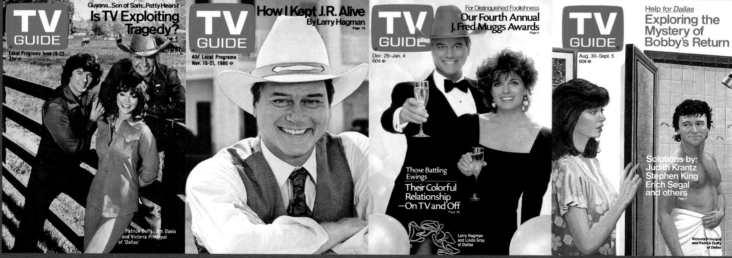

DALLAS
J.R. Ewing (Larry Hagman), Cliff Barnes (Ken Kercheval), Bobby Ewing (Patrick Duffy). CBS, 1978–91
COVERS: BY ROBERT PHILLIPS, JUNE 16, 1979. BY GENE TRINDL, NOVEMBER 15, 1980. BY MARIO CASILLI, DECEMBER 29, 1984. BY TERESA FASOLINO, AUGUST 30, 1986

Dormant since the 1960s, the prime-time soap opera roared back to life like an oil-rig gusher with *Dallas*. Standing out even among such outsize characters as alcoholic Sue Ellen Ewing (Linda Gray) and upright Pam Ewing (Victoria Principal) was the gleefully amoral oilman J.R. Ewing. His attempted murder in a season-ending cliff-hanger inspired the burning question of the summer of '80: Who shot J.R.? "Villainy could be fun, and that's how I played it," Larry Hagman wrote of his character in TV GUIDE that year. In the article, Hagman also described how he fled to London in order to leverage his sudden popularity into a more lucrative contract—a successful ploy that surely would have made J.R. cackle with delight.

DYNASTY
Krystle Jennings Carrington (Linda Evans), Alexis Carrington Colby (Joan Collins). ABC, 1981–89
COVERS: BY ROBERT PHILLIPS, FEBRUARY 27, 1982. BY MARIO CASILLI, NOVEMBER 10, 1984; MARCH 23, 1985; AND DECEMBER 27, 1986

Big oil, big hair and big troubles were already proven winners on CBS's *Dallas* when ABC launched *Dynasty* as a challenger in 1981. "Trash with flash," TV GUIDE said of the new Denver-set prime-time soap. In addition to an eye-popping budget for extravagant clothing and furnishings, *Dynasty* also enjoyed one of television's great female rivalries: the pitting of lovely Krystle (Linda Evans), second wife of silky skunk Blake Carrington (John Forsythe), against his rapacious, vengeful-vamp first wife, Alexis, played to the hilt by Joan Collins. In 1985, *Dynasty* finished No. 1 in the ratings, having out-trashed and out-flashed even J.R. Ewing and Co.

THE MAD BUSINESS OF RUNNING FOR PRESIDENT
By Edward P. Morgan

TV GUIDE

**LOCAL PROGRAMS
OCTOBER 3-9**

15¢

MIA FARROW
OF 'PEYTON PLACE'

PEYTON PLACE
ABC, 1964–69
COVER: BY DENNIS CAMERON,
OCTOBER 3, 1964

Daytime soap-opera mores moved to prime time in 1964 with the debut of *Peyton Place*, based on the popular novel by Grace Metalious. (The 1957 feature-film adaptation starred Lana Turner.) Airing twice a week and then three times a week in its second season, the series tracked the shenanigans of citizens in a small but prodigiously frisky New England town. Over the show's run, TV GUIDE's opinion paralleled the public's: A review in 1964 was enthusiastic—"We are not ones to equate bigness with goodness, but this show is, for once, both"— but by 1966, it had cooled toward the "single-minded monotony with which Peyton people face life, hunching over the ghastly sins and secrets that have taken place off screen and long ago." Still, the magazine asked, "who among us will deny the eternity in Mia Farrow's wide, wide eyes?" The show itself, however, would have far less than an eternity with its breakout star—Farrow quit shortly thereafter. Her character, Allison MacKenzie, mysteriously disappeared, and was kept alive by the arrival in town of other characters toting clues to her existence: a bracelet on one occasion, a baby on another. But even the mama Mia story line couldn't save *Peyton*'s place in the ratings—or ABC's schedule.

TWIN PEAKS
Laura Palmer (Sheryl Lee). ABC, 1990–91
COVER: BY MARIO CASILLI, SEPTEMBER 8, 1990

Who killed Laura Palmer? That was the question that millions of mesmerized fans wanted answered in the spring of 1990, when this astonishing, unearthly vision of life in a Pacific Northwest logging town shimmered into view. On the surface, the plot outline sounded at least reasonably conventional: The murder of a homecoming queen sparks an investigation led by FBI agent Dale Cooper (Kyle MacLachlan), who uncovers dark secrets in a town where characters are jumping in and out of one another's beds and where the rich folks are greedy and duplicitous. But that doesn't begin to suggest the hypnotic strangeness of creator David Lynch's vision, or the sense of warped normalcy conveyed by characters like Cooper. No one familiar with Lynch's truly twisted movies (*Eraserhead, Blue Velvet*) would ever have guessed he would turn up on television. But here he was, creeping us out with a fetishist's-eye view of everyday objects and reveling in his ability to manipulate the camera, his characters and the audience. Lynch rejected charges that he was merely perpetrating a camped-up soap opera: "Camp is not only not creative," he told TV GUIDE in '90, "it is putting yourself above something else that has already been done and poking fun at it. To me, that is a lower kind of humor." What Lynch was striving for, he said, was to create "a fantastic mood and sense of place...and hopefully you want to go back and feel it each week." Viewers did just that, and *Twin Peaks* was given a second season on ABC—which turned out to be a mistake. The stylish tricks and contorted plotlines quickly began to look like self-parody. That's too bad, because if the show had ended after its first six-week run, *Twin Peaks* might easily have been remembered as the coolest thing ever on television.

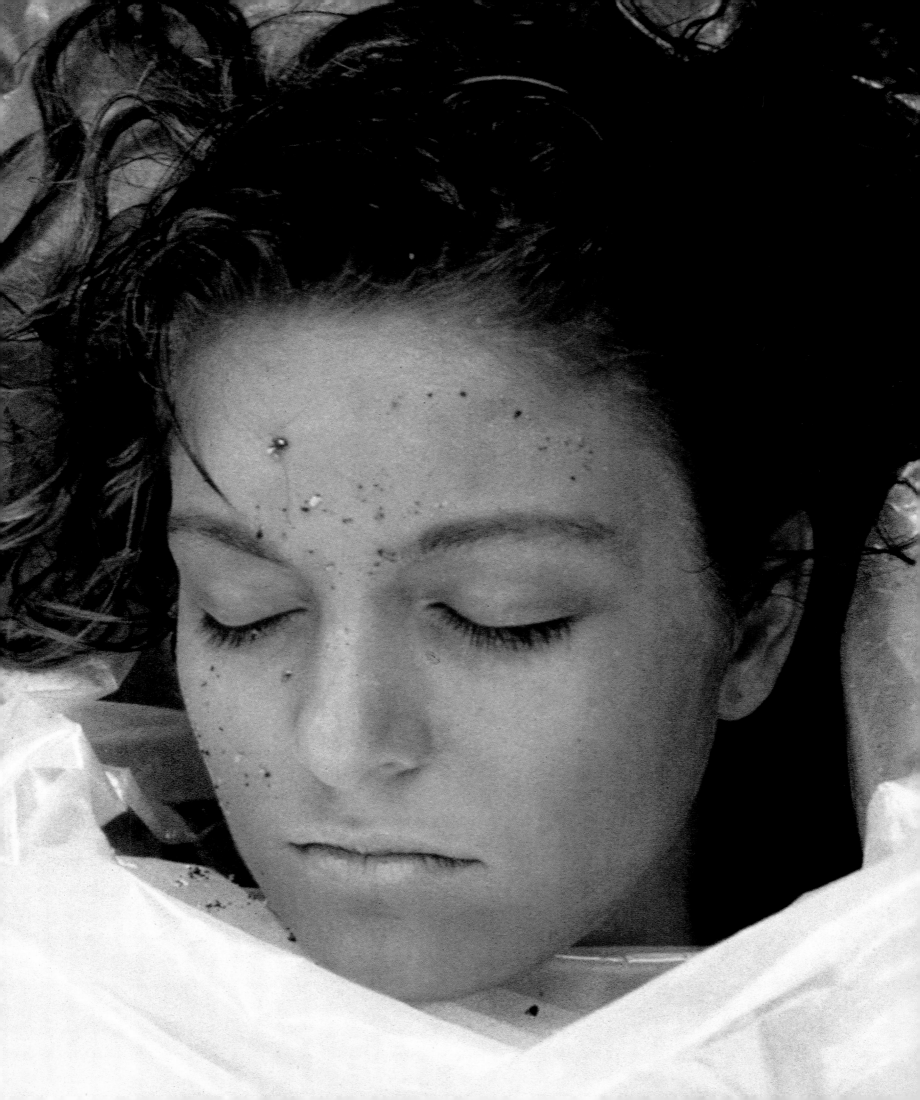

BEWITCHED
Samantha Stephens (Elizabeth Montgomery), Endora (Agnes Moorehead), Darrin Stephens (Dick York).
ABC, 1964–72
COVER: BY IVAN NAGY, MAY 29, 1965

Just in case some grad student in the semiotics of pop culture is contemplating a paper on the situation comedy and how it influences social evolution, here's an excellent candidate for deconstruction: *Bewitched*. Consider this: In 1964, as cultural upheaval was rocking the nation, we were presented with Darrin Stephens (Dick York), a '50s-style soldier in the gray-flannel army who diligently marched off to work every day while, back at home, *everybody else was on acid*. At least that's how it looked sometimes in this comedy about a straitlaced ad man who discovered that his well-scrubbed, all-American wife, Samantha (Elizabeth Montgomery), was really a witch. Darrin, worried about what his boss and neighbors would think, insisted that she suppress her nose-twitching power to alter the world. But Samantha couldn't resist using her magic to sort out a few

problems—and indeed, her supernatural family members *did* complicate life, like when Julius Caesar showed up instead of a Caesar salad. Audiences adored the show and especially Montgomery. But York may have had his own spooky powers. In a 1964 TV GUIDE article, he said there was only one way to tell for sure if he was overshadowed on the show by Montgomery because of his role or his acting ability: "Kill me off in one show, give the witch another husband and see if I'm missed." As it turned out, York, ailing with a chronic back injury, left the series in 1969 and was replaced by Dick Sargent—without an explanation to viewers. *Bewitched*'s ratings quickly eroded, and it was canceled in 1972. The show became a syndication favorite, as did the pastime of comparing the merits of old Darrin and new Darrin.

BUFFY THE VAMPIRE SLAYER
Buffy Summers (Sarah Michelle Gellar). WB, 1997–2001; UPN, 2001–
COVER: BY FRANK OCKENFELS 3, AUGUST 2, 1997

TV GUIDE had a thing for *Buffy the Vampire Slayer*, putting the show—OK, Sarah Michelle Gellar—on the cover twice in two and a half years, publishing an exhaustive guide to every episode of the first three seasons and even commissioning a five-page comic-book-style *Buffy* adventure. And why not? The series (based on the 1992 feature film of the same name) delectably combined the adolescent coming-of-age saga with horror-movie excess, then seasoned it with a dash of postmodern knowing-ness. Buffy Summers faced the usual trials of trying to fit in at a new school when the series began (a popular girl gave her this test: "John Tesh?" Buffy correctly answered: "The devil"), but she faced the added burden of being a vampire slayer in her spare time. Her assignment, which continued even after she moved on to college and beyond, was protecting Sunnydale, a town that had the misfortune of being located at the mouth of hell itself. Guided by her "Watcher," the peculiar school librarian, and assisted by pals known as the Scooby Gang, Buffy battled various fiends with wooden stakes, crucifixes and the occasional kick upside their slavering heads. *Buffy*'s writing was a marvel, swinging easily from droll comedy to the moving romantic trauma of Buffy's ill-fated liaison with the dark Angel (David Boreanaz). Series creator Joss Whedon even memorably crafted an hour-long episode without a word of dialogue for 30 minutes and another composed almost entirely of original song-and-dance numbers. Gellar speculated in TV GUIDE in 2000 that girls liked her Buffy character because she's "not the smartest or the most beautiful. She's kind of awkward, but she is OK with who she is." Guys were attracted to the character, Gellar said, because "they see Buffy as a take-charge, kick-ass girl who has never lost her femininity."

THE TWILIGHT ZONE
Rod Serling; Virginia Gregg, Milton Selzer, Alan Sues, Brooke Hayward; Julie Newmar, Albert Salmi; William Shatner; Agnes Moorehead. CBS, 1959–64

Thanks to Rod Serling's sterling reputation as a drama writer in the 1950s, he was able to interest CBS in an anthology of half-hour shows that shared only one trait: an unadulterated love of the strange. Although Serling took advantage of the anything-eerie-goes format to delve into social issues—like neo-Nazism in an episode starring a young Dennis Hopper—more often *The Twilight Zone* just reveled in unnerving fables with dramatic plot twists. These are the shows that get kicked around whenever a group of baby boomers turns to that beloved parlor game, My Creepiest *Twilight Zone* Episode (bonus points: name the celebrity-to-be). Was it the one where a guy on an airplane (played by the then-unknown William Shatner) goes nuts thinking he sees a creature out on the wing trying to tear it apart? (As they lead him away to the loony bin, he looks up and sees the mangled evidence that he was not hallucinating after all.) Or maybe it was the one where we're told that a hideously deformed woman has undergone a last-chance operation to make her look presentable enough to live among "normal people." (The operation is a horrific failure when the bandages are peeled away to reveal that she's still a beautiful woman—it's the doctors and nurses who look like gargoyles.) As Stephen King wrote in *Danse Macabre*, a collection of his meditations on horror that was excerpted in TV GUIDE in 1981, *The Twilight Zone* "generated a kind of existential weirdness that no other series has been able to match."

There is a fifth dimension beyond that which is known to man. It is a dimension as vast as space and as timeless as infinity. It is the middle ground between light and shadow, between science and superstition, and it lies between the pit of man's fears and the summit of his knowledge. This is the dimension of imagination. It is an area which we call **The Twilight Zone**

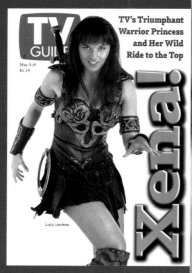

XENA: WARRIOR PRINCESS
Xena (Lucy Lawless).
Syndication, 1995–2001
COVER: BY GARY HEERY, MAY 3, 1997

When Xena hurled her last razor-sharp chakram disk after six years of syndicated success, TV GUIDE noted "X Things We'll Miss" about her and Lucy Lawless, the actress behind the Amazonian sci-fi/fantasy babe. They included: "The Grrrl Power" (Xena once kicked the entire Persian army's collective butt); "The Fashions" ("We were always a sucker for a gal in a wrought-iron bra"); and "The Lesbian Subtext" (Xena's unstated relationship with comic-relief sidekick Gabrielle titillated many fans). As if those attributes weren't enough, the magazine also celebrated *Xena*'s message: "The show's plea for tolerance and its timeless advice—be true to yourself—are the ultimate cool."

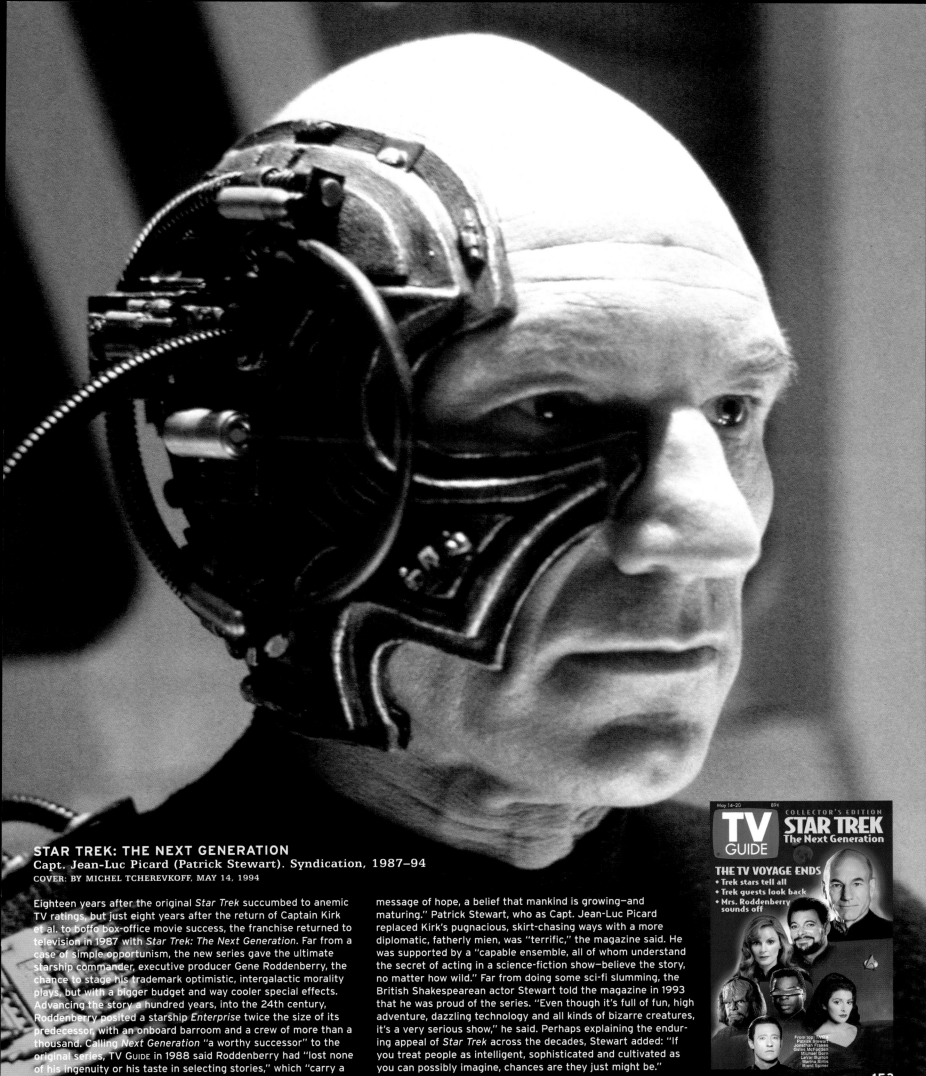

STAR TREK: THE NEXT GENERATION
Capt. Jean-Luc Picard (Patrick Stewart). Syndication, 1987–94
COVER: BY MICHEL TCHEREVKOFF, MAY 14, 1994

Eighteen years after the original *Star Trek* succumbed to anemic TV ratings, but just eight years after the return of Captain Kirk et al. to boffo box-office movie success, the franchise returned to television in 1987 with *Star Trek: The Next Generation*. Far from a case of simple opportunism, the new series gave the ultimate starship commander, executive producer Gene Roddenberry, the chance to stage his trademark optimistic, intergalactic morality plays, but with a bigger budget and way cooler special effects. Advancing the story a hundred years, into the 24th century, Roddenberry posited a starship *Enterprise* twice the size of its predecessor, with an onboard barroom and a crew of more than a thousand. Calling *Next Generation* "a worthy successor" to the original series, TV GUIDE in 1988 said Roddenberry had "lost none of his ingenuity or his taste in selecting stories," which "carry a

message of hope, a belief that mankind is growing—and maturing." Patrick Stewart, who as Capt. Jean-Luc Picard replaced Kirk's pugnacious, skirt-chasing ways with a more diplomatic, fatherly mien, was "terrific," the magazine said. He was supported by a "capable ensemble, all of whom understand the secret of acting in a science-fiction show—believe the story, no matter how wild." Far from doing some sci-fi slumming, the British Shakespearean actor Stewart told the magazine in 1993 that he was proud of the series. "Even though it's full of fun, high adventure, dazzling technology and all kinds of bizarre creatures, it's a very serious show," he said. Perhaps explaining the enduring appeal of *Star Trek* across the decades, Stewart added: "If you treat people as intelligent, sophisticated and cultivated as you can possibly imagine, chances are they just might be."

ANIMAL MAGNETISM

1) **THE LONE RANGER** (Clayton Moore) with Silver, Tonto (Jay Silverheels) with Scout. ABC, 1949-57

2) **THE ADVENTURES OF RIN TIN TIN** Native American (actor unknown), Rusty (Lee Aaker) with Rin Tin Tin. CBS, 1954-59

3) **THE PEOPLE'S CHOICE** Socrates "Sock" Miller (Jackie Cooper) with Cleo. NBC, 1955-58

4) **MY THREE SONS** Steve Douglas (Fred MacMurray) with Tramp. ABC, 1960-65; CBS, 1965-72

5) **THE JETSONS** George Jetson with Astro. ABC, 1962-63

6) **FLIPPER** Bud Ricks (Tommy Norden) with Flipper. NBC, 1964-68

7) **DAKTARI** Paula Tracy (Cheryl Miller), Bart Jason (Ross Hagen) with Clarence. CBS, 1966-69

8) **GENTLE BEN** Mark Wedloe (Clint Howard) with Ben. CBS, 1967-69

9) **LANCELOT LINK, SECRET CHIMP** Undercover simians. ABC, 1970-72

10) **BARETTA** Det. Tony Baretta (Robert Blake) with Fred. ABC, 1975-78

11) **MAD ABOUT YOU** Paul Buchman (Paul Reiser), Jamie Buchman (Helen Hunt) with Murray. NBC, 1992-99

12) **THE CROCODILE HUNTER** Steve Irwin, Terri Irwin with title creature. ANIMAL PLANET, 1996-

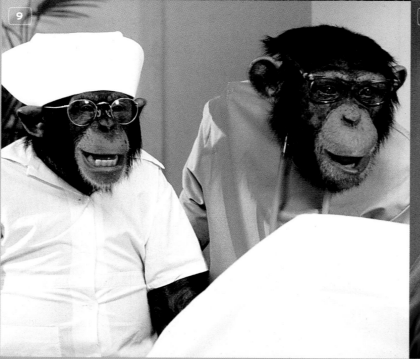

AN AMERICAN FAMILY

Clockwise from top left:
Lance Loud, Delilah Loud,
Grant Loud, Kevin Loud,
Michele Loud, Pat Loud,
Bill Loud. PBS, 1973

Long before *Big Brother* or *The Real World*, there was *An American Family*—a 12-part PBS documentary that riveted the country in 1973. For an hour every week, we stepped into the home of the Loud family of Santa Barbara, California, seeing first-hand the quotidian events and emotional dramas that occurred during the seven months that they lived under the unblinking gaze of the camera. The two signal moments of the series were the parents' breakup, when Pat Loud asked her philandering husband, Bill, to move out of the house, and Pat's trip to New York City. There, her son Lance—one of five Loud children—revealed he was gay, appeared on screen wearing blue lipstick and introduced his mom to the transvestite netherworld. Anthropologist Margaret Mead, writing in TV GUIDE, called the camera-as-witness programming "as new and as significant as the invention of drama or the novel—a new way in which people can learn to look at life." But *An American Family* also provoked a storm of criticism. The Louds themselves disavowed the documentary as a distorted view of their life. As TV GUIDE reported in a two-part investigation: "The family feels that [producer Craig] Gilbert and the editors were too eager to include pessimistic scenes." Pat added: "Knowing what I know now, I wouldn't go through it again." Other sniping came from critics who debated whether "the beleaguered family," as TV GUIDE called them, was being used "as an example of nearly everything that is supposedly going wrong with American society." For his part, Gilbert insisted that he wasn't trying to "propound universal truths" about families. But perhaps one universal truth of television did emerge from the affair: Whatever its controversies, "reality" programming—like a train wreck—holds an enduring fascination all its own.

THE OSBOURNES

Kelly Osbourne, Ozzy Osbourne, Sharon Osbourne, Jack Osbourne. MTV, 2002–

These things are hard to pin down, but TV GUIDE appears to have coined the subsequently ubiquitous phrase "Ozzy and Harried" to describe the cult TV hit of 2002, *The Osbournes*. That was the headline for a prescient late-February story about a show that didn't debut until March 5—and quickly became the biggest hit MTV had ever seen. Ozzy Osbourne, the middle-aged British heavy-metal star with a leaky brainpan, was the foul-mouthed, befuddled centerpiece of this genre salad: equal parts anti-*Ozzie and Harriet* family comedy, reality-TV show and special Beverly Hills edition of *This Is Spiñal Tap*. Osbourne worried aloud to TV GUIDE that fans of his old bat-gnawing excess might be disappointed to see him at home flummoxed by the remote control—"I wonder if it will crush their illusion about me"—but his wife and manager, the sardonic Sharon, reassured him: "People know you're not some mystical bloodsucking creature. You're a cottage-cheese eater." One of the Osbournes' teenagers, Aimee, opted out of the series, but second-generation rock and roll kids Kelly and Jack clomped through the dog-clogged Osbourne manse in a perpetual adolescent funk. "I have the foulest mouth on earth, and I don't really care," Kelly told TV GUIDE in April 2002, proving she's a *bleep* off the old block.

"It's 25 minutes of bleeps. It made me realize that we live in Beverly Hills and we sound like we live in a f---ing trailer park. What you see is the way it is; none of it's been doctored. None of it's hammed up. It's real. It's The Ozzy Osbourne Real World."
—Ozzy Osbourne

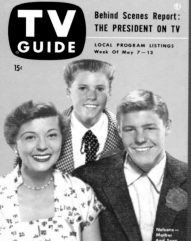

TV GUIDE

Behind Scenes Report:
THE PRESIDENT ON TV

LOCAL PROGRAM LISTINGS
Week Of May 7—13

15¢

*Nelsons—
Mother
And Sons*

THE ADVENTURES OF OZZIE & HARRIET
Harriet Nelson, Ozzie Nelson, David Nelson, Ricky Nelson.
ABC, 1952–66
COVER: PHOTOGRAPHER UNKNOWN, MAY 7, 1954

Here's an idea for a reality-TV series: Lock a family of four in a house and come back with a TV camera once a week for 14 years to see what goes on. That's essentially what happened with *The Adventures of Ozzie & Harriet*, except the premise didn't inspire any secret alliances or backstabbing. Or, for that matter, much in the way of adventure. But the addictively pleasant comedy starring the real-life Nelson family enjoyed an epic run anyway (after eight years on radio) and provided a window for America into an idealized suburbia. The country watched as Ozzie and Harriet's two sons, David and Ricky, grew up in real time in a pleasant middle-class house modeled on the Nelsons' own Hollywood home. If one of the boys took up singing, it went into the show–and it turned Ricky Nelson into a pop star. If the boys got married, then their real-life wives joined their on-air family too. "Occasionally, critics have complained that everyone on our show is a nice person," Ozzie, the series' creator, director and cowriter, told TV GUIDE in 1963. "I don't understand this type of complaint. Most people are pretty nice." It was just such unquestioning optimism that would forever make *Ozzie & Harriet* the cultural archetype of its era.

THE ADDAMS FAMILY
Gomez Addams (John Astin), Uncle Fester Frump (Jackie Coogan), Cousin Itt. ABC, 1964–66
COVER: ILLUSTRATION BY CHARLES ADDAMS, PHOTOGRAPHS BY IVAN NAGY, OCTOBER 30, 1965

When social change in the mid-'60s started chipping away at the institution of the traditional family, TV did its part by mocking Ozzie-and-Harriet values with two comedies launched in 1964: *The Munsters* (on CBS) and *The Addams Family*. Both shows wanted to wring laughs from the ghoul-next-door conceit, but as TV GUIDE pronounced at the time, "*The Addams Family* is far and away the most delectable." The show, inspired by Charles Addams's creepy-funny cartoons for *The New Yorker* magazine, stood conventional family life on its head: The morbid kids, Pugsley and Wednesday, skipped school because the class reading, *Grimms' Fairy Tales*, unfairly depicted cruelty to dragons, and their mother, the sepulchral Morticia, gushed wanly over her garden of deadly nightshade. Gomez, meanwhile, put a stake in the heart of the traditional neutered TV dad with a passionate, even carnal, devotion to his wife. Addams applauded what had become of his creations. "The casting has been superb," Addams wrote in TV GUIDE in 1965, "and Carolyn Jones and John Astin, as heads of this household, are beyond my reproach." The show left a pop-cultural legacy—two *Addams Family* feature films were released in the '90s—that lingered, like the undead, far beyond its two seasons on the air.

"WE HAPPENED TO HAVE A SHOW DURING A CULTURAL REVOLUTION

and a political revolution in this country. It was serendipitous, really. We were at the scene of the accident, and the times form you a little bit. And so we used comedy for our politics. Things had heated up in the Vietnam War and protests were out there, so we started reflecting more of what younger people were thinking. We were in our late twenties at that time and most of our writers were in their early twenties, so there was a certain passion there, and it showed up in sketches on the war and voter registration. And also in 1968, Martin Luther King Jr. was shot, Bobby Kennedy was shot, the riots at the Democratic Convention in Chicago—all that stuff happened during the time we were on the air. So basically, we expressed those alternative points of view that weren't being reflected, and it became a battle with the network censors. We'd put up a sign, ANOTHER MOTHER FOR PEACE. They'd say, well, you can't do that because it could be a Communist front organization or something like that. We played some games and had some fun. The last season, I said, 'If you're that unhappy with us, then don't pick us up.' They picked us up. But about three months later the election was over, Richard M. Nixon won over Hubert Humphrey, and in April we were fired. The Nixon administration wasn't going to have the Smothers Brothers critiquing their war effort."

—TOM SMOTHERS

THE SMOTHERS BROTHERS COMEDY HOUR
Tom Smothers, Dick Smothers. CBS, 1967–69
COVER: BY BOB PEAK, FEBRUARY 10, 1968

TV GUIDE applauded the arrival of *The Smothers Brothers Comedy Hour* in 1967, even though it wasn't sure if they were "folksinging comedians or comedy folksingers." Dick plucked the stand-up bass and was the level-headed foil for guitar-playing Tom's flights of fuzzy, convoluted logic—which somehow always led to his blurting out, "Mom always liked you better!" TV GUIDE's review, just a couple of months into the show, did issue a caveat: "One area in which this show could be improved is in the matter of taste." The magazine scolded the duo for using the rock group Paul Revere and the Raiders to lampoon Revolutionary War heroes. But if the magazine was sensi- tive about such matters, CBS was downright sore. The network fought to expunge anything controversial, particularly about religion or contemporary politics, despite the fact that the show's irreverence had made it immediately popular with viewers. The battles escalated until CBS canceled the series mid-hit after two seasons. The show "is much better in people's memories than it ever really was," Dick told TV GUIDE in 1988. Indeed, as the magazine noted, its martyrdom to the cause of free- dom of expression was "in its way, a blessing. The Smothers Brothers were forever fixed in public consciousness, a part of American cultural history."

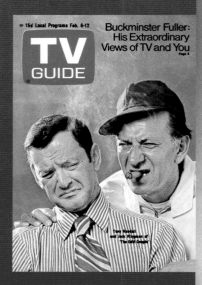

THE ODD COUPLE

Felix Unger (Tony
Randall), Oscar Madison
(Jack Klugman).
ABC, 1970–75
COVER: BY GENE TRINDL,
FEBRUARY 6, 1971

Neil Simon's conceit about two
mismatched roommates, Felix the
finicky photographer and Oscar the
slobby sportswriter, played on
Broadway and in movie theaters
before moving to TV in 1970. Art
Carney and Walter Matthau took
the dueling duo on stage, while
Jack Lemmon and Matthau were
on the big screen. Tough acts to
follow. But Tony Randall and Jack
Klugman "are actually better than
their predecessors" in the roles,
said TV GUIDE, bringing subtler
shadings to their characters:
Randall delivered "something
besides neurosis," and Klugman
"something besides vulgarity."
Those accomplishments aside, the
magazine noted, "they never forget
that the main point is to be funny."

KE JUDGE

HEH HEH
HEH

THE BEAVIS AND BUTT-HEAD SHOW
Butt-head, Beavis. MTV, 1993–97

"These characters are like guys I knew in junior high," *Beavis and Butt-head Show* creator Mike Judge told TV GUIDE shortly after its attention-grabbing debut on MTV. "Vulgar schoolyard humor is just the way they are." Critics deplored the proudly moronic duo's antics, such as using frogs for batting practice, urinating in swimming pools and starting fires (a rite of passage into juvenile delinquency that may have prompted copycat torchings among young viewers). But the cartoon cretins were in fact deftly satirizing the sex-obsessed, violence-fascinated, dumbbell layabouts in MTV's own audience. When the series ended, there was only one way to describe the announcement: It sucked.

SOUTH PARK
Mrs. Broflovski, Kenny McCormick. Comedy Central, 1997–
COVER: BY *SOUTH PARK*, MARCH 28, 1998

A town that might be visited by aliens one day and a diarrhea epidemic the next. A school-cafeteria cook who croons his advice to schoolchildren in songs dripping with sexually explicit lyrics. A kid who vomits whenever he gets near the girl he adores; another who's a fat, foul-mouthed bully; and yet another who met a grisly death in nearly every episode (until his final gasp in the show's fifth season). Welcome to *South Park*, the playground of animation team Trey Parker and Matt Stone. "What we're trying to say is, nothing is sacred," Stone told TV GUIDE shortly after the show's 1997 debut. The Comedy Central series, with animation that was rivaled in crudeness only by its language, immediately provoked outrage from guardians of the culture—and sheer delight among fans. The *South Park* buzz was so strong that cable companies not carrying Comedy Central were deluged with phone calls demanding that they add it. Within months, T-shirts and other merchandise featuring *South Park*'s four third-graders—Kyle, Stan, Cartman and Kenny—were pouring out of stores, and in addition to countless obscenities, the show had its own catchphrase: "Oh, my God, they killed Kenny!" The quiet kid buried deep inside his hooded parka had to die over and over again, Stone told the magazine, because "we just like to kill him. And we really like the line." Despite the cartoon's joyously juvenile humor, TV GUIDE called *South Park* "one of the most sophisticated shows on TV these days" for its send-up of life in small-town Colorado. "There are some things that are kind of wholesome about *South Park*," Parker told the magazine. "The bottom line is that as insane as it gets, right always sort of wins."

LEAVE IT TO BEAVER
Wally Cleaver (Tony Dow), Theodore "Beaver" Cleaver (Jerry Mathers).
CBS, 1957–58; ABC, 1958–63
COVER: BY GARRETT-HOWARD, JUNE 28, 1958

This show achieved a minor miracle during its run: It built a TV franchise on a simple, gimmick-free depiction of the domestic life of a nice family in a pleasant small town. TV GUIDE called the half hours with the Cleaver family in mythical Mayfield "one of the most honest, most human and most satisfying situation comedies on TV." While Ward Cleaver (Hugh Beaumont) was the sensible dad and his wife, June (Barbara Billingsley), the sweet-tempered and patient mom, the heart of *Leave It to Beaver* was the kids—Wally (Tony Dow), who was 12 and on the cusp of adolescence as the series began, and Theodore (Jerry Mathers), aka Beaver, whose 7-year-old's perspective on the world suffused the show with the innocent joys of everyday life. Beaver was forever stumbling into one mild crisis after another, such as losing the money entrusted to him by his father for a haircut and resolving to cut his own hair—a few days before appearing in a school play. Wally, impatient to grow up, fumed at being drawn back into Beaver's childish predicaments, but invariably helped out his brother despite the heckling of his friend Eddie Haskell (Ken Osmond). Though you sometimes still hear references to "June Cleaver" to describe the perfect mom, "Eddie Haskell" remains a vivid shorthand for a two-faced weasel, in this case a teenager whose elaborate politeness to adults ("*Good evening*, Mr. and Mrs. Cleaver") masks real contempt. *Leave It to Beaver* was a reliable performer, but it was during years of reruns that the show, with a characteristic lack of fanfare, gently won over viewers' affection.

1) **THE MAN FROM U.N.C.L.E.**
Napoleon Solo
(Robert Vaughn),
Illya Kuryakin
(David McCallum).
NBC, 1964-68

2) **I SPY**
Kelly Robinson (Robert Culp),
Alexander Scott
(Bill Cosby).
NBC, 1965-68

3) **IRONSIDE**
Robert Ironside
(Raymond Burr).
NBC, 1967-75

4) **CANNON**
Frank Cannon
(William Conrad).
CBS, 1971-76

5) **KOJAK**
Lt. Theo Kojak
(Telly Savalas).
CBS, 1973-78

6) **STARSKY AND HUTCH**
Det. Dave Starsky (Paul Michael
Glaser), Det. Ken "Hutch"
Hutchinson (David Soul).
ABC, 1975-79

7) **QUINCY, M.E.**
Dr. Quincy (Jack Klugman).
NBC, 1976-83

8) **POLICE SQUAD**
Det. Frank Drebin
(Leslie Nielsen).
ABC, 1982

9) **MACGYVER**
MacGyver
(Richard Dean Anderson).
ABC, 1985-92

10) **WISEGUY**
Vinnie Terranova (Ken Wahl).
CBS, 1987-90

11) **MYSTERY!: "POIROT"**
Hercule Poirot (David Suchet).
PBS, 1989-99

12) **MYSTERY!: "PRIME SUSPECT"**
DCI Jane Tennison
(Helen Mirren).
PBS, 1991-94

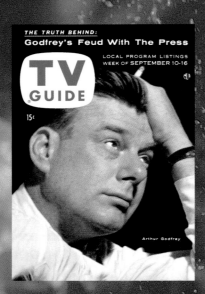

THE TRUTH BEHIND:
Godfrey's Feud With The Press
LOCAL PROGRAM LISTINGS
WEEK OF SEPTEMBER 10-16

TV GUIDE

15¢

Arthur Godfrey

ARTHUR GODFREY
Date unknown
COVER: PHOTOGRAPHER UNKNOWN,
SEPTEMBER 10, 1955

It's probably safe to say that no one whose only talent was a charismatic personality will ever dominate television the way Arthur Godfrey loomed over TV in the early 1950s. In addition to his radio show, which was being televised, he hosted two monster hit series, *Arthur Godfrey's Talent Scouts* and *Arthur Godfrey and His Friends*, which in 1952-53 finished second and third in the ratings behind *I Love Lucy*. *Talent Scouts* was just what the name implied, a showcase for amateurs and rising pros (Pat Boone and the McGuire Sisters among them); *Friends* was a variety show of performers, mostly singers, who got their break with Godfrey. But in both cases, the real attraction was the host himself, whose avuncular charm made him famous on '40s radio and translated deftly to television. Godfrey's championing of unknown performers, and his needling of corporate sponsors, established "the old redhead" as the little guy's best friend—a bond that endured until 1953, when Godfrey fired singer Julius LaRosa on the air. "That, folks, was Julie's swan song," Godfrey said after the unsuspecting LaRosa finished a number. LaRosa was an unknown when Godfrey discovered him, but had become a recording star and fan favorite on *Friends*. The press reaction to his canning was thunderously negative, particularly after Godfrey explained that LaRosa had been dumped for lacking "humility." The host then lashed out at his disapproving critics and started firing more stars and staff. The affair "ultimately shrank his TV empire almost to the dimensions of a doghouse," TV GUIDE said in '63, noting that "the conflict of amiability and ill temper has always raged within Godfrey." For his part, Godfrey may have learned the first lesson of modern celebrity, telling the magazine, "I did not have a well-organized public relations outfit."

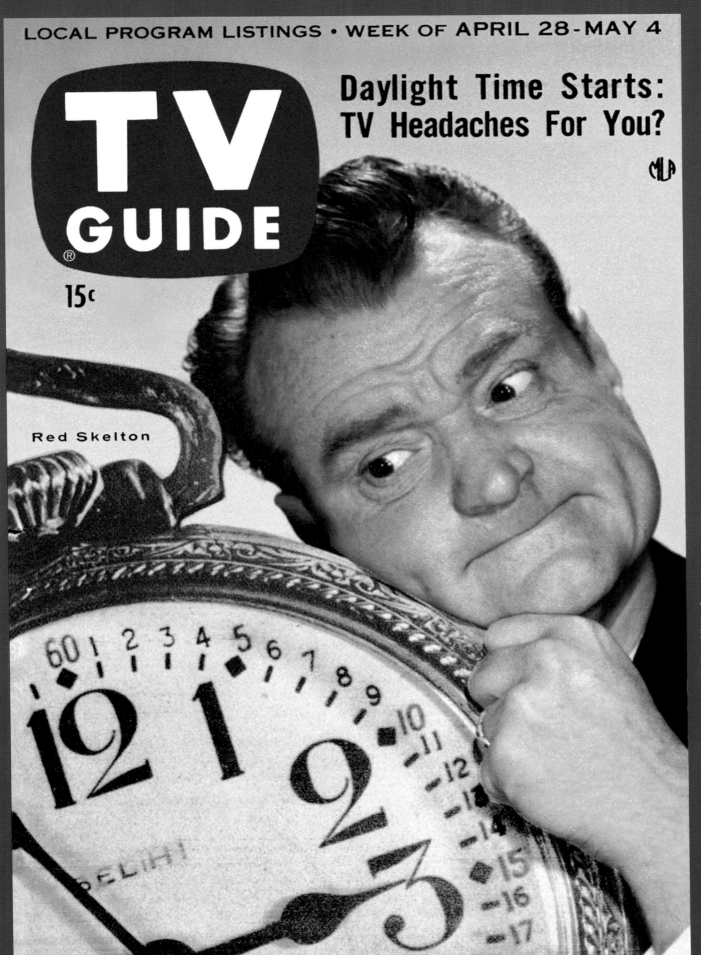

LOCAL PROGRAM LISTINGS • WEEK OF APRIL 28 - MAY 4

TV GUIDE

®

15¢

Daylight Time Starts: TV Headaches For You?

MLP

Red Skelton

THE RED SKELTON SHOW
NBC, 1951–53 and
1970–71; CBS, 1953–70
COVER: BY GARRETT-HOWARD,
APRIL 28, 1956

Kindhearted, tirelessly inventive
clown Red Skelton appeared on
TV GUIDE covers five times over
the course of his comedy-variety
show's 20-year history. The
comedian may have kept a file
cabinet full of tens of thousands
of jokes, but Skelton was most
beloved for the characters he
created, including the hobo
Freddie the Freeloader, country
bumpkin Clem Kadiddlehopper,
and the excessively bird-brained
seagulls Gertrude and Heath-
cliffe. When Skelton died in 1997,
frequent collaborator Marcel
Marceau wrote in TV GUIDE: "Red
Skelton brought joy, happiness
and poetry to millions of children
and grown-ups. In his field he
had no peer."

THE GEORGE BURNS AND GRACIE ALLEN SHOW
CBS, 1950–58
COVER: BY AL HIRSCHFELD, DECEMBER 1, 1956

By the time George Burns and Gracie Allen took their act to television—he was the cigar-puffing, bemused straight man to her endearing scatterbrain—it had been refined to perfection by decades of work in vaudeville and on radio. They could have easily coasted on the goodwill of their built-in audience, but *The George Burns and Gracie Allen Show* proved that they didn't need to: They had an apparently bottomless well of humor on which to draw. Only Gracie's decision to say good-night for the last time in '58 ended the show—though four years later, TV GUIDE was still celebrating the couple for finding so much comedy in "a husband and a wife who (miracle of miracles in these days!) seem to love each other."

'My Wife Jayne,' By Steve Allen

TV GUIDE

LOCAL PROGRAM LISTINGS
WEEK OF DECEMBER 1-7

15¢

George Burns
Gracie Allen

THE SONNY AND CHER COMEDY HOUR
Sonny Bono, Cher Bono. CBS, 1971–74 and 1976–77
COVER: BY ROGER PRIGENT, JUNE 5, 1976

Yes, there was plenty of controversy (Cher Bono's outlandish, flesh-revealing Bob Mackie outfits), lots of talent (guest stars like Teri Garr and Steve Martin) and dependable fun (regular
skits such as "Sonny's Pizza" and Cher's vamp segment). But the heart of *The Sonny and Cher
Comedy Hour* was the husband-and-wife ribbing between the puppyish Sonny Bono and sardonic
Cher. "In a word, it's terrific," TV GUIDE said of the show in 1972, singling out Cher for praise: "Is
there anything she can't do?" Yes, apparently: get along with Sonny. The couple's 1974 divorce
scuttled *Sonny and Cher* at the height of its popularity. The two tried solo shows and then
reunited two years later for a reprise of the original series, but the divorced duo never recaptured the magic of the "I Got You, Babe" years.

MONTY PYTHON'S FLYING CIRCUS
John Cleese. BBC, 1969–74

In 1974, just as it was ending a five-year stint on the BBC, *Monty Python's Flying Circus* rolled into America, bringing its brilliantly loony brand of humor to public television. No subject was safe from the freewheeling, smarty-pants slapstick of the five British Oxford and Cambridge grads (Graham Chapman, John Cleese, Terry Jones, Eric Idle and Michael Palin) and their rarely seen American pal, Terry Gilliam, who provided the show's crudely executed but wickedly funny animated segments. Pretentious TV talk-show hosts, stuffy bureaucrats, Hollywood directors, harridan housewives, sadistic shop clerks—they all got skewered in sketches, blackouts, faux documentaries and anything else the troupe could cram into half hours that were the comic equivalent of five years' worth of *Saturday Night Live* episodes. "The fact that our satire was never specific makes it last," Gilliam told TV GUIDE in 1990. "Our targets are cosmically silly forever." To its eternal shame, TV GUIDE back in 1975 just didn't get the joke. "It was all so far-fetched that it was pathetic," the magazine said, singling out for criticism "The Ministry of Silly Walks," a now-classic Cleese performance. "Plodded on endlessly," the magazine har-rumphed, just begging for someone to apply the trademark Python silencer, a smack in the face with a large fish.

THE ERNIE KOVACS SHOW
CBS, 1952–53; NBC, 1956
COVER: BY PHILLIPE HALSMAN, MAY 14, 1960

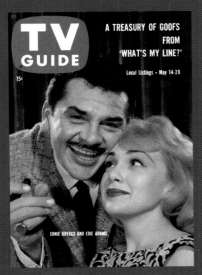

It's difficult to say which was more stunning: *The Ernie Kovacs Show* itself, or the fact that it only ran for a grand total of eight months (five in 1952-53 and three in 1956). Kovacs, still regarded by many as one of the most inventive, iconoclastic and funny comedians in television history, flouted virtually every convention of the medium, then and now. There was simply no one else on television to whom it would occur, for instance, to let the screen go black—except for the lines of an oscilloscope undulating to the sound of "Mack the Knife" sung in the original German. Further absurdist adventures in musical comedy included regularly convening the Nairobi Trio: Three guys, always dressed in gorilla suits, slowly played the same tune until one got bonked on the head. They would pause, then return to their song. Kovacs's sense of humor was indeed lost on some people—he was never a ratings giant—but anyone who saw his work never forgot it. He parodied other TV shows and commercials, brilliantly adapted TV technology to create surreal special effects and dreamed up recurring characters like the pricelessly fey poet Percy Dovetonsils. "While Sid Caesar and Imogene Coca were keeping millions in stitches over a domestic quarrel," Chevy Chase wrote in a TV GUIDE tribute in 1977, "Ernie was tilting sets, doing entire specials with no dialogue whatsoever and daringly working without a studio audience. He was, and remains, fresh and innovative, and above all—because this is the bottom line—funny." Although his series was short-lived, Kovacs was wonderfully prolific, bringing his trademark comedy to *The Tonight Show* as a fill-in for Steve Allen, creating TV specials and even hosting a game show. Kovacs's life was cut short: He died in 1962, at age 42, in a car accident in Los Angeles.

ROWAN AND MARTIN'S LAUGH-IN

**Clockwise from top right: Ruth Buzzi,
Goldie Hawn, Henry Gibson; Dick Martin,
Judy Carne, Dan Rowan; Arte Johnson.
NBC, 1968–73**

COVER: BY JACK DAVIS, MARCH 28, 1970

Early in the second season of *Rowan and Martin's
Laugh-In*, hosts Dan Rowan (the suave one) and Dick
Martin (the goofy playboy) presented a plaque to executive producer George Schlatter that read: IN SKATING OVER
THIN ICE—OUR SAFETY IS OUR SPEED. *Laugh-In* was nothing if
not fast: a whirling kaleidoscope of pratfalls, trapdoors,
one-liners, bikini-clad and body-painted dancers, and
joke-spouting celebrity guests that slipped daring (for
the time) humor about politics and sex into scripts
teeming with pure silliness. The show went to No. 1 in
the ratings in its first two full seasons at the end of the
'60s. Then it imploded as stars departed, behind-the-
scenes bickering escalated and, most likely, the frenetic
show simply wore out its welcome and its audience. But
for two exhilarating years, *Laugh-In* was a major pop-
cultural presence. (The show's reach was vividly demonstrated when presidential candidate Richard M. Nixon
appeared on *Laugh-In* saying, "Sock it to *me*?") Judy
Carne as the sock-it-to-me waif, Goldie Hawn as the
endearingly giggly dumb blond, Lily Tomlin's coyly
snorting telephone operator, Arte Johnson's "Verrrry
interesting" Nazi—these characters became instant
classics of American comedy. "Whatever happens to
the show now," TV GUIDE said in 1970, "it has earned its
niche as a genuine phenomenon of the 1960s, breaking
the stale old mold of the standard host-guest-comic-
choreography variety show, and substituting, instead,
irreverence, bawdiness and topical 'today' humor, aimed
like buckshot at children and intellectuals alike." Hawn
was already feeling nostalgic in 1972, two years after
leaving the show and a year before it ended: "The farther
away I get, the more beautiful it becomes," she told
TV GUIDE. "When I look at the old pictures, I could cry."

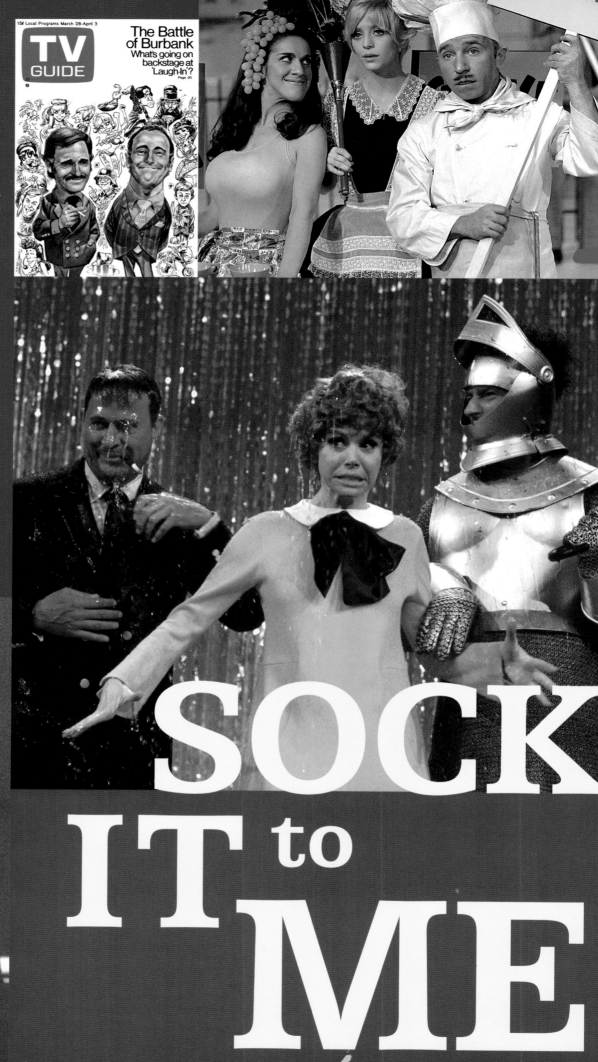

SOCK IT to ME

IN LIVING COLOR
Clockwise from near left: Jim Carrey; Damon Wayans, David Alan Grier; Wayans; the Fly Girls. Fox, 1990–94

The upstart Fox network, anxious to distinguish itself from the TV big boys in the early '90s, accomplished just that with *In Living Color*. It was the anti–*Saturday Night Live*: mostly black instead of mostly white, and a half hour crammed full of funny sketches instead of 90 minutes of sometimes spotty humorous moments. Creative multi-tasker Keenen Ivory Wayans was the engine behind the show and its main star, though he was surrounded by plenty of talent, from his brother Damon to Fly Girl dancer Jennifer Lopez to force-of-nature comedian Jim Carrey (working under the name James). Sketches to look forward to every week included "Men on Film," with the gayest cineasts around ("Two snaps up!"), and Damon's humorless Homey the Clown ("Homey don't play that"). Unfortunately, *In Living Color* went on life support after just two seasons when Keenen quit the show (followed by four of his siblings on the payroll) because of a dispute with Fox over the network's use of reruns, which he felt damaged the show's value in syndication. *In Living Color* left the air in '94 after one more season, but the memory remains: a dazzling example of a comedy-variety series brimming with energy and take-no-prisoners humor.

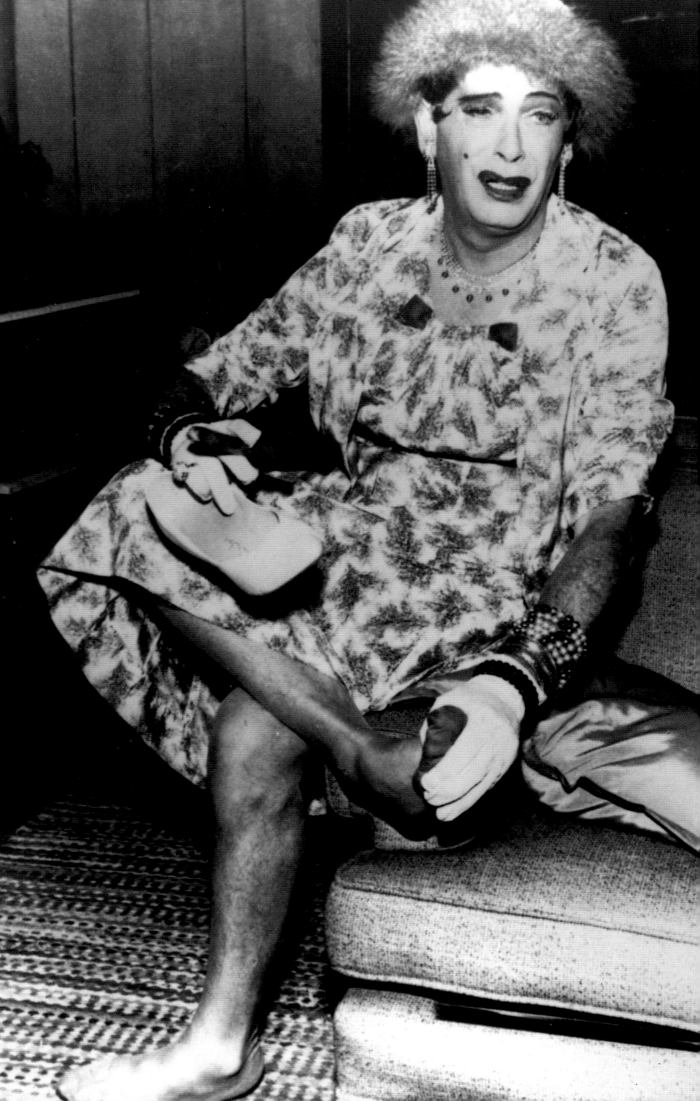

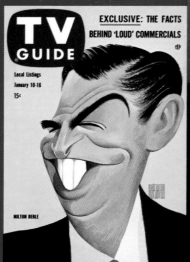

MILTON BERLE
Date unknown
COVER: BY AL HIRSCHFELD,
JANUARY 10, 1959

If you were one of the few hundred thousand people in America who owned a television set in 1948, on Tuesday nights at 8 P.M. you were almost by definition watching—probably in the company of a few friends and neighbors—*Texaco Star Theater*, better known as *The Milton Berle Show*. Berle would himself soon become better known as Mr. Television, or Uncle Miltie, as consumers anxious to watch the anything-for-a-joke-comedian sent the sale of TV sets soaring across the country. Municipalities reported drastic surges in water usage the moment the comedy-variety series left the air at 9 P.M. One theater owner in Ohio hung a sign in the lobby that said: CLOSED TUESDAY. I WANT TO SEE BERLE TOO. And what was everyone so excited about seeing? A vaude-ville and radio veteran madly exploiting the new television medium with an avalanche of puns, one-liners and, above all, sight gags. Berle would black out his front teeth, don a dress, take a shot of seltzer or a pie in the face, stumble into a juggler's act or come out on stage as a caveman after being introduced as "the man with the jokes from the Stone Age." The frantic shows were all live, with Berle so completely involved in the production that he was often shot from the waist up so the TV audience couldn't see his hands signaling the cameras. In 1959, three years after his phenomenal run ended, Berle told TV GUIDE, "I'm the kind of greasepaint bum—not 'bum'; make that 'ham'—who likes to hear the sound of applause."

I'M SO GLAD WE HAD this TIME TOGETHER

THE CAROL BURNETT SHOW
CBS, 1967–78
COVER: BY AL HIRSCHFELD, APRIL 11, 1970

One of the secrets of Carol Burnett's immense appeal was that she always imagined herself performing for a very specific middle-American couple that she named "Fred and Marge." The couple was "smart, they know everything," Burnett told TV GUIDE in 1972. You couldn't play down to them, she said, you couldn't be too risqué and you couldn't get away with a mediocre production. Hence *The Carol Burnett Show*, television's last great variety series. By 1963, TV GUIDE had already dubbed Burnett "America's most raucous female comic," but her gifts for clowning, singing and dancing found their ideal showcase in the variety show that launched four years later. The series was packed with marvelous performers, including Harvey Korman, Lyle Waggoner, Tim Conway and Vicki Lawrence. Among the many terrific regular features, the movie parodies got some of the biggest laughs. "Went With the Wind," a satire of a certain Civil War classic, itself became a classic with moments like the one where "Ratt" admires the dress that "Starlett" has made out of curtains (including the rod) and she replies, "I saw it in a window and I just couldn't resist it." The shows often started informally, with Burnett and that week's guest star answering the studio audience's questions; each broadcast ended with Burnett singing "It's Time to Say Goodbye" and tugging on her earlobe, originally a secret signal to her grandmother. The public's affection for Burnett endured long after the show left the air. A CBS special 23 years later in November 2001, with the former cast members chatting in between old outtakes, was the week's top-rated show, drawing 30 million viewers.

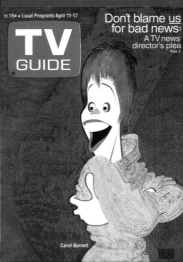

THE '70s

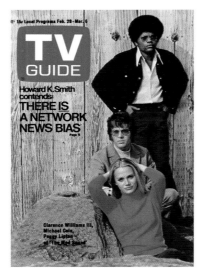

February 28, 1970
By Raphael
Clarence Williams III, Michael Cole and
Peggy Lipton of *The Mod Squad*

June 27, 1970
By Raphael
Liza Minnelli

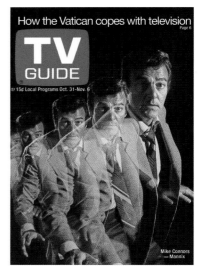

October 31, 1970
By Gene Trindl
Mike Connors of *Mannix*

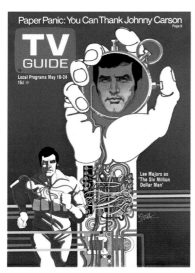

May 18, 1974
By Bob Peak
Lee Majors of *The Six Million Dollar Man*

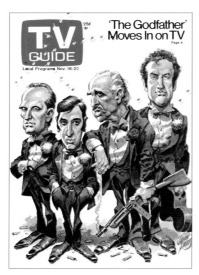

November 16, 1974
By Jack Davis
Cast of *The Godfather*

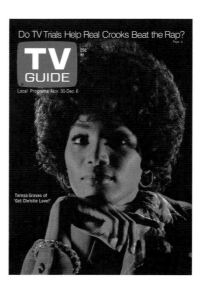

November 30, 1974
By Philippe Halsman
Teresa Graves of *Get Christie Love!*

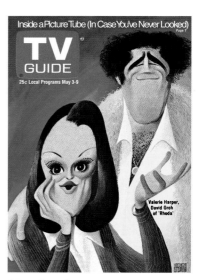

May 3, 1975
By Al Hirschfeld
Valerie Harper and David Groh of *Rhoda*

January 1, 1977
By Gene Trindl
John Travolta of *Welcome Back, Kotter*

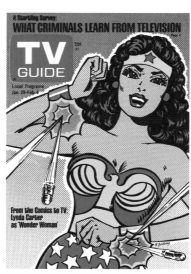

January 29, 1977
By William Goldberg
Lynda Carter of *Wonder Woman*

May 21, 1977
By Douglas Kirkland
Farrah Fawcett-Majors of *Charlie's Angels*

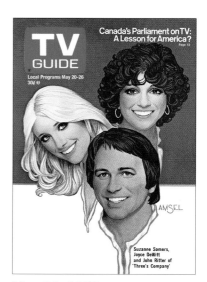

May 20, 1978
By Richard Amsel
Suzanne Somers, Joyce DeWitt and
John Ritter of *Three's Company*

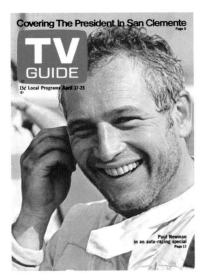

April 17, 1971
By Raphael
Paul Newman

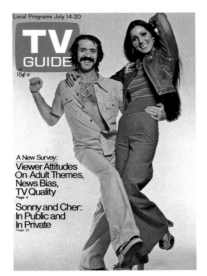

July 14, 1973
By Prigent
Sonny Bono and Cher Bono of
The Sonny and Cher Comedy Hour

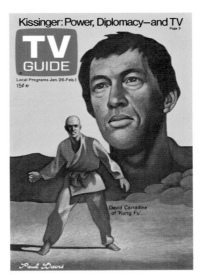

January 26, 1974
By Paul Davis
David Carradine of *Kung Fu*

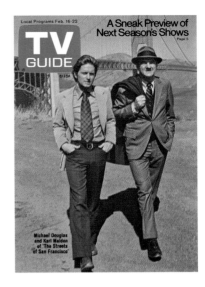

February 16, 1974
By Curt Gunther
Michael Douglas and Karl Malden
of *The Streets of San Francisco*

June 21, 1975
By Mario Casilli
Sherman Hemsley, Isabel Sanford and
Mike Evans of *The Jeffersons*

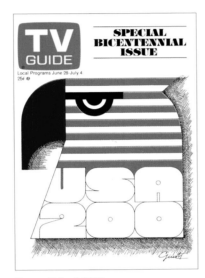

June 28, 1975
By George Giusti
Bicentennial

May 22, 1976
By Dorthy Tanous
Cindy Williams and Penny Marshall
of *Laverne & Shirley*

August 7, 1976
By Peter Kredenser
Marie Osmond and Donny Osmond
of *Donny & Marie*

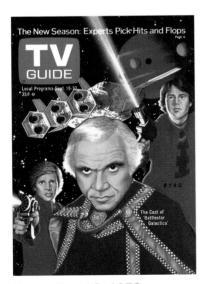

September 16, 1978
By David Byrd
Dirk Benedict, Lorne Greene and
Richard Hatch of *Battlestar Galactica*

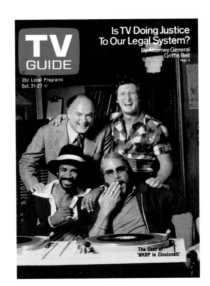

October 21, 1978
By Robert Phillips
Cast of *WKRP in Cincinnati*

October 28, 1978
By Peter Kredenser
Pam Dawber and Robin Williams of
Mork & Mindy

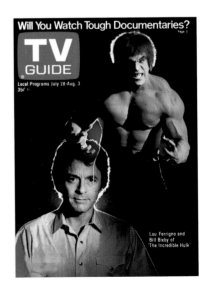

July 28, 1979
By Pete Turner
Bill Bixby and Lou Ferrigno of
The Incredible Hulk

ROLLER DERBY
Gerry Murray (No. 22) of the New York Chiefs in New York City, 1958

For sheer good-versus-evil theatrics with a sweaty subtext—not to mention a rabid TV following—pro wrestlers Stone Cold Steve Austin and the Rock ain't got nothing on the Roller Derby stars of the 1950s and '60s. San Francisco Bay Bombers Charlie O'Connell and Joanie "the Blonde Bomber" Weston were superstars of the men's and women's divisions, and hell-on-wheels Midge "Toughie" Brasuhn an early antihero of the banked-track oval. "Hostile Roller Derby women," TV GUIDE recalled in 1971, "meant as much to the early growth of television as Gorgeous George, Howdy Doody and Uncle Miltie."

MONDAY NIGHT FOOTBALL
Howard Cosell.
ABC, 1970–
COVER: BY JACK DAVIS,
NOVEMBER 29, 1980

The history of sports in America can be divided into two eras: pre- and post-*Monday Night Football*. Before *MNF*'s debut in 1970, football on TV looked like it was being broadcast through a 7-Eleven security camera. The president of ABC Sports, Roone Arledge, perceived that the Sunday-afternoon staple of NFL football could instead be presented as flashy nighttime entertainment. That insight—which has since spread to other sports and remade the industry into the multibillion-dollar marketing and entertainment juggernaut it is today—found its ideal packaging with the *MNF* broadcast team of Howard Cosell, "Dandy" Don Meredith and Frank Gifford. Meredith's folksy-cowboy shtick was the perfect antidote to Cosell's obnoxious "telling it like it is" style, a pleasure for millions to hate, and Giff's smooth neutrality made him the perfect play-by-play guy between them. "Sports is maybe the primary means in the United States for sustaining illusion and delusion," Cosell told TV GUIDE in 1971, explaining his mission to puncture those fantasies. But even as Cosell pursued his prickly crusade, *MNF* was building a myth about itself, and football in general, that would remake the sports business in America.

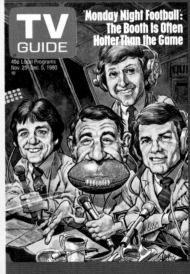

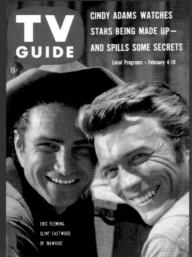

RAWHIDE
Rowdy Yates (Clint Eastwood). CBS, 1959–66
COVER: BY RUSS HALFORD, FEBRUARY 4, 1961

For once, the herd mentality in television was a good thing: *Rawhide* depicted life on the cattle drives of the 1860s, telling the low-key stories of the cowpokes and the folks they encountered along the way. Eric Fleming played the leather-tough trail boss Gil Favor, but the main attraction was the man who portrayed ramrod Rowdy Yates, his second-in-command. "We're doing stories as they pretty much happened," Clint Eastwood told TV Guide in 1961. "Oh, occasionally I guess we hoke one up for dramatic purposes, but generally speaking we're doing the kind of things that guys on the cattle drives really did." Head 'em up, move 'em out!

WRESTLING
The Rock, Stone Cold Steve Austin, 1999
COVER: BY MARK HANAUER, DECEMBER 5, 1998

Beefy guys engaged in titanic battles of good and evil have been a TV staple almost since the first ratings-hungry television producer landed a job. In the 1940s and '50s, viewers watched cartoonish characters such as Gorgeous George, Argentina Rocca and Lou Thesz sweating their way through scrapes "as rigidly stylized as a Greek tragedy," TV GUIDE wrote in 1959. It was a bonanza for promoters—though they caught flak for solemnly insisting that the matches weren't rigged, a fiction that kept the skeptical out of their audiences. In the 1980s, however, Vince McMahon had the brilliant idea to embrace the fakery and reposition pro wrestling as "sports entertainment," plunging wholeheartedly into all-out spectacle. That decision "was the turning point," McMahon told TV GUIDE in 2000, when his World Wrestling Federation (later World Wrestling Entertainment) was virtually minting money from its pay-per-view events. The phenomenon created superstars out of musclebound hams like Stone Cold Steve Austin, the Rock and a menagerie of "babyface" good guys and "heel" bad guys who acted out story lines involving sex, homophobia and racism, and made old-time wrestling look like episodes of *Romper Room.* "Once you say you're an entertainment," McMahon told the magazine, in a rare understatement, "it allows you to entertain in a much broader spectrum."

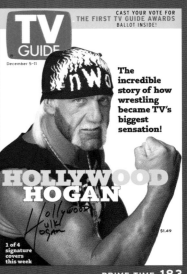

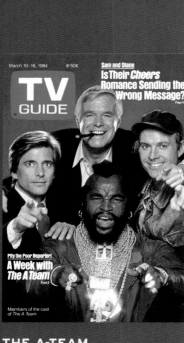

THE A-TEAM
B.A. "Bad Attitude"
Bosco Baracus (Mr. T).
NBC, 1983–87
COVER: BY MARIO CASILLI,
MARCH 10, 1984

Pity the fool who underestimated
the joys of a show about blowing
stuff up. George Peppard as Col.
John "Hannibal" Smith was the
putative centerpiece of this hit,
in which a group of heavily armed
Vietnam vets shuttled around the
world righting wrongs. But the
scowling, gold-chained Mr. T was
its breakout star. TV GUIDE wondered
in 1983 about the effect of *The
A-Team*'s unabashed love of
destruction, but acknowledged
that this "blue-collar *Mission:
Impossible*" could be "an uncom-
plicated diversion." If you didn't
say that with a smile, you better
watch out, sucka!

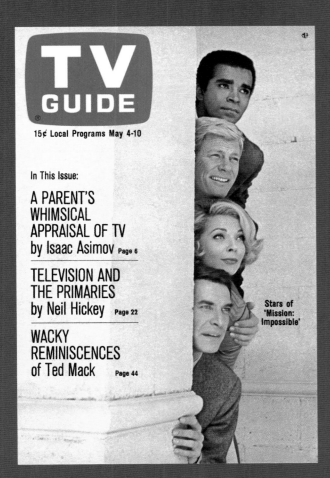

MISSION: IMPOSSIBLE
CBS, 1966–73
COVER: BY PHILLIPE HALSMAN,
MAY 4, 1968

Mission: Impossible had just about everything to satisfy the '60s taste for spy dramas: ingenious gadgetry, noble missions to throw a monkey wrench into the plans of America's enemies, Martin Landau as a master of disguise and an about-to-self-destruct tape giving the Impossible Missions Force its marching orders. What the show didn't have, despite its seven years on the air, was stability. Peter Graves replaced the first-year team leader, Steven Hill; Landau and his wife, Barbara Bain (who played sexy spy Cinnamon Carter), left in 1969 over a contract dispute; and even Landau's replacement, Leonard Nimoy, ditched after two seasons. But two actors—Greg Morris, as electronics pro Barney Collier, and Peter Lupus, as brawny Willie Armitage—decided to accept all seven seasons' worth of missions. Perhaps it was the cool theme song?

"WHEN I WAS A KID, WE DIDN'T HAVE A TV,

so I went to my neighbor's house and hoped he wanted to stay inside and watch television. I really liked *The Untouchables* with Walter Winchell doing the narration. But [mainly] we liked to watch Westerns like *The Wild Wild West*, *Wanted—Dead or Alive* with Steve McQueen, *The Rebel* with Nick Adams and *Gunsmoke*. The best action shows had characters who were likable, so people could feel in that character's shoes. [Shows have] got to be exciting—that's the key.

"Coolness, I think, is better than violence. We would watch them get the bad guys and then we would laugh a little bit, but nobody said, 'I want that type of gun.' At that time, we just saw it as entertainment, and we left it on the TV. We didn't fight with guns. I could watch action at my neighbor's house and then go back home and just forget about it."

—MR. T

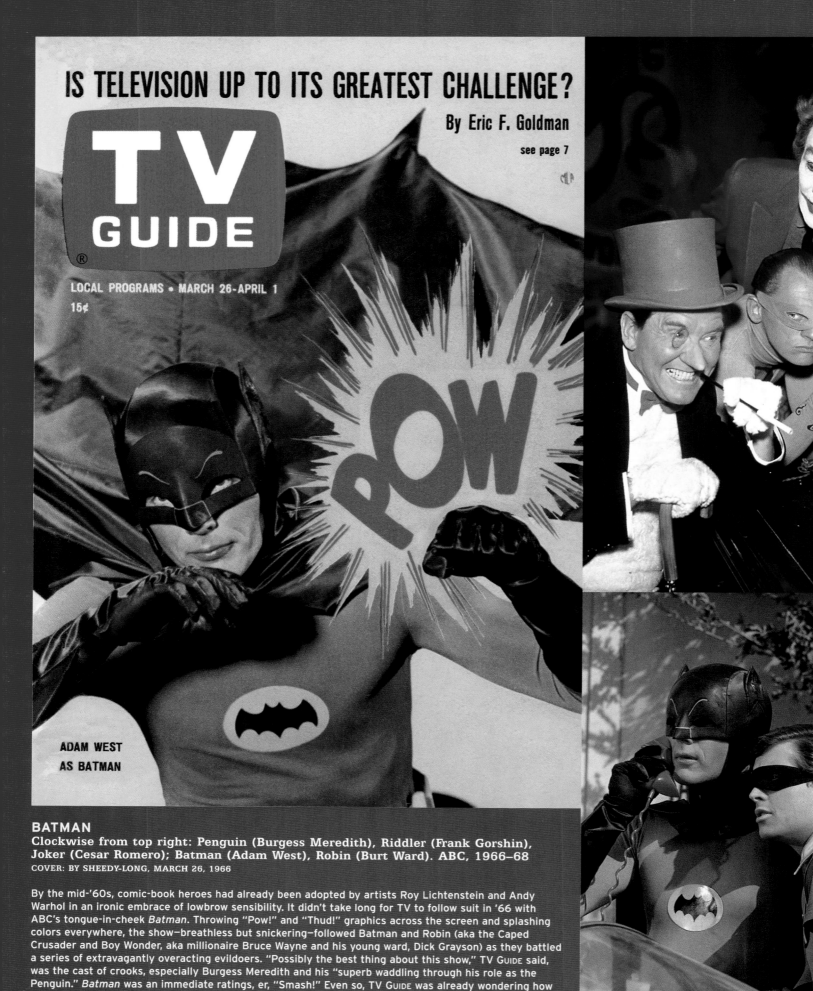

IS TELEVISION UP TO ITS GREATEST CHALLENGE?

By Eric F. Goldman

see page 7

TV GUIDE

LOCAL PROGRAMS • MARCH 26–APRIL 1

15¢

POW

ADAM WEST
AS BATMAN

BATMAN
Clockwise from top right: Penguin (Burgess Meredith), Riddler (Frank Gorshin), Joker (Cesar Romero); Batman (Adam West), Robin (Burt Ward). ABC, 1966–68
COVER: BY SHEEDY-LONG, MARCH 26, 1966

By the mid-'60s, comic-book heroes had already been adopted by artists Roy Lichtenstein and Andy Warhol in an ironic embrace of lowbrow sensibility. It didn't take long for TV to follow suit in '66 with ABC's tongue-in-cheek *Batman*. Throwing "Pow!" and "Thud!" graphics across the screen and splashing colors everywhere, the show—breathless but snickering—followed Batman and Robin (aka the Caped Crusader and Boy Wonder, aka millionaire Bruce Wayne and his young ward, Dick Grayson) as they battled a series of extravagantly overacting evildoers. "Possibly the best thing about this show," TV GUIDE said, was the cast of crooks, especially Burgess Meredith and his "superb waddling through his role as the Penguin." *Batman* was an immediate ratings, er, "Smash!" Even so, TV GUIDE was already wondering how long the hit could last: Children loved it, but "for the adults the joke could very quickly run thin." Holy prescience! By the show's second season, the numbers were dropping, and in '68 the Batmobile was towed off the TV schedule.

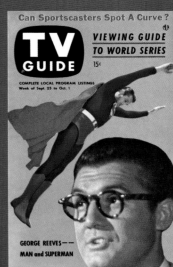

THE ADVENTURES OF SUPERMAN
Lois Lane (Phyllis Coates), Superman (George Reeves). Syndication, 1952–57
COVER: PHOTOGRAPHER UNKNOWN, SEPTEMBER 25, 1953

Superman has demonstrated his superpowers in every media, but for many people it was George Reeves's performance in *The Adventures of Superman* during the '50s that became the definitive portrayal of the defender of truth, justice and the American way. Certainly, only a real Man of Steel could get away with wearing those tights and that cape. And as TV GUIDE said in 1953, Reeves "carries the *Superman* role on his broad shoulders with a delicate sense of balance, kidding himself when among adults but taking it dead seriously when among the younger fry."

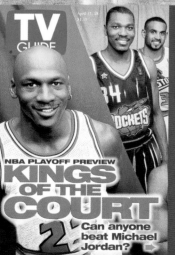

NBA
Michael Jordan (No. 23), June 14, 1998
COVER: BY GREGORY HEISLER, APRIL 12, 1997

In the 1940s and '50s, TV sports was all about baseball. In the 1960s and '70s, the medium discovered football. Then, in the 1980s, basketball finally scored a slam dunk. Suddenly, people who'd never even watched a game before were gripped with an undeniable urge to watch the National Basketball Association. Well, not the NBA so much as two superstars: Los Angeles Laker Earvin "Magic" Johnson and Boston Celtic Larry Bird. The league expertly promoted the rivalry between these two charismatic players, and in the process mightily expanded its fan base in the United States and around the world—preparing the ground, as it turned out, for the dazzling decade of Michael Jordan. In 1994, TV GUIDE observed that "from Madison Avenue to Main Street, basketball has bypassed baseball and set its sights on football in the quest to be America's most popular sport." It certainly seemed that way at the time. The Jordan dynasty had plenty of riches yet to offer, including his storybook final shot in '98 against the Utah Jazz to complete the Chicago Bulls' second championship three-peat. Although the NBA's buzz soon subsided, hardcore fans knew that the game would continue to offer jaw-dropping moments of athletic achievement. And TV would still be there to witness them.

MAJOR LEAGUE BASEBALL
Carlton Fisk, October 21, 1975
COVER: BY ROBERT GUISTI, OCTOBER 6, 1979

The New York Giants' Willie Mays making his fabled over-the-shoulder catch to rob the Cleveland Indians' Vic Wertz of an extra-base hit in Game 1 of the '54 World Series. Carlton Fisk, in the bottom of the 12th, *willing* his long ball to stay fair and win the Boston Red Sox the sixth game against the Cincinnati Reds in the '75 series. Kirk Gibson hobbling to the plate and drilling the game-winning homer for the Los Angeles Dodgers in the first game of the '88 series with the Oakland Athletics. Great, Hall of Fame moments—amazing to have seen in person, to be sure, but known to the world, savored over and over again, thanks only to television. Of course, the national pastime wasn't truly nationwide until every small town in America could see the sport. Writing in TV GUIDE in 1954, pitcher-turned-broadcaster "Dizzy" Dean described a recent trip to his home state, Arkansas: "I'm a son of a buck if they didn't have television. People can see big-league games now that never could before." Not that they had major-league owners to thank for that. For years, the proprietors of the sport were leery of giving the game away for free on television. TV GUIDE even ran editorials during the '50s urging these "obstacles to the 20th century" to understand that "exposing as many people as possible to baseball—through television—will make the future take care of itself." Football, better able to exploit the development of TV technology, learned the lesson quickly and eventually surpassed baseball in popularity. Even so, nowadays baseball's future does indeed take care of itself. Whether you're on the sofa or in the next room, you know the rhythm of a ball game on television just as surely as you know the pulse of American life.

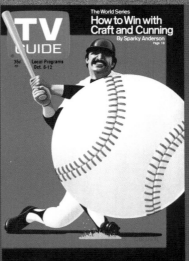

DESK OFFICER

HILL STREET BLUES
Sgt. Henry Goldblume (Joe Spano), Officer Bobby Hill (Michael Warren), Officer Andy Renko (Charles Haid). NBC, 1981–87
COVER: BY GENE TRINDL, JUNE 19, 1982

Hill Street Blues never cracked the Nielsen ratings' Top 20 during its six years, but creator Steven Bochco's innovative approach to the ossified cop-show genre paved the way for such '90s hits as *NYPD Blue* and *Homicide: Life on the Street*. In fact, *Hill Street* did make one Top 20 list: TV GUIDE's best shows of the '80s. What earned the magazine's admiration was its "new style of gritty, grimy urban realism" and "one of television's great ensemble casts. On *Hill Street*, viewers learned to expect the unexpected—hilarity could turn to horror in an instant—but the writing and acting were consistently fine." Capt. Frank Furillo (Daniel J. Travanti) was the calm eye in the hurricane of life at the Hill Street station in a seamy, drug-infested district of an unidentified city. When he wasn't dealing with the squad room full of vividly

drawn cops or the puffed-up bureaucrat Chief Daniels (Jon Cypher), he was coping with the hectoring of his bitter ex-wife, Fay (Barbara Bosson) or escaping into the arms of pretty, no-nonsense public defender Joyce Davenport (Veronica Hamel). (Sharp-eyed fans will also recall that future *NYPD Blue*-man Dennis Franz played not one but two separate rabid cops over the series' lifespan.) As it turned out, the show's backstage dramas were as chaotic and acrimonious as its on-screen ones, and a year before its demise, TV GUIDE was already writing the show's epitaph: "*Hill Street* wasn't about events but about how people responded to them," the magazine said, "so there were never any simple answers, any neat endings." It was an approach that, long after *Hill Street Blues*'s own ending, still endures.

"WHEN HILL STREET BLUES CAME ON,

it set a new standard for television drama. When I go back and look at *Hill Street*—then look at any shows prior to it—there's nothing that matches it in terms of the complexity of the storytelling or the abundance of characters we can invest in. They had flaws that we could identify with. They came to life as human beings, as opposed to TV characters.

"On *NYPD Blue*, we have stayed with that tradition and taken it a step further with our character studies. We've gone deeper into what makes up these people's personal lives, seeing them as troubled at times and perhaps having difficulty doing their jobs and living their lives. I think viewers enjoy investing in characters they can relate to.

"Some shows get criticized for playing up the realities of life, but those are the shows that set new benchmarks, the shows that everybody seems to watch. We say there is too much vulgarity and sexuality and violence on TV, and then we talk about the brilliance of *The Sopranos* and *The Shield*. We are very hypocritical as an audience.

"Television dramas have evolved with our society. If we look back at a show like *Dragnet* now, it's like looking at a black-and-white movie. Earlier dramas are enjoyable to watch as an artifact of their time. Now we try to make them more realistic; the characters aren't black-and-white—there are more shades of gray. I think the more gray matter there is, the more interesting the show is.

"My character [on *NYPD Blue*, Det. Andy Sipowicz] would have died off in the first episode if the show had been in the *Dragnet* days. I don't fit the mold—my character has too many problems and doesn't always show himself in the best light. Yet those types are the ones viewers are often most interested in. We're a wiser audience now. We have evolved as television has evolved."

—DENNIS FRANZ

LAW & ORDER

Assistant D.A. Ben Stone (Michael Moriarty), Det. Mike Logan (Christopher Noth), Det. Phil Cerreta (Paul Sorvino), Assistant D.A. Paul Robinette (Richard Brooks). NBC, 1990–

COVER: BY MICHAEL DAKS, MARCH 28, 1998

In the spring of 2000, NBC signed a deal with *Law & Order*—which at 10 years old was already gray in TV terms—that would keep it on the air through 2005, making it second only to *Gunsmoke* in prime-time-drama longevity. It was a remarkable accomplishment for a series that took five years to crack the weekly Nielsen Top 20, and it further burnished *Law & Order*'s reputation for not only surviving major cast changes, but getting better with the passage of time. (The show even spun off two series, *Law & Order: Special Victims Unit* in 1999 and *Law & Order: Criminal Intent* in 2001.) The bust-'em-and-try-'em approach had been attempted before, in the early '60s with *Arrest and Trial* (starring the unlikely duo of Ben Gazzara and Chuck Conners), but *Law & Order* offered something unusual in police dramas: almost zero interest in the personal lives of its characters. The show preferred instead to concentrate on a realistic depiction—heightened by handheld camera-

work and a bureaucratically drab palette—of the step-by-occasional-misstep legal process. "There's an unspoken desire on a lot of people's parts to go back to a more understandable morality," creator Dick Wolf told TV GUIDE in 1996, explaining *Law & Order*'s building popularity. "And cop shows are morality plays." The series' keystones were Jerry Orbach, as the seen-it-all Det. Lennie Briscoe, and Sam Waterston, as Assistant D.A. Jack McCoy; they joined in '92 and '94 respectively and—unlike several other stars, such as Benjamin Bratt and Carey Lowell—never left. The show stayed fresh by ripping many of its plotlines from the headlines, presenting its own versions of real-life stories like the Mike Tyson rape trial. And there was one other ingredient in the success of *Law & Order*, which was shot on the streets of the Big Apple. As TV GUIDE said in 1990: "There's even something of a New York attitude in the show's style: Hey, ya want crime? Here it is. Now shuddup."

ER

Dr. Elizabeth Corday (Alex Kingston), Dr. Kerry Weaver (Laura Innes), Dr. Peter Benton (Eriq La Salle), Dr. Doug Ross (George Clooney), Dr. Mark Greene (Anthony Edwards), Head Nurse Carol Hathaway (Julianna Margulies), Physician's Assistant Jeanie Boulet (Gloria Reuben), Dr. John Carter (Noah Wyle), Dr. Anna Del Amico (Maria Bello). NBC, 1994–

COVER: BY LANCE STAEDLER, OCTOBER 14, 1995

"The reason our show took off," George Clooney told TV GUIDE in 1995, "was because it was something you hadn't seen before." Sure, portraits of overworked but heroic doctors and nurses were nothing new to television. But no audience this side of a cable documentary had ever seen as much blood, guts and chaos as there was in this emergency room, where gurneys were forever bursting through doors as the camera careened down the halls. Michael Crichton, the *Jurassic Park* author, drew on his real-life experience as a hospital intern to create the Chicago-set series, but was unsure whether the idea would work. So he showed it to a friend: "He said, 'It doesn't follow any of the rules–but you're not going to be able to take your eyes away from it,'" Crichton recalled in TV GUIDE in 1994. That's what backer Steven Spielberg thought, too, as he sat at home screening the unedited *ER* footage, which was even bloodier than what aired: "I don't want my kids to watch it," he told TV GUIDE. As it turned out, it was hard to say which action was more riveting: the operating-room ordeals or the bedroom romance between Clooney's hard-partying, self-redeeming screwup, Dr. Doug Ross, and suicidal head nurse Carol Hathaway (Julianna Margulies). When Clooney left *ER* in 1999, it had been first in the ratings for three out of its five years. By 2002, thanks to its inventive writing and strong, revolving ensemble cast, the show was still in the Top 10–proof that viewers still couldn't take their eyes away from it.

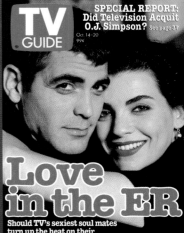

TV GUIDE

SPECIAL REPORT: Did Television Acquit O.J. Simpson? See page 37

Oct 14-20 99¢

Love in the ER

Should TV's sexiest soul mates turn up the heat on their passion? George Clooney and Julianna Margulies say...

ST. ELSEWHERE
Dr. Victor Ehrlich (Ed Begley Jr.), Dr. Mark Craig (William Daniels).
NBC, 1982–88

St. Elsewhere broke with TV's tradition of depicting the medical profession as a well-scrubbed haven for virtuous miracle workers. Instead of paging Drs. Kildare or Welby, the hour-long drama called on a gritty ensemble cast to portray the rough goings-on in a Boston city hospital disparagingly known as St. Elsewhere, a dumping ground for patients shunned by fancier medical centers. The series came from the same MTM Productions shop that produced *Hill Street Blues*, and it was rightly likened to that groundbreaking cop show for its lack of a major star (though cast member Denzel Washington certainly went on to become one), its multiple story lines that carried over from week to week and its roaming camera, which picked up snippets of conversation in a simulation of life in an intense workplace. TV GUIDE singled out William Daniels's performance as the arrogant heart surgeon Dr. Mark Craig for praise a few months after the show's 1982 debut (he "plays this impervious boob to perfection"). While not exactly raving about *St. Elsewhere*, calling it only "interesting," the magazine did "hope it survives." That was certainly in doubt after the first season, when it finished 86th out of 98 prime-time series. But as TV GUIDE reported after the show was miraculously renewed for a second season, *St. Elsewhere* set a precedent that would have far-reaching implications for the industry. NBC had decided not to cancel the series after newfangled audience-composition reports revealed that the show's fans were high-income viewers between the ages of 18 and 49, a fact that could be hyped to advertisers. "Thank God for people who like cleansers," actor Ed Begley Jr., who played the clumsy Dr. Victor Ehrlich, told the magazine. "It is programming by a new kind of numbers," TV GUIDE said. "Maybe that will be *St. Elsewhere*'s legacy."

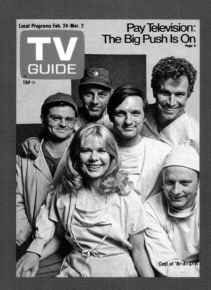

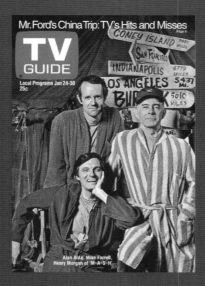

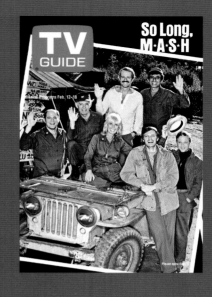

M*A*S*H
Cpl. Maxwell Klinger (Jamie Farr). CBS, 1972–83

COVERS: BY SHERMAN WEISBURD, FEBRUARY 24, 1973. BY SCOTT ENYART, JANUARY 24, 1976. BY AL HIRSCHFELD, APRIL 25, 1981. BY MARIO CASILLI, FEBRUARY 12, 1983

When TV GUIDE asked Alan Alda in 1983 to write about his favorite episode of *M*A*S*H*, he couldn't limit himself to just one—instead he described more than a dozen. Many fans certainly felt the same way regarding this black comedy about the insanity of war—specifically, the Korean War—as seen through the eyes of the troops in the 4077th Mobile Army Surgical Hospital. "Clearly, even in our most antic moments," Alda wrote, "death is usually lurking just behind the door, even if sometimes he's wearing a fright wig and carrying a pig's bladder." The fighting in Korea, of course, was a surrogate for the Vietnam War in a series that began in 1972 (two years after Robert Altman's feature film of the same name), when antiwar sentiment had moved into the mainstream. *M*A*S*H* entertained, even as it appalled, with tales that centered around Alda as the gifted but rebellious surgeon-prankster, Capt. Benjamin Franklin "Hawkeye" Pierce. Over the course of the show's 11 years, he and the rest of the colorful crew became utterly familiar to TV audiences. As Alda—who won Emmys for acting, writing and directing—proudly pointed out in TV GUIDE, *M*A*S*H* experimented in its storytelling. One episode was presented as a black-and-white war documentary, for instance, and another was told in real time, with a clock ticking in the corner of the screen as the doctors performed a vein-graft operation. The final episode, a two-and-half-hour special called "Goodbye, Farewell and Amen," was seen in 77 percent of the households watching television that night. In terms of number of viewers, it's the most-watched program of all time. The show's "multitude of fans," TV GUIDE said, could take some comfort in knowing "that on TV, at any rate, old soldiers never die...they just go on rerunning from here to eternity."

M*A*S*H WAS
ONE OF A KIND

It is one of the unsolved mysteries of American television that *M*A*S*H*, a tragicomedy about an unpopular war almost as dire in its effects as Vietnam, should have retained for more than a decade a popular rating way up there in a catalog of trash of many varieties. Night after night, week after week, year after year, its siren song of "incoming wounded!" beckoned 33 million or so away from teary soaps, drug sagas, frantic sitcoms and marshmallow porn. It is not the intention of this piece to unravel the knotty problem, except to identify some of the elements that made *M*A*S*H*—as the song says—"an isle of joy" in an ocean of junk.

War movies of two sorts—the knockabout farce and the grimly sentimental "pity-of-it-all" epic—have been standard products of the American film industry from *Shoulder Arms* to *Apocalypse Now*. Their usual elements were predictable enough to guarantee for each kind an audience that knew exactly what it was going to get. In most of the epics, against a background of artillery fire and ruined woods (World War I), or mopped-up villages and Pacific jungles (World War II), we had half a dozen or so familiar types: the solemn colonel, the hip-hup sergeant, the rough diamond, the goldbrick, the gentle weakling, the company comic, the plucky kid and his mentor—our hero—the clean-limbed star, played by John Gilbert, Gary Cooper, Kirk Douglas, Burt Lancaster, et al. In the farces, the blood-and-guts action had to be indicated as unpleasantness far in the future, while Wheeler and Woolsey or Bob Hope made adorable asses of themselves in basic training.

Apart from a glut of shameless morale-builders made during WWII—in which the

Nazis were always bullies, the Japanese always shifty and our chaps decent and heroic, if in cantankerous ways—most war movies were made in retrospect, when the real thing was comfortably over. The fact that Chaplin's *Shoulder Arms* came out while WWI was still on can now be seen as one freakish consequence of a frontline censorship so ironclad that the chuckling audiences had only the faintest notion of the scale and hideousness of the enormous slaughter. Offhand, I don't recall any uproarious comedies about Vietnam. So, all right, *M*A*S*H* started, also, when the Korean War was all over. Even so, Ring Lardner Jr.'s original movie script, filmed and shown 17 years after the fighting ended, was enough of a shocker (joking surgeons whose hands, just below the frame, were fiddling with intestines) to cause the British film historian Leslie Halliwell to call it "the great anti-everything film, certainly very funny for those who can take it"; and Judith Crist to write: "The laughter is blood soaked and the comedy cloaks a bitter and terrible truth." Not, you would say, the sort of thing likely to spawn a television series that would last 11 years.

But we have come to take its "blood-soaked" scene for granted and to adopt a whole family of characters who were novel and astonishing in many ways. Let me count the ways.

First, instead of a commanding officer who looks like a gray-flecked "man of distinction" in a whiskey ad, we had, first, Henry Blake, half-dolt, half locker-room buddy; and then Sherman Potter, a sentimental, bandy-legged holdover from WWI. Both of them, however, were soldiers of much horse sense who knew—

as COs came to know in any war later than WWII—that parade and discipline are impossible to maintain in conscripts bogged down in a jungle clearing. The colonels' tolerance of Klinger's idiotic transvestism was a big shock to early viewers. But it provided a constant reminder of how much eccentricity had to be put up with in a small group of often overworked human beings pushed to the limit of sanity by nothing but boredom. One veteran doctor of a Mobile Army Surgical Hospital unit recalled to me that above everything else boredom was the pitiless enemy, so that childish entertainment, dressing up, lotteries, cartoon movies, casual sex, petty racketeering and practical jokes became essential therapy.

(The actual boredom came to include hideous routines—having to do with the disposal of human wastes and the daily examination of the Korean "service" girls on the line—that even M*A*S*H chose to sidestep.)

This basic condition of life in the 4077 must have been grasped by the writers early in the series, and it made us accept a wildly varied cast of characters and wildly unmilitary behavior that the training manuals and all previous army scripts had never imagined. Thus, the CO's ranking subordinates offered the startling novelties of a woman major and her light of love, the asinine chauvinist and reluctant husband, Maj. Frank Burns—both, I should guess, impossible bits of casting in any previous war movie. And, just to ram home the lesson that excessive devotion to "loyalty" and "security" was an almost obscene nuisance, we had the paranoid CIA snooper.

Offsetting these weirdos was a group of comparative innocents such as every soldier has encountered, though perhaps not in the movies: Father Mulcahy, no heroic priest he, in the mold of Bing Crosby or Pat O'Brien, but a limited, slow-witted nice man; Radar, befogged, unsure even of his virginity; Dr. Freedman, the sensible, believable psychia-

trist, a million miles away from the Hollywood fusspot with the Viennese accent; the absurd Winchester, to remind us of another world—ours—and other values, preposterous maybe, but the values we all pretend to aspire to. Finally, Trapper and B.J.—two amiable variations on the smart-ass's sidekick, the smart-ass being no one but Hawkeye.

Hawkeye was the hinge. Played less well, by an actor less high-strung, less deeply forlorn, the whole series could have expired in its infancy. Somebody had the wit to spot him at the beginning as Hamlet and Horatio rolled into one: the brilliant neurotic and the normal antihero. He was the one who kept the place in a happy ferment: the enviable expert surgeon and also the mischief maker all pent-up soldiers yearn to be.

And yet. Hawkeye represented, more than most, the one quality that held the whole family together, the quality of fundamental decency. This was the sheet anchor of a crew awash in exhaustion, emergencies, bad temper, physical peril. The patient came first, the patient of either side and any color. And the only golden rule that everybody recognized was that no big brass, no visiting congressman, no CIA inquisitor or other busybody must be allowed to forget it. It was here that every viewer, according to personal taste and judgment, had to decide how often the series ignored the messiness of life and spilled over into the neatness of sentimentality.

All in all, the series was remarkable, something of a marvel, in staying so close to ordinary life and peopling a formula with what in television is something of a curiosity: a company of recognizable human beings. Let us stifle a starting tear and bid farewell to M.A.S.H. 4077, and pray that no Hollywood smarties are licking their chops and drafting some carbon-copy series. M*A*S*H, like The Honeymooners and Upstairs, Downstairs, was one of a kind. Let it stay that way.

—ALISTAIR COOKE, EXCERPT FROM TV GUIDE, FEBRUARY 12, 1983

THE '80s

February 9, 1980
By Wilson McLean
The Olympics

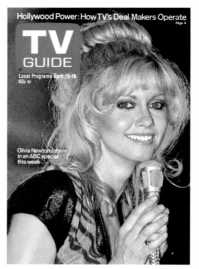

April 12, 1980
By Herb Ritts
Olivia Newton-John

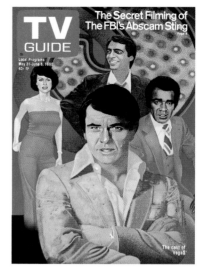

May 31, 1980
Illustrator unknown
Cast of *Vegas*

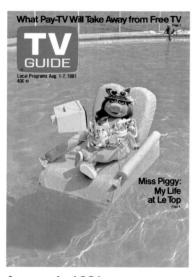

August 1, 1981
By John E. Barrett
Miss Piggy of *The Muppet Show*

October 24, 1981
By Robert Giusti
"Blind Spot in the Middle East"

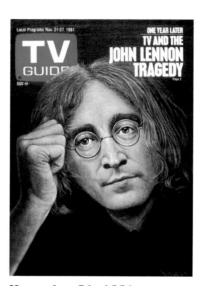

November 21, 1981
By Richard Hess
John Lennon

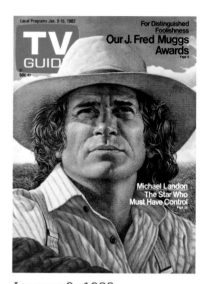

January 9, 1982
By Richard Hess
Michael Landon of *Little House on the Prairie*

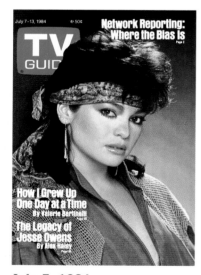

July 7, 1984
By Mario Casilli
Valerie Bertinelli of *One Day at a Time*

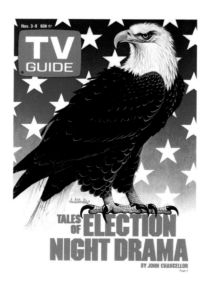

November 3, 1984
By Braldt Bralds
"Tales of Election Night Drama"

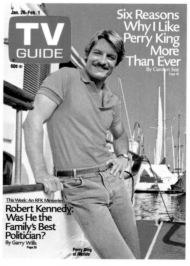

January 26, 1985
By Jim Shea
Perry King of *Riptide*

March 9, 1985
By Richard Amsel
Angela Lansbury of *Murder, She Wrote*

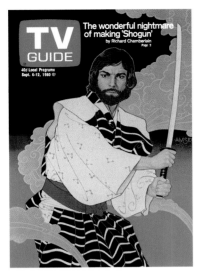

September 6, 1980
By Richard Amsel
Richard Chamberlain in *Shogun*

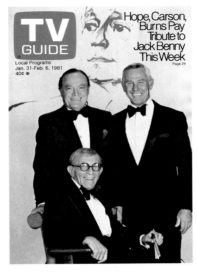

January 31, 1981
By Gene Trindl
Bob Hope, George Burns and
Johnny Carson

February 7, 1981
By Peter Kredenser
Jane Seymour in *East of Eden*

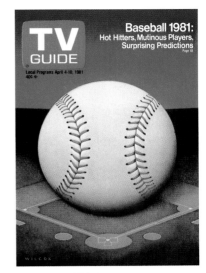

April 4, 1981
By David Wilcox
"Baseball 1981"

January 14, 1984
By Ken Whitmore
Emmanuel Lewis of *Webster*

January 28, 1984
By Peter Kredenser
Cybill Shepherd of *The Yellow Rose*

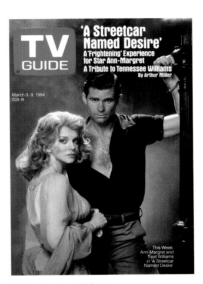

March 3, 1984
By Mario Casilli
Ann-Margret and Treat Williams in
A Streetcar Named Desire

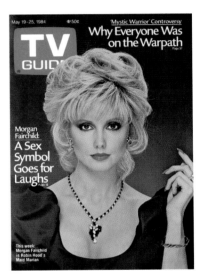

May 19, 1984
By Robert Phillips
Morgan Fairchild in *The Zany
Adventures of Robin Hood*

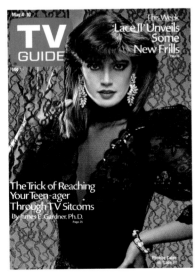

May 4, 1985
By Roger Prigent
Phoebe Cates in *Lace II*

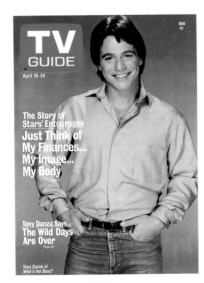

April 18, 1987
By Tony Costa
Tony Danza of *Who's the Boss*

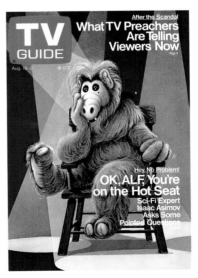

August 15, 1987
By John Eggert
ALF of *ALF*

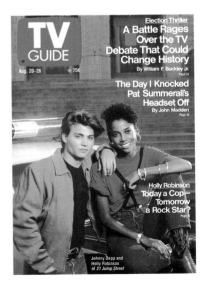

August 20, 1988
By Tony Costa
Johnny Depp and Holly Robinson
of *21 Jump Street*

THAT GIRL
ABC, 1966–71
COVER: BY KEN WHITMORE,
NOVEMBER 12, 1966

That Girl "is not exactly going to keep you on the edge of your chair," TV GUIDE said in 1966 about the comedy starring the "very pretty and very funny" Marlo Thomas. She played the upbeat but struggling actress Ann Marie, who dated nerdy magazine exec Donald Hollinger (Ted Bessell) while trying to make it in New York City. The show aired for five years, but it had a more dramatic and lasting effect in Hollywood: Its success paved the way for such independent-woman comedies as *The Mary Tyler Moore Show* and *Rhoda*.

How Television's Rich Actors Stay That Way
see page 14

LOCAL PROGRAMS · NOVEMBER 12-18

TV GUIDE
®

15¢

MARLO THOMAS OF 'THAT GIRL'

"THE MOST REVOLUTIONARY THING ABOUT THAT GIRL

was that my father on the show would continually say to me, 'When are you going to get married?' and I would say, 'Daddy, I don't want to get married yet. I want to have my career.' That was the single most radical element of the show, even more than having her living on her own. In essence, we were saying out loud that a woman didn't have to get married in order to be fulfilled. Not that you shouldn't get married, but you didn't *have* to—there were others things you could do. This was groundbreaking at the time.

"You can really see the progression of women in comedies after *That Girl*. There were single mothers in *Kate & Allie*. Murphy Brown was a not-so-perfect woman who was a drinker, screamed at people and had a baby without being married. Even Rachel on *Friends*—who also is not married—talks about sex and had a baby.

"Ironically, in real life, young people in the '60s were behaving exactly how the characters on *Friends* are behaving now. It's not like we were any more pure than girls are today. But we weren't reflecting that behavior—or even talking about it—on TV comedies. I remember we did a whole episode on *That Girl* about the fact that Donald's dry cleaning was quite innocently hanging in my closet, and my father came over and saw it and it became this big deal. These were people in their twenties—come on!

"There was a certain dishonesty about all this. Remember Lucy and Ricky didn't sleep in the same bed? And when she got pregnant, they used all sorts of phrases to describe her condition because you couldn't say 'pregnant' on TV? They even called the episode in which she finds out she's expecting 'Lucy Is *Enceinte*'—which is French for pregnant—just to get around using the word. Since when did pregnancy become a bad word? It was all really backward, and it infantilized the audience.

"Now, of course, reality has caught up with television and television has caught up with reality. Now *The Vagina Monologues* is on TV. At last!"

—MARLO THOMAS

TV GUIDE

®

15¢

PATTY DUKE

THE PATTY DUKE SHOW
Frank Sinatra Jr., Patty Duke. ABC, 1963–66
COVER: BY PHILLIPE HALSMAN, DECEMBER 28, 1963

Patty Duke turned from her movie triumph in 1962's *The Miracle Worker* to perform a mini-miracle of comedy on TV. She was the youngest performer, at 17, ever to get her name in the title of a prime-time show. For three years, she portrayed identical cousins: Cathy, a serious Scot who had lived "ev'rywhere from Zanzibar to Berk'ley Square"—as the show's theme song explained—and Patty, the quintessential pre-hippie '60s teen, who had "only seen the sights a girl can see from Brooklyn Heights." Cathy lived with Patty's family, and the girls' frequent identity swapping seemed to flummox everyone within a 10-block radius. Duke did such a delightful job that TV GUIDE said in '64: "As far as we are concerned, she could play *all* the parts."

MY SO-CALLED LIFE
Angela Chase (Claire Danes), Jordan Catalano (Jared Leto). ABC, 1994–95

For all the grown-ups who ever lectured a miserable teenager about these being *the best years of your life*, here was the ultimate retort. *My So-Called Life* "is adolescence as adolescents see it: gritty, mean, real and only occasionally fun," TV GUIDE said in 1994. "It's the scholastic *NYPD Blue*." Actress Claire Danes, as 15-year-old Angela Chase, seemed like teen agony incarnate, electrified by life's possibilities but apprehensive as she balanced awkwardly on the cusp between childhood and young adulthood. "School is a battlefield for your heart. You are lucky to get out alive," she said. Angela started hanging out with a dicey crowd and found herself drawn—in the classic good-girl/bad-boy tango—to Jordan Catalano (Jared Leto), who sang in a rock band but was otherwise inscrutable. At home, Angela had to deal with a sniping mother and a father who was beginning to withdraw from her as she began to mature sexually. *My So-Called Life*, from Ed Zwick and Marshall Herskovitz, the creators of *thirtysomething*, scored well with critics and teens but wasn't lucky enough to graduate to a second season. MTV astutely picked up the episodes and replayed them for three years to an audience for whom Danes's poignant portrayal must have resonated like no other young actress's on television.

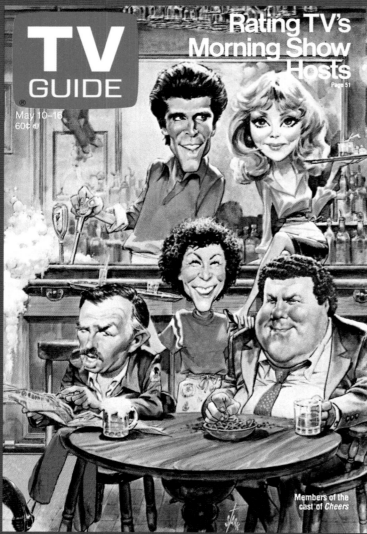

CHEERS
Sam Malone (Ted Danson), Diane Chambers (Shelley Long). NBC, 1982–93
COVER: BY BRUCE STARK, MAY 10, 1986

A few months after the show's debut, TV Guide tried to convey how terrific the dialogue among the *Cheers* patrons was by citing their colloquium on the sweatiest movies of all time—"*Body Heat*"? "*Cool Hand Luke*"?—but then concluded: "The jokes don't reproduce on paper, mostly because they arise out of character instead of out of a gag file. It's a healthy sign. This one should be around awhile." Although it took more than three years for *Cheers* to catch on with audiences, the characters did indeed become some of the most familiar in TV history. They included Sam (Ted Danson), the cocky ex-Red Sox pitcher who owned the Boston bar; Diane (Shelley Long), the pretty and pretentious grad student/waitress; Carla (Rhea Perlman), the tough-talking broad who delivered as many insults as drinks; lovable but dim bartender Coach (Nicholas Colasanto), who was followed by the younger but just as clueless Woody (Woody Harrelson); and Norm and Cliff (George Wendt and John Ratzenberger), the Tweedledee and Tweedledumber accountant and postal worker who were bar-stool fixtures. At what appeared to be the height of the show's popularity, in 1987, Long left to pursue a movie career. It seemed like a disaster for *Cheers*—the mercurial relationship between Sam and Diane had been one of the great antagonistic TV romances, a fact made abundantly clear when their long-anticipated first kiss seemed to electrify the entire nation as well as the couple. But Long's departure turned out to be disastrous only for the actress's own fortunes. *Cheers* thrived with the arrival of Kirstie Alley as Rebecca Howe, the corporate climber who became Sam's boss after he sold the bar. The only indispensable player was Danson: *Cheers* finally ended with his departure in 1993, when it was still one of the top-rated shows in television—a testament to the powerful pull of a place where you were so well-acquainted with the characters, you'd swear everybody knew *your* name.

FRIENDS
Rachel Green (Jennifer Aniston), Ross Gellar (David Schwimmer). NBC, 1994–
COVER: BY DAVIS FACTOR, SEPTEMBER 23, 1995

Critics groaned at the debut of *Friends* in 1994–TV GUIDE called the comedy about a bunch of pals sitting around cracking jokes just another *Seinfeld/Cheers* hybrid that was "born more of marketing than of imagination." The only part of *Friends* that seemed original was the focus on twentysomethings who were ambivalent about plunging fully into the grown-up world of careers and commitment. But the show also had two secret weapons: truly first-rate writing, led by series creators David Crane and Marta Kauffman, and a talented cast of six actors, who also just happened to be insufferably attractive. The combo captivated viewers, and critics soon came along, too. A year into the show, TV GUIDE admitted that you "just couldn't resist liking these guys." Led by ravishing amateur den mother Monica (Courteney Cox Arquette), the gang—Monica's brainiac brother Ross (David Schwimmer), aromatherapized ditz Phoebe (Lisa Kudrow), spoiled rich kid Rachel (Jennifer Aniston), good-hearted meathead Joey (Matt LeBlanc) and jokester Chandler (Matthew Perry)—all got together to kvetch entertainingly about dating, sex, work, parents and one another. "When the six of us filmed the pilot, there was something inexplicable about the chemistry among us, like we were six pieces of a puzzle that naturally came together," Schwimmer told TV GUIDE in 2001. Indeed, the palpable affinity between cast members helped make *Friends* a ratings hit in its first season. It remained at or near the top of the Nielsens for eight years, and in 2002 its popularity showed no signs of flagging. New plotlines kept viewers hooked (Monica and Chandler were married, Ross and Rachel were on-again, off-again; she had his baby). But as Perry told TV GUIDE in '95: "The show is really at its best when it's just the six of us in a room talking, making each other laugh."

WHY I CONSIDER CAGNEY & LACEY
THE BEST
SHOW ON TELEVISION

I consider *Cagney & Lacey* the best show on television. Launched as a CBS TV-movie in 1981 and as a series in 1982, it honors women's friendships and represents a radical departure from the myth that women can't get along.

Before that, women on TV tended to be tokens in a man's world or else rivals for a man's affections. In the few instances when women were permitted to be friends (e.g., Lucy Ricardo and Ethel Mertz), the relationship was comedic and often catty. And the women weren't working together. Christine Cagney and Mary Beth Lacey, two New York City police officers, are work buddies in a way that only male characters have been in the past.

The quality of their friendship has humanized cop shows. In fact, along with NBC's *Hill Street Blues*, *Cagney & Lacey* has brought a human resonance to TV police work that renders the simple good-guy/bad-guy cop shows of the past hopelessly obsolete.

I particularly like the fact that the scripts usually don't take the easy way out. Some scripts are so strong that they might actually change people's attitudes.

The most authentic touches are found in the wonderfully strong acting of Sharon Gless, as Cagney, and Tyne Daly, as Lacey. The characters are so convincing that one can imagine them growing and changing, like real people. It's this human accuracy that makes the show attractive to women, who tend not to care for the usual cop shows.

In fact, one hears that women identify strongly with both the very married Lacey and the very single Cagney. After all, even though few women are police detectives, most women have demanding jobs, whether inside or outside the home, and they rely for support on close women friends. *Cagney & Lacey* is one of those rare shows that reflect the reality of women's lives.

—GLORIA STEINEM, EXCERPT FROM TV GUIDE, JANUARY 16, 1988

CAGNEY & LACEY
CBS, 1982–88
COVER: BY DAVID BYRD, JANUARY 16, 1988

If it had simply come and gone like other series, *Cagney & Lacey* would have earned a place in TV history as the first buddy cop show that starred two women. But *Cagney & Lacey* was also notable for the very fact that after it came and went, it came back again—stronger than ever, thanks to a letter-writing campaign that persuaded CBS to reverse its decision to cancel the show in 1983 after one season. Sharon Gless was the fun-loving but ambitious Christine Cagney, and Tyne Daly the more settled wife and mom, Mary Beth Lacey. The show eagerly tried to approximate real life, embracing the personal struggles—not just the jobs—of its two New York City police detectives. That approach won it no shortage of well-known champions: *Ms.* magazine founder Gloria Steinem and *Love Story* author Erich Segal both wrote valentines to *Cagney & Lacey* in TV GUIDE. Segal praised the show upon its return to the air for offering "real characters with real emotions," calling it "one of the best series ever to hit the tube." As Segal might have put it, loving *Cagney & Lacey* meant never having to change the channel.

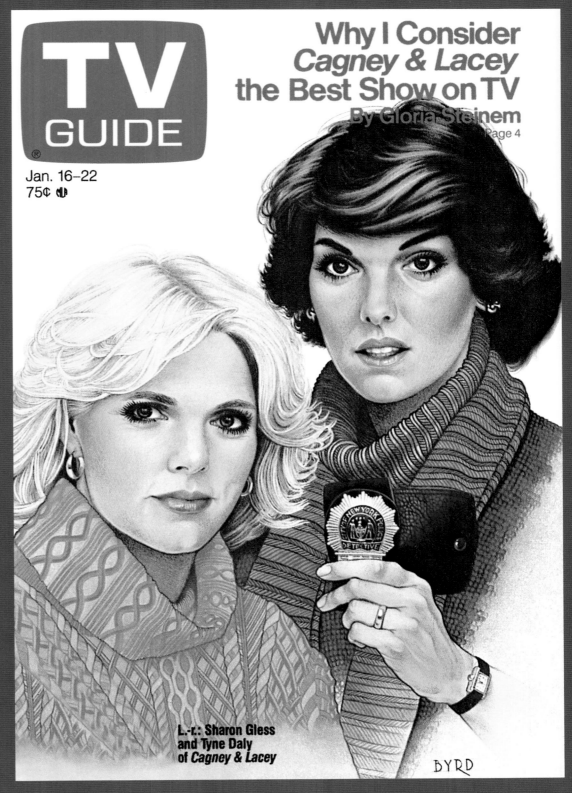

TV GUIDE

Jan. 16–22
75¢

Why I Consider
Cagney & Lacey
the Best Show on TV
By Gloria Steinem
Page 4

L.-r.: Sharon Gless
and Tyne Daly
of *Cagney & Lacey*

BYRD

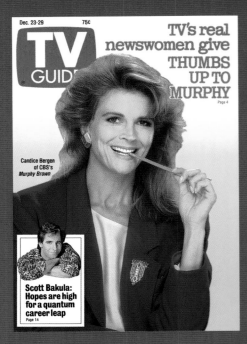

Dec. 23-29   75c

TV GUIDE

TV's real
newswomen give
THUMBS
UP TO
MURPHY
Page 4

Candice Bergen
of CBS's
Murphy Brown

Scott Bakula:
Hopes are high
for a quantum
career leap
Page 14

MURPHY BROWN
CBS, 1988–98
COVER: BY BERNARD BOUDREAU, DECEMBER 23, 1989

This comedy ("put together like a fine watch," TV GUIDE said in 1989) about a TV newsmagazine called *FYI* had many memorable elements: Candice Bergen as a glam-but-tough journalist, her glacially slow housepainter-in-residence, the stream of Murphy's hapless secretaries. But despite a 10-year run, the show is most likely to be remembered for a single plot development—Murphy's single parenthood—and its denunciation in 1992 by Vice President Dan Quayle as an example of Hollywood's hostility toward family values. "I'm the last person to think fathers are obsolete," Bergen told TV GUIDE at the time, but having the baby was "absolutely the right decision," she said. "For Murphy and the show."

DEPT. OF TRANSPORTATION

1) **77 SUNSET STRIP** Merry Anders (Herself), Stuart Bailey (Efrem Zimbalist Jr.) with 1961 Thunderbird. ABC, 1958-64

2) **CAR 54, WHERE ARE YOU?** Officer Francis Muldoon (Fred Gwynne), Officer Gunther Toody (Joe E. Ross) with Car 54. NBC, 1961-63

3) **MY MOTHER THE CAR** Dave Crabtree (Jerry Van Dyke) with 1928 Porter. NBC, 1965-66

4) **GIDGET** Francine "Gidget" Lawrence (Sally Field) with 'board. ABC, 1965-66

5) **LOST IN SPACE** *Jupiter II.* CBS, 1965-68

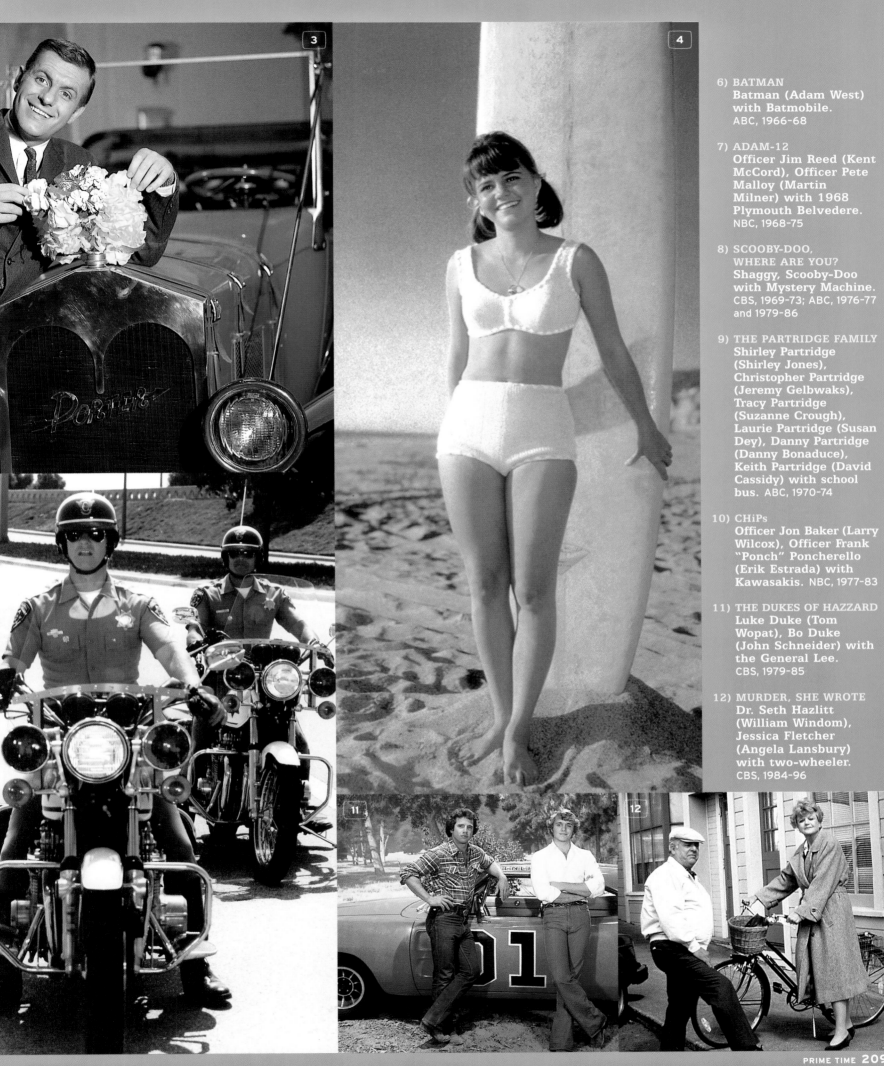

6) BATMAN
Batman (Adam West) with Batmobile.
ABC, 1966-68

7) ADAM-12
Officer Jim Reed (Kent McCord), Officer Pete Malloy (Martin Milner) with 1968 Plymouth Belvedere.
NBC, 1968-75

8) SCOOBY-DOO, WHERE ARE YOU?
Shaggy, Scooby-Doo with Mystery Machine.
CBS, 1969-73; ABC, 1976-77 and 1979-86

9) THE PARTRIDGE FAMILY
Shirley Partridge (Shirley Jones), Christopher Partridge (Jeremy Gelbwaks), Tracy Partridge (Suzanne Crough), Laurie Partridge (Susan Dey), Danny Partridge (Danny Bonaduce), Keith Partridge (David Cassidy) with school bus. ABC, 1970-74

10) CHiPs
Officer Jon Baker (Larry Wilcox), Officer Frank "Ponch" Poncherello (Erik Estrada) with Kawasakis. NBC, 1977-83

11) THE DUKES OF HAZZARD
Luke Duke (Tom Wopat), Bo Duke (John Schneider) with the General Lee.
CBS, 1979-85

12) MURDER, SHE WROTE
Dr. Seth Hazlitt (William Windom), Jessica Fletcher (Angela Lansbury) with two-wheeler.
CBS, 1984-96

TAXI
Latka Gravas (Andy Kaufman), Louie De Palma (Danny DeVito). ABC, 1978–82; NBC, 1982–83
COVER: BY BOB PEAK, JULY 26, 1980

It might have been known as the Sunshine Cab Company, but when Elaine Nardo (Marilu Henner) showed up for her first day of work there, she nailed the mood of the place when she asked: "Why is everyone here just a little bit angry?" Perhaps it was because like her—an aspiring art-gallery owner—several of her fellow drivers regarded their jobs as nothing more than annoying pit stops on the way to great success. Tough guy Tony Banta (Tony Danza) pursued a boxing career even though he'd been knocked down so many times he had "a cauliflower back," and bushy blond Bobby Wheeler (Jeff Conaway) dreamed of unlikely fame and fortune as an actor. As it turned out, the show proved to be an excellent showcase for several performers who did indeed go on to bigger and better things. Danny DeVito shined as a short, stout tyrant whose sadistic barbs were issued from inside the dispatcher's cage—he was Lou Grant with a whiff of Hannibal Lecter. Christopher Lloyd played "Reverend Jim" Ignatowski—a wobbly, recovering '60s burnout—to perfection. And

the extraordinary Andy Kaufman created the gentle immigrant mechanic Latka. But the show truly revolved around the one driver, Alex Reiger, who actually worked full-time there and thought of himself as nothing more than a cabby. Judd Hirsch played the role with good-hearted grimness: "His delivery is flat as a slab but somehow wonderful," TV GUIDE said after *Taxi*'s 1978 debut. For all of its supposed animus, the show had a heart of gold, reflected in its prickly yet always sweet-natured scripts, as when Alex, mercilessly ribbed by his coworkers, follows through on his blind date with an obese woman whom he ends up hugging. "Come to think of it, *Taxi* often ends with someone hugging someone else," the magazine noted. Viewers, however, didn't exactly embrace the show. ABC canceled it after four years; NBC gave it a try for one more and fared no better. But the proof was in the prizes: *Taxi*'s sparkling ensemble acting and sharp writing won it three Emmy awards for Outstanding Comedy Series.

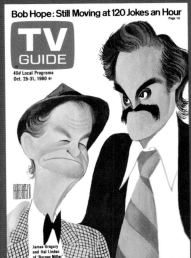

BARNEY MILLER
Capt. Barney Miller (Hal Linden), Det. Stanley Wojehowicz (Maxwell Gail), Det. Phil Fish (Abe Vigoda), bomber (actor unknown). ABC, 1975–82
COVER: BY AL HIRSCHFELD, OCTOBER 25, 1980

The early returns weren't good, and you didn't have to be a detective to pick up the clues: First, TV GUIDE (among others) panned this 1975 mid-season replacement about a New York City precinct house ("an awful lot going on, and most of the lot is awful"). Then, in a profile, it dubbed the show's sweet-tempered star, Hal Linden, "an optimist in the midst of disaster" because "practically nobody" was watching. But Linden's faith paid off: *Barney Miller* soon climbed into the Nielsen ratings' Top 20 and stayed there for four years as audiences—and critics—managed to get past the show's contrivances (a rigorously multiethnic mix of characters and a formula that required three plotlines in each half hour). The atmosphere was more social club than police headquarters, a hangout for a few guys with a crime-fighting hobby: Abe Vigoda's Detective Fish was the epic complainer, Maxwell Gail's "Wojo" an earnest striver, Jack Soo's Detective Yemana a hilarious deadpan philosopher. When viewers finally wandered away, the series ended with a plot about the city declaring the precinct house a landmark and dispersing the cops to new assignments. Nevertheless, *Barney Miller* itself remained a landmark for reminding us that comedy doesn't have to be mean-spirited.

THE LARRY SANDERS SHOW
Sanders (Garry Shandling). HBO, 1992–98

For six years in the 1990s, comedian Garry Shandling administered the definitive antidote to the age of celebrity with this lacerating satire of Hollywood self-loathing. Shandling played Larry Sanders, the host of a late-night show who managed to simulate Johnny Carson-like amiability on camera, but who backstage—and even on stage, during commercial breaks—was a wreck of insecurity and anxiety. Clustered around him was a pitch-perfect choir of Tinseltown types, particularly the brilliant Rip Torn as Artie, a glad-handing, string-pulling producer, and Jeffrey Tambor as Larry's repellent sidekick, Hank (catchphrase: "Hey, now!"), who was equal parts preening arrogance and pathetic desperation. *The Larry Sanders Show* so hilariously skewered the bitter, backstabbing insincerities of show business that real-life celebrities clamored to appear on the show, playing themselves in some sort of cathartic truth telling about the industry. Two of the most memorable guest appearances came in the dazzling final episode in 1998, when Shandling decided to quit while he was ahead. David Duchovny reprised a previous appearance when his tenderly solicitous treatment of Larry drove the host batty trying to figure out if Duchovny was coming on to him. And Jim Carrey belted out an over-the-top "Dreamgirls" anthem in a farewell tribute—and then, the moment after the cameras switched off, icily said to the host, "What are you going to do now? Movies? I'll *crush* you." For all the belly laughs *Larry Sanders* inspired, its star found a moral in all the amoral grasping. "I think it's a metaphor for a wrong way to live," Shandling told TV GUIDE near the end of the series. "Worrying too much about what people think and wanting to appeal to the most number of people" was a bad idea whether you are "in show business or in high school." There is no doubt, however, that it made for fabulous television.

FRASIER
Dr. Frasier Crane (Kelsey Grammer). NBC, 1993–
COVER: BY KATE GARNER, OCTOBER 3, 1998

Quick, name the only five-time winner of the Emmy award for best comedy. *The Dick Van Dyke Show? Cheers? All in the Family?* Nope. They all pulled down four. *Frasier* won five Emmys in a row in the mid-'90s, cementing its reputation as the most successful comedy spin-off ever. Frasier Crane (Kelsey Grammer) afforded us plenty of laughs on *Cheers* as a pompous psychiatrist bumping up against regular-guy sensibilities. The genius of *Frasier* was to relocate him to Seattle as a radio call-in therapist and pair him with his brother, Niles (David Hyde Pierce), also a psychiatrist and, if anything, even pickier and more pretentious. "Such unlikely characters," Grammer told TV GUIDE in 1998, "so forbidding and elite, and yet we are so adrift in the same sea of pettiness that all brothers go through." Frasier's cranky ex-cop father, Martin (John Mahoney),

who lived with Frasier in his gorgeous high-rise apartment, had a retirement hobby of puncturing the Crane brothers' effete balloons, while Daphne (Jane Leeves), the English home-care worker who tended to Martin, unwittingly pierced the shy Niles's heart. That infatuation simmered for years, peaking in a grand, *Graduate*-like gesture in which Niles stole away with bride-to-be Daphne in a Winnebago. In 1998, executive producer Christopher Lloyd described the essence of *Frasier* to TV GUIDE: "It's really about these guys who have an idea of this utopian world where people are polished and smart and treat each other well, and every week they get strong evidence to the contrary. It's very winning to root for them." When it comes to Emmys and audiences, winning is clearly the right word.

"PEANUTS" HOLIDAY SPECIALS
A Charlie Brown Christmas (1965). CBS, 1965–
COVER: BY CHARLES SCHULZ, OCTOBER 28, 1972

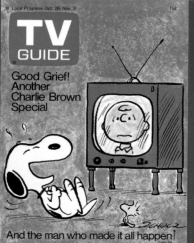

Charles Schulz was never really comfortable translating his "Peanuts" comic strip to television. "In TV there is no time for talk," he griped to TV GUIDE in 1972. "Everything has to lead to action." And eight years later, he wrote an article in the magazine complaining that too little "low-key poetry finds its way into the script." None of that mattered to audiences, who embraced his first foray into the medium, *A Charlie Brown Christmas* (which seemed to be graced with plenty of low-key poetry in its tale of Charlie Brown's homely tree and the true spirit of Christmas). Charlie Brown, Snoopy and friends quickly became something of a TV staple. As the magazine reported in '72, the first seven "Peanuts" specials each averaged a 40 to 44 percent share of the television audience, with about 35 million households tuned in—and, amazingly, drew similar numbers on their first few reruns. "I'll say this: The specials have brought children in more," Schulz grudgingly told TV GUIDE. Thirty years later, many of those children have their own families and still make viewing a vintage "Peanuts" special—say, the Halloween classic *It's the Great Pumpkin, Charlie Brown*—a holiday tradition.

TV GUIDE

LOCAL PROGRAMS
JAN. 26—FEB. 1

15¢

Bob Hope

BOB HOPE
Date unknown
COVER: BY AL HIRSCHFELD,
JANUARY 26, 1957

"What's an American institution?"
TV GUIDE asked in 1965. "Well,
there's Mount Rushmore...baseball...
Mom's apple pie...and Bob Hope."
Hope thrived in vaudeville, on stage,
in radio and in feature films—
particularly in the marvelous *Road*
movies with Bing Crosby—but found
his greatest success on television.
The star-laden Christmas shows he
put on to entertain troops deployed
around the world kept soldiers and
TV audiences laughing from World
War II all the way through the Gulf
War. As the perfect, classy-yet-
teasing host, Hope was practically a
permanent fixture at the Academy
Awards throughout the '50s and
'60s. His countless other specials,
guest appearances and TV series
were for decades simply an
essential element of television
entertainment, as were his needling
topical humor and jibes at
politicians. But of all the great
moments show business afforded
him, Hope told TV GUIDE that the
greatest ones were with the GIs. "If
only they knew," he said, "what *they
do for me*." One of the comedian's
most enduring contributions, the
magazine said in 1996, was that
"Hope made it possible to be
irreverent *and* patriotic."

FAMILY TIES

Alex P. Keaton (Michael J. Fox), Elyse Keaton (Meredith Baxter-Birney), Jennifer Keaton (Tina Yothers), Steven Keaton (Michael Gross), Mallory Keaton (Justine Bateman). NBC, 1982–89

COVER: BY PETER KREDENSER, SEPTEMBER 21, 1985

The quintessential television comedy of the Reagan era showed us just how far the culture had traveled since the days of *All in the Family* in the early '70s: Now, instead of an old grouchy reactionary versus a young liberal, we had *Family Ties*, where the parents were leftover lefties continuously needled by their *Wall Street Journal*-reading Republican teenage son, Alex P. Keaton. *Family Ties* became a hit after surviving several "squalls," TV GUIDE said in 1985. They included initially sorry ratings and Michael J. Fox's "unexpected, potentially disconcerting burst into stardom." The public's infatuation with him and his character spurred a "realignment of the show's dramatic thrust," the magazine said, a move that helped cement its status as one of the biggest hits of the 1980s. Talking to TV GUIDE in 1985 about his newfound fame, Fox said: "I'm afraid someone will take it away if I'm a jerk about it." It was that sort of self-policing modesty that made Fox such an appealing actor, despite Alex's undeniable obnoxiousness. The goodwill he earned from viewers did not wane: Seven years after *Family Ties* left the air in 1989, they were delighted to see Fox return to television as the even more politically

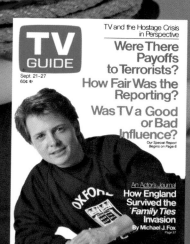

MARRIED...
WITH CHILDREN

Front row: Al Bundy
(Ed O'Neill), Peg Bundy
(Katey Sagal). **Back row:**
Kelly Bundy (Christina
Applegate), Bud Bundy
(David Faustino).
Fox, 1987–97
COVER: BY E.J. CAMP,
DECEMBER 12, 1992

Every time *Married...With
Children* aired in the late 1980s,
the fledgling Fox channel sent a
shot across the bow of the established networks. In an era ruled
by *Cosby Show* coziness,
Married... chronicled the unholy
Bundy household. It was less a
family than it was a nest of rabid
backbiting and viciousness,
moronic gloating and sexual
ridicule. The show seemed intent
not only on breaking every law of
old-school TV censorship (even
Fox balked at running the 1988
season premiere episode in which
all three women on a camping
trip start menstruating at the
same time; it aired later in the
season), but also breaking
Hollywood's golden rule that
every script have at least one
character the audience can root
for. Nevertheless, it all somehow
worked. "It's packed with sharp,
funny lines and comic acting,"
TV GUIDE said during the debut
season. The show ran for 10
years, defying the efforts of well-
connected Michigan housewife
Terry Rakolta to cripple it with an
advertiser boycott. As it happened, that was long enough for
son Bud (David Faustino) to finally
lose his virginity—on the series
that may have marked the
deflowering of network television.

THE '90s

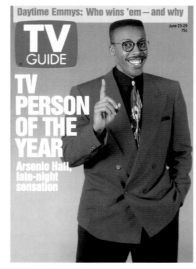

June 23, 1990
By Charles William Bush
Arsenio Hall of *The Arsenio Hall Show*

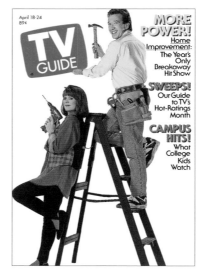

April 18, 1992
By Philip Saltonstall
Patricia Richardson and Tim Allen of *Home Improvement*

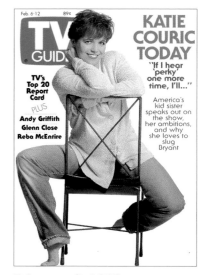

February 6, 1993
By Timothy White
Katie Couric of *Today*

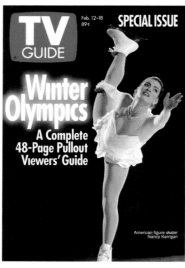

February 12, 1994
By Nancie Battaglia
Nancy Kerrigan

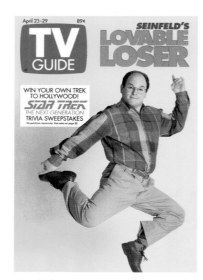

April 23, 1994
By Jeffery Newbury
Jason Alexander of *Seinfeld*

July 9, 1994
By Jeff Katz
Red Ranger of *Mighty Morphin Power Rangers*

July 16, 1994
By Deborah Feingold
Cindy Crawford of *House of Style*

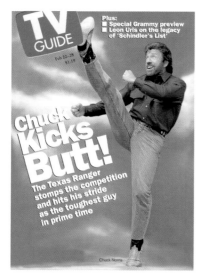

February 22, 1997
By Wyatt McSpadden
Chuck Norris of *Walker, Texas Ranger*

March 1, 1997
By Greg Lavy
Cast of *3rd Rock From the Sun*

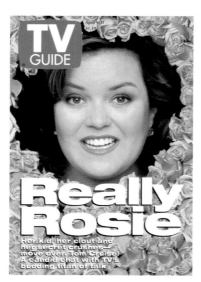

April 5, 1997
By Michael Daks
Rosie O'Donnell of *The Rosie O'Donnell Show*

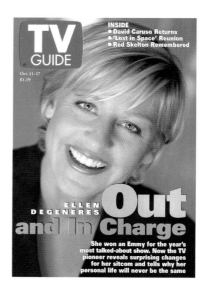

October 11, 1997
By Gregory Heisler
Ellen DeGeneres of *Ellen*

March 27, 1993
By Theo Westenberger
Billy Crystal

May 29, 1993
By Timothy White
Richard Simmons

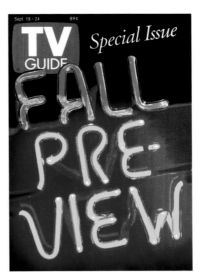

September 18, 1993
Photographer unknown
Fall Preview

January 8, 1994
By Jeff Katz
David Caruso of *NYPD Blue*

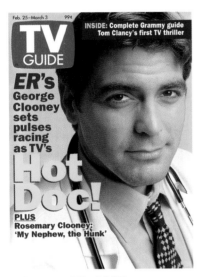

February 25, 1995
By Jeffery Newbury
George Clooney of *ER*

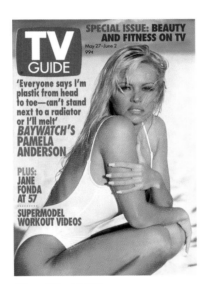

May 27, 1995
By Steve Wayda
Pamela Anderson of *Baywatch*

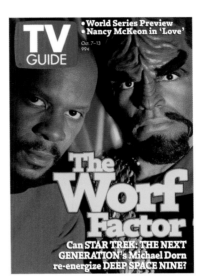

October 7, 1995
By Darryl Estrine
Avery Brooks and Michael Dorn of
Star Trek: Deep Space Nine

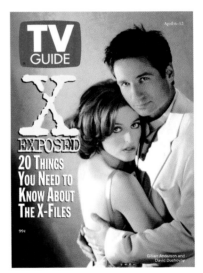

April 6, 1996
By William Hawkes
Gillian Anderson and David
Duchovny of *The X-Files*

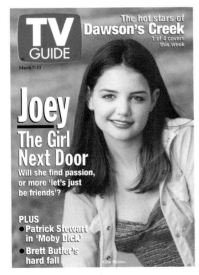

March 7, 1998
By Fergus Greer
Katie Holmes of *Dawson's Creek*

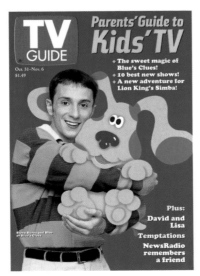

October 31, 1998
By John-Frances Burke
Steve Burns and Blue of *Blue's Clues*

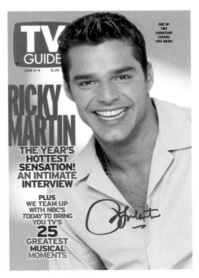

June 5, 1999
By Jose Molina
Ricky Martin

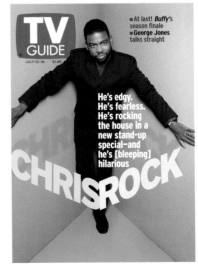

July 10, 1999
By Frank W. Ockenfels 3
Chris Rock in *Bigger & Blacker*

"L.A. LAW
WAS ONE OF THE FIRST

hour-long dramas with so much humor in it. When I think back to *All in the Family*—one of the shows that I loved so much—I realize it was the opposite. It was a comedy that was very dramatic. To me, the mix is more realistic, it's what life is about. In the worst moments, there can still be humor.

"Grace was tough and she was serious, and yet there was this vulnerable side that was dying to come out but was so afraid to. She has a line where she says, 'You know, I always wanted to be taken seriously. All my life, that's all I wanted, and now that's the only way people take me.' That's a great line, isn't it?"

–SUSAN DEY

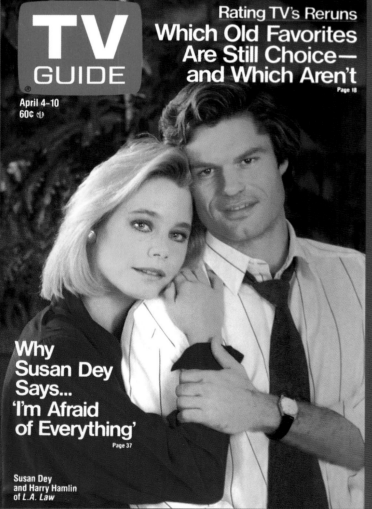

Susan Dey
and Harry Hamlin
of *L.A. Law*

L.A. LAW
NBC, 1986–94
COVER: BY GENE TRINDL, APRIL 4, 1987

L.A. Law was hardly the first series about the legal profession, but as creator Steven Bochco told TV Guide in 1986, he envisioned his show as a departure from the *Perry Mason* tradition. Old-school legal dramas were too "earnest," Bochco said, with "precious little humor," and "the cases were all resolved, usually heroically, by the end of each episode." The *Hill Street Blues* executive producer lifted many of that show's techniques out of the dank police precinct and transferred them to the bright, cool *L.A. Law* offices: an ensemble cast, intertwined story lines that sometimes spanned several episodes, lots of humor, thinly veiled variants on headline-grabbing real-life cases (dwarf tossing, the outing of closeted homosexuals) and plenty of on-the-job romantic tension. Middle-aged viewers everywhere rooted for dumpy tax lawyer Stuart Markowitz (Michael Tucker) and his use of the never-explained Venus Butterfly sex maneuver to win over colleague Ann Kelsey (real-life wife Jill Eikenberry), but the major loveline involved good-looking younger partner Michael Kuzak (Harry Hamlin) and fetching assistant district attorney Grace Van Owen (Susan Dey). The only hotter romance on the show was the infatuation of sleazy divorce lawyer Arnie Becker (Corbin Bernsen) with himself. Just two months after *L.A. Law*'s launch in late '86, TV Guide was championing the show, urging readers to support it and send a message to Hollywood that "this is the right direction for television."

THIRTYSOMETHING

Front row: Nancy Weston (Patricia Wettig), Elliot Weston (Timothy Busfield), Ethan Weston (Jason Nagler). Back row: Ellyn Warren (Polly Draper), Prof. Gary Shepherd (Peter Horton), Janey Steadman (Brittany and Lacey Craven), Michael Steadman (Ken Olin), Hope Murdoch Steadman (Mel Harris), Melissa Steadman (Melanie Mayron). ABC, 1987–91
COVER: BY TONY COSTA, JUNE 11, 1988

Not many television shows have their very titles enshrined in the language— we'll be hearing people described as "thirtysomething" long after the characters in this show reach fiftysomething. And it was just as unusual for a series to provoke such a love-hate passion from TV audiences: You were either riveted by the emotional lives and often low-anxiety domestic dramas of its seven financially comfortable friends, or you were "one of those who say they have enough troubles without having to watch a show about yuppie angst," as TV GUIDE put it in 1988. Over the course of its four years, buddies Michael and Elliot opened up their own ad agency and forever pondered if they were making the right choices in life, while their wives, ambitious Hope and artistic Nancy, raised the kids and forever wondered if *they* were making the right choices in life. Such was the confidence of *thirtysomething*—in its writing and in its hold on viewers' attention—that story lines that might be resolved in a single episode on other series here were allowed to unfold over months. (Nancy spent an entire season in the slow-motion collapse of her relationship with Elliot, and another in her struggle with ovarian cancer.) Though each character represented some aspect of not-old/not-young adulthood, Ken Olin's Michael was the mouthpiece for creators Ed Zwick and Marshall Herskovitz. Rather than worrying about his daughter's eventual first date, Olin told TV GUIDE, Michael "is filled with self-questioning and self-doubts. How often do you see a father like that on television?" It was that accomplishment—defining the young ambivalent professional—that would establish *thirtysomething* as a monument to the 1980s.

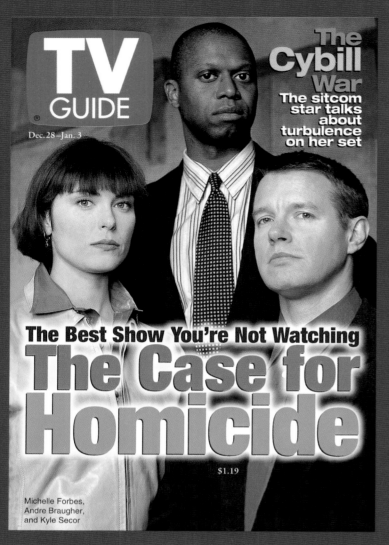

TV GUIDE

Dec. 28–Jan. 3

The Cybill War
The sitcom star talks about turbulence on her set

The Best Show You're Not Watching

The Case for Homicide

$1.19

Michelle Forbes,
Andre Braugher,
and Kyle Secor

HOMICIDE: LIFE ON THE STREET
NBC, 1993–99
COVER: BY STEVE DANELIAN, DECEMBER 28, 1996

There have been more popular cop shows, but none better than *Homicide: Life on the Street*, where gunfights were infrequent, car chases almost unheard of and corpses plentiful. Not every case from the drug-ravaged inner city of Baltimore was solved—the killing of a child named Adena Watson haunted the squad room—but every new murder was approached with a *Homicide*-al mixture of missionary zeal, mordant humor and Sisyphean doggedness by the show's vivid collection of sharply observed characters. If *Miami Vice*'s detectives were "MTV cops," Richard Belzer told TV GUIDE in 1993, then *Homicide*'s were "Tolstoy cops." Belzer, a stand-up comedian, eagerly signed up to play the squad's foul-tempered cynic, John Munch: "It's the difference between being Zippy the dumb neighbor in a sitcom or a fully realized homicide cop working in a very gritty, real situation." Though many actors performed brilliantly in the Barry Levinson-produced series—Ned Beatty as the veteran "Big Man" Det. Stanley Bolander, for instance, and Yaphet Kotto as the perfect no-nonsense boss—Andre Braugher topped them all. As TV GUIDE said in '98, Braugher's "electrifying" performance as Det. Frank Pembleton made him "*Homicide*'s most provocative and prickly detective, a master of intuition and intimidation. His operatic interrogations in 'the box' rank among the blistering highlights of any TV season." Despite almost uniformly ecstatic reviews, the show never drew ratings that measured up to the stature of its writing or performances. After seven years, NBC finally and officially closed the *Homicide* case for good.

106 C

COPS
Zane Schuberger, John Cosgrove. Fox, 1989–

Crime never looked more deglamorized than on *Cops*, the ride-along documentary series showing police officers on the job. Since its 1989 beginning, the show has been filmed in more than 100 American cities, as well as overseas precincts like London and Hong Kong. But no matter where the cameras went, the message was always the same: Police officers are by and large dedicated, low-key heroes, and criminals—whether a wife-beating drunk or a drug-dealing sleazeball—are almost uniformly miserable numbskulls. You just couldn't take your eyes off the banal but enthralling struggle between the good guys in blue (and gray and brown) and these car wrecks of humanity.

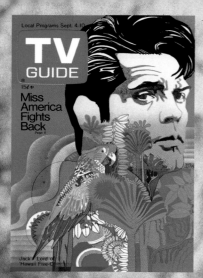

HAWAII FIVE-O
Det. Steve McGarrett (Jack Lord).
CBS, 1968–80
COVER: BY BOB PEAK, SEPTEMBER 4, 1971

Brooklyn-born Jack Lord always looked like a film-noir refugee who had wandered onto the set of a beach-blanket movie. He was Det. Steve McGarrett, wearing a suit and a scowl, battling crime in the land of leisurewear. And it worked. In 1971, three years into what would become one of television's longest-running cop shows, Lord told TV GUIDE: "People wonder why he doesn't get himself more girls. Our form is as rigid as a sonnet. Romance just doesn't work." Ah, but there was the romance of luscious Hawaii itself, and the irresistible theme song, which could keep you sitting around for an hour, waiting for the final credits just so you could hear it again.

BOOK 'EM, DANNO

134

COLUMBO
Lt. Columbo (Peter Falk). NBC, 1971–77; ABC, 1989–93
COVER: BY AL HIRSCHFELD, AUGUST 14, 1976

The only mystery in the detective drama *Columbo* was how, precisely, a shambling cop who appeared to sleep in his raincoat could outfox his wealthy, polished adversaries (one possibility: Columbo's deceptively casual request for "just one more thing"–the question that often tripped up his suspects). Even so, it wasn't the "how" as much as the "who" that explained the lasting appeal of this show. Director John Cassavetes talked to TV GUIDE in 1972 about series star Peter Falk: "He's archaic. He's deep. He's gentle. He's 2,000 years old. He's also somebody everybody falls in love with." That included the magazine, which lauded him as the "highly irregular–and highly wonderful–Mr. Peter Falk."

TV GUIDE — Republican Convention: Complete Details of TV Coverage — Local Programs Aug. 14–2 — 25¢

Peter Falk of 'Columbo'

MAGNUM, P.I.
Thomas Magnum (Tom Selleck). CBS, 1980–88
COVER: BY GENE TRINDL,
JANUARY 2, 1982

CBS decided it needed a crime-fighting series set in the Aloha State to pick up where *Hawaii Five-O* left off in 1980. But its chosen star, Tom Selleck, wasn't happy with the overly macho-heroic tenor of the pilot script he was shown. "I wanted the guy to make mistakes, to have flaws," Selleck told TV GUIDE shortly after *Magnum, P.I.*'s debut. That turned out to be a masterstroke—Selleck looked the part of a hunky private investigator, but as the magazine noted, he was endearing as "a guy who, running from a gang of thugs, forgets where he parked his car."

TV GUIDE

Critic's Choice
The 10 Best TV-Movies of 1981
By Judith Crist
Page 4

Local Programs Jan. 2-8, 1982
50¢

John Hillerman
and Tom Selleck
of 'Magnum, P.I.'

"PEOPLE REALLY UNDERSTOOD MAGNUM AND THEY RELATED TO HIM.

He didn't always get the girl. In fact, most of the time he did what most guys do, which is screw it up. Magnum said that one day he woke up as a Navy SEAL at age 33 and realized he'd never been 23. So the eight years represented in *Magnum* were the least responsible period in that character's life. He owed everybody money. He was always having to trick his friends into doing him favors. He was living for free and he drove somebody else's really expensive car. But the show seemed to have this universal audience where women found Magnum very attractive and men weren't offended by him. And I think that his fallibility and his humanness were big keys to the success.

"*Magnum* was really an ensemble piece about four characters and their relationships. But Hawaii was also a character in the show, and we treated it as such. *Hawaii Five-0* and *Magnum, P.I.* literally followed each other—*Five-0* went off the air and we came on—and both were hugely successful series. Hawaii is a state of mind for some people. If you're in Minnesota in the winter, it's kind of nice to watch this guy running around in a Hawaiian shirt and shorts.

"*Magnum, P.I.* was like *The Rockford Files*, because it dealt with problems of the human condition. Rockford was a neat character, and he influenced me a lot. He was an ex-con; people forget that. Magnum was a Navy SEAL—highly trained, highly lethal if he wanted to be—and had a lot of tragedy and heartache in his life. There's a timelessness to shows like *Rockford* and *Magnum*. I meet a lot of high school kids who know more lines from the show than I knew. I'm proud of the fact that the show has been around for so long and they still think Magnum is cool.

"I was fortunate enough to win an Emmy as best dramatic actor, but it was a show with an enormous amount of humor. I know somebody told me you have to find the comedy in tragedy and the tragedy in comedy, and I think *Magnum* did that pretty well. And we're in the Smithsonian. Magnum's Hawaiian shirt, his Detroit Tigers hat and his ring are all in there along with Archie Bunker's chair. And we were recognized officially by the Smithsonian as the first show that [portrayed] Vietnam veterans in a positive light. We did something right."

—TOM SELLECK

GET SMART
NBC, 1965–69;
CBS, 1969–70
COVER: BY KEN WHITMORE,
AUGUST 27, 1966

The 007-fueled secret-agent fad of the 1960s begged for lampooning, and comic masters Mel Brooks and Buck Henry obliged with *Get Smart*, about the world's dimmest spy. They found the ideal Maxwell Smart in comedian Don Adams, who could keep a straight face while talking into his shoe-phone or endlessly milking catchphrases like "Sorry about that, Chief." "I don't want to change the thinking of the world," Adams told TV GUIDE in 1965. "I just want to make people laugh." Sure enough, with the help of Barbara Feldon as brainy beauty Agent 99, he had the country in stitches.

HOW I FOUND A WIFE ON TELEVISION

By Richard Warren Lewis

See page 20

TV GUIDE

15¢ • Local Programs
Aug. 27 – Sept. 2

BARBARA FELDON,
DON ADAMS AND K-13
OF 'GET SMART'

Jan. 14-20   75¢

TV GUIDE
®

Cybill and the *Moonlighting* Mess—
Behind the Feuding That Almost Killed the Show

Delta Burke and Gerald McRaney
Their First Screen Kiss Turned into Real-Life Love

Memo to President Bush: How to Use TV— and Not Be Abused by It
By Richard Nixon

Cybill Shepherd
and Bruce Willis
of *Moonlighting*

MOONLIGHTING
ABC, 1985–89
COVER: BY ABC, JANUARY 14, 1989

Moonlighting's ostensible focus was the Blue Moon detective agency, but the cases were incidental to the exhilarating verbal sparring between Cybill Shepherd, as reluctant owner and glam ex-fashion model Maddie Hayes, and pre–*Die Hard* Bruce Willis, as cocksure detective David Addison. "Few television shows had ever been so heralded by audiences and critics alike," TV GUIDE said in 1987, already speaking in the past tense about a series just two years old. As it happened, production delays and backstage acrimony on *Moonlighting* would take another two years to actually bring the show down.

Local Programs • March 27-April 2

TV
GUIDE

15¢

This season's
most jinxed show
page 6

Edith Efron beards
Lawrence E. Spivak
page 14

Political leaders,
broadcasters debate
the Minow plan
page 30

Mary Tyler Moore
and Dick Van Dyke

THE DICK VAN DYKE SHOW
Laura Petrie (Mary Tyler Moore), Rob Petrie (Dick Van Dyke). CBS, 1961–66
COVER: BY MARIO CASILLI, MARCH 27, 1965

When this show made its 1961 debut, TV GUIDE was so sure that readers would be unfamiliar with the comedian who supposedly merited name-in-the-title treatment that it ran an article called "What's a Dick Van Dyke?" (Answer: "He is a long, elegant string bean of a man with a knack for doing almost everything interestingly, whether playing a love scene or taking the most explosive falls since Buster Keaton.") By the end of the show's five-year run on CBS, of course, millions of people knew not only Van Dyke and his portrayal of Rob Petrie, head writer for a comedy-variety series in New York City, but also Mary Tyler Moore, as his high-strung but lovable wife, Laura, and his writing partners, played by Rose Marie and Morey Amsterdam. Though plenty of action took place behind the scenes of the fictional *Alan Brady Show* (*Your Show of Shows* vet Carl Reiner, who played the egomaniacal Brady, created *The Dick Van*

Dyke Show), the moments that endeared a generation of viewers to the series occurred back home in suburban New Rochelle, New York. There, Rob was forever plunging into situations armed with the wrong information or a missing vital fact: Laura actually hates the gaudy piece of jewelry he thinks she loves; after an embarrassing display of jealousy, Rob discovers that a former suitor of Laura's is now a priest; Rob demands to meet a couple he is certain got the Petries' baby by mistake at the hospital—and discovers they are black. "We found it unfunny," TV GUIDE said in 1964 of the hospital mix-up episode, "but the producers undoubtedly felt it was all very modern and adult." On the whole, though, the magazine agreed that the show was "fresh, fast and frolicsome"—thanks primarily to the lucky fact that this series about a comedy writer happened to enjoy terrific comedy writing.

ROSEANNE
Roseanne Conner (Roseanne Barr), Dan Conner (John Goodman). ABC, 1988–97
COVER: BY TIMOTHY WHITE, AUGUST 29, 1992

In 1988, before the crotch-grabbing national anthem, before the startling declaration of multiple personalities and before the less than salutary marriage to Tom Arnold, there was simply Roseanne—star of a new comedy that was so resonantly "real" that it rose to second place in the Nielsen ratings in its fourth week (and stayed in the Top 5 for the next six years). "I'm not Lucy tryin' to hide 20 bucks from Ricky or June Cleaver glidin' around a dust-proof house in pearls and heels," Roseanne Barr told TV GUIDE during her show's first season. "I'm a woman who works hard and loves her family, but they can drive her nuts." It was precisely that unsentimental view of family and married life that had propelled the sarcastic "domestic goddess" to fame as a stand-up comedian in the mid-'80s. With *Roseanne*, she also

wanted to create "a portrait of working folks with a little warmth and dignity, not buffoons. Bad grammar doesn't mean you're an idiot." The working folks in this case were Roseanne and Dan Conner of Lanford, Illinois: overweight, underpaid and trying to make ends meet while raising three kids. Dan, adeptly played by John Goodman, was a small-time contractor, and Roseanne was a production-line drone at a plastics factory (reflecting the way people really live, both changed jobs over the years). But the focus was usually back home, on the thorny but loving relationships between mom, dad and the kids. Other comedies had working-class premises, of course, but not even *The Honeymooners* or *All in the Family* nailed what it was like to be a blue-collar family in America as effectively as *Roseanne*.

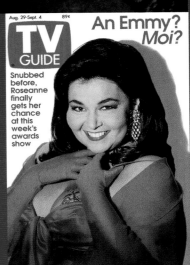

Aug. 29-Sept. 4   894
TV GUIDE
An Emmy? Moi?
Snubbed before, Roseanne finally gets her chance at this week's awards show

TO THE
MOON,
ALICE'

THE HONEYMOONERS

Above, left: Ralph Kramden (Jackie Gleason), Alice Kramden (Audrey Meadows), Ed Norton (Art Carney), Trixie Norton (Joyce Randolph). CBS, 1955–56
COVERS (FROM TOP): BY TOM CAFFREY, MARCH 19, 1955, AND MAY 21, 1955

"To the moon, Alice." "One of these days, Alice, one of these days: Pow! Right in the kisser." "Baby, you're the greatest." These lines have been repeated so many times on television over the past five decades that they're practically ingrained in our DNA. But it wasn't just the sheer repetition of *The Honeymooners* that made Jackie Gleason's trademark phrases so familiar; it was the vividness of his performance as Ralph Kramden, the pop-eyed, big-bellied bus driver who stormed around his grim Brooklyn, New York, apartment scheming to strike it rich, raging at the world and chafing at the skepticism of his sardonic wife. TV GUIDE loved *The Honeymooners* ("a rollicking, slapsticky, fast-paced situation comedy, played for the big reaction") but was so perplexed by its popularity in light of Ralph's aspiring-wife-beater shtick that the magazine consulted a psychiatrist to help explain its success. "The psychiatrist thinks that the American male has a feeling he is being submerged by his mate," the magazine reported in 1955, when the show moved from being a segment on *The Jackie Gleason Show* to its own half-hour slot on CBS, "and that he recognizes his own submission in Ralph Kramden's comic exasperation." That, plus the fact that the show was simply damned hilarious, week after week. There's an argument to be made that the real genius of *The Honeymooners* lay not in the relationship between Ralph and Alice (Audrey Meadows), but between him and his pal and upstairs neighbor, sewer worker Ed Norton, played by the incomparable Art Carney. There was an inherent comedy in big baby Ralph having to take care of someone else even more handicapped in life than he was (even in sleep, "Nah'en" needed Ralph to save him from his night walking). They were alike in their burning desire to get rich quick—and in the brain-cell deficit that kept them from accomplishing the dream—but where Ralph almost frantically veered between pure hope and utter despair, Norton seemed to glide through life with an improbable confidence. It's surprising Ralphie-boy never sent *him* to the moon.

SEX AND THE CITY

Miranda Hobbes (Cynthia Nixon), Samantha Jones (Kim Cattrall), Charlotte York (Kristin Davis), Carrie Bradshaw (Sarah Jessica Parker). HBO, 1998–

COVERS: BY DAH LEN, JUNE 17, 2000

Sure, *Sex and the City* featured four comely women whose frank sexual chat turned chic New York City bistros into the female equivalent of a guys' locker room, and of course it *had* to be on cable, because there's no way characters on a broadcast network could have gotten away with saying and doing the graphic stuff routinely showcased here. But as TV GUIDE said in 2000, HBO "also got a sharply written, seamlessly acted and, at times, poignant adult comedy." The show revolved around newspaper columnist and self-titled "sexual anthropologist" Carrie Bradshaw (Sarah Jessica Parker) and her three frisky friends: publicist Samantha

(Kim Cattrall), lawyer Miranda (Cynthia Nixon) and art dealer-turned-museum volunteer Charlotte (Kristin Davis). Though only Samantha was as promiscuous as the hype suggested, the women certainly upended conventional depictions of relations between the sexes. "The men are playing all the women's roles in this show," Parker told TV GUIDE in 1998. "The women are in control." Among their potential dates—"toxic bachelors," "modelizers" and others—a guy occasionally broke out of the pack (Chris Noth's Mr. Big, for instance), but generally, Parker said, "men are objectified the way we often are." In terms of ratings, it was a *Sex* technique that worked.

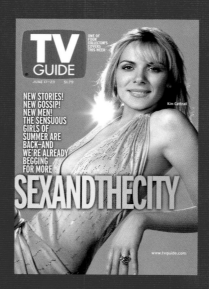

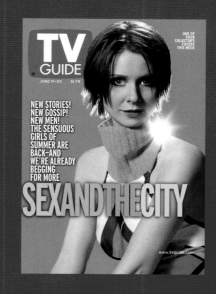

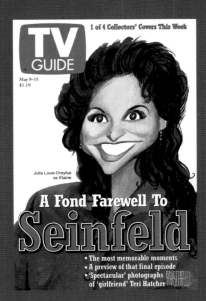
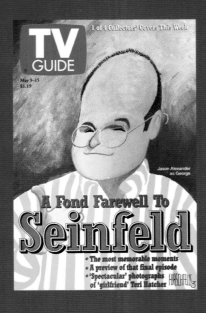
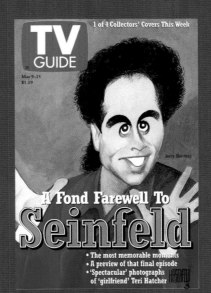
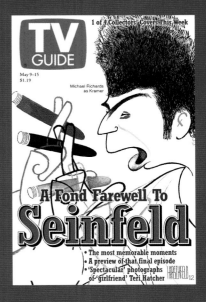

SEINFELD
George Costanza (Jason Alexander), Elaine Benes (Julia Louis-Dreyfus), Cosmo Kramer (Michael Richards), Jerry Seinfeld (Jerry Seinfeld). NBC, 1990–98
COVERS: BY AL HIRSCHFELD, MAY 9, 1998

Mary Tyler Moore, who knows a few things about television comedy, summed up her thoughts about *Seinfeld* for TV GUIDE in 1996: "The unexpected turns, the complete dedication to the multiple layers of the characters, the chances that each actor takes—it's like watching each one of them on the high wire, and when they make it to the end, you cheer." Neil Simon, who knows a few things about *writing* comedy, was more succinct: "It's a terrific show. It's just *funny*." As put forth on the series itself, *Seinfeld* was a comedy about nothing. But in reality it was about the very worthy subject of modern manners—waiting interminably for a table at a Chinese restaurant, for instance, or trying to find your car in a parking garage—and it addressed these issues with all the acute observation and satirical brilliance of a Restoration comedy. It's just that the manners of Jerry (Jerry Seinfeld), George (Jason Alexander), Elaine (Julia

Louis-Dreyfus) and Kramer (Michael Richards) were often atrocious. Seinfeld told TV GUIDE in 1992 that it was "micro-concept TV," as if, the magazine said, they had taken "the fourth wall off not just the apartment, but the *life* of an urbane 38-year-old, and invited the audience in." What you saw wasn't always pretty, but it was almost uniformly hilarious. (Has any show ever contributed more catchphrases to the national discourse? "Not that there's anything wrong with that," "sponge-worthy," "master of my domain," "yada, yada, yada"—if you need them explained, you missed the '90s.) When *Seinfeld* finally signed off in '98, TV GUIDE said: "In the end we're left with nothing. Nothing but a comic afterglow: echoes of shamelessly loud guffaws, laugh lines etched over years of sustained smirking at the unlikely fates and unseemly follies of four chronically maladjusted Manhattanites."

IS SEINFELD THE BEST COMEDY EVER?

In the beginning was *The Honeymooners*. Then *I Love Lucy*. It's about time to elect *Seinfeld* to the Sitcom Hall of Fame. Now that half the shows on prime time bear a striking familial resemblance to the show about Jerry and his friends, it behooves us to honor this *Citizen Kane* of situation comedies, and to propose that it may be—as Ralph Kramden would say—the greatest.

I wish to go on record as saying that the first time I saw *Seinfeld* I predicted that it would die a quick and quiet death. Not because I didn't think it was great; I just thought it was way too good to be on TV. I thought they'd cancel it. Generally, if I like a new television show, it's quickly devoured by a mid-season replacement. And *Seinfeld* seemed too weird to survive on the tube. Or rather, too much like real life, which is actually far more peculiar than life in sitcom land. It was also outrageously funny, the humor arising out of mundane situations of failed communication and everyday embarrassment, like being caught picking

your nose by your new girlfriend. *Seinfeld* pays homage to the fact that embarrassment is funny. Men probably laughed louder than women at the episode in which Elaine discovered that her nipple was exposed on her Christmas-card photo, while women presumably had a huge laugh when George was caught with his pants down after a dip in a cold swimming pool. This stuff happens to all of us. And it's funny—particularly when it happens to someone else. But who ever thought they'd put it on TV?

It's easy to forget after seven seasons just how strange *Seinfeld* seemed at first. Remember the show in which Jerry and George are trying to come up with an idea for a TV show to pitch to NBC? George suggests that they pitch a show about nothing: "No story, just talking." Kramer, on the other hand, proposes a show in which Jerry plays a circus manager. The characters will be circus freaks. "People love to watch freaks," says Kramer. Like the candy mint that is also a breath mint, *Seinfeld* is both of these things. It's a show about nothing in particular, which is to say, everyday life as we know it. And Jerry is the bemused ringmaster of a genuine freak show.

"We are all queer fish," F. Scott Fitzgerald once said. The revelation of *Seinfeld*, as distinct from most sitcoms, is that normal life is actually quite peculiar. Kramer, lurching around Jerry's apartment like a cross between Baby Huey and Frankenstein's monster, isn't the only freak; Newman, the Pillsbury Sourdoughboy, certainly qualifies. And George is neurotic enough to make Woody Allen seem positively serene and WASPy. I know people like this. But before *Seinfeld*, I don't recall anyone like George or Elaine or even Jerry on TV.

Yankees owner George Steinbrenner, who will have a cameo on the show next season, declared recently, "George Costanza is a nice guy." He was also quoted as saying, "This Seinfeld is the nicest young man." Steinbrenner is wrong as usual. One of the nicest things about *Seinfeld* is its portrayal of George and Jerry and Elaine in their not-so-niceness. Unlike your average sitcom protagonists, George and Jerry are not especially nice to the women they date, or even to sweet little old ladies, like the one who happens to have purchased the last loaf of rye bread from the bakery right before Jerry tries to buy one; Jerry knocks her over on the street and steals it. Mind you, he had a good reason, as we all do when we do something lousy. But let's not rob Jerry of his own obnoxious charm by calling him a nice guy. He'd sell Kramer down the river in a minute for a date with the buxom heiress to the O'Henry candy fortune. As would many of my closest friends. And George, in last month's season finale, doesn't see any harm in calling Marisa Tomei for a date just hours after learning that his fiancée has died.

As a New Yorker, I appreciate the fact that although it's filmed in L.A., *Seinfeld* actually has the lumpy texture of life in the city, the random looniness of the street, the idioms (Jerry waits on line, not in line) and speech inflections of Manhattan. But I don't necessarily expect the rest of the country to share my taste. Perhaps there is something inherently funny about the claustrophobia of New York apartment living, which is the backdrop that the three greatest sitcoms of all time—including *The Honeymooners* and *I Love Lucy*—have in common. (My only complaint vis-à-vis *Seinfeld*'s authenticity is the fact that all the characters seem to own and drive cars. This is nuts. No New Yorker in his right mind drives a car around the city. We ride around in foul-smelling yellow limos with bad shocks.)

Car quibbles aside, I still don't know how Jerry Seinfeld and cocreator Larry David managed to talk the network into a show about nothing except a bunch of neurotic New Yorkers. But from my own experience meeting with network types around the time *Seinfeld* was hatched, I can only assume they must have kidnapped an NBC executive and held him hostage until they got the green light. It presumably made things easier for the creators of subsequent quirky New York shows. *Mad About You*? No sweat—like *Seinfeld*, except Jerry and Elaine are married. *Friends*? *Seinfeld* with great-looking actors. *Caroline in the City*? Jerry Seinfeld with breasts.

However Jerry and Larry pitched the show, you have to hand it to the person who approved the *Seinfeld* pilot, which wasn't like *anything* on the tube. That's the most frightening concept in Hollywood—a genuine original.

—JAY McINERNEY, EXCERPT FROM TV GUIDE, JUNE 1, 1996

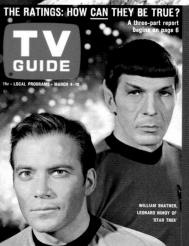

STAR TREK
Capt. James T. Kirk (William Shatner), Spock (Leonard Nimoy). NBC, 1966–69
COVER: BY SHEEDY-LONG, MARCH 4, 1967

With its debut in 1966, *Star Trek* boldly went where no television adventure series had gone before. Sure, other shows, like *Captain Video*, had ventured into outer space, but none combined special effects with an interest in social commentary. Series creator Gene Roddenberry made the U.S.S. *Enterprise* the vessel of his '60s idealism, and Capt. James T. Kirk (William Shatner) his spokesman. That is, except when Kirk was too busy fending off the attacks of enemy Klingons, trying to goad a smile out of the reserved Mr. Spock (Leonard Nimoy) or requesting a hailing frequency from communications officer Uhura (Nichelle Nichols, a rare African-American on '60s TV but in keeping with *Star Trek*'s One World sensibility). Writing in

TV GUIDE in 1967, science-fiction master Isaac Asimov called the show a "noble and successful effort to present good science fiction to the American public." The American public—at least the adult segment—did not appreciate the gesture; the foundering series was canceled by NBC after just three seasons. But the phasers-set-on-stun gadgetry and abundance of women in skin-tight synthetic mini-dresses were catnip for teenage boys. Thanks largely to these "Trekkers," *Star Trek* relaunched a decade later as a movie franchise, followed by four TV series spin-offs and possibly the most lucrative worldwide merchandising effort in television history. Live long enough, the message seemed to be, and eventually you will prosper.

APOLLO 11
Edwin "Buzz" Aldrin, July 20, 1969
COVER: BY NORMAN ADAMS, JULY 19, 1969

The TV GUIDE headline read simply: "Live–from the Moon." It was a jaw-dropping concept. Not only did the United States succeed in putting astronauts on the Moon on July 20, 1969, but it transmitted the event on television to a worldwide audience of 600 million who, gathered in their living rooms, watched the event as virtually one family. A black-and-white camera mounted near the base of *Apollo 11*'s lunar landing module recorded 38-year-old Neil Armstrong's slow climb down a ladder to the Moon's surface. We saw Armstrong reach the ground and heard him announce, "That's one small step for man, one giant leap for mankind." Fifteen minutes later, Edwin "Buzz" Aldrin joined Armstrong, who mounted the camera on a tripod so that the world could watch the most astonishing nature program ever broadcast: two guys collecting soil and rocks, setting up experiments, taking photographs and planting the American flag. "This combination of the television camera, which does not lie, and the Age of Apollo seems to me the most dramatic coupling of events in man's history," Walter Cronkite wrote in TV GUIDE the week of the landing. "It has sophisticated and educated our children to a world we thought existed only on the pulp pages of science fiction."

ONE SMALL STEP for MAN, ONE GIANT LEAP for MANKIND

Local Programs August 15-21

TV GUIDE

15¢

How One-Parent
TV Shows
Affect Your Family
—A psychologist's report
page 6

Johnny Carson

norman rockwell

THE TONIGHT SHOW STARRING JOHNNY CARSON
From below: Carson with Woody Allen; Don King; Bette Midler.
NBC, 1962–92
COVER: BY NORMAN ROCKWELL, AUGUST 15, 1970

Other shows stayed on the air longer, made more news, got higher ratings. But no television show—no television personality—was more thoroughly woven into the American conscious than *The Tonight Show* and its host of 30 years, Johnny Carson. Hearing the Carson theme song alone can instantly evoke an avalanche of pop-culture touchstones: bandleader Doc Severinsen's preposterous outfits; chortling second banana Ed McMahon and his "Heeeere's Johnny" introduction; the inimitable Carson monologue (OK, it was imitable for Rich Little); Carson in the audience playing "Stump the Band"; Carson decked out as the psychic Carnac the Magnificent; Carson warily handling exotic San Diego Zoo creatures. Carson was so utterly familiar because, in an often repeated phrase, the whole country went to bed with him every night. When he finally decided to end his remarkable run in 1992, a few months short of his 30th anniversary, TV GUIDE spoke with dozens of celebrities eager to praise the man whose show was a compulsory stop for Hollywood royalty. Mel Brooks: "Johnny is the greatest audience known to man because he listens and he *gets* it." Charlton Heston: "He is probably the best stand-up comic in America." Milton Berle: "He speaks a language that all America understands." As the magazine said at the time, one of Carson's greatest attractions was that "he frequently made failure funnier than the really funny stuff, because he accepted defeat with grace and self-deprecation. He taught America how to tell a joke—and how to get away with telling it badly. In this very important job, there is no successor to Johnny. And because all America no longer watches the same show every night, there may never be another Johnny."

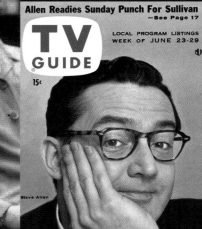

Allen Readies Sunday Punch For Sullivan
—See Page 17

TV GUIDE

LOCAL PROGRAM LISTINGS
WEEK OF JUNE 23-29

15¢

Steve Allen

PAAR'S STRANGE HOLD ON STAY-UP-LATE AMERICA

by Samuel Grafton

TV GUIDE

15¢

LOCAL PROGRAMS
MARCH 10-16

Jack Paar

HIRSCHFELD

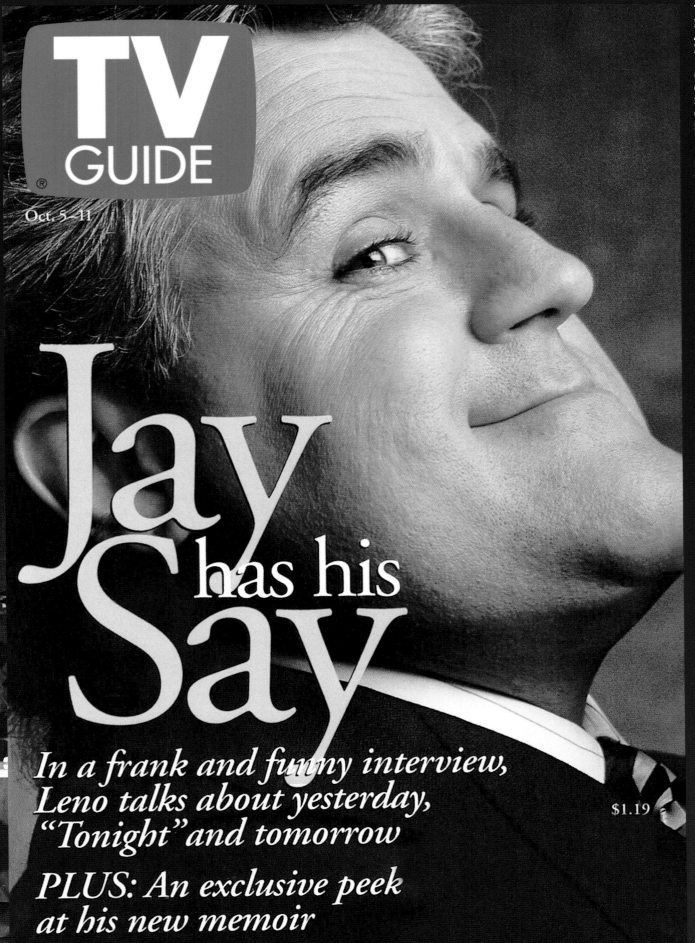

TV GUIDE

Oct. 5–11

Jay has his Say

In a frank and funny interview, Leno talks about yesterday, "Tonight" and tomorrow

PLUS: An exclusive peek at his new memoir

$1.19

THE TONIGHT SHOW
From far left: Steve Allen; Jack Paar, Hugh Downs. NBC, 1954–57 (Allen), 1957–62 (Paar) and 1992– (Jay Leno)
COVERS: BY AL HIRSCHFELD, MARCH 10, 1962. BY HOWELL CONANT, JUNE 23, 1956. BY MARK HANAUER, OCTOBER 5, 1996

When Steve Allen opened his late-night talk show on NBC in the mid-1950s, sitting at a piano and often playing his song, "This Could Be the Start of Something Big," it really *was* the start of something big: a TV institution that would still be flourishing half a century later. Johnny Carson, of course, was the *Tonight* king, but Allen, Jack Paar and Jay Leno contributed mightily to the show's legend. The innovative Allen made on-the-street remotes and audience participation reliably entertaining elements of *The Tonight Show*. (In a TV GUIDE tribute to the late Allen in 2000, comedian Jerry Stiller, a frequent guest, recalled the time the host spied someone sleeping in the back row and conducted an interview with the snoozing man. "That, to me, was classic," Stiller said.) When Paar took over in 1957, his more urbane humor still got plenty of laughs, but it was the host's mercurial emotions that made the show compelling. Paar cried if a song moved him, and spewed venom at his critics. He famously quit for a month in 1960, enraged that NBC censored a joke involving a "water closet." Paar "discovered that people like to see human beings being human. It was one of the most sensational discoveries in the history of show business," TV GUIDE said in 1962 after the host, easily bored, left *Tonight* for good. Then came Carson's phenomenal 30-year run. Though it was the very definition of a hard act to follow, genial Leno poured his heart into sustaining the franchise after landing the job in '92. Critics preferred rival David Letterman, but Leno consistently won the ratings war. "It's that old American adage," Leno told the magazine in 2002. "I'll take ambition over genius any day of the week." And for almost 50 years, Americans have taken *The Tonight Show* over the competition any night of the week.

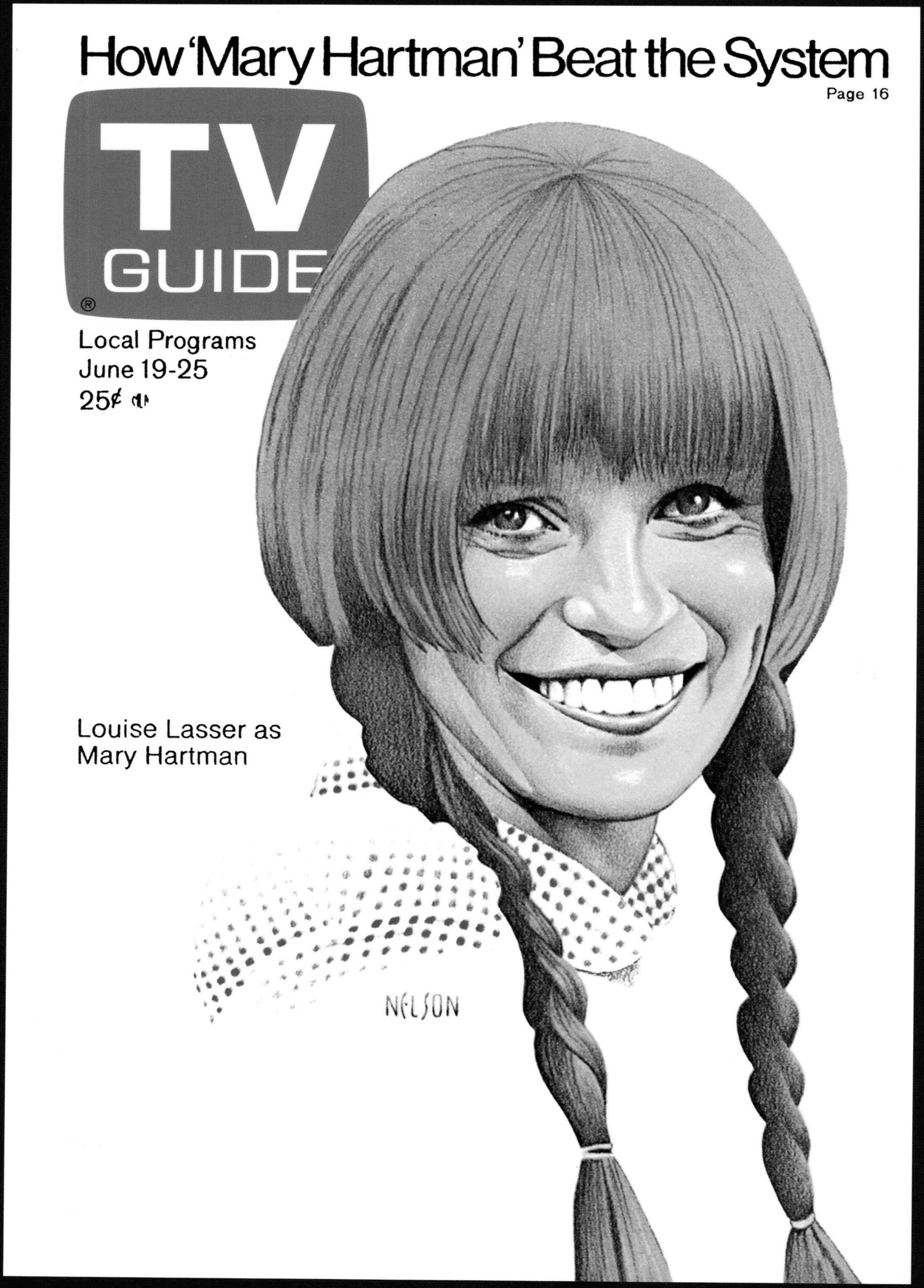

How 'Mary Hartman' Beat the System

Page 16

TV GUIDE

®

Local Programs
June 19-25
25¢

Louise Lasser as
Mary Hartman

NELSON

**MARY HARTMAN,
MARY HARTMAN**
Syndication, 1976–77
COVER: BY BILL NELSON,
JUNE 19, 1976

Over the course of 325 delicious
episodes in the mid-'70s, the
Norman Lear-produced satire
Mary Hartman, Mary Hartman
carried soap-opera sensibilities
to their logical but preposterous
conclusions. Louise Lasser
played a perpetually bewildered,
somnambulant housewife in fictional Fernwood, Ohio. Thanks to
her unquestioning acceptance of
advertising messages, Mary was
as troubled by the "waxy yellow
buildup" on her kitchen floor as
she was by her father's disap-
pearance, her daughter's kidnap-
ping or her husband's impotence.
"At its best," TV GUIDE said in
1976, "this show is the funniest
program on the air this year."

THE DICK CAVETT SHOW
ABC, 1968–75
COVER: BY BERNIE FUCHS, DECEMBER 5, 1970

"I hate the fact that I ever got labeled as an intellectual," late-night talk-show host Dick Cavett told TV GUIDE in 1973, when his being tagged with a career-blunting reputation as a smarty-pants was a fait accompli (that's a "done deal" to you). He might have hated the classification, but it's hard to imagine Johnny Carson presiding, as Cavett did in 1971, over the verbal brawling between literary enemies Norman Mailer and Gore Vidal. Critics loved Cavett, relishing his witty wordplay and often startling selection of guests—Groucho Marx was as likely to turn up as John Lennon. Ultimately, though, despite ABC's repeated attempts to sell Cavett to viewers, the *I* word did indeed do him in.

SPORTSCENTER
Keith Olbermann, Dan Patrick. ESPN, 1979–

Like a stop at the water fountain after coming off the basketball court, ESPN's *SportsCenter* has been a compulsory destination for news-thirsty sports fans. The guys who made it so were Keith Olbermann and Dan Patrick, who teamed up in 1992 to host the scores-and-highlights show and promptly transformed the genre. A baseball player on a hitting tear wasn't simply on fire; in Patrick's patois, he was *"en fuego."* An injured player was listed as day-to-day, Olbermann reported, adding, "But then again, aren't we all?" The duo's dry delivery and amused asides launched a thousand imitators—many of whom later turned up as deadpan *SportsCenter* hosts themselves—but no one could beat the Dan 'n' Keith combo (though Kenny Mayne probably takes the batting doughnut for weirdly vivid home-run calls, like "I'm not sure what this pitch is, but it tastes like chicken"). Olbermann and Patrick would probably scoff at the "pioneer" label, but their knee-jerk scoffery was precisely their appeal—especially with Olbermann, whom TV GUIDE called "the patron saint of smart-ass sportscasting." That was in 2001, after he'd become a free agent and mystified fans by shuttling unhappily from one TV job to another. The still *SportsCenter*ed Patrick, however, wisely decided to stay with the home team.

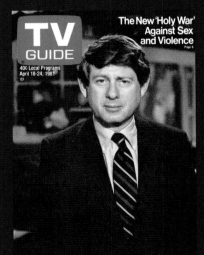

ABC NEWS NIGHTLINE
Ted Koppel. ABC, 1980–
COVER: BY DAVID HUME KENNERLY, APRIL 18, 1981

The near-death experience of *ABC News Nightline* early in 2002, when the network aggressively courted CBS's David Letterman to take over its late-night time slot, prompted a renewed appreciation for *Nightline*'s many achievements over the course of two decades. ABC established a beachhead for late-night news in 1979 with *The Iran Crisis: America Held Hostage*. After it became clear that the standoff wasn't going to be resolved soon, the broadcast was rechristened *ABC News Nightline* in March 1980. By then, the hosting duties had been taken over by former diplomatic correspondent Ted Koppel, whose impressive showing as a substitute for anchorman Frank Reynolds (he'd taken a night off to celebrate his birthday) landed him the full-time job. Much like the *MacNeil-Lehrer Report* on PBS, *Nightline* focused on a single major news story of the day, presenting taped reports and live interviews with the principal players. The difference was the presence of Koppel. As author

David Halberstam wrote in TV GUIDE in 1985, "He is television's best interviewer, immensely skilled at keeping a show going, making it move, cutting to the heart of an issue, not letting people bore or blather on, minimizing ideology and bureaucratese." A trademark *Nightline* moment would pit two leading proponents of diametrically opposed ideas against each other, with Koppel as the serene yet impatient referee. Or as Koppel himself explained it in the magazine in '87: "Take two cables, put them together and watch the sparks fly." That describes the unprecedented debate over apartheid between South African foreign minister R.F. "Pik" Botha and Bishop Desmond Tutu in 1985, part of a series of broadcasts from South Africa that Halberstam called "the best use of television journalism in some 10 years." *Nightline*'s future may have been made uncertain by the era of the 24-hour news channel, but its contributions have never been in doubt.

DAVID LETTERMAN

Below: Letterman with Drew Barrymore. Left: Richard Simmons. Far left, bottom: with Madonna. NBC, 1982–93; CBS, 1993–

COVER: BY GREGORY HEISLER, FEBRUARY 15, 1997

Six days after September 11, 2001, David Letterman went back on the air from New York City, bewildered and visibly saddened, and explained why, at a moment like this, he was doing his show: "Mayor Giuliani encouraged us...to go back to our lives, go on living, continue trying to make New York City the place that it should be.... It's very simple. There is only one requirement for any of us, and that is to be courageous, because courage, as you might know, defines all other human behavior." It was one of the most moving statements of any delivered during that terrible time, and it was a cathartic, necessary show that reminded millions of viewers why they cherish—a word that would probably make him wince—Letterman as a familiar presence in their lives. As with a good friend, you never had to wonder what kind of mood Letterman was in. He could be cranky and miserable, but he was sweet with kids and the canine stars of "Stupid Pet Tricks," and his remote-camera chats with his mother, Dorothy, were lovely glimpses of a son's long-standing, teasing affection for his mom. It was Letterman's sensibility as an entertainer, though, that made him indispensable to his fans. On *Late Night With David Letterman* (NBC) and *Late Show With David Letterman* (CBS), he relentlessly mocked showbiz artifice, and then demonstrated his own idea of entertainment with a warped brilliance that evoked Ernie Kovacs at his best: He was the man in the Velcro suit and the fizzing Alka-Seltzer outfit, the guy who'd drop watermelons from a rooftop just to watch them pop, who'd commandeer a Taco Bell drive-through to torment customers. He played nicely with guests if they seemed to be making an effort but couldn't mask his boredom with the pretentious or preening. Critics called him mean—which left him "just crushed," Letterman told TV GUIDE in '97. "I don't want to be on TV and be mean. I just want to be funny." Dan Rather, a guest on that first show after the terrorist attacks of September 11, told TV GUIDE earlier in 2001: "Dave is always irrepressibly and unavoidably himself, and exactly what that means seems to change from night to night. In a copycat world, he is a true original."

AND THE NO. 1 SIGN SOMETHING IS WRONG WITH YOUR SCHOOL LUNCH...

While growing up in Canada, I slowly became aware of the little box that had moving pictures in it. But it was the product of *that* country to the south, and I was involved in school and working in the most important medium, the one that was bound to last forever: radio. Radio, the theater of the mind, the source of employment for many Canadian actors, especially me. I put myself through college with my radio fees. But then I grew up, immigrated to America and after years of theater found myself doing stage performances in front of large boxy cameras. Now I was in live tele-

vision, putting myself through life on my television fees. The cameras, with their internal ventilation systems, sounded like cooing, warm little animals, and I thought of them as friendly, too, even with their red eyes. I was not intimidated when they would zoom in on me for a close-up—they meant no harm. After several years of live TV, my boyish visage began to show evidence of wear and tear.

And so I came of age on television. I went from shows like *Studio One*, *Playhouse 90* and *The US Steel Hour*, all coming out of New York City, to shows like *The Twilight Zone* and *Alfred Hitchcock Presents* in Los Angeles. I shuttled between coasts during those years as the industry evolved from live productions to filmed projects. I found myself doing movies of the week on location. There was more money in it because advertisers saw a novel way to reach buyers and pumped money into the emerging medium. More and more people were turning off their radio sets and not going to the movies; they were sitting at home in front of the magic square.

Steve McQueen leaped from *Wanted—Dead or Alive* to major screen stardom; that was the seminal moment when actors realized that doing a series was not a detriment to one's career, but could be used to one's advantage. So several actors made the jump from movies to television or from television to movies. TV was no longer a second-class citizen. I performed in *For the People* out of New York, one of the last of the shows to be filmed in that great city for a long time, and flew to Los Angeles when it closed, in time to do the second pilot for a show called *Star Trek*. For the next three years, we were a moderate success. And finally, it seemed, oblivion closed in.

But no, not on TV. Ten years later, *Star Trek* returned not only unscathed, but exalted. People began to look at me sideways. It went from, "Aren't you?" to "You are?" to "It's, it's…!" to "Well, I am, but hey, more than that." I had taken off the uniform and put on a tux.

And television, too, had gone to another level—the worldwide stage. It became the instrument of education and illumination. Kennedy was assassinated; wars were fought, won and lost on TV. History turned as a result of that omnipotent eye. I, along with the rest of the world, became hooked—at the expense of reading, conversation and sometimes original thought—because there in front of us lay the world, in all its glory and devastation.

But you see, TV is a mass of contradictions.

I love television. I am fascinated by looking at the screen and seeing people and events with which I could never and would never be otherwise acquainted. TV has opened my mind to philosophies, to issues, to politics and, yes, to tragedy. We are bound closer as human beings because of TV, and we are separated further as the haves and have-nots become bitterly aware of each other.

The thing that causes me as much concern and bewilderment as anything else is the sight of me aging gracelessly through the years. You've got to look at it from my perspective. I started in TV when I was practically a teenager. I'm now, by most measurements of time, an old man. And it's all happened in front of the American audience. I've watched my body go from slim adolescence to rippling manhood to (let's be kind) a middle-aged profile. I've watched my skin go from a youthful glow segueing to a flop-sweat sheen and finally to a moisturized opaqueness. I make it a point never to watch myself, whether it's something I did years ago or something I've just done.

Now, mind you, I'm also looking at a host of other people who are on the same journey. Don't you marvel at what Barbara Walters looked like when she was breaking in? Doesn't David Letterman's hairline make you curiously interested? Is Peter Falk decaying under that raincoat? And the one I really can't figure out is Regis. He looks exactly the same. Botox?

Anyway, you understand what I'm saying. Television is a chronicler of time. We see the good, the bad and the Howard Sterns move across those pixels and finally into oblivion… except for reruns.

—WILLIAM SHATNER

THE BEST OF
ACCORDING TO TV GUIDE

THE 50 GREATEST SHOWS

1. *Seinfeld*
2. *I Love Lucy*
3. *The Honeymooners*
4. *All in the Family*
5. *The Sopranos*
6. *60 Minutes*
7. *Late Show With David Letterman*
8. *The Simpsons*
9. *The Andy Griffith Show*
10. *Saturday Night Live*
11. *The Mary Tyler Moore Show*
12. *The Tonight Show Starring Johnny Carson*
13. *The Dick Van Dyke Show*
14. *Hill Street Blues*
15. *The Ed Sullivan Show*
16. *The Carol Burnett Show*
17. *Today*
18. *Cheers*
19. *thirtysomething*
20. *St. Elsewhere*
21. *Friends*
22. *ER*
23. *ABC News Nightline*
24. *Law & Order*
25. *M*A*S*H*
26. *The Twilight Zone*
27. *Sesame Street*
28. *The Cosby Show*
29. *Donahue*
30. *Your Show of Shows*
31. *The Defenders*
32. *An American Family*
33. *Playhouse 90*
34. *Frasier*
35. *Roseanne*
36. *The Fugitive*
37. *The X-Files*
38. *The Larry Sanders Show*
39. *The Rockford Files*
40. *Gunsmoke*
41. *Buffy the Vampire Slayer*
42. *Rowan and Martin's Laugh-In*
43. *Bonanza*
44. *The Bob Newhart Show*
45. *Twin Peaks*
46. *Star Trek: The Next Generation*
47. *Rocky and His Friends*
48. *Taxi*
49. *The Oprah Winfrey Show*
50. *Bewitched*

Originally published in TV GUIDE, May 4, 2002

THE 25 GREATEST MUSICAL MOMENTS

1. The Beatles on *The Ed Sullivan Show* (1964)
2. *Motown 25: Yesterday, Today, Forever* (1983)
3. Elvis Presley's TV special "comeback," *Elvis* (1968)
4. James Brown on *The T.A.M.I. Show* (1973)
5. Barbra Streisand's special *My Name Is Barbra* (1965)
6. Elvis Presley on *The Ed Sullivan Show* (1957)
7. Marvin Gaye sings the national anthem at the NBA All-Star Game (1983)
8. Julie Andrews and Carol Burnett in the special *Julie and Carol at Carnegie Hall* (1962)
9. Bette Midler sings "One for My Baby (and One More for the Road)" on Johnny Carson's final *Tonight Show* (1992)
10. Frank Sinatra in the special *Sinatra: The Main Event* (1974)
11. Leonard Bernstein sings the Beatles on *Leonard Bernstein's Young People's Concert* (1964)
12. The Notorious B.I.G. tribute on the MTV Video Music Awards (1997)
13. Frank Sinatra and Dean Martin on *The Judy Garland Show* (1962)
14. David Bowie on *Bing Crosby's Merrie Olde Christmas* (1977)
15. The Who on *The Smothers Brothers Comedy Hour* (1967)
16. Bruce Springsteen sings "Streets of Philadelphia" on the Academy Awards (1994)
17. Nirvana on *MTV Unplugged* (1993)
18. Isaac Hayes sings "Theme From *Shaft*" on the Academy Awards (1972)
19. Mary Martin in the special *Peter Pan* (1955)
20. Ricky Nelson sings "I'm Walkin'" on *The Adventures of Ozzie & Harriet* (1957)
21. *A Charlie Brown Christmas* (1965)
22. Cast sings "You've Really Got a Hold on Me" on *Roseanne* (1991)
23. The debut of *The Nat King Cole Show* (1956)
24. Ernie sings "Rubber Duckie" on *Sesame Street* (1970)
25. The special *This Is Garth Brooks, Too!* (1994)

Originally published in TV GUIDE, June 5, 1999

THE 50 GREATEST CHARACTERS

1. Louie De Palma / *Taxi*
2. Ed Norton / *The Honeymooners*
3. Lucy Ricardo / *I Love Lucy*
4. Fonzie / *Happy Days*
5. Archie Bunker / *All in the Family*
6. Mr. Spock / *Star Trek*
7. Lt. Columbo / *Columbo*
8. Emma Peel / *The Avengers*
9. Barney Fife / *The Andy Griffith Show*
10. George Costanza / *Seinfeld*
11. J.R. Ewing / *Dallas*
12. Felix Unger and Oscar Madison / *The Odd Couple*
13. Ralph Kramden / *The Honeymooners*
14. Homer Simpson / *The Simpsons*
15. Lilly Harper / *I'll Fly Away*
16. Sgt. Bilko / *The Phil Silvers Show*
17. Alex P. Keaton / *Family Ties*
18. Theo Kojak / *Kojak*
19. Maxwell Smart / *Get Smart*
20. Eddie Haskell / *Leave It to Beaver*
21. Mary Richards / *The Mary Tyler Moore Show*
22. Maynard G. Krebs / *The Many Loves of Dobie Gillis*
23. Andy Sipowicz / *NYPD Blue*
24. Paladin / *Have Gun, Will Travel*
25. Jim Rockford / *The Rockford Files*
26. Roseanne / *Roseanne*
27. Steve Urkel / *Family Matters*
28. Edina Monsoon / *Absolutely Fabulous*
29. Ted Baxter / *The Mary Tyler Moore Show*
30. Frank Pembleton / *Homicide: Life on the Street*

TELEVISION

THE 25 GREATEST COMMERCIALS

1. Apple Computer / "1984" (1984)
2. Alka-Seltzer / "Atsa spicy meatball!" (1969)
3. Volkswagen / Funeral procession (1969)
4. Volkswagen / Volkswagen driver helps out snowplow driver (1963)
5. Federal Express / "Fast-Paced World" with motormouth (1981)
6. American Tourister / Gorilla bashes luggage (1970)
7. Coca-Cola / Mean Joe Greene and young fan (1979)
8. Miller Lite / Bob Uecker brags in a bar (1975)
9. Wendy's / "Where's the beef?" (1984)
10. Life cereal / "He likes it! Hey, Mikey!" (1971)
11. Partnership for a Drug-free America / "Fried Egg": Your brain on drugs (1987)
12. Coca-Cola / "I'd Like to Teach the World to Sing" (1971)
13. California Milk Board / Who shot Alexander Hamilton: "Got Milk?" (1993)
14. Alka-Seltzer / Prison cafeteria (1970)
15. Benson & Hedges / "The Dis-advantages" (1966)
16. Keep America Beautiful / "Crying Indian" (1971)
17. Cracker Jack / Box of Cracker Jack is passed on a train (1965)
18. Nike / "Bo, you don't know diddly" (1989)
19. Energizer Batteries / Bunny keeps going...and going... (1989)
20. Lyndon B. Johnson for President / Daisy petals and nuclear countdown (1964)
21. Pepsi / Coke deliveryman sneaks a Pepsi (1996)
22. ESPN / "This is *SportsCenter*" campaign (1995)
23. Xerox / Monk forsakes hand copying for xeroxing (1975)
24. Pepsi / Archaeologists find long-forgotten Coke can (1985)
25. Levi's / "The 501 Blues" (1984)

Originally published in TV GUIDE, July 3, 1999

THE 25 GREATEST MUSIC VIDEOS

1. "Thriller" / Michael Jackson / John Landis, director
2. "Vogue" / Madonna / David Fincher, director
3. "Smells Like Teen Spirit" / Nirvana / Samuel Bayer, director
4. "Sledgehammer" / Peter Gabriel / Stephen R. Johnson, director
5. "Walk This Way" / Run DMC and Aerosmith / Jon Small, director
6. "Sweet Child o' Mine" / Guns N' Roses / Nigel Dick, director
7. "Sabotage" / Beastie Boys / Spike Jonze, director
8. "Addicted to Love" / Robert Palmer / Terence Donovan, director
9. "California Love" / 2Pac with Dr. Dre / Hype Williams, director
10. "Express Yourself" / Madonna / David Fincher, director
11. "Hungry Like the Wolf" / Duran Duran / Russell Mulcahy, director
12. "Beat It" / Michael Jackson / Bob Giraldi, director
13. "Losing My Religion" / R.E.M. / Tarsem, director
14. "Take On Me" / A-Ha / Steve Barron, director
15. "The Rain (Supa Dupa Fly)" / Missy "Misdemeanor" Elliot / Hype Williams, director
16. "Every Breath You Take" / The Police / Kevin Godley and Lol Creme, directors
17. "Closer" / Nine Inch Nails / Mark Romanek, director
18. "Freedom" / George Michael / David Fincher, director
19. "Jeremy" / Pearl Jam / Mark Pellington, director
20. "Put Your Hands Where My Eyes Can See" / Busta Rhymes / Hype Williams, director
21. "Need You Tonight"-"Mediate" / INXS / Richard Lowenstein, director
22. "No Rain" / Blind Melon / Samuel Bayer, director
23. "Mo Money, Mo Problems" / The Notorious B.I.G. with Puff Daddy and Mase / Hype Williams, director
24. "Virtual Insanity" / Jamiroquai / Jonathan Glazer, director
25. "You Might Think" / The Cars / Jeff Stein, director

Originally published in TV GUIDE, December 4, 1999

31. Niles Crane / *Frasier*
32. Jim Ignatowski / *Taxi*
33. Diane Chambers / *Cheers*
34. Mork / *Mork & Mindy*
35. Kramer / *Seinfeld*
36. Fred Sanford / *Sanford and Son*
37. Hawk / *Spenser: For Hire*
38. Jane Hathaway / *The Beverly Hillbillies*
39. Artie / *The Larry Sanders Show*
40. Alexis Carrington / *Dynasty*
41. Dr. Mark Craig / *St. Elsewhere*
42. Bill Bittinger / *Buffalo Bill*
43. Adam / *Northern Exposure*
44. David Addison / *Moonlighting*
45. Jane Tennison / *Prime Suspect*
46. Xena / *Xena: Warrior Princess*
47. Douglas Wambaugh / *Picket Fences*
48. Miles Drentell / *thirtysomething*
49. Elliot Carlin / *The Bob Newhart Show*
50. Maurice "Buddy" Sorrell / *The Dick Van Dyke Show*

Originally published in TV GUIDE, October 16, 1999

THE 25 GREATEST GAME SHOWS

1. *The Price Is Right*
2. *Jeopardy!*
3. *G.E. College Bowl*
4. *Password*
5. *What's My Line?*
6. *$25,000 Pyramid*
7. *Who Wants to Be a Millionaire*
8. *Masquerade Party*
9. *To Tell the Truth*
10. *Match Game*
11. *The Newlywed Game*
12. *Survivor*
13. *Queen for a Day*
14. *Family Feud*
15. *Twenty One*
16. *The Gong Show*
17. *Video Village*
18. *Let's Make a Deal*
19. *The Hollywood Squares*
20. *Concentration*
21. *Truth or Consequences*
22. *The $64,000 Question*
23. *Beat the Clock*
24. *You Bet Your Life*
25. *Wheel of Fortune*

Originally published in TV GUIDE, January 27, 2001

Index
OF COVERS

A COMPLETE, YEAR-BY-YEAR LISTING OF ALL TV GUIDE COVERS FROM APRIL 3, 1953, TO APRIL 6, 2002

1953–57

1953

April 3	Lucille Ball and Desiderio Alberto Arnaz IV of *I Love Lucy*
April 10	Jack Webb of *Dragnet*
April 17	"TV Ratings–Fact or Fraud?": Lucille Ball, Arthur Godfrey, Milton Berle, Imogene Coca and Sid Caesar
April 24	Ralph Edwards of *This Is Your Life*
May 1	Eve Arden of *Our Miss Brooks*
May 8	Arthur Godfrey of *Arthur Godfrey's Talent Scouts*
May 15	David Nelson and Ricky Nelson of *The Adventures of Ozzie & Harriet*
May 22	Red Buttons of *The Red Buttons Show*
May 29	Queen Elizabeth II
June 5	Dean Martin and Jerry Lewis of *The Colgate Comedy Hour*
June 12	Eddie Fisher of *Coke Time With Eddie Fisher*
June 19	Ed Sullivan of *The Ed Sullivan Show*
June 26	Dinah Shore of *The Dinah Shore Show*
July 3	Perry Como of *The Perry Como Show*
July 10	Dave Garroway and Mr. Muggs of *Today*
July 17	Lucille Ball and Desi Arnaz of *I Love Lucy*
July 24	Groucho Marx of *You Bet Your Life*
July 31	Max Liebman, Sid Caesar and Imogene Coca of *Your Show of Shows*
August 7	Ray Milland of *Meet Mr. McNutley*
August 14	Patti Page of *Scott Music Hall*
August 21	Mary Hartline and Claude Kirchner of *Super Circus*
August 28	Jayne Meadows of *I've Got a Secret* and Audrey Meadows of *The Jackie Gleason Show*
September 4	Wally Cox of *Mr. Peepers*
September 11	Joan Caulfield and Ralph Edwards of *This Is Your Life*
September 18	Fall Preview
September 25	George Reeves of *The Adventures of Superman*
October 2	Red Skelton of *The Red Skelton Show*
October 9	Bishop Fulton J. Sheen of *Life Is Worth Living*
October 16	T-Venus winners
October 23	Arthur Godfrey of *Arthur Godfrey's Talent Scouts*
October 30	Buelah Witch, Kukla and Ollie of *Kukla, Fran and Ollie*
November 6	Warren Hull of *Strike It Rich*
November 13	Jimmy Durante of *The Colgate Comedy Hour*
November 20	Dorothy McGuire and Julius LaRosa of *Arthur Godfrey's Talent Scouts*
November 27	Lugene Sanders of *The Life of Riley*
December 4	Loretta Young of *The Loretta Young Show*
December 11	Jack Webb of *Dragnet*
December 18	Bob Hope
December 25	Christmas: Perry Como, Patti Page and Eddie Fisher

1954

January 1	Bing Crosby
January 8	Joan Caulfield of *My Favorite Husband*
January 15	Martha Raye in *The Martha Raye Show*
January 22	Jayne Meadows, Henry Morgan and Joan Bennett of *I've Got a Secret*
January 29	Robert Montgomery of *Robert Montgomery Presents*
February 5	Jack Benny of *The Jack Benny Show*
February 12	Red Buttons of *The Red Buttons Show*
February 19	Ann Sothern of *Private Secretary*
February 26	Liberace of *The Liberace Show*
March 5	Frank Parker and Marion Marlowe of *Arthur Godfrey's Talent Scouts*
March 12	Maria Riva of *Studio One*
March 19	Groucho Marx of *You Bet Your Life*
March 26	Jackie Gleason of *The Jackie Gleason Show*
April 2	Eve Arden of *Our Miss Brooks*
April 9	Charlie Applewhite and Milton Berle of *The Milton Berle Show*
April 16	TV Guide Gold Medal Awards
April 23	Lucille Ball of *I Love Lucy*
April 30	Ben Alexander and Jack Webb of *Dragnet*
May 7	Harriet Nelson, Ricky Nelson and David Nelson of *The Adventures of Ozzie & Harriet*
May 14	Frank Sinatra in *Anything Goes*
May 21	Patricia Benoit and Wally Cox of *Mr. Peepers*
May 28	Gale Storm of *My Little Margie*
June 4	Arthur Godfrey of *Arthur Godfrey's Talent Scouts*
June 11	Ben Blue and Alan Young of *Saturday Night Revue*
June 18	Rise Stevens and Ed Sullivan of *Toast of the Town*
June 25	Bob Smith and Howdy Doody of *Howdy Doody*
July 2	Joan Davis and Jim Backus of *I Married Joan*
July 9	Arlene Francis of *What's My Line?*
July 17	Roy Rogers of *The Roy Rogers Show*
July 24	Jack Webb and Ann Robinson of *Dragnet*
July 31	William Bendix of *The Life of Riley*
August 7	Perry Como and friends of *The Perry Como Show*
August 14	Dean Martin and Jerry Lewis
August 21	Jayne Meadows and Steve Allen of *What's My Line?*
August 28	Roxanne of *Beat the Clock*
September 4	Eddie Fisher of *Coke Time With Eddie Fisher*
September 11	Betty Hutton
September 18	Liberace of *The Liberace Show*
September 25	Fall Preview
October 2	Teresa Wright and Dick Powell of *Climax*
October 9	Lucille Ball of *I Love Lucy*
October 16	Red Buttons of *The Red Buttons Show*
October 23	Walt Disney of *Disneyland*
October 30	Joan Caulfield and Barry Nelson of *My Favorite Husband*
November 6	George Burns and Gracie Allen of *The George Burns and Gracie Allen Show*
November 13	Liberace of *The Liberace Show* and Joanne Rio
November 20	Bebe Daniels and Ralph Edwards of *This Is Your Life*
November 27	Marcia Henderson and Peter Lawford of *Dear Phoebe*
December 4	George Gobel of *The George Gobel Show*
December 11	Marion Marlowe of *Arthur Godfrey and His Friends*
December 18	Imogene Coca of *The Imogene Coca Show*
December 25	Ozzie Nelson, Harriet Nelson, David Nelson and Ricky Nelson of *The Adventures of Ozzie & Harriet*

1955

January 1	Loretta Young of *The Loretta Young Show*
January 8	Arthur Godfrey of *The Arthur Godfrey Show*
January 15	Garry Moore, Bill Cullen, Jayne Meadows, Henry Morgan and Faye Emerson of *I've Got a Secret*
January 22	Ed Sullivan of *Toast of the Town*
January 29	Martha Raye of *The Martha Raye Show*
February 5	Edward R. Murrow of *Person to Person*
February 12	Dorothy Collins, Snooky Lanson, Russell Arms and Gisele MacKenzie of *Your Hit Parade*
February 19	Sid Caesar of *Caesar's Hour*
February 26	Steve Allen of *Tonight* and Judy Holliday
March 5	Liberace of *The Liberace Show*
March 12	Dinah Shore of *The Dinah Shore Show*
March 19	Art Carney of *The Honeymooners*
March 26	Gale Gordon and Eve Arden of *Our Miss Brooks*
April 2	Tony Martin of *The Tony Martin Show*
April 9	Gloria Marshall and Bob Cummings of *The Bob Cummings Show*
April 16	Garry Moore of *The Garry Moore Show*
April 23	Gale Storm of *My Little Margie*
April 30	Buddy Ebsen and Fess Parker of *Davy Crockett*
May 7	Peggy Wood and Robin Morgan of *Mama*
May 14	Perry Como of *The Perry Como Show*
May 21	Audrey Meadows and Jackie Gleason of *The Honeymooners*
May 28	Ralph Edwards of *This Is Your Life*
June 4	Eddie Fisher of *Coke Time With Eddie Fisher*
June 11	Gail Davis of *Annie Oakley*
June 18	Danny Thomas of *Make Room for Daddy*
June 25	Barbara Nichols, Sid Caesar and Cliff Norton of *Caesar Presents*
July 2	Lee Aaker and Rin Tin Tin of *The Adventures of Rin Tin Tin* and Tommy Rettig and Lassie of *Lassie*
July 9	Patti Page of *The Patti Page Show*
July 16	Julius LaRosa of *The Julius LaRosa Show*
July 23	Jack Webb and Janet Leigh of *Dragnet*
July 30	Barbara Whiting and Margaret Whiting of *Those Whiting Girls* and Lucille Ball and Desi Arnaz of *I Love Lucy*
August 6	Art Linkletter of *People Are Funny*
August 13	Roxanne and Bud Collyer of *Beat the Clock*
August 20	Hal March of *The $64,000 Question*
August 27	Groucho Marx of *You Bet Your Life*
September 3	Johnny Carson and Jody Carson of *The Johnny Carson Show*
September 10	Arthur Godfrey of *Arthur Godfrey and His Friends and Talent Scouts*
September 17	Milton Berle and Esther Williams of *The Milton Berle Show*
September 24	Fall Preview
October 1	Mickey Mouse, Jiminy Cricket, David Stollery and Tim Considine of *Mickey Mouse Club*
October 8	George Burns and Gracie Allen of *The George Burns and Gracie Allen Show*
October 15	Richard Boone of *Medic*
October 22	Peggy King and George Gobel of *The George Gobel Show*
October 29	Phil Silvers of *You'll Never Get Rich*
November 5	Nanette Fabray of *Your Show of Shows*
November 12	Liberace of *The Liberace Show*
November 19	Jack Benny of *Shower of Stars*
November 26	Martha Raye of *The Martha Raye Show*
December 3	Peter Lind Hayes and Mary Healy
December 10	Lucille Ball of *I Love Lucy*
December 17	Robert Montgomery of *Robert Montgomery Presents*
December 24	Christmas
December 31	Cleo of *The People's Choice*

1956

January 7	Arthur Godfrey and Goldie of *Arthur Godfrey and His Friends* and *Talent Scouts*
January 14	Loretta Young of *The Loretta Young Show*
January 21	Lawrence Welk of *The Lawrence Welk Show*
January 28	Janis Paige of *It's Always Jan*
February 4	Judy Tyler and Ed Sullivan of *The Ed Sullivan Show*
February 11	Perry Como of *The Perry Como Show*
February 18	Jimmy Durante of *The Jimmy Durante Show*
February 25	Gisele MacKenzie of *Your Hit Parade*
March 3	Lynn Dollar and Hal March of *The $64,000 Question*
March 10	Frances Rafferty and Spring Byington of *December Bride*
March 17	Maurice Evans and Lilli Palmer in *The Taming of the Shrew*
March 24	Dave Garroway of *Today*
March 31	Arlene Francis and John Daly of *What's My Line*
April 7	Jayne Meadows, Garry Moore and Faye Emerson of *I've Got a Secret*
April 14	Grace Kelly
April 21	Nanette Fabray of *Caesar's Hour*
April 28	Red Skelton of *The Red Skelton Show*
May 5	Mitzi Gaynor and George Gobel of *The George Gobel Show*
May 12	Bernadette O'Farrell and Richard Greene of *The Adventures of Robin Hood*
May 19	Phil Silvers and Elisabeth Fraser of *The Phil Silvers Show*
May 26	Alice Lon and Lawrence Welk of *The Lawrence Welk Show*
June 2	Sid Caesar and Janet Blair of *Caesar's Hour*
June 9	Patti Page of *The Patti Page Show*
June 16	Elinor Donahue, Robert Young, Lauren Chapin and Billy Gray of *Father Knows Best*
June 23	Steve Allen of *The Steve Allen Show*
June 30	Bob Cummings of *The Bob Cummings Show*
July 7	Lassie of *Lassie*
July 14	Gordon MacRae and Sheila MacRae of *The Gordon MacRae Show*
July 21	Bill Lundigan and Mary Costa of *Climax*
July 28	Gail Davis of *Annie Oakley*
August 4	Jackie Cooper and Cleo of *The People's Choice*
August 11	Democratic Convention
August 18	GOP Convention
August 25	Esther Williams
September 1	Alice Lon of *The Lawrence Welk Show*
September 8	Elvis Presley
September 15	Fall Preview
September 22	Hal March of *The $64,000 Question*
September 29	Jackie Gleason of *The Jackie Gleason Show*
October 6	Gale Storm of *The Gale Storm Show*
October 13	Harriet Nelson, Ozzie Nelson, David Nelson and Ricky Nelson of *The Adventures of Ozzie & Harriet*
October 20	Perry Como and Phyllis Goodwind of *The Perry Como Show*
October 27	Alfred Hitchcock of *Alfred Hitchcock Presents*
November 3	Edward R. Murrow of *Person to Person*
November 10	Loretta Young of *The Loretta Young Show*
November 17	Buddy Hackett of *Stanley*
November 24	Nanette Fabray in *High Button Shoes*
December 1	George Burns and Gracie Allen of *The George Burns and Gracie Allen Show*
December 8	Victor Borge
December 15	Dinah Shore of *The Dinah Shore Show*
December 22	Christmas
December 29	Jeannie Carson of *Hey, Jeannie*

1957

January 5	Arthur Godfrey of *Arthur Godfrey's Talent Scouts*
January 12	Lucille Ball of *I Love Lucy*
January 19	Jerry Lewis
January 26	Bob Hope
February 2	Jane Wyman of *Jane Wyman Theater*
February 9	Hugh O'Brian of *The Life and Legend of Wyatt Earp*
February 16	Robert Young and Jane Wyatt of *Father Knows Best*
February 23	Charles Van Doren of *Twenty One*
March 2	Dorothy Collins and Gisele MacKenzie of *Your Hit Parade*
March 9	Arthur Godfrey and Pat Boone of *The Arthur Godfrey Show*
March 16	The Emmy Awards
March 23	Tennessee Ernie Ford of *The Ford Show*
March 30	Julie Andrews in Rodgers & Hammerstein's *Cinderella*
April 6	Lawrence Welk of *The Lawrence Welk Show*
April 13	Nanette Fabray of *The Kaiser Aluminum Hour*
April 20	Loretta Young of *The Loretta Young Show*
April 27	Groucho Marx of *You Bet Your Life*
May 4	Hal March and Robert Strom of *The $64,000 Question*
May 11	James Arness of *Gunsmoke*
May 18	Esther Williams of *Lux Video Theatre*
May 25	Sid Caesar of *Caesar's Hour*
June 1	Ida Lupino and Howard Duff of *Mr. Adams and Eve*
June 8	Lassie of *Lassie*
June 15	Red Skelton of *The Red Skelton Show*
June 22	Jack Bailey of *Queen for a Day*

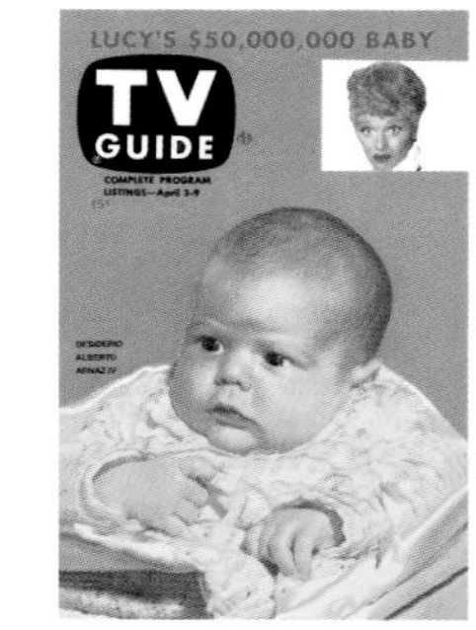

April 3, 1953
PHOTOGRAPHER UNKNOWN

The very first cover of TV Guide featured Lucy and Desi's son, Desiderio Alberto Arnaz IV. Lucille Ball timed her cesarean so that she gave birth the same night Lucy Ricardo did.

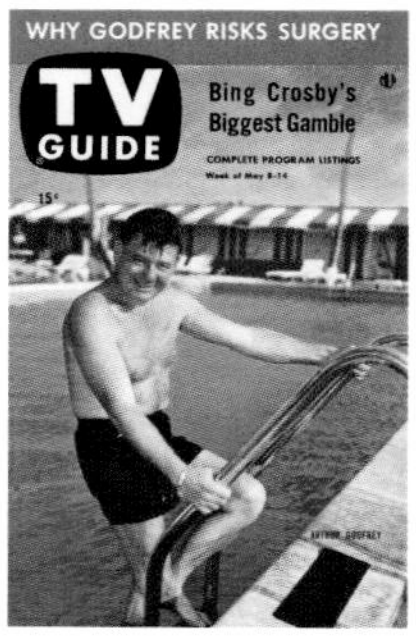

May 8, 1953
PHOTOGRAPHER UNKNOWN

Despite running away from home at 15, Arthur Godfrey became one of the most powerful men in early TV. It is estimated that at one point he was responsible for 12 percent of CBS's TV revenue.

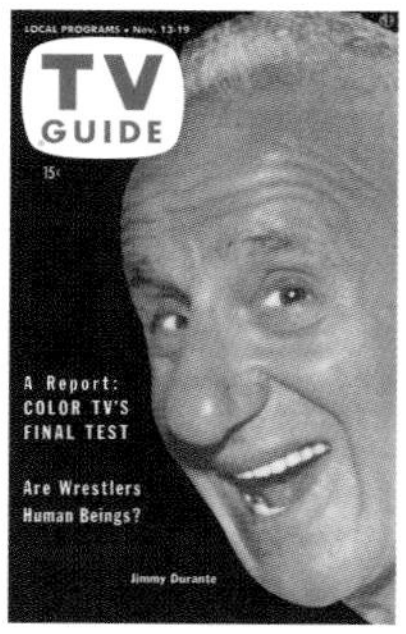

November 13, 1953
PHOTOGRAPHER UNKNOWN

Known as "the Schnoz," beloved vaudeville veteran Jimmy Durante closed each episode of his show with the signature phrase "And good night Mrs. Calabash, wherever you are."

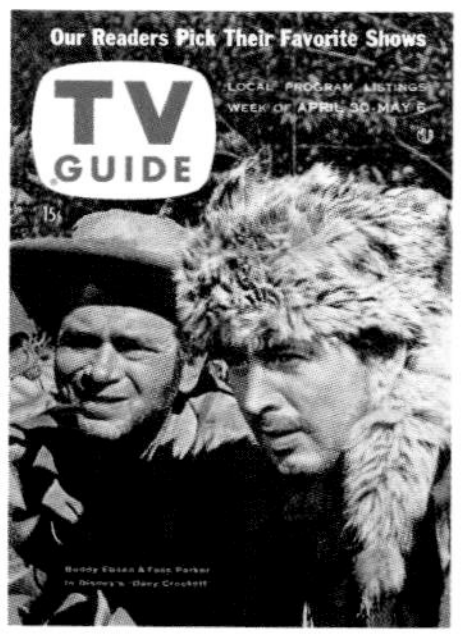

April 30, 1955
BY WALT DISNEY PRODS.

Davy Crockett, starring Fess Parker and Buddy Ebsen, was an early example of Disney programming and a national phenomenon. Ebsen went on to *The Beverly Hillbillies* and *Barnaby Jones*.

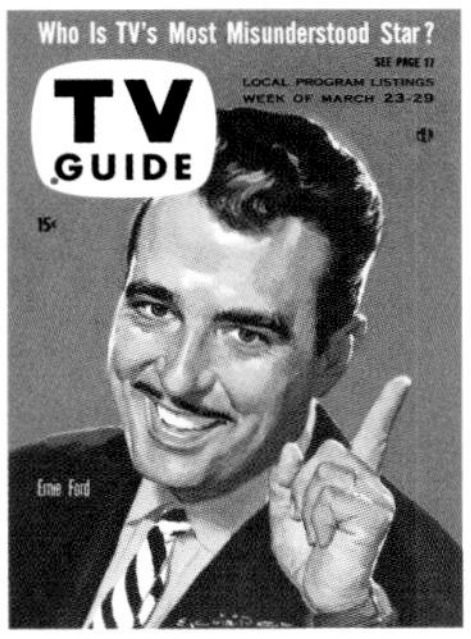

March 23, 1957
BY ERNEST CHIRIAKA

Tennessee Ernie Ford's folksy country charm made him a fixture on the small screen. His star was brightest during his eponymous mid-'50s show, but this comical singer also shined on *I Love Lucy* and *Hee Haw*.

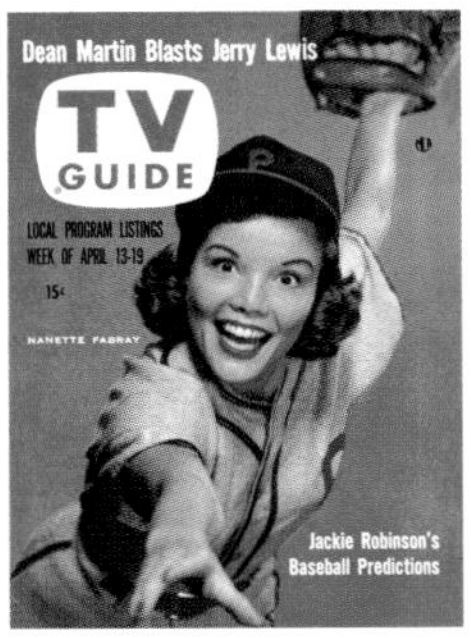

April 13, 1957
BY HERB BALL

Despite a childhood stint in vaudeville, a part in *Our Gang* and time on Broadway, Nanette Fabray found her biggest success on television, including her turn as Sid Caesar's partner-in-laughs on *Your Show of Shows*.

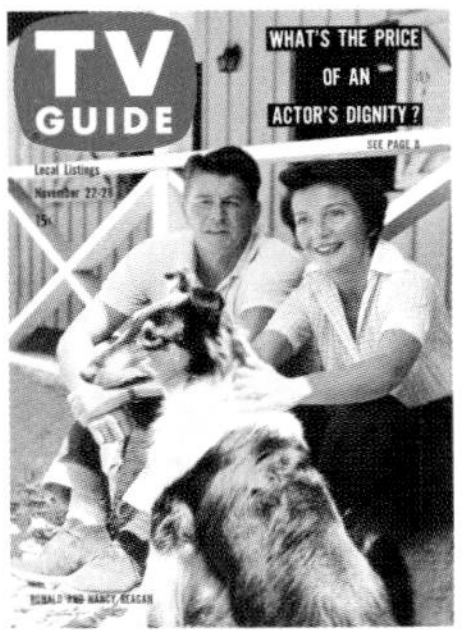

November 22, 1958
BY GARRETT-HOWARD

Originally a minor matinee idol, Ronald Reagan developed his oratorical skills hosting several 1950s TV shows, including *General Electric Theater*. He married aspiring starlet Nancy Davis in 1952.

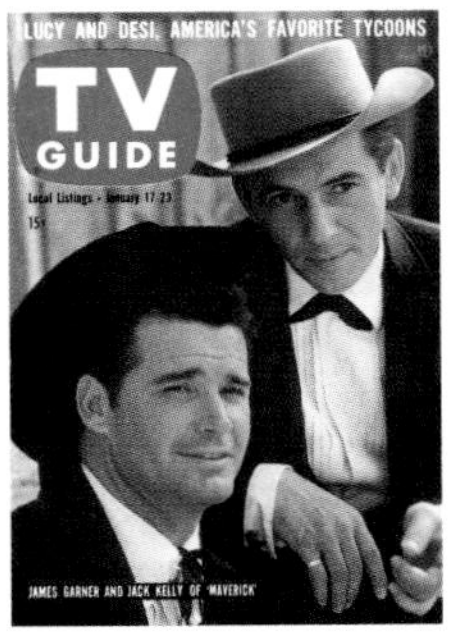

January 17, 1959
BY GENE TRINDL

Before he was an irreverent private detective on *The Rockford Files*, James Garner (with Jack Kelley) was an irreverent gambler in the Old West on *Maverick*.

June 29 Gale Storm of *Oh! Susanna*
July 6 John Daly, Arlene Francis, Bennett Cerf and Dorothy Kilgallen of *What's My Line?*
July 13 Gail Davis of *Annie Oakley*
July 20 Julius LaRosa of *The Julius LaRosa Show*
July 27 Garry Moore of *I've Got a Secret*
August 3 Cleo of *The People's Choice*
August 10 Ann B. Davis and Bob Cummings of *The Bob Cummings Show*
August 17 Phil Silvers of *The Phil Silvers Show*
August 24 Marjorie Lord and Danny Thomas of *The Danny Thomas Show*
August 31 Clint Walker of *Cheyenne*
September 7 Janette Davis and Arthur Godfrey of *Arthur Godfrey's Talent Scouts*
September 14 Fall Preview
September 21 Pat Boone of *The Pat Boone-Chevy Showroom*
September 28 George Burns and Gracie Allen of *The George Burns and Gracie Allen Show*
October 5 Joan Caulfield of *Sally*
October 12 "This Is the Week to Watch": Mickey Rooney, Queen Elizabeth II, Rosemary Clooney, Bing Crosby, Jane Powell and Eddie "Rochester" Anderson
October 19 Loretta Young of *The Loretta Young Show*
October 26 Peter Lawford and Phyllis Kirk of *The Thin Man*
November 2 Lucille Ball of *I Love Lucy*
November 9 James Garner of *Maverick*
November 16 Patti Page of *The Big Record*
November 25 Mary Martin in *Annie Get Your Gun*
November 30 Alfred Hitchcock of *Alfred Hitchcock Presents*
December 7 Dinah Shore of *The Dinah Shore Show*
December 14 Walt Disney, Jiminy Cricket, Mickey Mouse, Pluto, Tinkerbell and Donald Duck of *Disneyland*
December 21 Christmas
December 28 Ricky Nelson of *The Adventures of Ozzie & Harriet*

1958
January 4 Lawrence Welk of *The Lawrence Welk Show*
January 11 Gisele MacKenzie of *The Gisele MacKenzie Show*
January 18 John Payne of *The Restless Gun*
January 25 Sid Caesar and Imogene Coca of *The Sid Caesar Show*
February 1 Walter Winchell
February 8 Tab Hunter and Peggy King in *Hans Brinker*
February 15 "A Great Week"
February 22 Rosemary Clooney of *The Lux Show Starring Rosemary Clooney*
March 1 Lassie of *Lassie*
March 8 Arthur Godfrey of *Arthur Godfrey's Talent Scouts*
March 15 Amanda Blake and James Arness of *Gunsmoke*
March 22 Perry Como of *The Perry Como Show*
March 29 Tennessee Ernie Ford of *The Ford Show*
April 5 Gale Storm of *Oh! Susanna*
April 12 Hugh O'Brian of *The Life and Legend of Wyatt Earp*
April 19 Polly Bergen of *To Tell the Truth*
April 26 Guy Williams of *Zorro*
May 3 Shirley Temple of *Shirley Temple's Storybook*
May 10 Richard Boone of *Have Gun, Will Travel*
May 17 Danny Thomas, Marjorie Lord, Angela Cartwright and Sherry Jackson of *The Danny Thomas Show*
May 24 Dick Clark of *American Bandstand* and *The Dick Clark Show*
May 31 Phyllis Kirk of *The Thin Man*
June 7 Pat Boone of *The Pat Boone-Chevy Showroom*
June 14 Robert Young and Jane Wyatt of *Father Knows Best*
June 21 Ed Sullivan of *The Ed Sullivan Show*
June 28 Jerry Mathers of *Leave It to Beaver*
July 5 Bill Cullen of *The Price Is Right*
July 12 Lucille Ball of *The Lucy-Desi Comedy Hour*
July 19 Dale Robertson of *Tales of Wells Fargo*
July 26 Marvin Miller and Paula Raymond of *The Millionaire*
August 2 Walter Brennan of *The Real McCoys*
August 9 Steve Lawrence and Eydie Gorme of *Steve Allen Presents the Steve Lawrence-Eydie Gorme Show*
August 16 Robert Horton and Ward Bond of *Wagon Train*
August 23 Edie Adams and Janet Blair of *The Chevy Show*
August 30 Polly Bergen, Bud Collyer and Kitty Carlisle of *To Tell the Truth*
September 6 Arthur Godfrey of *The Arthur Godfrey Show*
September 13 Kathy Lennon, Dianne Lennon, Peggy Lennon, Janet Lennon and Lawrence Welk of *The Lawrence Welk Show*
September 20 Fall Preview
September 27 Garry Moore of *The Garry Moore Show*
October 4 Dick Clark of *American Bandstand* and *The Dick Clark Show*
October 11 Fred Astaire and Barrie Chase
October 18 Perry Como of *The Perry Como Show*
October 25 George Burns of *The George Burns Show*
November 1 Jack Paar of *The Jack Paar Show*
November 8 Loretta Young of *The Loretta Young Show*
November 15 Warner Anderson and Tom Tully of *The Lineup*
November 22 Ronald Reagan and Nancy Reagan of *General Electric Theater*
November 29 Victor Borge in *Comedy and Music*
December 6 James Arness of *Gunsmoke*
December 13 Danny Thomas of *The Danny Thomas Show*
December 20 Christmas
December 27 David Nelson and Ricky Nelson of *The Adventures of Ozzie & Harriet*

1959
January 3 Lola Albright and Craig Stevens of *Peter Gunn*
January 10 Milton Berle of *The Kraft Music Hall*
January 17 James Garner and Jack Kelly of *Maverick*
January 24 Red Skelton of *The Red Skelton Show*
January 31 George Gobel of *The George Gobel Show*
February 7 Johnny Crawford and Chuck Connors of *The Rifleman*
February 14 Alfred Hitchcock of *Alfred Hitchcock Presents*
February 21 Barbara Hale and Raymond Burr of *Perry Mason*
February 28 Richard Boone of *Have Gun, Will Travel*
March 7 Walter Brennan of *The Real McCoys*
March 14 Arthur Godfrey of *Arthur Godfrey and His Friends*
March 21 Ann Sothern of *The Ann Sothern Show*
March 28 Tennessee Ernie Ford of *The Ford Show*
April 4 Efrem Zimbalist Jr. and Roger Smith of *77 Sunset Strip*
April 11 Ward Bond of *Wagon Train*
April 18 Dinah Shore of *The Dinah Shore Show*
April 25 Dick Powell of *Dick Powell's Zane Grey Theater*
May 2 Hugh O'Brian of *The Life and Legend of Wyatt Earp*
May 9 Edd Byrnes of *77 Sunset Strip*
May 16 Loretta Young of *The Loretta Young Show*
May 23 Bob Hope in *Frances Langford Presents*
May 30 Steve McQueen of *Wanted—Dead or Alive*
June 6 Gale Storm of *The Gale Storm Show*
June 13 Pat Boone of *The Pat Boone Show*
June 20 Robert Young and Lauren Chapin of *Father Knows Best*
June 27 Lloyd Bridges of *Sea Hunt*
July 4 Jon Provost and Lassie of *Lassie*
July 11 Lola Albright and Craig Stevens of *Peter Gunn*
July 18 Janet Blair of *The Blair & Raitt Show*
July 25 John Russell of *The Lawman*
August 1 Dave Garroway of *Today*
August 8 Donna Reed of *The Donna Reed Show*
August 15 Lawrence Welk of *The Lawrence Welk Show*
August 22 Bess Myerson, Henry Morgan, Betsy Palmer and Bill Cullen of *I've Got a Secret*
August 29 Dick Clark of *American Bandstand*
September 5 James Garner and Jack Kelly of *Maverick*
September 12 Arthur Godfrey of *Arthur Godfrey and His Friends*
September 19 Fall Preview
September 26 Jackie Cooper and Abby Dalton of *Hennesey*
October 3 June Allyson of *The June Allyson Show*
October 10 Robert Taylor of *The Detectives*
October 17 Ingrid Bergman in *The Turn of the Screw*
October 24 Jay North of *Dennis the Menace*
October 31 Fred Astaire and Barrie Chase in *Astaire Time*
November 7 Jack Benny of *The Jack Benny Show*
November 14 Perry Como of *The Perry Como Show*
November 21 Clint Walker of *Cheyenne*
November 28 Art Carney of *The Honeymooners*
December 5 Gayle Polayes, Joan Chandler and Dwayne Hickman of *The Many Loves of Dobie Gillis*
December 12 Danny Thomas of *The Danny Thomas Show*
December 19 Christmas
December 26 Loretta Young of *The Loretta Young Show*

1960
January 2 Dennis Weaver, Amanda Blake, Milburn Stone and James Arness of *Gunsmoke*
January 9 Jane Wyatt and Elinor Donahue of *Father Knows Best*
January 16 Cliff Arquette of *The Charley Weaver Show*
January 23 Walter Brennan and Kathy Nolan of *The Real McCoys*
January 30 Garry Moore of *The Garry Moore Show*
February 6 Richard Boone of *Have Gun, Will Travel*
February 13 John Vivyan and Pippa Scott of *Mr. Lucky* and Lola Albright and Craig Stevens of *Peter Gunn*
February 20 Red Skelton of *The Red Skelton Show*
February 27 Robert Stack of *The Untouchables*
March 5 Jay North of *Dennis the Menace*
March 12 Chuck Connors of *The Rifleman*
March 19 Raymond Burr and Barbara Hale of *Perry Mason*
March 26 Donna Reed of *The Donna Reed Show*
April 2 Tennessee Ernie Ford of *The Tennessee Ernie Ford Show*
April 9 Efrem Zimbalist Jr. of *77 Sunset Strip*
April 16 Ann Sothern of *The Ann Sothern Show*
April 23 Hoagy Carmichael, John Smith, Bobby Crawford Jr. and Robert Fuller of *Laramie*
April 30 June Lockhart, Jon Provost and Lassie of *Lassie*
May 7 Elvis Presley and Frank Sinatra
May 14 Ernie Kovacs and Edie Adams of *Take a Good Look*
May 21 Gene Barry of *Bat Masterson*
May 28 Poncie Ponce and Connie Stevens of *Hawaiian Eye*
June 4 Darren McGavin of *Riverboat*
June 11 Noreen Corcoran, John Forsythe and Sammee Tong of *Bachelor Father*
June 18 Gardner McKay of *Adventures in Paradise*
June 25 Lorne Greene, Pernell Roberts, Dan Blocker and Michael Landon of *Bonanza*
July 2 Lawrence Welk of *The Lawrence Welk Show*
July 9 David Brinkley and Chet Huntley of *The Huntley-Brinkley Report*
July 16 Lucille Ball
July 23 John Daly of *What's My Line?*
July 30 Mike Connors and Ruta Lee of *Tightrope*
August 6 Esther Williams
August 13 Nick Adams of *The Rebel*
August 20 Betsy Palmer
August 27 Roger Smith, Efrem Zimbalist Jr., Edd Byrnes and Richard Long of *77 Sunset Strip*
September 3 Arlene Francis of *What's My Line?*
September 10 Dick Clark of *American Bandstand*
September 17 June Allyson and Dick Powell of *The DuPont Show With June Allyson*
September 24 Fall Preview
October 1 Dinah Shore of *The Dinah Shore Chevy Show*
October 8 Arthur Godfrey of *Candid Camera*
October 15 Marion Lorne and Carol Burnett of *The Garry Moore Show*
October 22 Debbie Reynolds
October 29 Danny Kaye
November 5 Loretta Young of *The Loretta Young Show*
November 12 Fred MacMurray and Tramp of *My Three Sons*
November 19 Ward Bond of *Wagon Train*
November 26 Abby Dalton, Jackie Cooper, Roscoe Karns and Henry Kulky of *Hennesey*
December 3 Shirley Temple of *The Shirley Temple Show*
December 10 Amanda Blake and James Arness of *Gunsmoke*
December 17 Sebastian Cabot, Anthony George and Doug McClure of *Checkmate*
December 24 Christmas
December 31 Dorothy Provine of *The Roaring Twenties*

1961
January 7 Richard Boone of *Have Gun, Will Travel*
January 14 Perry Como of *The Perry Como Show*
January 21 Barbara Stanwyck of *The Barbara Stanwyck Show*
January 28 Andy Griffith and Ronny Howard of *The Andy Griffith Show*
February 4 Eric Fleming and Clint Eastwood of *Rawhide*
February 11 Lola Albright and Craig Stevens of *Peter Gunn*
February 18 Nanette Fabray of *Westinghouse Playhouse*
February 25 Dorothy Collins, Allen Funt and Arthur Godfrey of *Candid Camera*
March 4 Raymond Burr of *Perry Mason*
March 11 Robert Stack of *The Untouchables*
March 18 Marjorie Lord of *The Danny Thomas Show*
March 25 Alfred Hitchcock of *Alfred Hitchcock Presents*
April 1 Roger Smith of *77 Sunset Strip*
April 8 Lori Martin and King of *National Velvet*
April 15 Mitch Miller of *Sing Along With Mitch*
April 22 Garry Moore of *The Garry Moore Show*
April 29 Rod Taylor of *Hong Kong*
May 6 Donna Reed of *The Donna Reed Show*
May 13 Lorne Greene of *Bonanza*
May 20 Walter Brennan and Richard Crenna of *The Real McCoys*
May 27 Ronald Reagan and Dorothy Malone of *General Electric Theater*
June 3 Paul Burke and Horace McMahon of *Naked City*
June 10 Nanette Fabray and Efrem Zimbalist Jr.
June 17 Lawrence Welk of *The Lawrence Welk Show*
June 24 John McIntire and Robert Horton of *Wagon Train*
July 1 The Flintstones of *The Flintstones*
July 8 Harry Morgan and Cara Williams of *Pete and Gladys*
July 15 Gardner McKay of *Adventures in Paradise*
July 22 Martin Milner and George Maharis of *Route 66*
July 29 Bob Keeshan of *Captain Kangaroo*
August 5 Fred MacMurray, William Frawley and Stanley Livingston of *My Three Sons*
August 12 "The World of Soap Opera"
August 19 Troy Donahue of *Surfside 6*
August 26 Hugh Downs of *The Jack Paar Show*
September 2 Dwayne Hickman and Bob Denver of *The Many Loves of Dobie Gillis*
September 9 Sebastian Cabot, Anthony George and Doug McClure of *Checkmate*
September 16 Fall Preview
September 23 Mitch Miller of *Sing Along With Mitch*
September 30 Carol Burnett of *The Garry Moore Show*
October 7 Walter Cronkite of *CBS Reports* and Dwight D. Eisenhower
October 14 Red Skelton of *The Red Skelton Show*
October 21 Joe E. Ross and Fred Gwynne of *Car 54, Where Are You?*
October 28 "This Is the Week to Watch": Ernie Kovacs, Bob Hope in *The World of Bob Hope*, Joan Crawford in *The Ziegfeld Touch* and Sir Laurence Olivier in *The Power and the Glory*
November 4 Dorothy Provine of *The Roaring Twenties*
November 11 Robert Stack of *The Untouchables* and Mrs. Robert Stack
November 18 Garry Moore, Durward Kirby and Marion Lorne of *The Garry Moore Show*
November 25 Amanda Blake and James Arness of *Gunsmoke*
December 2 Joey Bishop of *The Joey Bishop Show*
December 9 Dick Van Dyke and Mary Tyler Moore of *The Dick Van Dyke Show*
December 16 Raymond Massey and Richard Chamberlain of *Dr. Kildare*

December 23 Christmas
December 30 Cynthia Pepper of *Margie*

1962

January 6 Vince Edwards of *Ben Casey*
January 13 Bobby Buntrock, Shirley Booth and dog of *Hazel*
January 20 Chuck Connors of *The Rifleman*
January 27 Myrna Fahey of *Father of the Bride*
February 3 Mark Richman of *Cain's Hundred*
February 10 Jacqueline Kennedy
February 17 Danny Thomas of *The Danny Thomas Show*
February 24 Troy Donahue of *Surfside 6*
March 3 Raymond Burr and Barbara Hale of *Perry Mason*
March 10 Jack Paar of *The Jack Paar Show*
March 17 E.G. Marshall and Robert Reed of *The Defenders*
March 24 Dick Powell of *The Dick Powell Show*
March 31 Alan Young and Mister Ed of *Mister Ed*
April 7 John McIntire of *Wagon Train*
April 14 George Maharis and Martin Milner of *Route 66*
April 21 Connie Stevens of *Hawaiian Eye*
April 28 Ron Harper and Robert Lansing of *87th Precinct*
May 5 Sheila James and Dwayne Hickman of *The Many Loves of Dobie Gillis*
May 12 Don Knotts of *The Andy Griffith Show*
May 19 Paul Burke of *Naked City*
May 26 Fred MacMurray and Stanley Livingston of *My Three Sons*
June 2 Mary Tyler Moore of *The Dick Van Dyke Show*
June 9 Efrem Zimbalist Jr. of *77 Sunset Strip*
June 16 Raymond Massey and Richard Chamberlain of *Dr. Kildare*
June 23 Arlene Francis of *What's My Line?*
June 30 Mitch Miller of *Sing Along With Mitch*
July 7 David Brinkley of NBC News
July 14 Sebastian Cabot and Anthony George of *Checkmate*
July 21 Donna Reed of *The Donna Reed Show*
July 28 Bill Cullen and Barbara Benner of *The Price Is Right*
August 4 Gale Gordon and Jay North of *Dennis the Menace*
August 11 Robert Stack of *The Untouchables*
August 18 Garry Moore, Bess Myerson, Betsy Palmer, Henry Morgan and Bill Cullen of *I've Got a Secret*
August 25 Lawrence Welk of *The Lawrence Welk Show*
September 1 Connie Stevens and Troy Donahue of *Hawaiian Eye*
September 8 Lorne Greene, Michael Landon and Dan Blocker of *Bonanza*
September 15 Fall Preview
September 22 Vincent Edwards of *Ben Casey*
September 29 Lucille Ball of *The Lucy Show*
October 6 Shirley Booth and Don DeFore of *Hazel*
October 13 Jackie Gleason of *The Jackie Gleason Show*
October 20 Loretta Young of *The Loretta Young Show*
October 27 Richard Rust and Edmond O'Brien of *Sam Benedict*
November 3 Stanley Holloway of *Our Man Higgins*
November 10 Donna Douglas, Max Baer Jr., Buddy Ebsen and Irene Ryan of *The Beverly Hillbillies*
November 17 Jack Lord of *Stoney Burke*
November 24 Jacqueline Kennedy
December 1 Marty Ingels and John Astin of *I'm Dickens—He's Fenster*
December 8 Dick Van Dyke of *The Dick Van Dyke Show*
December 15 Zina Bethune and Shirl Conway of *The Nurses*
December 22 Christmas
December 29 Edie Adams

1963

January 5 Bettye Ackerman, Vincent Edwards and Sam Jaffe of *Ben Casey*
January 12 Arnold Palmer
January 19 Joe E. Ross and Fred Gwynne of *Car 54, Where Are You?*
January 26 George Maharis and Martin Milner of *Route 66*
February 2 Jack Webb of *Dragnet*
February 9 Ernest Borgnine of *McHale's Navy*
February 16 Princess Grace
February 23 Carol Burnett of *The Garry Moore Show*
March 2 Wendell Corey and Jack Ging of *The Eleventh Hour*
March 9 Donna Douglas and Buddy Ebsen of *The Beverly Hillbillies*
March 16 Richard Chamberlain of *Dr. Kildare*
March 23 Andy Williams of *The Andy Williams Show*
March 30 Michael Landon, Dan Blocker, Lorne Greene and Pernell Roberts of *Bonanza*
April 6 Lucille Ball of *The Lucy Show*
April 13 Richard Egan of *Empire*
April 20 Red Skelton of *The Red Skelton Show*
April 27 William Talman and Raymond Burr of *Perry Mason*
May 4 Roberta Shore, Lee J. Cobb and James Drury of *The Virginian*
May 11 Don Knotts, Ronny Howard and Andy Griffith of *The Andy Griffith Show*
May 18 E.G. Marshall and Robert Reed of *The Defenders*
May 25 Lawrence Welk of *The Lawrence Welk Show*
June 1 Dorothy Loudon and Garry Moore of *The Garry Moore Show*
June 8 Johnny Carson of *The Tonight Show*
June 15 Vic Morrow and Rick Jason of *Combat*
June 22 Durward Kirby, Allen Funt and Marilyn Van Derber of *Candid Camera*
June 29 Donna Reed and Carl Betz of *The Donna Reed Show*
July 6 Martin Milner and Glenn Corbett of *Route 66*
July 13 Vic Damone, Gloria Neil and Quinn O'Hara of *The Lively Ones*
July 20 Dennis Weaver and James Arness of *Gunsmoke*
July 27 "The Odd Science of Picking Game-Show Contestants"
August 3 Morey Amsterdam and Richard Deacon of *The Dick Van Dyke Show*
August 10 Garry Moore, Betsy Palmer, Bill Cullen, Henry Morgan and Bess Myerson of *I've Got a Secret*
August 17 Fred MacMurray of *My Three Sons*
August 24 June Lockhart, Lassie and Jon Provost of *Lassie*
August 31 Richard Boone of *The Richard Boone Show*
September 7 Irene Ryan and Donna Douglas of *The Beverly Hillbillies*
September 14 Fall Preview
September 21 Richard Chamberlain of *Dr. Kildare*
September 28 Inger Stevens of *The Farmer's Daughter*
October 5 Phil Silvers of *The New Phil Silvers Show*
October 12 Ben Gazzara and Chuck Connors of *Arrest and Trial*
October 19 Judy Garland of *The Judy Garland Show*
October 26 Roberta Shore and Lee J. Cobb of *The Virginian*
November 2 Bill Bixby and Ray Walston of *My Favorite Martian*
November 9 Carol Burnett in *Calamity Jane*
November 16 James Franciscus and Dean Jagger of *Mr. Novak*
November 23 Gene Barry, Joan Staley, Eileen O'Neill and Sharyn Hillyer of *Burke's Law*
November 30 George C. Scott of *East Side/West Side*
December 7 John McIntire and Robert Fuller of *Wagon Train*
December 14 Rosemary Clooney, Frank Sinatra, Dean Martin, Kathryn Crosby and Bing Crosby
December 21 Christmas
December 28 Patty Duke of *The Patty Duke Show*

1964

January 4 Mary Tyler Moore, Dick Van Dyke and Carl Reiner of *The Dick Van Dyke Show*
January 11 "Hollywood's Favorite Second Tomatoes": Marjorie Lord, June Lockhart, Amanda Blake and Barbara Hale
January 18 Pernell Roberts and Kathie Browne of *Bonanza*
January 25 "America's Long Vigil"
February 1 Danny Kaye and Laurie Ichino of *The Danny Kaye Show*
February 8 Linda Kaye, Pat Woodell, Jeannine Riley and Bea Benadaret of *Petticoat Junction*
February 15 Claudine Longet and Andy Williams of *The Andy Williams Show*
February 22 David Janssen of *The Fugitive*
February 29 Zina Bethune and Shirl Conway of *The Nurses*
March 7 Richard Chamberlain of *Dr. Kildare*
March 14 Irene Ryan, Donna Douglas and Buddy Ebsen of *The Beverly Hillbillies*
March 21 Don Knotts, Andy Griffith and Jim Nabors of *The Andy Griffith Show*
March 28 Lawrence Welk of *The Lawrence Welk Show*
April 4 Vince Edwards of *Ben Casey*
April 11 Bill Bixby and Ray Walston of *My Favorite Martian*
April 18 Dean Jagger and James Franciscus of *Mr. Novak*
April 25 Danny Thomas of *The Danny Thomas Show*
May 2 William Windom and Inger Stevens of *The Farmer's Daughter*
May 9 Vic Morrow and Rick Jason of *Combat*
May 16 Alfred Hitchcock of *Alfred Hitchcock Presents*
May 23 Mary Tyler Moore of *The Dick Van Dyke Show*
May 30 Ernest Borgnine, Tim Conway and Joe Flynn of *McHale's Navy*
June 6 Amanda Blake of *Gunsmoke*
June 13 Fred Flintstone of *The Flintstones*
June 20 Donna Reed of *The Donna Reed Show*
June 27 Johnny Carson of *The Tonight Show* and Joanne Carson
July 4 Raymond Burr of *Perry Mason* and Erle Stanley Gardner
July 11 "The Anchor Men": Howard K. Smith, David Brinkley, Chet Huntley, Edward P. Morgan and Walter Cronkite
July 18 Doug McClure, Roberta Shore and James Drury of *The Virginian*
July 25 Fred MacMurray of *My Three Sons*
August 1 Hugh Downs, Maureen O'Sullivan, Frank Blair and Jack Lescoulie of *Today*
August 8 Gene Barry and Gary Conway of *Burke's Law*
August 15 Frank McGrath, Robert Fuller, Terry Wilson and John McIntire of *Wagon Train*
August 22 E.G. Marshall of *The Defenders*
August 29 Patty Duke, William Schallert and Jean Byron of *The Patty Duke Show*
September 5 Lucille Ball of *The Lucy Show*
September 12 David Janssen and Barry Morse of *The Fugitive*
September 19 Fall Preview
September 26 Dan Blocker of *Bonanza*
October 3 Mia Farrow of *Peyton Place*
October 10 Gig Young, David Niven and Charles Boyer in *The Rogues*
October 17 Lassie and Robert Bray of *Lassie*
October 24 Robert Vaughn of *The Man From U.N.C.L.E.*
October 31 John Astin and Carolyn Jones of *The Addams Family*
November 7 Richard Chamberlain and Daniela Bianchi of *Dr. Kildare*
November 14 Cara Williams of *The Cara Williams Show*
November 21 Jim Nabors of *Gomer Pyle, U.S.M.C.*
November 28 Elizabeth Montgomery of *Bewitched*
December 5 Sammy Jackson and Laurie Sibbald of *No Time for Sergeants*
December 12 Julie Newmar of *My Living Doll*
December 19 Christmas
December 26 Juliet Prowse

1965

January 2 Al Lewis, Fred Gwynne and Yvonne DeCarlo of *The Munsters*
January 9 Kathy Nolan, Lois Roberts, Sheila James and Joan Staley of *Broadside*
January 16 Bob Hope
January 23 Chuck Connors of *Branded*
January 30 Inger Stevens of *The Farmer's Daughter*
February 6 Jackie Gleason of *The Jackie Gleason Show*
February 13 Andy Williams of *The Andy Williams Show*
February 20 Burgess Meredith and James Franciscus of *Mr. Novak*
February 27 Donna Douglas, Irene Ryan and Nancy Kulp of *The Beverly Hillbillies*
March 6 David Janssen of *The Fugitive*
March 13 Lorne Greene, Michael Landon, Dan Blocker and Pernell Roberts of *Bonanza*
March 20 Dorothy Malone of *Peyton Place* with daughters
March 27 Mary Tyler Moore and Dick Van Dyke of *The Dick Van Dyke Show*
April 3 Vince Edwards and Kathy Kersh of *Ben Casey*
April 10 Janet Lake and Walter Brennan of *The Tycoon*
April 17 Robert Vaughn and David McCallum of *The Man From U.N.C.L.E.*
April 24 Andy Griffith of *The Andy Griffith Show*
May 1 Connie Stevens of *Wendy and Me*
May 8 Bob Denver and Tina Louise of *Gilligan's Island*
May 15 Robert Lansing of *Twelve O'Clock High*
May 22 Julie Andrews
May 29 Elizabeth Montgomery and Dick York of *Bewitched*
June 5 Flipper and Brian Kelly of *Flipper*
June 12 Milburn Stone and Amanda Blake of *Gunsmoke*
June 19 Richard Basehart and David Hedison of *Voyage to the Bottom of the Sea*
June 26 Donna McKechnie, Lada Edmund Jr. and Barbara Monte of *Hullabaloo*
July 3 Jimmy Dean of *The Jimmy Dean Show*
July 10 Yvonne DeCarlo and Fred Gwynne of *The Munsters*
July 17 Carl Ballantine, Ernest Borgnine, Tim Conway, Gary Vinson and Joe Flynn of *McHale's Navy*
July 24 Raymond Burr of *Perry Mason*
July 31 Fred MacMurray, Stanley Livingston and Barry Livingston of *My Three Sons*
August 7 Gene Barry of *Burke's Law*
August 14 Robert Bray and Lassie of *Lassie*
August 21 Fess Parker and Patricia Blair of *Daniel Boone*
August 28 Lucille Ball of *The Lucy Show* with Splash
September 4 Dan Blocker, Lorne Greene and Michael Landon of *Bonanza*
September 11 Fall Preview
September 18 "1966 TV Set Buyers' Guide": Adrianne
September 25 Jackie Gleason of *The Jackie Gleason Show*
October 2 Don Adams and Barbara Feldon of *Get Smart*
October 9 Anne Francis of *Honey West*
October 16 Red Skelton of *The Red Skelton Show*
October 23 Chuck Connors of *Branded*
October 30 John Lynn and Carolyn Jones of *The Addams Family*
November 6 June Lockhart and Guy Williams of *Lost in Space*
November 13 Joey Heatherton
November 20 Efrem Zimbalist Jr. of *The F.B.I.*
November 27 Cynthia Lynn and Bob Crane of *Hogan's Heroes*
December 4 Juliet Prowse of *Mona McCluskey*
December 11 Forrest Tucker, Melody Patterson, Ken Berry and Larry Storch of *F Troop*
December 18 Jim Nabors of *Gomer Pyle, U.S.M.C.*
December 25 Christmas

1966

January 1 Carol Channing
January 8 Eva Gabor and Eddie Albert of *Green Acres*
January 15 Robert Culp and Bill Cosby of *I Spy*
January 22 David Janssen of *The Fugitive*
January 29 Patricia Crowley, Mark Miller and Ladadog of *Please Don't Eat the Daisies*
February 5 Barbara Eden and Larry Hagman of *I Dream of Jeannie*
February 12 Ryan O'Neal and Barbara Parkins of *Peyton Place*
February 19 Ben Gazzara of *Run for Your Life*
February 26 Charles Briles, Linda Evans and Barbara Stanwyck of *The Big Valley*
March 5 Barbara Feldon of *Get Smart*
March 12 Donna Douglas, Irene Ryan, Buddy Ebsen and Max Baer Jr. of *The Beverly Hillbillies*
March 19 David McCallum and Robert Vaughn of *The Man From U.N.C.L.E.*
March 26 Adam West of *Batman*
April 2 Dean Martin of *The Dean Martin Show*
April 9 Roy Thinnes of *The Long, Hot Summer*
April 16 Lori Saunders, Linda Kaye and Gunilla Hutton of *Petticoat Junction*
April 23 Andy Williams of *The Andy Williams Show*
April 30 Lucille Ball of *The Lucy Show*
May 7 Lyndon B. Johnson and Ray Scherer
May 14 Frank Sinatra
May 21 Robert Conrad and Ross Martin of *The Wild Wild West*
May 28 Sally Field of *Gidget*

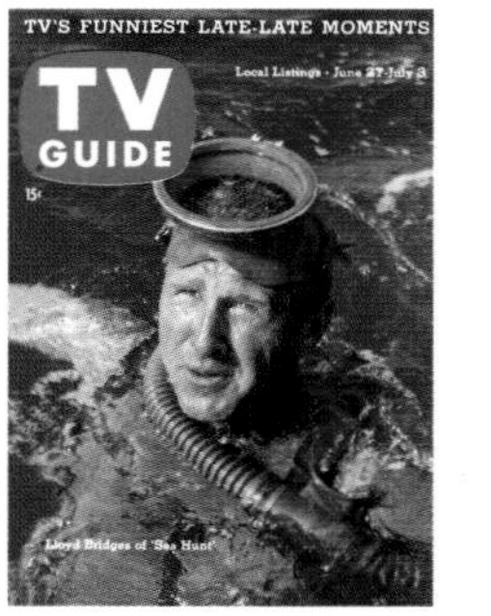

June 27, 1959
BY RUSS HALFORD

One of the most popular shows of the '50s, *Seahunt* starred, almost exclusively, Lloyd Bridges, patriarch of the Bridges family—though son Beau made several appearances as a boy.

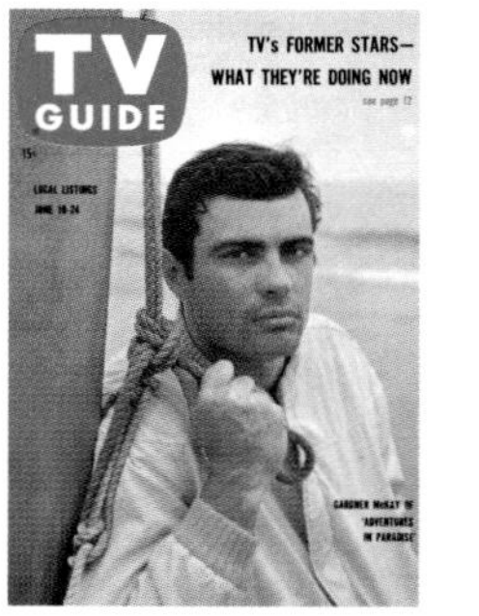

June 18, 1960
BY SHERMAN WEISBURD

James Michener created *Adventures in Paradise* and then dropped out. Viewers, though, stuck around for three seasons to watch the South Seas adventures of hunky Gardner McKay.

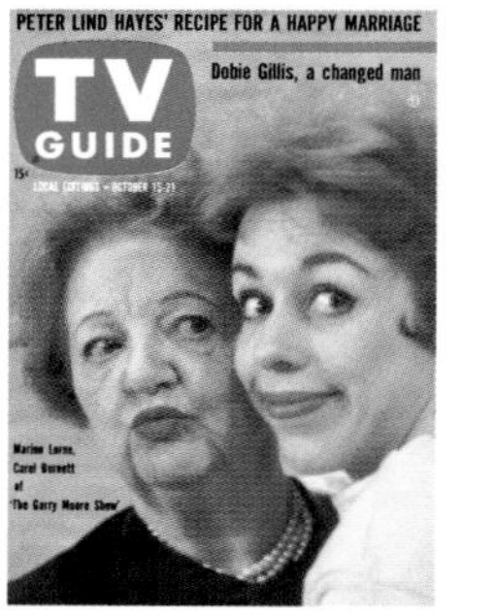

October 15, 1960
BY CURT GUNTHER

Carol Burnett's first of 16 appearances on TV Guide's cover came thanks to her star-making role on *The Garry Moore Show*. Also shown is Marion Lorne, who went on to play Aunt Clara on *Bewitched*.

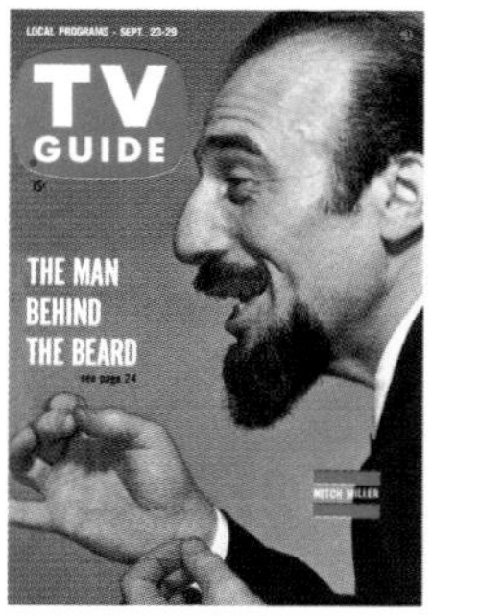

September 23, 1961
BY PHILIPPE HALSMAN

Even after rock and roll had taken hold, *Sing Along With Mitch* (Mitch Miller, that is) made it OK to love the old standards. With the help of the lyrics flashing on the TV screen, anyone could be a star in their own living room.

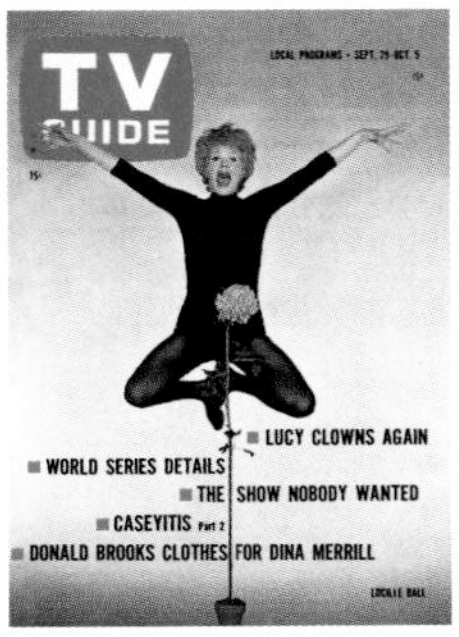

September 29, 1962
BY PHILIPPE HALSMAN

Lucille Ball holds the distinction of gracing more covers of TV Guide than any other individual: 34, as of the magazine's 50th anniversary. It's a record she'll most likely keep.

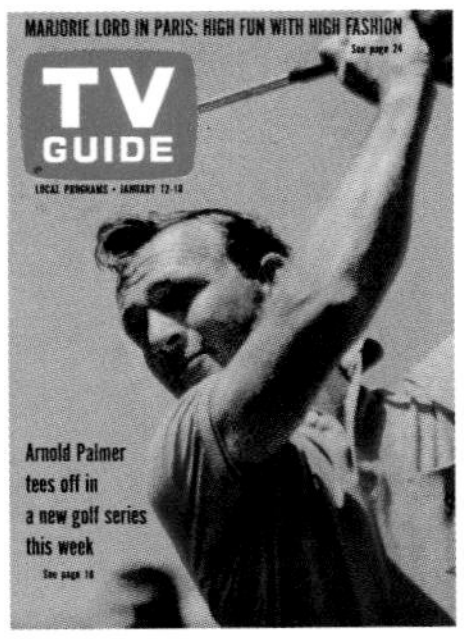

January 12, 1963
BY RUSS HALFORD

Before Arnold Palmer, golfers were known for being cool and quiet. With his passion and charisma, this telegenic pro has been called the perfect figure to usher in golf's television era.

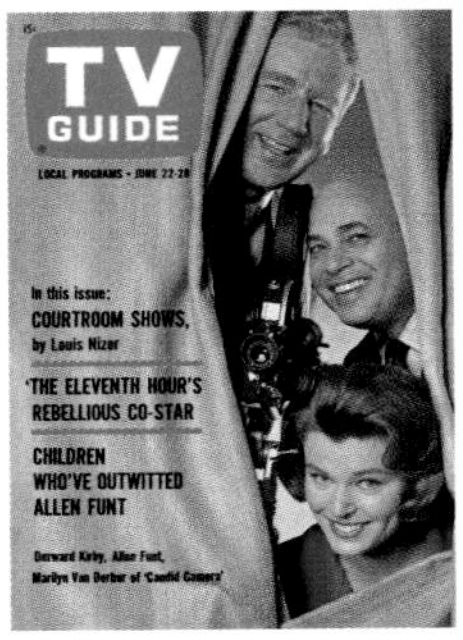

June 22, 1963
BY PHILIPPE HALSMAN

One of the original "reality" shows, *Candid Camera* filmed unsuspecting folks set up in odd and crazy pranks. Allen Funt (center) hosted various incarnations since its 1948 debut.

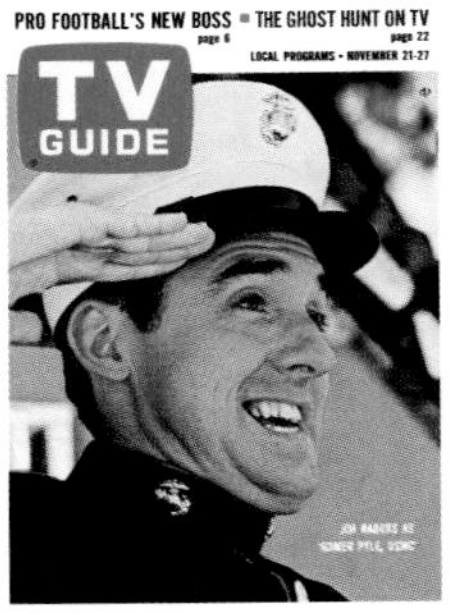

November 21, 1964
BY GENE TRINDL

The Andy Griffith Show spun off two popular comedies: *Mayberry R.F.D.* and *Gomer Pyle, U.S.M.C.*, with Jim Nabors as the dim but lovable bumpkin gone military.

June 4	Andy Griffith of *The Andy Griffith Show*
June 11	Tina Louise, Alan Hale Jr. and Bob Denver of *Gilligan's Island*
June 18	Elizabeth Montgomery, Agnes Moorehead and Tabitha of *Bewitched*
June 25	William Smith, Peter Brown, Philip Carey and Neville Brand of *Laredo*
July 2	Walter Cronkite of *CBS Evening News*
July 9	Brian Kelly and Flipper of *Flipper*
July 16	Fred MacMurray and William Demarest of *My Three Sons*
July 23	Efrem Zimbalist Jr. and Stephen Brooks of *The F.B.I.*
July 30	Johnny Carson of *The Tonight Show*
August 6	Marshall Thompson and Clarence of *Daktari*
August 13	Melody Patterson and Larry Storch of *F Troop*
August 20	Red Skelton of *The Red Skelton Show*
August 27	Barbara Feldon, Don Adams and K-13 of *Get Smart*
September 3	Eva Gabor of *Green Acres*
September 10	Fall Preview
September 17	"1967 TV Set Buyers' Guide": Joey Heatherton
September 24	Barbara Eden of *I Dream of Jeannie*
October 1	"The Vietnam War: Is TV Giving Us the Picture?"
October 8	Jim Nabors of *Gomer Pyle, U.S.M.C.*
October 15	Peter Deuel and Judy Carne of *Love on a Rooftop*
October 22	Lucille Ball of *The Lucy Show*
October 29	Van Williams and Bruce Lee of *The Green Hornet*
November 5	Robert Vaughn and David McCallum of *The Man From U.N.C.L.E.*
November 12	Marlo Thomas of *That Girl*
November 19	Bob Crane and Robert Clary of *Hogan's Heroes*
November 26	Ron Ely of *Tarzan*
December 3	Lawrence Casey, Chris George and Justin Tarr of *The Rat Patrol*
December 10	James Arness of *Gunsmoke*
December 17	Michael Callan and Patricia Harty of *Occasional Wife*
December 24	Christmas
December 31	Stefanie Powers of *The Girl From U.N.C.L.E.*

1967

January 7	Ben Gazzara of *Run for Your Life*
January 14	Art Carney of *The Jackie Gleason Show*
January 21	Diana Rigg and Patrick Macnee of *The Avengers*
January 28	Mickey Dolenz, Peter Tork, Mike Nesmith and Davy Jones of *The Monkees*
February 4	Dale Robertson of *The Iron Horse*
February 11	Steven Hill, Barbara Bain and Martin Landau of *Mission: Impossible*
February 18	Dean Martin of *The Dean Martin Show*
February 25	Phyllis Diller of *The Pruitts of Southampton*
March 4	William Shatner and Leonard Nimoy of *Star Trek*
March 11	Dorothy Malone of *Peyton Place*
March 18	Jackie Gleason of *The Jackie Gleason Show*
March 25	Robert Culp and Bill Cosby of *I Spy*
April 1	Cheryl Miller and Judy of *Daktari*
April 8	Dick Van Dyke
April 15	"The Starlet, 1967": Karen Jensen and Jeff Scott
April 22	Anissa Jones, Sebastian Cabot and Brian Keith of *Family Affair*
April 29	Lawrence Welk of *The Lawrence Welk Show*
May 6	Harry Morgan and Jack Webb of *Dragnet '67*
May 13	Elizabeth Montgomery of *Bewitched*
May 20	Andy Griffith and Aneta Corsaut of *The Andy Griffith Show*
May 27	Ken Berry, Forrest Tucker and Larry Storch of *F Troop*
June 3	Dennis Cole and Howard Duff of *Felony Squad*
June 10	Dick and Tom Smothers of *The Smothers Brothers Comedy Hour*
June 17	Ed Sullivan of *The Ed Sullivan Show*
June 24	Barbara Feldon and Don Adams of *Get Smart*
July 1	Chet Huntley and David Brinkley of *The Huntley-Brinkley Report*
July 8	Efrem Zimbalist Jr. of *The F.B.I.* and J. Edgar Hoover
July 15	Lucille Ball of *The Lucy Show*
July 22	Michael Landon, Dan Blocker and Lorne Greene of *Bonanza*
July 29	Justin Tarr, Gary Raymond, Lawrence Casey and Chris George of *The Rat Patrol*
August 5	Hugh Downs and Barbara Walters of *Today*
August 12	Mike Douglas of *The Mike Douglas Show*
August 19	Barry Morse and David Janssen of *The Fugitive*
August 26	Jim Nabors of *Gomer Pyle, U.S.M.C.*
September 2	Eddie Albert and Eva Gabor of *Green Acres*
September 9	Fall Preview
September 16	Raymond Burr of *Ironside*
September 23	Mickey Dolenz, Peter Tork, Mike Nesmith and Davy Jones of *The Monkees*
September 30	Sally Field of *The Flying Nun*
October 7	Richard Benjamin, Jack Cassidy and Paula Prentiss of *He & She*
October 14	Johnny Carson of *The Tonight Show*
October 21	Mia Farrow in *Johnny Belinda*
October 28	"Who Killed Hollywood Society?"
November 4	Stuart Whitman of *Cimarron Strip*
November 11	Yvette Mimieux
November 18	William Shatner and Leonard Nimoy of *Star Trek*
November 25	Christopher Carey, Cesare Danova, Rudy Solari, Brendon Boone and Ron Harper of *Garrison's Gorillas*
December 2	Danny Thomas of *The Danny Thomas Hour* and Marlo Thomas of *That Girl*
December 9	Kaye Ballard and Eve Arden of *The Mothers-in-Law*
December 16	Sebastian Cabot of *Family Affair*
December 23	Christmas
December 30	Carol Burnett of *The Carol Burnett Show*

1968

January 6	Robert Conrad of *The Wild Wild West*
January 13	Bob Hope
January 20	Leif Erickson, Linda Cristal and Cameron Mitchell of *The High Chaparral*
January 27	Elizabeth Montgomery of *Bewitched*
February 3	Ben Gazzara in *Run for Your Life*
February 10	Dick and Tom Smothers of *The Smothers Brothers Comedy Hour*
February 17	Efrem Zimbalist Jr. and William Reynolds of *The F.B.I.*
February 24	Joey Bishop of *The Joey Bishop Show*
March 2	David Canary and Lorne Greene of *Bonanza*
March 9	Jackie Gleason of *The Jackie Gleason Show*
March 16	Sally Field and Alejandro Rey of *The Flying Nun*
March 23	Bill Cosby and Robert Culp of *I Spy*
March 30	Lucille Ball of *The Lucy Show*
April 6	Barbara Anderson and Raymond Burr of *Ironside*
April 13	Carl Betz of *Judd, for the Defense*
April 20	Barbara Feldon of *Get Smart*
April 27	Leslie Uggams
May 4	Greg Morris, Peter Graves, Barbara Bain and Martin Landau of *Mission: Impossible*
May 11	Fess Parker, Darby Hinton and Patricia Blair of *Daniel Boone*
May 18	Mike Connors of *Mannix*
May 25	Diana Hyland of *Peyton Place*
June 1	Ed Sullivan of *The Ed Sullivan Show*
June 8	"Salvador Dali's View of Television": Hugh Downs and Johnny Carson
June 15	Linda Cristal and Leif Erickson of *The High Chaparral*
June 22	Toni Helfer
June 29	Robert Wagner of *It Takes a Thief*
July 6	Barbara Eden of *I Dream of Jeannie*
July 13	"The Wondrous Andy Griffith TV Machine": Jim Nabors, Griffith and Don Knotts
July 20	Barbara Stanwyck, Richard Long and Linda Evans of *The Big Valley*
July 27	Joey Heatherton and Frank Sinatra Jr. of *Dean Martin Presents the Golddiggers*
August 3	David Brinkley, Chet Huntley, Walter Cronkite and Howard K. Smith
August 10	Dennis Weaver, Ben, Clint Howard and Beth Brickell of *Gentle Ben*
August 17	Milburn Stone, James Arness and Amanda Blake of *Gunsmoke*
August 24	DeForest Kelley, William Shatner and Leonard Nimoy of *Star Trek*
August 31	Johnny Carson of *The Tonight Show*
September 7	Anissa Jones, Johnnie Whitaker, Kathy Garver and Sebastian Cabot of *Family Affair*
September 14	Fall Preview: Darren McGavin, Doris Day and Tommie Smith
September 21	Dan Rowan and Dick Martin of *Rowan and Martin's Laugh-In*
September 28	Dean Martin of *The Dean Martin Show*
October 5	Fred MacMurray, Tina Cole and Don Grady of *My Three Sons*
October 12	The Olympics
October 19	Jim Nabors
October 26	Hope Lange of *The Ghost and Mrs. Muir*
November 2	Peggy Lipton, Clarence Williams III and Michael Cole of *The Mod Squad*
November 9	Barbara Feldon of *Get Smart*
November 16	Bob Denver and Herb Edelman of *The Good Guys*
November 23	Frank Sinatra
November 30	Ann-Margret
December 7	E.J. Peaker and Robert Morse of *That's Life*
December 14	Diahann Carroll of *Julia*
December 21	Christmas
December 28	Doris Day of *The Doris Day Show*

1969

January 4	David Soul, Bridget Hanley, Bobby Sherman and Robert Brown of *Here Come the Brides*
January 11	Bob Hope
January 18	Darren McGavin in *The Outsider*
January 25	Deanna Lund and Gary Conway of *Land of the Giants*
February 1	Cameron Mitchell, Henry Darrow, Mark Slade and Leif Erickson of *The High Chaparral*
February 8	Peter Lupus, Greg Morris, Peter Graves, Barbara Bain and Martin Landau of *Mission: Impossible*
February 15	Raymond Burr of *Ironside*
February 22	James Stacey, Wayne Maunder and Andrew Duggan of *Lancer*
March 1	Lucille Ball, Desi Arnaz Jr. and Lucie Arnaz of *Here's Lucy*
March 8	Ruth Buzzi, Jo Anne Worley, Goldie Hawn, Arte Johnson, Chelsea Brown, Judy Carne and Henry Gibson of *Rowan and Martin's Laugh-In*
March 15	Buddy Foster and Ken Berry of *Mayberry R.F.D.*
March 22	Elizabeth Montgomery of *Bewitched*
March 29	Tony Franciosa, Gene Barry and Robert Stack of *The Name of the Game*
April 5	Tom and Dick Smothers of *The Smothers Brothers Comedy Hour*
April 12	Dick Van Dyke and Mary Tyler Moore
April 19	Lawrence Welk of *The Lawrence Welk Show*
April 26	Jack Paar
May 3	Madeleine Sherwood and Sally Field of *The Flying Nun*
May 10	"The Raging Controversy Over TV's Role in Space Shots"
May 17	Marlo Thomas of *That Girl*
May 24	Hugh Downs, Barbara Walters, Joe Garagiola and Frank Blair of *Today*
May 31	Anissa Jones, Sebastian Cabot and Johnnie Whitaker of *Family Affair*
June 7	"The Hollywood Dancer": Debbie Macomber
June 14	Glen Campbell of *The Glen Campbell Goodtime Hour*
June 21	Jackie Gleason of *The Jackie Gleason Show*
June 28	Marc Copage and Diahann Carroll of *Julia*
July 5	Kent McCord and Martin Milner of *Adam 12*
July 12	Peggy Lipton, Clarence Williams III and Michael Cole of *The Mod Squad*
July 19	"The First Live Telecast From the Moon"
July 26	June Lockhart, Edgar Buchanan, Lori Saunders, Meredith MacRae and Linda Kaye of *Petticoat Junction*
August 2	Andrew Duggan of *Lancer*
August 9	"Will Soaring Costs Knock Sports Off TV?"
August 16	Merv Griffin of *The Merv Griffin Show*
August 23	Linda Cristal and Leif Erickson of *The High Chaparral*
August 30	Johnny Cash of *The Johnny Cash Show*
September 6	Eddie Albert and Eva Gabor of *Green Acres*
September 13	Fall Preview
September 20	Jim Nabors of *The Jim Nabors Show*
September 27	Robert Young and James Brolin of *Marcus Welby, M.D.*
October 4	Bill Cosby of *I Spy*
October 11	"What Is TV Doing to Them [children]?"
October 18	Peter Lupus, Greg Morris, Leonard Nimoy and Peter Graves of *Mission: Impossible*
October 25	Joan Hotchkis, William Windom and Lisa Gerritsen of *My World and Welcome to It*
November 1	Denise Nicholas, Michael Constantine and Lloyd Haynes of *Room 222*
November 8	Andy Williams of *The Andy Williams Show*
November 15	Dan Dailey and Julie Sommars of *The Governor & J.J.*
November 22	Barbara Eden of *I Dream of Jeannie*
November 29	Michael Landon, Lorne Greene, Dan Blocker and David Canary of *Bonanza*
December 6	Doris Day of *The Doris Day Show*
December 13	Michael Parks of *Then Came Bronson*
December 20	Christmas
December 27	"Remember 1969?": Richard Nixon, Spiro Agnew, Dick and Tom Smothers, astronauts and New York Mets

1970

January 3	"Here Come the '70s: How They Will Change the Way You Live"
January 10	Fred MacMurray and Beverly Garland of *My Three Sons*
January 17	Don Mitchell, Barbara Anderson, Don Galloway and Raymond Burr of *Ironside*
January 24	Tom Jones of *This Is Tom Jones*
January 31	Debbie Reynolds of *The Debbie Reynolds Show*
February 7	Elizabeth Montgomery and Dick Sargent of *Bewitched*
February 14	Linda Harrison, Laraine Stephens and Karen Jensen of *Bracken's World*
February 21	James Daly and Chad Everett of *Medical Center*
February 28	Clarence Williams III, Michael Cole and Peggy Lipton of *The Mod Squad*
March 7	Gordie Tapp, Louis Jones, Jeannine Riley, Diana Scott, David Akeman, Lulu Roman, Buck Owens, Roy Clark and Cathy Baker of *Hee Haw*
March 14	Diahann Carroll of *Julia*
March 21	Jackie Gleason of *The Jackie Gleason Show*
March 28	Dan Rowan and Dick Martin of *Rowan and Martin's Laugh-In*
April 4	Florence Henderson, Robert Reed, Maureen McCormick, Ann B. Davis, Mike Lookinland, Barry Williams, Eve Plumb, Susan Olsen and Christopher Knight of *The Brady Bunch*
April 11	Carol Burnett of *The Carol Burnett Show*
April 18	Burl Ives, James Farentino and Joseph Campanella of *The Bold Ones*
April 25	Raquel Welch and John Wayne in *Raquel!*
May 2	Glen Campbell of *The Glen Campbell Goodtime Hour*
May 9	David Frost of *The David Frost Show*
May 16	Vice President Spiro T. Agnew
May 23	Mike Wallace, Tricia Nixon and Harry Reasoner
May 30	Julie Sommars of *The Governor & J.J.*
June 6	Robert Young of *Marcus Welby, M.D.*
June 13	Johnny Cash of *The Johnny Cash Show*
June 20	John Forsythe, Joyce Menges, Susan Neher and Melanie Fullerton of *To Rome With Love*
June 27	Liza Minnelli
July 4	Miyoshi Umeki, Brandon Cruz and Bill Bixby of *The Courtship of Eddie's Father*
July 11	Raymond Bailey, Donna Douglas, Max Baer Jr., Irene Ryan and Buddy Ebsen of *The Beverly Hillbillies*
July 18	Jackie Chidsey, Michelle della Fave, Paula Cinko, Pauline Antony, Tara Leigh, Wanda Bailey, Rosetta Cox, Patricia Mickey, Micki McGlone and Susan Lund of *Dean Martin Presents the Golddiggers*
July 25	Buddy Foster, George Lindsey, Jack Dodson, Arlene Golonka, Paul Hartman and Ken Berry of *Mayberry R.F.D.*
August 1	Chet Huntley of *The Huntley-Brinkley Report*
August 8	Ted Bessell and Marlo Thomas of *That Girl*
August 15	Johnny Carson of *The Tonight Show*
August 22	James Arness, Amanda Blake, Milburn Stone and Ken Curtis of *Gunsmoke*
August 29	Eddie Albert of *Green Acres*
September 5	Richard Burton and Elizabeth Taylor with Lucille Ball of *Here's Lucy*
September 12	Fall Preview
September 19	Mary Tyler Moore of *The Mary Tyler Moore Show*
September 26	Lloyd Haynes, Denise Nicholas, Karen Valentine and Michael Constantine of *Room 222*

October 3 Red Skelton of *The Red Skelton Show*
October 10 Herschel Bernardi of *Arnie*
October 17 David Cassidy, Danny Bonaduce, Suzanne Crough, Jeremy Gelbwaks, Susan Dey and Shirley Jones of *The Partridge Family*
October 24 Don Knotts of *The Don Knotts Show*
October 31 Mike Connors of *Mannix*
November 7 Renne Jarrett, John Fink and Celeste Holm of *Nancy*
November 14 Christopher George of *The Immortal*
November 21 "What It Takes to Be a Starlet in the '70s": Sally Marr
November 28 John Wayne, Lorne Greene, Phyllis Diller, Dean Martin, Greg Morris, Bob Hope, Red Skelton, Bing Crosby, Dan Rowan, Dick Martin, Johnny Cash, Dan Blocker, Jack Benny and Ann-Margret
December 5 Dick Cavett of *The Dick Cavett Show*
December 12 The Muppets and Ed Sullivan of *The Ed Sullivan Show*
December 19 Christmas
December 26 Diahann Carroll and Fred Williamson of *Julia*

1971
January 2 "Remember 1970?"
January 9 Andy Griffith of *The Headmaster*
January 16 June Carter and Johnny Cash of *The Johnny Cash Show*
January 23 Flip Wilson of *The Flip Wilson Show*
January 30 James Arness of *Gunsmoke*
February 6 Tony Randall and Jack Klugman of *The Odd Couple*
February 13 Goldie Hawn
February 20 Doris Day of *The Doris Day Show*
February 27 Sharon Acker and Hal Holbrook of *The Senator*
March 6 Broderick Crawford of *The Interns*
March 13 Gene Barry and Robert Stack of *The Name of the Game*
March 20 Harry Reasoner of *ABC Evening News*
March 27 Michael Landon, Dan Blocker, Lorne Greene and Mitch Vogel of *Bonanza*
April 3 "Cable TV: What's All the Talk About?"
April 10 Bob Hope
April 17 Paul Newman
April 24 Elena Verdugo and Robert Young of *Marcus Welby, M.D.*
May 1 Lisa Gerritsen and Mary Tyler Moore of *The Mary Tyler Moore Show*
May 8 Henry Fonda of *The Smith Family*
May 15 "Television Journalism–an Inside Story"
May 22 David Cassidy of *The Partridge Family*
May 29 Carroll O'Connor, Jean Stapleton, Rob Reiner and Sally Struthers of *All in the Family*
June 5 Dan Rowan and Dick Martin of *Rowan and Martin's Laugh-In*
June 12 Lucille Ball of *Here's Lucy*
June 19 Brandon Cruz and Bill Bixby of *The Courtship of Eddie's Father*
June 26 Martin Milner and Kent McCord of *Adam 12*
July 3 Michael Cole, Peggy Lipton and Clarence Williams III of *The Mod Squad*
July 10 Cookie Monster of *Sesame Street*
July 17 Chad Everett of *Medical Center*
July 24 Lefty of *The Wonderful World of Disney*
July 31 "Henry VIII and His Six Wives Come to Television"
August 7 Nina Hart, Jerry Lacy, Larry Bryggman, Swoosie Kurtz, Ethel Remey, Fran Carlon, Henderson Forsythe, Marie Masters, Peter Galman, Eileen Fulton, Phoebe Dorin, Rita McLaughlin, Santos Ortega, Helen Wagner, Dan MacLaughlin and William Johnstone of *As the World Turns*
August 14 Mitch Vogel, Lorne Greene, Michael Landon and Dan Blocker of *Bonanza*
August 21 "Public Television: Is Anybody Watching?"
August 28 Howard Cosell, Don Meredith and Frank Gifford of *Monday Night Football*
September 4 Jack Lord of *Hawaii Five-O*
September 11 Fall Preview
September 18 Sandy Duncan of *Funny Face*
September 25 Shirley MacLaine of *Shirley's World*
October 2 Jimmy Stewart of *The Jimmy Stewart Show*
October 9 Hope Lange and Dick Van Dyke of *The New Dick Van Dyke Show*
October 16 Mia Farrow in *Goodbye, Raggedy Ann*
October 23 James Franciscus of *Longstreet*
October 30 Larry Hagman and Donna Mills of *The Good Life*
November 6 William Conrad of *Cannon*
November 13 Rupert Crosse and Don Adams of *The Partners*
November 20 Carroll O'Connor, Sally Struthers, Jean Stapleton and Rob Reiner of *All in the Family*
November 27 Joanne Woodward in *All the Way Home*
December 4 Julie Andrews and Carol Burnett in *Julie and Carol at Lincoln Center*
December 11 James Garner of *Nichols*
December 18 Brian Forster, Suzanne Crough, Danny Bonaduce, David Cassidy, Shirley Jones, Susan Dey and Dave Madden of *The Partridge Family*
December 25 Christmas

1972
January 1 "Remember 1971?": Rob Reiner, Sally Struthers, Jean Stapleton and Carroll O'Connor of *All in the Family*; Richard Nixon; Baltimore Colts; and astronauts
January 8 Flip Wilson of *The Flip Wilson Show*
January 15 "America Out of Focus: How–and Why–European Television Distorts Our Image"
January 22 Lynda Day George, Greg Morris, Peter Graves and Peter Lupus of *Mission: Impossible*
January 29 David Janssen of *O'Hara, U.S. Treasury*
February 5 Raymond Burr and Elizabeth Baur of *Ironside*
February 12 Arthur Hill of *Owen Marshall, Counselor at Law*
February 19 Richard Nixon and Chou En-lai
February 26 Mary Tyler Moore of *The Mary Tyler Moore Show*
March 4 Johnny Carson of *The Tonight Show*
March 11 James Brolin and Robert Young of *Marcus Welby, M.D.*
March 18 Sonny Bono and Cher Bono of *The Sonny and Cher Comedy Hour*
March 25 Peter Falk of *Columbo*
April 1 Glenn Ford of *Cade's County*
April 8 "TV Political Coverage: Fair or Biased?"
April 15 Thomas K. Mattingly, Charles M. Duke Jr. and John W. Young
April 22 Don Rickles of *The Don Rickles Show*
April 29 Susan Saint James and Rock Hudson of *McMillan and Wife*
May 6 Sandy Duncan of *Funny Face*
May 13 Demond Wilson and Redd Foxx of *Sanford and Son*
May 20 Efrem Zimbalist Jr. and J. Edgar Hoover of *The F.B.I.*
May 27 Carroll O'Connor and Jean Stapleton of *All in the Family*
June 3 Rod Serling of *Rod Serling's Night Gallery*
June 10 Doris Day of *The Doris Day Show*
June 17 Julie London of *Emergency!*
June 24 Mike Connors of *Mannix*
July 1 Carol Burnett of *The Carol Burnett Show*
July 8 Merv Griffin of *The Merv Griffin Show*
July 15 David Cassidy of *The Partridge Family*
July 22 Jack Webb, Martin Milner and Kent McCord of *Adam 12*
July 29 "All About *Love, American Style*"
August 5 "Countess Tolstoy Writes of Her Father– as *War and Peace* Comes to Television"
August 12 "*Leonardo da Vinci*: Unusual Drama Series"
August 19 Chad Everett of *Medical Center*
August 26 The Olympics
September 2 Jack Klugman and Tony Randall of *The Odd Couple*
September 9 Fall Preview
September 16 Yul Brynner and Samantha Eggar of *Anna and the King*
September 23 George Peppard of *Banacek*
September 30 Meredith Baxter and David Birney of *Bridget Loves Bernie*
October 7 Michael Landon, David Canary, Mitch Vogel, Lou Frizzel and Lorne Greene of *Bonanza*
October 14 Robert Conrad of *Assignment Vienna*
October 21 Carroll O'Connor and Cloris Leachman in *Of Thee I Sing*
October 28 Snoopy, Charlie Brown and Woodstock
November 4 John Wayne
November 11 Alistair Cooke of *Alistair Cooke's America*
November 18 Beatrice Arthur of *Maude*
November 25 Doug McClure, Tony Franciosa and Hugh O'Brian of *Search*
December 2 Mike Douglas of *The Mike Douglas Show*
December 9 Julie Andrews of *The Julie Andrews Hour*
December 16 Duke and Duchess of Windsor
December 23 Christmas
December 30 Barbara Walters of *Today*

1973
January 6 "1972: How It Looked on Television": Richard Nixon, Leonid Brezhnev, Chou En-lai and Mark Spitz
January 13 "China: Inside *The Forbidden City*"
January 20 Bob Newhart and Suzanne Pleshette of *The Bob Newhart Show*
January 27 Sam Melville, Georg Stanford Brown and Michael Ontkean of *The Rookies*
February 3 Bill Cosby of *The New Bill Cosby Show*
February 10 John Calvin, Paul Lynde and Jane Actman of *The Paul Lynde Show*
February 17 Susan Saint James and Rock Hudson of *McMillan and Wife*
February 24 Gary Burghoff, McLean Stevenson, Alan Alda, Wayne Rogers, Larry Linville and Loretta Swit of *M*A*S*H*
March 3 William Conrad of *Cannon*
March 10 Marlo Thomas in *That Girl in Wonderland*
March 17 Redd Foxx and Demond Wilson of *Sanford and Son*
March 24 Ann-Margret
March 31 Lucille Ball and Desi Arnaz IV
April 7 "When Is Children's TV Going to Grow Up?"
April 14 Shelley Fabares and Brian Keith of *The Little People*
April 21 Raymond Burr in *Portrait: A Man Whose Name Was John*
April 28 Eric Scott, Jon Walmsley, Richard Thomas, Will Geer, Ellen Corby, Kami Cotler, Ralph Waite, Michael Learned, David W. Harper, Judy Norton-Taylor and Mary Elizabeth McDonough of *The Waltons*
May 5 Peter Falk of *Columbo*
May 12 Shirley Booth of *A Touch of Grace*
May 19 Mary Tyler Moore of *The Mary Tyler Moore Show*
May 26 Karl Malden and Michael Douglas of *The Streets of San Francisco*
June 2 Mike Evans and Carroll O'Connor of *All in the Family*
June 9 Richard Widmark of *Madigan*
June 16 Beatrice Arthur and Bill Macy of *Maude*
June 23 David Carradine of *Kung Fu*
June 30 Dennis Weaver of *McCloud*
July 7 Dick Cavett of *The Dick Cavett Show*
July 14 Sonny Bono and Cher Bono of *The Sonny and Cher Comedy Hour*
July 21 Robert Young of *Marcus Welby, M.D.* and Chad Everett of *Medical Center*
July 28 "The Lie That Wouldn't Die: TV's Great Sex Movie Scare"
August 4 Martin Milner and Kent McCord of *Adam 12*
August 11 Roy Clark of *Hee Haw*
August 18 Robert Fuller of *Emergency!*
August 25 Buddy Ebsen of *Barnaby Jones*
September 1 Miss America
September 8 Fall Preview
September 15 Football Preview
September 22 Jack Lord and James MacArthur of *Hawaii Five-O*
September 29 "The War in Vietnam: What Happened Vs. What We Saw"
October 6 Diana Rigg of *Diana*
October 13 "Does TV Go Too Far?"
October 20 Telly Savalas of *Kojak*
October 27 Blythe Danner and Ken Howard of *Adam's Rib*
November 3 Deirdre Lenihan of *Needles and Pins*
November 10 "A Very Special Week": Princess Anne and Mark Phillips; Dean Martin; Bob Hope; Julie Andrews; Sammy Davis Jr.; Elvis Presley; William Holden; Jon Walmsey, Richard Thomas, Will Geer, Kami Cotler, Ralph Waite, Michael Learned and Judy Norton-Taylor
November 17 Frank Sinatra
November 24 Jacques Cousteau
December 1 Bill Bixby of *The Magician*
December 8 Mary Tyler Moore, Georgia Engel and Valerie Harper of *The Mary Tyler Moore Show*
December 15 Katharine Hepburn in *The Glass Menagerie*
December 22 Christmas
December 29 Mason Reese

1974
January 5 "How You Saw the World on Television in 1973"
January 12 Beatrice Arthur, Bill Macy and Conrad Bain of *Maude*
January 19 Bob Hope
January 26 David Carradine of *Kung Fu*
February 2 Dom DeLuise of *Lotsa Luck*
February 9 Loretta Swit, Alan Alda, McLean Stevenson, Larry Linville, Gary Burghoff and Wayne Rogers of *M*A*S*H*
February 16 Michael Douglas and Karl Malden of *The Streets of San Francisco*
February 23 Richard Boone of *Hec Ramsey*
March 2 Jimmy Stewart of *Hawkins*
March 9 "How Showbiz Takes Over Local News"
March 16 Carol Burnett and Vicki Lawrence of *The Carol Burnett Show*
March 23 James Franciscus of *Doc Elliot*
March 30 Susan Strasberg and Tony Musante of *Toma*
April 6 Carroll O'Connor of *All in the Family*, Bill Macy of *Maude*, Redd Foxx of *Sanford and Son* and Norman Lear
April 13 Richard Thomas, Michael Learned and Ralph Waite of *The Waltons*
April 20 Peter Falk of *Columbo*
April 27 Bruce Bould, Dan O'Herlihy, Anthony Quayle, Ben Gazzara and Lee Remick in *QB VII*
May 4 Sam Melville, Georg Stanford Brown and Michael Ontkean of *The Rookies*
May 11 Bob Newhart and Peter Bonerz of *The Bob Newhart Show*
May 18 Lee Majors of *The Six Million Dollar Man*
May 25 J.D. Cannon and Dennis Weaver of *McCloud*
June 1 Sonny Bono and Cher Bono of *The Sonny and Cher Comedy Hour*
June 8 Marilyn Baker
June 15 Kathy O'Dare and Ron Howard of *Happy Days*
June 22 John Chancellor of *NBC Nightly News*
June 29 Esther Rolle and John Amos of *Good Times*
July 6 Lucille Ball of *The Lucy Show*
July 13 Johnny Carson of *The Tonight Show*
July 20 "The Boom in Made-for-TV Films"
July 27 Lee McCain and Ronny Cox of *Apple's Way*
August 3 Kevin Tighe and Randolph Mantooth of *Emergency!*
August 10 "Games Viewers Play"
August 17 *Police Story*
August 24 Susan Blakely
August 31 Telly Savalas of *Kojak*
September 7 Fall Preview
September 14 "They're Off and Running! Experts Pick Winners of New-Show Handicap"
September 21 Football Preview
September 28 Paul Sand of *Friends and Lovers*
October 5 Redd Foxx and Demond Wilson of *Sanford and Son*
October 12 Valerie Harper of *Rhoda*
October 19 Freddie Prinze and Jack Albertson of *Chico and the Man*
October 26 Ralph Waite, Will Geer and Richard Thomas of *The Waltons*
November 2 Wayne Rogers, McLean Stevenson, Larry Linville, Alan Alda, Loretta Swit and Gary Burghoff of *M*A*S*H*
November 9 Sophia Loren
November 16 Robert Duvall, Al Pacino, Marlon Brando and James Caan in *The Godfather*
November 23 "What a Week!"
November 30 Teresa Graves of *Get Christie Love*
December 7 Michael Landon of *Little House on the Prairie*
December 14 Esther Rolle, Jimmie Walker, Ralph Carter, BerNadette Stanis and John Amos of *Good Times*

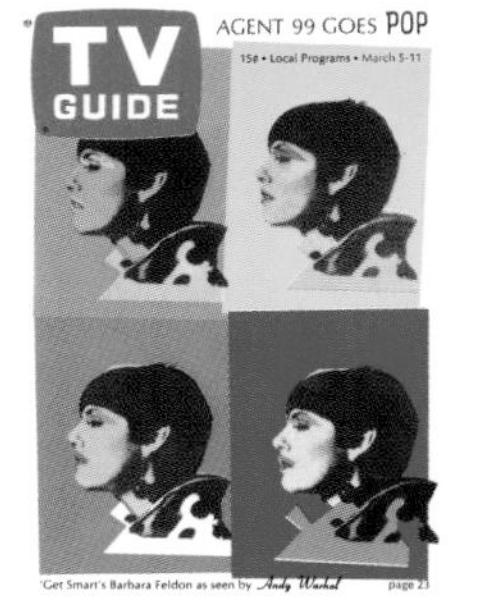

March 5, 1966
BY ANDY WARHOL

Get Smart's entire existence depended on the pop-culture phenomenon of 007, James Bond. Who better to put a pop stamp of approval on Barbara Feldon's Agent 99 than Andy Warhol?

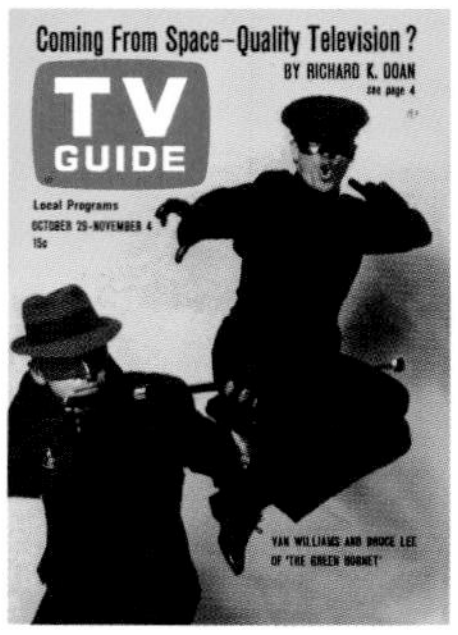

October 29, 1966
BY IVAN NAGY

Once a '40s radio program, *The Green Hornet*, starring Van Williams, was produced by the same team behind *Batman*. It also gave the world an early look at future martial-arts legend Bruce Lee.

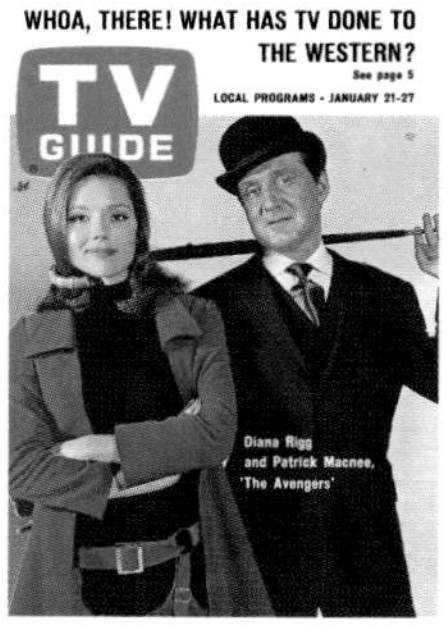

January 21, 1967
BY TERRY O'NEILL

A secret-agent import from the United Kingdom, *The Avengers* starred Patrick Macnee with trademark derby and cane. The first year, actress Honor Blackman was by his side; then Diana Rigg stepped into the catsuit.

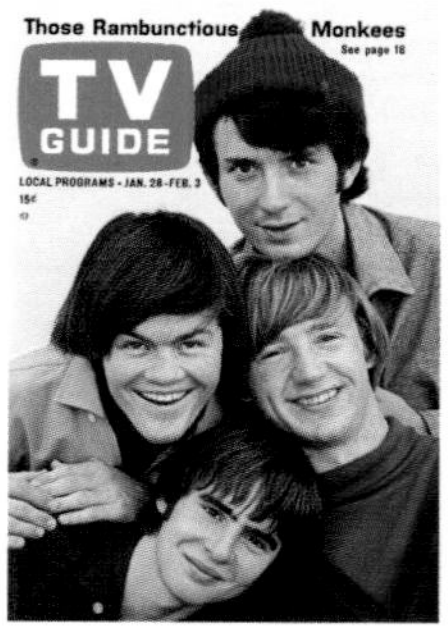

January 28, 1967
BY GENE TRINDL

Pre-MTV, the Monkees were a fabricated boy band in the mold of the Beatles whose show featured a lot of fast edits, surreal imagery and slap-stick humor. The kids bought it.

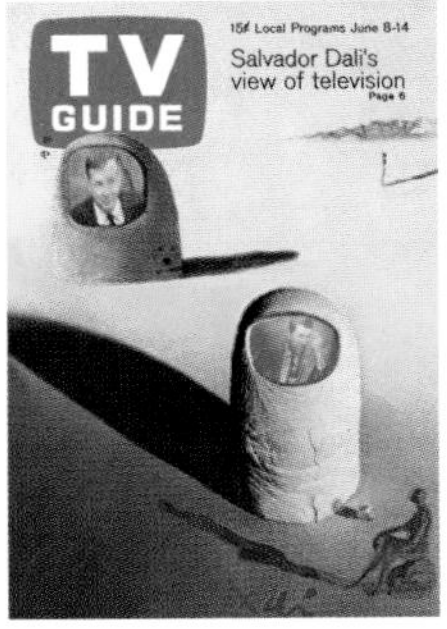

June 8, 1968
ILLUSTRATION BY SALVADOR DALI, PHOTOGRAPHS BY PHILIPPE HALSMAN

The late '60s were a crazy time, so why not a cover from a crazy surrealist? Dali's "Today, Tonight and Tomorrow" featured Johnny Carson and Hugh Downs on thumbnail TV screens.

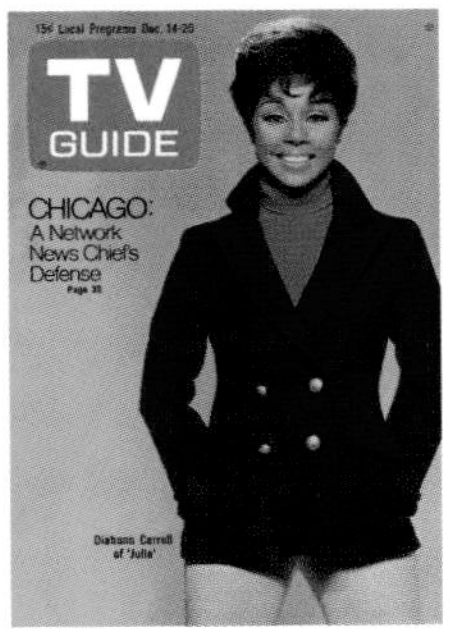

December 14, 1968
BY PRIGENT

While not a bad comedy, *Julia* is best known for being the first show to star an African-American woman, Diahann Carroll, in a lead role where she wasn't hired help. The public accepted the integrated show with no problem.

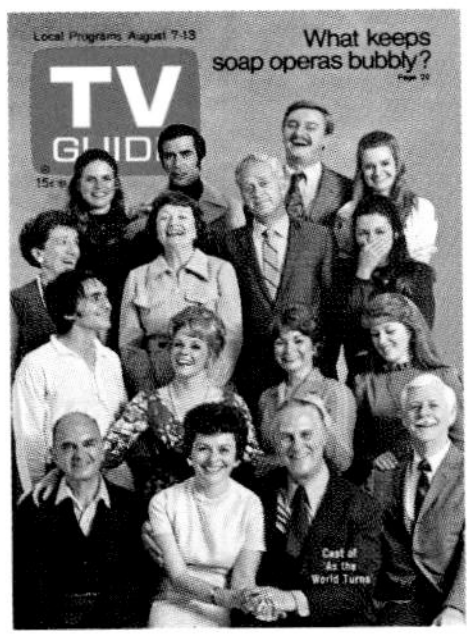

August 7, 1971
BY SHELDON SECUNDA

As the World Turns premiered in 1956 and has been a springboard for some major talent. Just a few of the headline names include Julianne Moore, Meg Ryan, Marisa Tomei and Lauryn Hill.

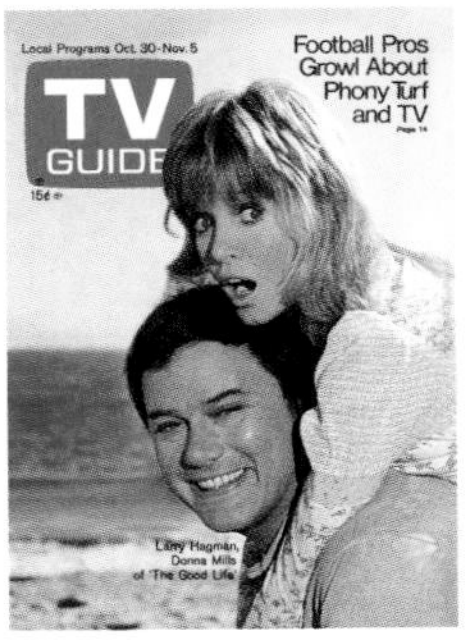

October 30, 1971
BY RAPHAEL

On the short-lived comedy *The Good Life*, Larry Hagman and Donna Mills played a husband and wife working as butler and cook. Seven years later, he was *Dallas*'s mogul, J.R. Ewing, and she was his sister-in-law on *Knots Landing*.

December 21 Christmas
December 28 "Memorable Bowl Games, Wacky Parades"

1975

January 4 Angie Dickinson of *Police Woman*
January 11 David Janssen of *Harry-O*
January 18 Theresa Merritt and Clifton Davis of *That's My Mama*
January 25 Gene Shalit, Jim Hartz and Barbara Walters of *Today*
February 1 James Garner of *The Rockford Files*
February 8 Valerie Harper of *Rhoda*, Bob Newhart of *The Bob Newhart Show* and Mary Tyler Moore of *The Mary Tyler Moore Show*
February 15 Georg Stanford Brown, Bruce Fairbairn, Sam Melville and Gerald S. O'Loughlin of *The Rookies*
February 22 Telly Savalas of *Kojak*
March 1 Jack Albertson and Freddie Prinze of *Chico and the Man*
March 8 Chad Everett of *Medical Center*
March 15 Karen Valentine of *Karen*
March 22 Karl Malden and Michael Douglas of *The Streets of San Francisco*
March 29 Beatrice Arthur and Hermione Baddeley of *Maude*
April 5 Baseball Preview
April 12 Cher of *Cher*
April 19 Frank Converse and Claude Akins of *Movin' On*
April 26 Dennis Weaver, J.D. Cannon and Terry Carter of *McCloud*
May 3 Valerie Harper and David Groh of *Rhoda*
May 10 Muhammad Ali
May 17 Barry Newman of *Petrocelli*
May 24 Jason Robards and Colleen Dewhurst in *A Moon for the Misbegotten*
May 31 Bill Daily, Suzanne Pleshette, Marcia Wallace, Bob Newhart, Pat Finley and Peter Bonerz of *The Bob Newhart Show*
June 7 Melissa Gilbert, Melissa Sue Anderson, Lindsay Greenbush, Sidney Greenbush, Michael Landon and Karen Grassle of *Little House on the Prairie*
June 14 "Violence on TV–Does It Affect Our Society?"
June 21 Sherman Hemsley, Isabel Sanford and Mike Evans of *The Jeffersons*
June 28 Bicentennial
July 5 Tony Orlando, Joyce Vincent Wilson and Telma Hopkins of *Tony Orlando and Dawn*
July 12 "Apollo/Soyuz Mission on Television"
July 19 Hal Linden, Abe Vigoda, Jack Soo, Gregory Sierra, Ron Glass, Maxwell Gail and Barbara Barrie of *Barney Miller*
July 26 Howard K. Smith and Harry Reasoner of *The CBS Evening News*
August 2 Mike Douglas of *The Mike Douglas Show*
August 9 Buddy Ebsen of *Barnaby Jones*
August 16 Bobby Troup, Kevin Tighe, Randolph Mantooth, Robert Fuller and Julie London of *Emergency!*
August 23 Ralph Waite, Richard Thomas and Michael Learned of *The Waltons*
August 30 Carroll O'Connor of *All in the Family*
September 6 Fall Preview
September 13 "Experts Pick Hit Shows, NFL Winners"
September 20 Barbara Walters
September 27 Howard Cosell of *Saturday Night Live with Howard Cosell*
October 4 Lee Remick in *Jennie*
October 11 Glenn Ford, Lance Kerwin, Elizabeth Cheshire and Julie Harris of *The Family Holvak*
October 18 "TV's Sex Crisis: A Thoughtful Analysis of a Stormy Controversy"
October 25 Cloris Leachman of *Phyllis*
November 1 Lloyd Bridges of *Joe Forrester*
November 8 Julie Kavner and Valerie Harper of *Rhoda*
November 15 David Soul and Paul Michael Glaser of *Starsky and Hutch*
November 22 "A Banner Week!"
November 29 Tony Curtis of *McCoy*
December 6 "Does America Want Family Viewing Time?"
December 13 Robert Wagner and Eddie Albert of *Switch*
December 20 Christmas
December 27 Robert Blake and Fred of *Baretta*

1976

January 3 Telly Savalas of *Kojak*
January 10 Ron Howard and Henry Winkler of *Happy Days*
January 17 Angie Dickinson and Earl Holliman of *Police Woman*
January 24 Alan Alda, Mike Farrell and Harry Morgan of *M*A*S*H*
January 31 Steve Forrest of *S.W.A.T.*
February 7 Abe Vigoda, Hal Linden, Gregory Sierra, Maxwell Gail, Jack Soo, Ron Glass and Barbara Barrie of *Barney Miller*
February 14 Redd Foxx of *Sanford and Son*
February 21 William Conrad of *Cannon*
February 28 Bob Hope in *Joys*
March 6 Noah Beery Jr. and James Garner of *The Rockford Files*
March 13 Jack Albertson, Freddie Prinze and Scatman Crothers of *Chico and the Man*
March 20 Danny Thomas of *The Practice*
March 27 Jack Palance of *Bronk*
April 3 Baseball Preview
April 10 *Police Story*
April 17 Gabe Kaplan and Marcia Strassman of *Welcome Back, Kotter*
April 24 Beatrice Arthur of *Maude*
May 1 George Kennedy of *The Blue Knight*
May 8 Lindsay Wagner of *The Bionic Woman*
May 15 Jose Perez, Hal Williams, Bobby Sandler and Rick Hurst of *On the Rocks*
May 22 Cindy Williams and Penny Marshall of *Laverne & Shirley*
May 29 Michael Landon, Melissa Sue Anderson, Lindsay Greenbush, Sidney Greenbush and Melissa Gilbert of *Little House on the Prairie*
June 5 Sonny Bono and Cher of *The Sonny and Cher Show*
June 12 David Janssen and Anthony Zerbe of *Harry-O*
June 19 Louise Lasser of *Mary Hartman, Mary Hartman*
June 26 Mary Tyler Moore of *The Mary Tyler Moore Show*
July 3 Bicentennial
July 10 "Convention Coverage: Complete Details"
July 17 The Olympics
July 24 Bonnie Franklin of *One Day at a Time*
July 31 "Terrorism and Television–the Medium in the Middle"
August 7 Marie Osmond and Donny Osmond of *Donny and Marie*
August 14 Peter Falk of *Columbo*
August 21 Will Geer, Ellen Corby and Richard Thomas of *The Waltons*
August 28 Lee Majors of *The Six Million Dollar Man*
September 4 Football Preview
September 11 Bob Dylan
September 18 Fall Preview
September 25 Farrah Fawcett-Majors, Jaclyn Smith and Kate Jackson of *Charlie's Angels*
October 2 David Birney of *Serpico*
October 9 Bernadette Peters and Richard Crenna of *All's Fair*
October 16 World Series
October 23 Linda Lavin of *Alice*
October 30 Jimmy Carter and Gerald Ford
November 6 Clark Gable and Vivian Leigh in *Gone With the Wind*
November 13 Dorothy Hamill
November 20 "NBC Throws an All-Star 50th Birthday Party"
November 27 Paul Michael Glaser and David Soul of *Starsky and Hutch*
December 4 Tony Randall of *The Tony Randall Show*
December 11 Valerie Harper of *Rhoda*
December 18 John Chancellor and David Brinkley of *NBC Nightly News*
December 25 Christmas

1977

January 1 John Travolta of *Welcome Back, Kotter*
January 8 Super Bowl
January 15 "I, Jimmy Carter, Do Solemnly Swear..."
January 22 *Roots*
January 29 Lynda Carter of *Wonder Woman*
February 5 Barbara Walters of *ABC Evening News*
February 12 Telly Savalas and George Savalas of *Kojak*
February 19 Nancy Walker of *Blansky's Beauties*
February 26 Martha Raye and Rock Hudson of *McMillan and Wife*
March 5 Liv Ullmann in *Scenes From a Marriage*
March 12 Lauren Hutton in *The Rhinemann Exchange*
March 19 Mary Tyler Moore of *The Mary Tyler Moore Show*
March 26 Jack Klugman of *Quincy, M.E.*
April 2 Dinah Shore, Judy Rankin, Jane Blalock and JoAnne Carner
April 9 Baseball Preview
April 16 Frank Sinatra
April 23 Mike Wallace, Dan Rather and Morley Safer of *60 Minutes*
April 30 Richard M. Nixon and David Frost
May 7 Valerie Bertinelli, Mackenzie Phillips and Bonnie Franklin of *One Day at a Time*
May 14 Tom Brokaw of *Today*
May 21 Farrah Fawcett-Majors of *Charlie's Angels*
May 28 Robert Blake of *Baretta*
June 4 Alan Alda of *M*A*S*H*
June 11 Dan Haggerty and Bozo of *The Life and Times of Grizzly Adams*
June 18 Cindy Williams and Penny Marshall of *Laverne & Shirley*
June 25 Eric Scott, Jon Walmsley, Richard Thomas, Will Geer, Ellen Corby, Kami Cotler, Ralph Waite, Michael Learned, David W. Harper, Judy Norton-Taylor and Mary Elizabeth McDonough of *The Waltons*
July 2 Linda Lavin and Polly Holliday of *Alice*
July 9 Peter Isacksen and Don Rickles of *C.P.O. Sharkey*
July 16 Abe Vigoda, Ron Glass, Maxwell Gail, Hal Linden and Jack Soo of *Barney Miller*
July 23 "Public TV in Turmoil"
July 30 Johnny Carson of *The Tonight Show*
August 6 Fozzie Bear and Kermit the Frog of *The Muppet Show*
August 13 David Soul of *Starsky and Hutch*
August 20 James Garner and Joe Santos of *The Rockford Files*
August 27 "Sex and Violence: Hollywood Fights Back"
September 3 Andy Griffith, Cliff Robertson, Robert Vaughn and Jason Robards in *Washington: Behind Closed Doors*
September 10 Fall Preview
September 17 Football Preview
September 24 Betty White and John Hillerman of *The Betty White Show*
October 1 Squire Fridell and Tony Roberts of *Rosetti and Ryan*
October 8 Marie Osmond and Donny Osmond of *Donny and Marie*
October 15 Ed Asner of *Lou Grant*
October 22 Ron Palillo, Lawrence-Hilton Jacobs, John Travolta, Gabe Kaplan and Robert Hegyes of *Welcome Back, Kotter*
October 29 Beverly Archer of *We've Got Each Other*
November 5 Parker Stevenson and Shaun Cassidy of *The Hardy Boys Mysteries*
November 12 Al Pacino, Marlon Brando and Robert De Niro in *The Godfather Part II*
November 19 Frank Sinatra in *Contract on Cherry Street*
November 26 Arthur Peterson, Robert Mandan, Katherine Helmond, Robert Guillaume, Cathryn Damon, Jennifer Salt, Richard Mulligan, Diana Canova, Ted Wass, Billy Crystal, Jimmy Baio and Robert Urich of *Soap*
December 3 Patrick Duffy of *Man From Atlantis*
December 10 "What the Censors Cut...and Why"
December 17 Bonnie Franklin, Mackenzie Phillips, Pat Harrington and Valerie Bertinelli of *One Day at a Time*
December 24 Christmas
December 31 Kevin Dobson and Telly Savalas of *Kojak*

1978

January 7 Henry Winkler, Ron Howard, Donny Most and Anson Williams of *Happy Days*
January 14 Super Bowl
January 21 James Broderick, Meredith Baxter-Birney, Sada Thompson, Gary Frank and Kristy McNichol of *Family*
January 28 Dan Haggerty and Bozo of *The Life and Times of Grizzly Adams*
February 4 Lauren Tewes, Gavin MacLeod, Bernie Kopell, Ted Lange and Fred Grandy of *The Love Boat*
February 11 Jack Klugman and Garry Walberg of *Quincy, M.E.*
February 18 Kate Jackson, Jaclyn Smith and Cheryl Ladd of *Charlie's Angels*
February 25 David Ogden Stiers, Loretta Swit, Harry Morgan, Mike Farrell and Alan Alda of *M*A*S*H*
March 4 Lynnie Greene and Bess Armstrong of *On Our Own*
March 11 Kene Holliday and Victor French of *Carter County*
March 18 Lindsay Wagner of *The Bionic Woman*
March 25 "CBS Turns 50 With a Week of Nostalgia": Walter Cronkite and Mary Tyler Moore
April 1 Baseball Preview
April 8 Vic Tayback, Polly Holliday, Linda Lavin and Beth Howland of *Alice*
April 15 *Holocaust*
April 22 "How the Network Struggle Is Changing the Shape of Television"
April 29 Cindy Williams, Penny Marshall, Michael McKean and David L. Lander of *Laverne & Shirley*
May 6 Buddy Ebsen of *Barnaby Jones*
May 13 Merlin Olsen, Michael Landon, Karen Grassle, Melissa Gilbert, Melissa Sue Anderson, Lindsay Greenbush and Sidney Greenbush of *Little House on the Prairie*
May 20 Suzanne Somers, Joyce DeWitt and John Ritter of *Three's Company*
May 27 Phil Donahue of *The Phil Donahue Show*
June 3 Paul Michael Glaser and David Soul of *Starsky and Hutch*
June 10 "UFOs on TV: Flying in the Face of Logic"
June 17 Valerie Harper of *Rhoda*
June 24 "Can You Believe the Ratings? A New Perspective"
July 1 Ricardo Montalban and Herve Villechaize of *Fantasy Island*
July 8 Victoria Mallory, Brenda Dickson, David Hasselhoff and Jaime Lyn Bauer of *The Young and the Restless*
July 15 Robert Conrad of *Black Sheep Squadron*
July 22 Gavin MacLeod of *The Love Boat*
July 29 Gilda Radner, Bill Murray, Laraine Newman, Garrett Morris, Jane Curtin, Dan Aykroyd and John Belushi of *Saturday Night Live*
August 5 Paul Benedict, Isabel Sanford and Sherman Hemsley of *The Jeffersons*
August 12 David Hartman of *Good Morning America*
August 19 "America Speaks Out About Sports on TV"
August 26 Cheryl Ladd of *Charlie's Angels*
September 2 Football Preview
September 9 Fall Preview
September 16 Lorne Greene, Richard Hatch and Dirk Benedict of *Battlestar Galactica*
September 23 Mary Tyler Moore of *Mary*
September 30 Richard Chamberlain, Robert Conrad and Barbara Carrera in *Centennial*
October 7 World Series
October 14 Robert Urich of *Vegas*
October 21 Gary Sandy, Gordon Jump, Tim Reid and Howard Hesseman of *WKRP in Cincinnati*
October 28 Pam Dawber and Robin Williams of *Mork & Mindy*
November 4 John Travolta of *Welcome Back, Kotter*
November 11 Ron Leibman of *Kaz*
November 18 "Foreign Lobbyists: How They Try to Manipulate U.S. Television"
November 25 Suzanne Somers of *Three's Company*
December 2 "A Benji Special"
December 9 Linda Kelsey and Ed Asner of *Lou Grant*
December 16 Dick Van Patten, Grant Goodeve, Laurie Walters, Lani O'Grady, Connie Newton, Betty Buckley, Susan Richardson, Dianne Kay, Adam Rich and Willie Aames of *Eight Is Enough*
December 23 Christmas
December 30 Dick Clark of *Dick Clark's Live Wednesday*

1979

January 6 Carroll O'Connor and Jean Stapleton of *All in the Family*
January 13 "Network News Chiefs on the Hottest TV New Controversies": Roone Arledge, Richard Salent and Les Crystal
January 20 Super Bowl
January 27 Katharine Hepburn in *The Corn Is Green*

February 3 Larry Wilcox and Erik Estrada of *CHiPs*
February 10 *The Shakespeare Plays*
February 17 *Roots: The Next Generation*
February 24 James Arness of *How the West Was Won*
March 3 Gary Coleman of *Diff'rent Strokes*
March 10 Harry Reasoner, Dan Rather, Morley Safer and Mike Wallace of *60 Minutes*
March 17 Mike Farrell and Alan Alda of *M*A*S*H*
March 24 Ricardo Montalban of *Fantasy Island*
March 31 Baseball Preview
April 7 Maren Jensen of *Battlestar Galactica*
April 14 John S. Ragin and Jack Klugman of *Quincy, M.E.*
April 21 Walter Cronkite of *CBS Evening News*
April 28 Danny DeVito and Judd Hirsch of *Taxi*
May 5 James Stephens and John Houseman of *The Paper Chase*
May 12 "What Viewers Love/Hate About Television"
May 19 Penny Marshall and Cindy Williams of *Laverne & Shirley*
May 26 Ken Howard of *The White Shadow*
June 2 James Garner of *The Rockford Files*
June 9 Donna Pescow of *Angie*
June 16 Patrick Duffy, Jim Davis and Victoria Principal of *Dallas*
June 23 Johnny Carson of *The Tonight Show*
June 30 John Schneider, Catherine Bach and Tom Wopat of *The Dukes of Hazzard*
July 7 Maxwell Gail, Ron Carey, Ron Glass, Hal Linden, James Gregory and Steve Landesberg of *Barney Miller*
July 14 Michael Landon, Linwood Boomer and Melissa Sue Anderson of *Little House on the Prairie*
July 21 Greg Evigan and Sam of *B.J. and the Bear*
July 28 Lou Ferrigno and Bill Bixby of *The Incredible Hulk*
August 4 Joyce DeWitt of *Three's Company*
August 11 Rod Arrants of *Search for Tomorrow*
August 18 Ed Asner, Nancy Marchand and Mason Adams of *Lou Grant*
August 25 Football Preview
September 1 Miss America
September 8 Fall Preview
September 15 Robert Guillaume of *Benson*
September 22 Carroll O'Connor of *All in the Family*
September 29 Pope John Paul II
October 6 World Series
October 13 Tom Snyder of *Tomorrow*
October 20 Loni Anderson, Howard Hesseman and Gary Sandy of *WKRP in Cincinnati*
October 27 Muhammad Ali in *Freedom Road*
November 3 Stefanie Powers and Robert Wagner of *Hart to Hart*
November 10 The Bee Gees
November 17 Wilfrid Hyde-White and Shelley Smith of *The Associates*
November 24 Pernell Roberts of *Trapper John, M.D.*
December 1 Barbara Walters
December 8 "Talk Show Hosts: Who Are the Best–And Why?": Johnny Carson, Mike Douglas, Merv Griffin, Dick Cavett, Dinah Shore, Phil Donahue and Tom Snyder
December 15 Henry Winkler of *Happy Days*
December 22 Christmas
December 29 Jaclyn Smith, Cheryl Ladd and Shelley Hack of *Charlie's Angels*

1980
January 5 Jamie Farr, Alan Alda and Loretta Swit of *M*A*S*H*
January 12 Erik Estrada and Larry Wilcox of *CHiPs*
January 19 Super Bowl
January 26 Richard Mulligan and Cathryn Damon of *Soap*
February 2 Conrad Bain, Todd Bridges and Gary Coleman of *Diff'rent Strokes*
February 9 The Olympics
February 16 Buddy Ebsen and Lee Meriwether of *Barnaby Jones*
February 23 "Selecting Our Leaders: The TV Drama Begins"
March 1 Herve Villechaize and Ricardo Montalban of *Fantasy Island*
March 8 Mary Crosby, Larry Hagman and Linda Gray of *Dallas*
March 15 Meredith Baxter-Birney, Kristy McNichol, James Broderick, Quinn Cummings, Sada Thompson and Gary Frank of *Family*
March 22 Claude Akins, Brian Kerwin and Mills Watson of *The Misadventures of Sheriff Lobo*
March 29 Martin Balsam and Carroll O'Connor of *Archie Bunker's Place*
April 5 Baseball Preview
April 12 Olivia Newton-John
April 19 Linda Lavin, Vic Tayback, Beth Howland and Diane Ladd of *Alice*
April 26 Beau Bridges and Helen Shaver of *United States*
May 3 Robin Williams and Pam Dawber of *Mork & Mindy*
May 10 Mackenzie Phillips, Bonnie Franklin and Valerie Bertinelli of *One Day at a Time*
May 17 Franklin Cover, Roxie Roker, Sherman Hemsley and Isabel Sanford of *The Jeffersons*
May 24 "Situation Comedies: Are They Getting Better–or Worse?"
May 31 Bart Braverman, Greg Morris, Robert Urich and Phyllis Davis of *Vegas*
June 7 Joan Van Ark and Ted Shackelford of *Knots Landing*
June 14 Lynn Redgrave of *House Calls*
June 21 Robert Wagner and Stefanie Powers of *Hart to Hart*
June 28 Gregory Harrison and Pernell Roberts of *Trapper John, M.D.*
July 5 Michael Landon, Matthew Laborteaux, Melissa Gilbert, Karen Grassle, Wendy Turnbeaugh, Brenda Turnbeaugh, Lindsay Greenbush and Sidney Greenbush of *Little House on the Prairie*
July 12 John Schneider, Catherine Bach and Tom Wopat of *The Dukes of Hazzard*
July 19 Lauren Tewes, Gavin MacLeod and Ted Lange of *The Love Boat*
July 26 Judd Hirsch, Marilu Henner and Tony Danza of *Taxi*
August 2 Sarah Purcell of *Real People*
August 9 "Children's Television: Experts Pick the Best–and Worst–Shows": Fat Albert of *Fat Albert*, Ernie of *Sesame Street* and Fred Flintstone
August 16 "TV's Incredible Hunks": Tom Wopat of *The Dukes of Hazzard*, Erik Estrada of *CHiPs* and Greg Evigan of *B.J. and the Bear*
August 23 Genie Francis of *General Hospital*
August 30 Football Preview
September 6 Richard Chamberlain in *Shogun*
September 13 Fall Preview
September 20 Priscilla Presley of *Those Amazing Animals*
September 27 *Cosmos*
October 4 Ed Asner and Mason Adams of *Lou Grant*
October 11 World Series
October 18 Sophia Loren in *Sophia Loren: Her Own Story*
October 25 James Gregory and Hal Linden of *Barney Miller*
November 1 John Anderson, Ronald Reagan and Jimmy Carter
November 8 Polly Holliday of *Flo*
November 15 Larry Hagman of *Dallas*
November 22 Pam Dawber of *Mork & Mindy*
November 29 Don Meredith, Howard Cosell, Fran Tarkenton and Frank Gifford of *Monday Night Football*
December 6 Todd Bridges and Gary Coleman of *Diff'rent Strokes*
December 13 Diana Canova of *I'm a Big Girl Now*
December 20 Christmas
December 27 Tom Selleck of *Magnum, P.I.*

1981
January 3 Deborah Van Valkenburgh, Ted Knight and Lydia Cornell of *Too Close for Comfort*
January 10 David Hartman of *Good Morning America*
January 17 Ronald Reagan
January 24 Super Bowl
January 31 "Hope, Carson, Burns Pay Tribute to Jack Benny": Bob Hope, Johnny Carson, George Burns and Jack Benny
February 7 Jane Seymour in *East of Eden*
February 14 Richard Sanders, Jan Smithers, Loni Anderson, Gary Sandy, Frank Bonner, Gordon Jump, Tim Reid and Howard Hesseman of *WKRP in Cincinnati*
February 21 Faye Dunaway in *Evita Peron*
February 28 "Hollywood's Cocaine Connection"
March 7 Tom Wopat, John Schneider, Sorrell Booke and Catherine Bach of *The Dukes of Hazzard*
March 14 Suzanne Somers of *Three's Company*
March 21 Wayne Rogers and Lynn Redgrave of *House Calls*
March 28 Johnny Carson of *The Tonight Show*
April 4 Baseball Preview
April 11 Ed Asner of *Lou Grant*
April 18 Ted Koppel of *ABC News Nightline*
April 25 Alan Alda of *M*A*S*H*
May 2 John Davidson, Cathy Lee Crosby and Fran Tarkenton of *That's Incredible!*
May 9 Larry Hagman and Patrick Duffy of *Dallas*
May 16 Robert Wagner, Stefanie Powers and Lionel Stander of *Hart to Hart*
May 23 Barbara Eden of *Harper Valley P.T.A*
May 30 Dan Rather of *The CBS Evening News*
June 6 Judd Hirsch and Andy Kaufman of *Taxi*
June 13 Pernell Roberts, Charles Siebert and Gregory Harrison of *Trapper John, M.D.*
June 20 John Barbour, Skip Stephenson, Bill Rafferty, Byron Allen and Sarah Purcell of *Real People*
June 27 Linda Evans of *Dynasty*
July 4 Dana Plato and Gary Coleman of *Diff'rent Strokes*
July 11 "Prime-Time Vixens": Donna Mills of *Knots Landing*, Morgan Fairchild of *Flamingo Road* and Pamela Sue Martin of *Dynasty*
July 18 Greg Evigan, Judy Landers and the chimp of *B.J. and The Bear*
July 25 Prince Charles and Lady Diana Spencer
August 1 Miss Piggy of *The Muppets*
August 8 Carroll O'Connor of *Archie Bunker's Place*
August 15 Elvis Presley
August 22 Ann Jillian of *It's a Living*
August 29 Football Preview
September 5 Miss America
September 12 Fall Preview
September 19 Kate Mulgrew in *The Manions of America*
September 26 "The Battle for Northern Ireland: How TV Tips the Balance"
October 3 Valerie Bertinelli of *One Day at a Time*
October 10 Jaclyn Smith in *Jacqueline Bouvier Kennedy*
October 17 World Series
October 24 "Blind Spot in the Middle East"
October 31 Bruce Weitz, Daniel J. Travanti and Michael Conrad of *Hill Street Blues*
November 7 Mimi Kennedy and Peter Cook of *The Two of Us*
November 14 Loretta Lynn
November 21 "TV and the John Lennon Tragedy: One Year Later"
November 28 Merlin Olsen and Mine of *Father Murphy*
December 5 Lorna Patterson of *Private Benjamin*
December 12 "Video Games: A Shopper's Guide to 1981's Best"
December 19 Christmas
December 26 Henry Fonda

1982
January 2 John Hillerman and Tom Selleck of *Magnum, P.I.*
January 9 Michael Landon of *Little House on the Prairie*
January 16 "Bending the Rules in Hollywood: How TV's Movers and Shakers Operate"
January 23 Super Bowl
January 30 Robert Pine, Larry Wilcox and Erik Estrada of *CHiPs*
February 6 Sherman Hemsley of *The Jeffersons*
February 13 "A Noted Historian Judges TV's Holocaust Films"
February 20 Ed Bradley, Morley Safer, Mike Wallace and Harry Reasoner of *60 Minutes*
February 27 Pamela Sue Martin, John Forsythe and Linda Evans of *Dynasty*
March 6 Swoosie Kurtz, Tony Randall and Kaleena Kiff of *Love, Sidney*
March 13 Priscilla Barnes, John Ritter and Joyce DeWitt of *Three's Company*
March 20 Ronald Reagan
March 27 Larry Hagman of *Dallas*
April 3 Baseball Preview
April 10 Tom Brokaw of *NBC Nightly News*
April 17 Scott Baio, Henry Winkler and Erin Moran of *Happy Days*
April 24 Ingrid Bergman in *A Woman Called Golda*
May 1 John Schneider, Catherine Bach and Tom Wopat of *The Dukes of Hazzard*
May 8 Goldie Hawn
May 15 Ken Marshall in *Marco Polo*
May 22 Billy Moses, Lorenzo Lamas and Jane Wyman of *Falcon Crest*
May 29 "Anatomy of a Smear": Mike Wallace of *60 Minutes*, George Crile and Gen. William Westmoreland
June 5 Lauren Tewes and Gavin MacLeod of *The Love Boat*
June 12 "Why American TV Is So Vulnerable to Foreign Disinformation"
June 19 Daniel J. Travanti and Veronica Hamel of *Hill Street Blues*
June 26 Michele Lee of *Knots Landing*
July 3 Deborah Van Valkenburgh, Lydia Cornell and Ted Knight of *Too Close for Comfort*
July 10 Nancy McKeon, Charlotte Rae, Lisa Whelchel, Kim Fields and Mindy Cohn of *The Facts of Life*
July 17 Rick Springfield of *General Hospital*
July 24 William Katt of *The Greatest American Hero*
July 31 Katherine Cannon and Merlin Olsen of Father Murphy
August 7 Carroll O'Connor and Denise Miller of *Archie Bunker's Place*
August 14 William Shatner of *T.J. Hooker*
August 21 Nell Carter and Dolph Sweet of *Gimme a Break*
August 28 Penny Marshall and Cindy Williams of *Laverne & Shirley*
September 4 Miss America
September 11 Fall Preview
September 18 Victoria Principal of *Dallas*
September 25 "How Americans Rate TV Newspeople": Harry Reasoner, David Brinkley and John Chancellor
October 2 Genie Francis in *Bare Essence*
October 9 World Series
October 16 Erik Estrada and Morgan Fairchild in *Honeyboy*
October 23 Linda Evans and Joan Collins of *Dynasty*
October 30 Pernell Roberts of *Trapper John, M.D.*
November 6 Gene Anthony Ray and Erica Gimpel of *Fame*
November 13 *The Blue and the Gray*
November 20 Richard Kline, Joyce DeWitt, John Ritter and Priscilla Barnes of *Three's Company*
November 27 Meredith Baxter-Birney of *Family Ties*
December 4 "Video Games: A Shopper's Guide to 1982's Best"
December 11 Sally Struthers of *Gloria* and daughter Samantha
December 18 Deborah Van Valkenburgh, Ted Knight, Michael Phillip Cannon, William Thomas Cannon, Nancy Dussault and Lydia Cornell of *Too Close for Comfort*
December 25 Christmas

1983
January 1 Bob Newhart and Mary Frann of *Newhart*
January 8 John Madden
January 15 Rachel Dennison, Jean Marsh, Peter Bonerz, Valerie Curtin and Rita Moreno of *9 to 5*
January 22 "Rating TV's Investigative Reporters": Mike Wallace, Geraldo Rivera and Brian Ross
January 29 Robert Mitchum and Ali MacGraw in *The Winds of War*
February 5 Cheryl Ladd in *Grace Kelly*
February 12 David Ogden Stiers, Harry Morgan, Mike Farrell, Jamie Farr, Loretta Swit, Alan Alda and William Christopher of *M*A*S*H*
February 19 Armand Assante, Jaclyn Smith and Ken Howard in *Rage of Angels*
February 26 Kim Delaney, Laurence Lau and Susan Lucci of *All My Children*
March 5 Valerie Bertinelli of *One Day at a Time*
March 12 Bruce Weitz of *Hill Street Blues*
March 19 Gary Coleman of *Diff'rent Strokes* and Nancy Reagan
March 26 Richard Chamberlain and Rachel Ward in *The Thorn Birds*
April 2 Donna Mills of *Knots Landing*
April 9 Elvis Presley
April 16 Morley Safer, Ed Bradley, Harry Reasoner and Mike Wallace of *60 Minutes*

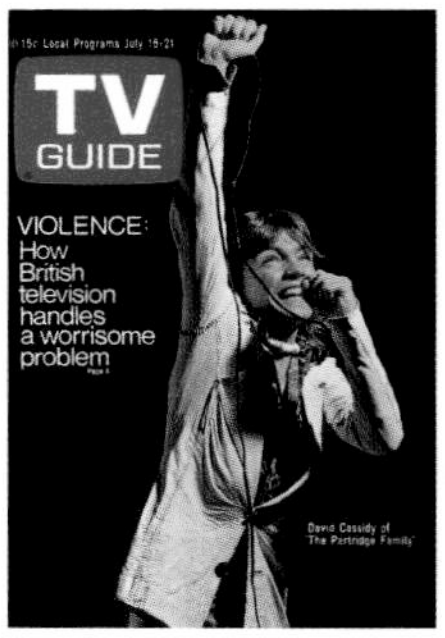

July 15, 1972
BY GENE TRINDL

One widow and five kids equaled TV's most famous family band, *The Partridge Family*. The show spawned a few hit singles and made David Cassidy a pinup for a generation.

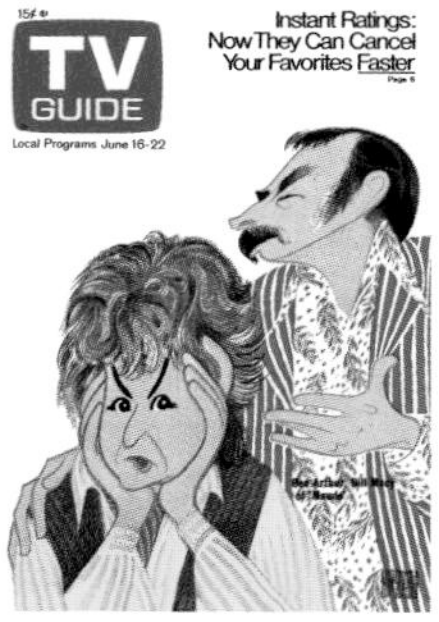

June 16, 1973
BY AL HIRSCHFELD

In *Maude*, Beatrice Arthur gave TV one of its strongest female figures. Even by today's standards, the comedy's subjects of abortion, alcoholism and facelifts were daring. So were the knee-length sweater-vests.

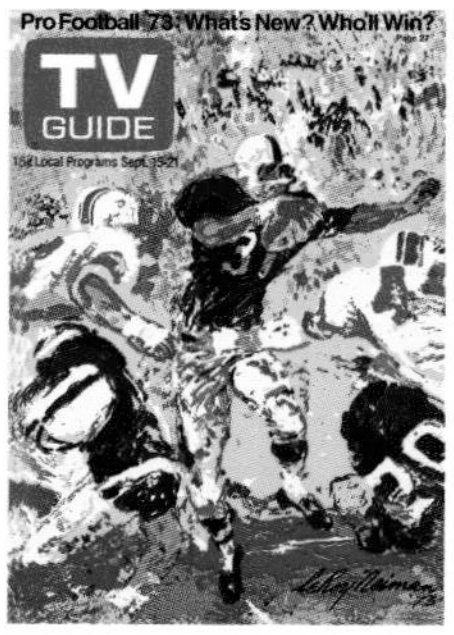

September 15, 1973
BY LEROY NEIMAN

The colorful and famed sports illustrator LeRoy Neiman painted a tribute to the Super Bowl in which the Miami Dolphins eventually beat the Washington Redskins, 14–7.

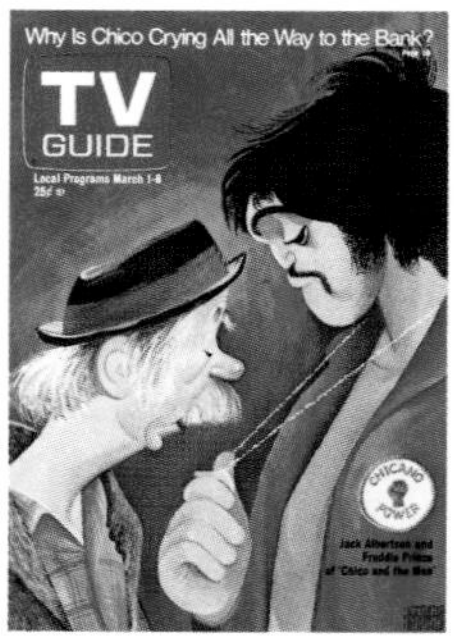

March 1, 1975
BY AL HIRSCHFELD

"Loooking goood!" Freddie Prinze (right) was a Latino sex symbol, but the *Chico and the Man* star was really named Frederick Pruetzel (Hungarian dad, Puerto Rican mom). Prinze was for "Prince of Comedy."

1983–87

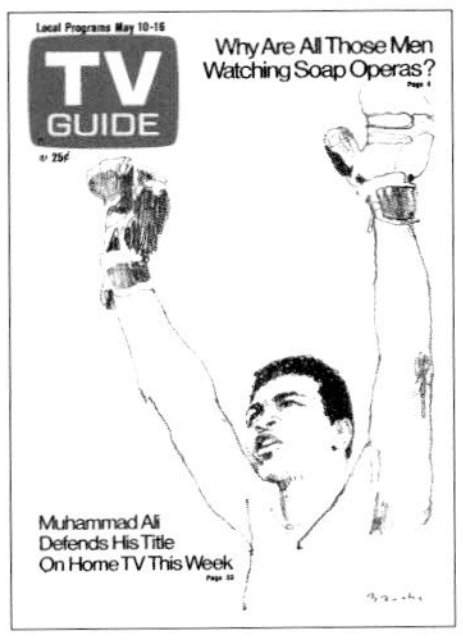

May 10, 1975
BY BERNARD FUCHS

If one athlete held the spotlight for the whole decade of the '70s, it was Muhammad Ali. Famous bouts with Joe Frazier, George Foreman and Leon Spinks had everyone watching.

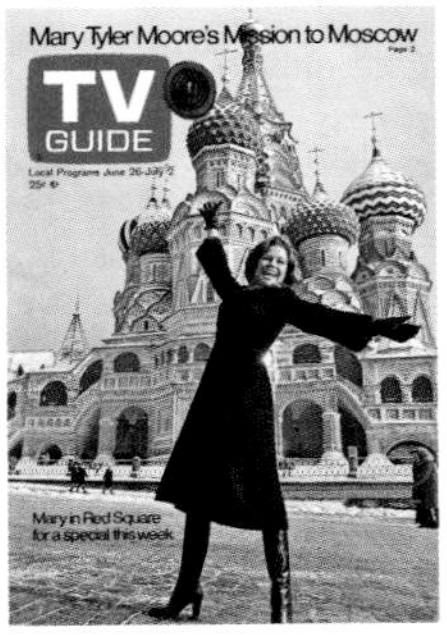

June 26, 1976
BY TONY ESPARZA

Third on the all-time list, Mary Tyler Moore has graced 24 TV GUIDE covers. Her first TV appearance, though, was as the Hotpoint Appliance elf on a commercial during *Ozzie & Harriet*.

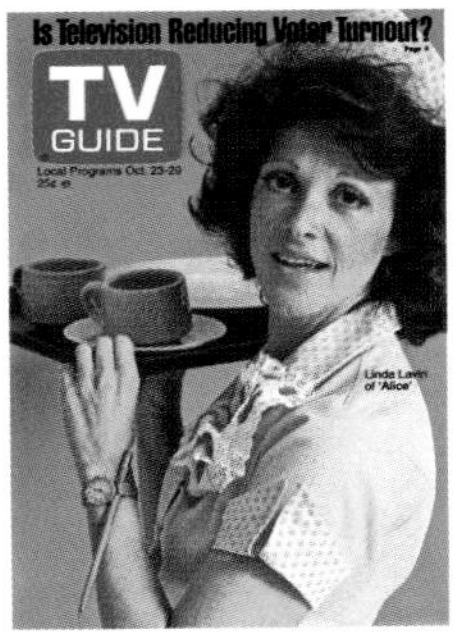

October 23, 1976
BY PETER KREDENSER

Based on the Martin Scorsese feature film *Alice Doesn't Live Here Anymore*, Linda Lavin's working-class comedy *Alice* ran for nine seasons and was guilty for the catchphrase "Kiss my grits."

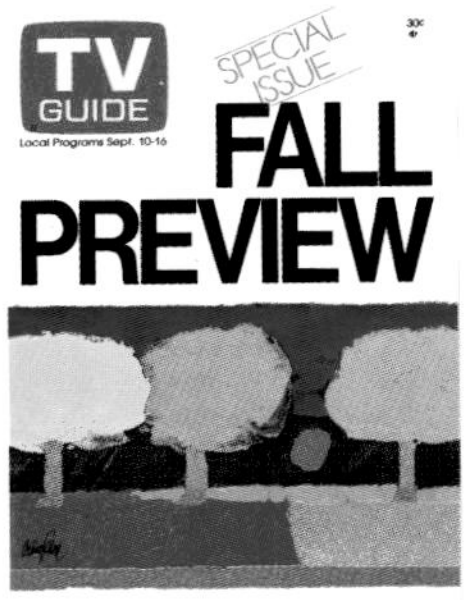

September 10, 1977
ILLUSTRATOR UNKNOWN

Don't let the quiet illustration of a few trees fool you—this is actually the cover of the best-selling issue in TV GUIDE's history. Obviously, it's what's on the inside that counts.

April 23 Linda Purl and Henry Winkler of *Happy Days*
April 30 Tom Selleck of *Magnum, P.I.*
May 7 Ricky Schroder, Erin Gray and Joel Higgins of *Silver Spoons*
May 14 Kathleen Beller and John James of *Dynasty*
May 21 Bob Hope
May 28 Audrey Landers, Ken Kercheval and Larry Hagman of *Dallas*
June 4 Lee Majors, Heather Thomas and Douglas Barr of *The Fall Guy*
June 11 "They're Stars–But Can They Act?": Alan Alda, Valerie Bertinelli, Linda Evans and Erik Estrada
June 18 Jameson Parker and Gerald McRaney of *Simon & Simon*
June 25 David Hasselhoff of *Knight Rider*
July 2 "The Best and Worst We Saw": Alan Alda, Mike Farrell and Harry Morgan of *M*A*S*H*; Joan Collins and Linda Evans of *Dynasty*; and Richard Chamberlain and Rachel Ward in *The Thorn Birds*
July 9 Ana Alicia, Lorenzo Lamas and Jane Wyman of *Falcon Crest*
July 16 "TV's Hunks–Isn't Something Missing?": Tom Selleck, Gregory Harrison, Pierce Brosnan and Lee Horsley
July 23 Ted Shackelford, Joan Van Ark and Donna Mills of *Knots Landing*
July 30 Isabel Sanford and Sherman Hemsley of *The Jeffersons*
August 6 "Why There Are Still No Female Dan Rathers": Judy Woodruff, Lesley Stahl and Anne Garrels
August 13 Deidre Hall and Wayne Northrop of *Days of Our Lives*
August 20 Stefanie Powers and Robert Wagner of *Hart to Hart*
August 27 "ABC/CBS/NBC: Who's Toughest on the White House–and Why"
September 3 Rob Reiner, Jean Stapleton, Carroll O'Connor and Sally Struthers of *All in the Family*
September 10 Fall Preview: William Christopher, Harry Morgan, Rosalind Chao and Jamie Farr of *AfterMASH*; Mr. Smith of *Mr. Smith*; Connie Sellecca, James Brolin and Bette Davis of *Hotel*
September 17 Miss America: Nancy Chapman, Elizabeth Ward and Debra Sue Maffett
September 24 Joyce DeWitt, John Ritter and Priscilla Barnes of *Three's Company*
October 1 Gregory Harrison of *Trapper John, M.D.*
October 8 The Country Music Awards: Anne Murray and Willie Nelson
October 15 "*Dallas* Vs. *Dynasty*": Larry Hagman of *Dallas* and Joan Collins of *Dynasty*
October 22 Mr. Smith of *Mr. Smith*
October 29 James Brolin and Connie Sellecca of *Hotel*
November 5 Marete Van Kamp in *Princess Daisy*
November 12 John F. Kennedy and Jacqueline Kennedy
November 19 Doug Scott and and John Cullum in *The Day After*
November 26 Linda Evans and Kenny Rogers in *The Gambler II: The Adventure Continues*
December 3 Barbara Walters and Johnny Carson
December 10 Tom Selleck of *Magnum, P.I.*
December 17 Erin Gray of *Silver Spoons*
December 24 Gavin MacLeod, Lauren Tewes, Ted Lange, Bernie Kopell, Jill Whelan and Fred Grandy of *The Love Boat*
December 31 Farrah Fawcett

1984
January 7 William Christopher, Harry Morgan, Rosalind Chao and Jamie Farr of *AfterMASH*
January 14 Emmanuel Lewis of *Webster*
January 21 "TV's Game-Show Hosts": Pat Sajak of *Wheel of Fortune*, Monty Hall of *Let's Make a Deal*, Bob Barker of *The Price Is Right*, Jack Barry of *The Joker's Wild*, Bill Cullen of *Hot Potato* and Wink Martindale of *Tic Tac Dough*
January 28 Cybill Shepherd of *The Yellow Rose*
February 4 The Olympics
February 11 Kate Jackson and Bruce Boxleitner of *Scarecrow & Mrs. King*
February 18 Ted Danson, Shelley Long and Rhea Perlman of *Cheers*
February 25 Harry Reasoner, Ed Bradley, Mike Wallace and Morley Safer of *60 Minutes*
March 3 Ann-Margret and Treat Williams in *A Streetcar Named Desire*
March 10 Dirk Benedict, George Peppard, Mr. T and Dwight Schultz of *The A-Team*
March 17 Priscilla Presley of *Dallas*
March 24 Veronica Hamel and Daniel J. Travanti of *Hill Street Blues*
March 31 Teri Copley of *We Got It Made*
April 7 Mike Wallace of *60 Minutes* and Barry Bostwick in *George Washington*
April 14 Rebecca Holden and David Hasselhoff of *Knight Rider*
April 21 Amy Irving and Ben Cross in *The Far Pavilions*
April 28 Donny Most, Henry Winkler, Anson Williams, Pat Morita, Al Molinaro, Marion Ross, Heather O'Rourke, Erin Moran, Tom Bosley, Ted McGinley, Cathy Silvers, Lynda Goodfriend, Ron Howard, Scott Baio and Crystal Bernard of *Happy Days*
May 5 Lesley-Anne Down in *The Last Days of Pompeii*
May 12 Crystal Gayle
May 19 Morgan Fairchild in *The Zany Adventures of Robin Hood*
May 26 Daniel Hugh-Kelly and Brian Keith of *Hardcastle & McCormick*
June 2 Victoria Principal of *Dallas*
June 9 Pierce Brosnan and Stephanie Zimbalist of *Remington Steele*
June 16 "A Social Climber's Guide to TV": Larry Hagman of *Dallas*, Stefanie Powers of *Hart to Hart* and Joan Collins of *Dynasty*
June 23 Connie Sellecca of *Hotel*
June 30 "The Best and Worst We Saw": Martin Sheen and Blair Brown in *Kennedy*; Arielle Dombasle, Brooke Adams, Bess Armstrong and Phoebe Cates in *Lace*; and *The Day After*
July 7 Valerie Bertinelli of *One Day at a Time*
July 14 Johnny Carson of *The Tonight Show*
July 21 Donna Mills, Ted Shackelford and Lisa Hartman of *Knots Landing*
July 28 The Olympics
August 4 Jameson Parker and Gerald McRaney of *Simon & Simon*
August 11 Elisabeth Shue, Cindy Pickett, Gabriel Damon, Craig T. Nelson and David Hollander of *Call to Glory*
August 18 Jane Pauley of *Today*
August 25 Lindsay Bloom and Stacy Keach of *Mickey Spillane's Mike Hammer*
September 1 "Who Shot Bobby?": Linda Gray, Larry Hagman, Victoria Principal and Patrick Duffy of *Dallas* with Morley Safer of *60 Minutes*
September 8 Fall Preview
September 15 George Burns and Catherine Bach of *The Dukes of Hazzard*
September 22 Philippine Leroy-Beaulieu and Stacy Keach in *Mistral's Daughter*
September 29 Mary Tyler Moore and James Garner in *Heart Sounds*
October 6 Nicollette Sheridan, Terry Farrell and Morgan Fairchild of *Paper Dolls*
October 13 Keshia Knight Pulliam and Bill Cosby of *The Cosby Show*
October 20 Daniel J. Travanti, Sophia Loren and Edoardo Ponti in *Aurora by Night*
October 27 Brooke Shields in *Wet Gold*
November 3 "Tales of Election Night Drama"
November 10 Michael Nader and Joan Collins of *Dynasty*
November 17 "What It's Like to Be a Top TV Model": Carol Alt, Kim Alexis and Kelly Emberg
November 24 Jane Curtin and Susan Saint James of *Kate & Allie*
December 1 Shari Belafonte-Harper of *Hotel*
December 8 Ana Alicia and Billy Moses of *Falcon Crest*
December 15 "TV's 10 Most Beautiful Women": Connie Sellecca, Priscilla Presley and Jaclyn Smith
December 22 Susan Clark, Emmanuel Lewis and Alex Karras of *Webster*
December 29 Larry Hagman and Linda Gray of *Dallas*

1985
January 5 Elvis Presley
January 12 Donna Mills and William Devane of *Knots Landing*
January 19 Super Bowl; Ronald Reagan
January 26 Perry King of *Riptide*
February 2 Sharon Gless and Tyne Daly of *Cagney & Lacey*
February 9 Ellen Foley and Harry Anderson of *Night Court*
February 16 Candice Bergen, Joanna Cassidy, Mary Crosby, Angie Dickinson, Stefanie Powers, Suzanne Somers, Catherine Mary Stewart and Frances Bergen in *Hollywood Wives*
February 23 The Grammys: Prince, Bruce Springsteen and Michael Jackson
March 2 Michael Landon of *Highway to Heaven*
March 9 Angela Lansbury of *Murder, She Wrote*
March 16 Lauren Tewes of *The Love Boat*
March 23 Diahann Carroll of *Dynasty*
March 30 *A.D.*
April 6 Richard Chamberlain in *Wallenberg: A Hero's Story*
April 13 Blair Brown, Harry Hamlin and James Garner in *Space*
April 20 Deborah Shelton of *Dallas*
April 27 Justine Bateman, Meredith Baxter-Birney, Michael Gross, Michael J. Fox and Tina Yothers of *Family Ties*
May 4 Phoebe Cates in *Lace II*
May 11 Cheryl Ladd in *A Death in California*
May 18 Gabriel Byrne in *Christopher Columbus*
May 25 Antony Hamilton and Jennifer O'Neill of *Cover Up*
June 1 Rene Enriquez, Taurean Blacque, Ed Marinaro, Bruce Weitz, James Sikking, Charles Haid, Michael Warren, Veronica Hamel, Daniel J. Travanti, Barbara Bosson, Robert Prosky, Robert Hirschfield, Joe Spano, Kiel Martin and Betty Thomas of *Hill Street Blues*
June 8 Jameson Parker and Gerald McRaney of *Simon & Simon*
June 15 Summer Preview: Mary Lou Retton, Roger Mudd, Connie Chung, Robert Redford and Teri Copley
June 22 Nancy Reagan
June 29 "The Best and Worst We Saw": Bill Cosby of *The Cosby Show*, Farrah Fawcett in *The Burning Bed* and Linda Evans, John Forsythe and Joan Collins of *Dynasty*
July 6 Shelley Long, Ted Danson and George Wendt of *Cheers*
July 13 Heather Thomas of *The Fall Guy*
July 20 "TV's Hottest Soap Couples": Kristina Malandro and Jack Wagner of *General Hospital*, Phil Morris and Stephanie Williams of *The Young and the Restless* and Kristian Alfonso and Peter Reckell of *Days of Our Lives*
July 27 Philip Michael Thomas and Don Johnson of *Miami Vice*
August 3 "Romance on the Set": Catherine Hickland and David Hasselhoff
August 10 Madonna
August 17 "Real Men on TV and the Wimps": Tom Selleck, Bob Newhart, Lee Majors, Mr. T, Ted Danson and Bill Cosby
August 24 Lisa Hartman and Alec Baldwin of *Knots Landing*
August 31 George Peppard and Mr. T of *The A-Team*
September 7 Phylicia Ayers-Allen and Bill Cosby of *The Cosby Show*
September 14 Fall Preview
September 21 Michael J. Fox of *Family Ties*
September 28 Howard Cosell, Frank Gifford, Don Meredith and O.J. Simpson of *Monday Night Football*
October 5 Cybill Shepherd and Don Johnson in *The Long Hot Summer*
October 12 Victoria Principal of *Dallas*
October 19 Betty White, Bea Arthur and Rue McClanahan of *The Golden Girls*
October 26 "Network News Today": Dan Rather, Tom Brokaw and Peter Jennings
November 2 Patrick Swayze, Wendy Kilbourne, James Read and Lesley-Anne Down in *North and South*
November 9 Prince Charles and Princess Diana
November 16 Charlton Heston, Stephanie Beacham, Barbara Stanwyck, Emma Samms and John James of *Dynasty II: The Colbys*
November 23 Judith Light, Katherine Helmond and Tony Danza of *Who's the Boss?*
November 30 "Is *Knots Landing* Now Better Than *Dallas* and *Dynasty*?": Joan Van Ark, Ted Shackelford and Donna Mills of *Knots Landing*; Linda Gray, Larry Hagman and Victoria Principal of Dallas; and Joan Collins, John Forsythe and Linda Evans of *Dynasty*
December 7 Cybill Shepherd of *Moonlighting*
December 14 Robert Blake of *Hell Town*
December 21 Victor French and Michael Landon of *Highway to Heaven*
December 28 John Rubinstein, Penny Peyser and Jack Warden of *Crazy Like a Fox*

1986
January 4 Connie Sellecca of *Hotel*
January 11 Bruce Boxleitner and Kate Jackson of *Scarecrow & Mrs. King*
January 18 John Larroquette, Harry Anderson and Markie Post of *Night Court*
January 25 Joan Collins in *Sins*
February 1 Maximilian Schell in *Peter the Great*
February 8 "Hollywood Love Scenes": Linda Evans and Rock Hudson of *Dynasty*, Patrick Duffy and Victoria Principal of *Dallas*; and Laura Johnson and Lorenzo Lamas of *Falcon Crest*
February 15 Angela Lansbury of *Murder, She Wrote*
February 22 Jane Seymour, Lee Horsley and Cheryl Ladd in *Crossings*
March 1 Linda Evans of *Dynasty*
March 8 Don Johnson and Philip Michael Thomas of *Miami Vice*
March 15 Madolyn Smith in *If Tomorrow Comes*
March 22 Bill Cosby of *The Cosby Show*
March 29 "Sexual Harassment in Hollywood"
April 5 Justine Bateman, Tina Yothers and Michael J. Fox of *Family Ties*
April 12 Alice Krige and Richard Chamberlain in *Dream West*
April 19 "The 10 Most Attractive Men on TV": Pierce Brosnan, Don Johnson and Tom Selleck
April 26 Jane Curtin and Susan Saint James of *Kate & Allie*
May 3 James Read and Patrick Swayze in *North and South: Book II* and Mark Harmon in *The Deliberate Stranger*
May 10 John Ratzenberger, Rhea Perlman, George Wendt, Ted Danson and Shelley Long of *Cheers*
May 17 Burt Lancaster in *On Wings of Eagles*
May 24 Larry Hagman of *Dallas*
May 31 Richard Dean Anderson of *MacGyver*
June 7 "The Most Talented Stars on TV": Bruce Willis, Sharon Gless and Michael J. Fox
June 14 Emmanuel Lewis of *Webster*
June 21 Teri Austin of *Knots Landing*
June 28 Ronald Reagan and Nancy Reagan
July 5 "The Goodwill Games: Will the U.S.-Soviet Matchup Make Them a Smash on TV?"
July 12 "The Best and Worst We Saw": Joan Collins of *Dynasty*, Cybill Shepherd and Bruce Willis of *Moonlighting* and Don Johnson in *The Long Hot Summer*
July 19 Robert Urich and Barbara Stock of *Spenser: For Hire*
July 26 "TV's Top Moneymakers": Bill Cosby, Richard Chamberlain, Linda Evans and John Forsythe
August 2 "How to Outfox TV's New Breed of Macho Man": Bruce Willis and Cybill Shepherd of *Moonlighting* and Ted Danson and Shelley Long of *Cheers*
August 9 Alan Thicke, Joanna Kerns, Jeremy Miller, Tracey Gold and Kirk Cameron of *Growing Pains*
August 16 Suzanne Somers
August 23 Valerie Harper of *Valerie*
August 30 Victoria Principal and Patrick Duffy of *Dallas*
September 6 "Rites of Fall": Susin Akin and Sharlene Wells of Miss America and Phil Simms of *Monday Night Football*
September 13 Fall Preview
September 20 *George Washington II: The Forging of a Nation*
September 27 Bronson Pinchot and Mark Linn-Baker of *Perfect Strangers*
October 4 "Two Old Favorites Return to Series TV": Lucille Ball of *Life With Lucy* and Andy Griffith of *Matlock*
October 11 Harry Hamlin, Jill Eikenberry and Corbin Bernsen of *L.A. Law*
October 18 Michael J. Fox and Brian Bonsall of *Family Ties*
October 25 Kim Novak of *Falcon Crest*
November 1 Jaclyn Smith and Ken Howard in *Rage of Angels: The Story Continues*
November 8 Joan Collins and George Hamilton in *Monte Carlo*
November 15 Carol Burnett, Charles Grodin, Teri Garr, Valerie Mahaffey, Gregory Harrison and Dabney Coleman in *Fresno*
November 22 Farrah Fawcett in *Nazi Hunter: The Beate Klarsfeld Story*
November 29 Tom Mason and Shelley Hack of *Jack and Mike*
December 6 Delta Burke of *Designing Women*
December 13 James Garner and James Woods in *Promise*
December 20 Deidre Hall, Chad Allen, Wilford Brimley, Keri Houlihan and Shannen Doherty of *Our House*
December 27 Heather Locklear of *Dynasty*

1987
January 3 Angela Lansbury of *Murder, She Wrote*
January 10 Ted Koppel of *ABC News Nightline*

January 17 Clifton Davis and Sherman Hemsley of *Amen*
January 24 Nicollette Sheridan of *Knots Landing*
January 31 Betty White, Rue McClanahan, Bea Arthur and Estelle Getty of *The Golden Girls*
February 7 Ann-Margret in *The Two Mrs. Grenvilles*
February 14 Robert Urich and Kris Kristofferson in *Amerika*
February 21 Tom Selleck of *Magnum, P.I.* and Frank Sinatra
February 28 Valerie Bertinelli in *I'll Take Manhattan*
March 7 Justine Bateman and Michael J. Fox of *Family Ties*
March 14 Victoria Principal of *Dallas*
March 21 Don Johnson and Philip Michael Thomas of *Miami Vice*
March 28 Kirk Cameron of *Growing Pains*
April 4 Susan Dey and Harry Hamlin of *L.A. Law*
April 11 Bob Newhart, Tom Poston, Mary Frann, Tony Papenfuss, William Sanderson, John Voldstad, Julia Duffy and Peter Scolari of *Newhart*
April 18 Tony Danza of *Who's The Boss?*
April 25 Fred Dryer and Stepfanie Kramer of *Hunter*
May 2 Woody Harrelson, Kelsey Grammer, John Ratzenberger, Rhea Perlman, George Wendt, Ted Danson and Shelley Long of *Cheers*
May 9 Pam Dawber and Rebecca Schaeffer of *My Sister Sam*
May 16 Howard Hesseman, Robin Givens, Dan Frischman, Daniel J. Schneider, Brian Robbins and Khrystyne Haje of *Head of the Class*
May 23 Edward Woodward of *The Equalizer*
May 30 Cybill Shepherd of *Moonlighting*
June 6 "Grading TV's Child Stars": Keshia Knight Pulliam of *The Cosby Show*, Jason Bateman of *Valerie* and Jeremy Miller of *Growing Pains*
June 13 Al Waxman and Sharon Gless of *Cagney & Lacey*
June 20 Markie Post of *Night Court*
June 27 "The Best and Worst We Saw": Kris Kristofferson in *Amerika*, Valerie Bertinelli in *I'll Take Manhattan*, ALF of *ALF* and Susan Dey and Harry Hamlin of *L.A. Law*
July 4 "Does She Push Too Hard: Interviewees' Report Card on Barbara Walters": Walters with Angela Lansbury, Patrick Duffy and Betty White
July 11 Tempestt Bledsoe and Malcolm-Jamal Warner of *The Cosby Show*
July 18 "Ambition in Hollywood": Kate Jackson of *Scarecrow & Mrs. King*, Victoria Principal of *Dallas* and Oprah Winfrey of *The Oprah Winfrey Show*
July 25 Blair Brown of *The Days and Nights of Molly Dodd*
August 1 Melody Thomas Scott, Eric Braeden and Eileen Davidson of *The Young and the Restless*
August 8 "Special Report: Is TV Sex Getting Bolder?"
August 15 ALF of *ALF*
August 22 "TV Is Opening Up the Soviet Bloc Nations...Whether They Like It or Not"
August 29 Sherman Hemsley and Anna Maria Horsford of *Amen*
September 5 Terri Garber of *Dynasty*
September 12 Fall Preview
September 19 Brooke Shields
September 26 Michael Tucker and Jill Eikenberry of *L.A. Law*
October 3 Victoria Principal in *Mistress*
October 10 "Which Are TV's Best Sitcoms and Worst": Michael J. Fox of *Family Ties*; Bob Newhart of *Newhart*; and Joanna Kerns, Alan Thicke and Kirk Cameron of *Growing Pains*
October 17 Dolly Parton of *Dolly*
October 24 Bruce Willis and Cybill Shepherd of *Moonlighting*
October 31 Courteney Cox and Michael J. Fox of *Family Ties*
November 7 Jacqueline Bisset and Armand Assante in *Napoleon and Josephine: A Love Story*
November 14 Ted Danson and Kirstie Alley of *Cheers*
November 21 Linda Gray, Kenny Rogers and Bruce Boxleitner in *The Gambler, III*
November 28 David Birney and Meredith Baxter-Birney in *The Long Journey Home*
December 5 Connie Sellecca in *Downpayment on Murder*
December 12 John Ritter and Bijoux of *Hooperman*
December 19 Keshia Knight Pulliam in *The Little Match Girl*
December 26 Amanda Peterson, Trey Ames and Richard Kiley of *A Year in the Life*

1988

January 2 Jane Wyman, Dana Sparks, Margaret Ladd, Ana Alicia and Susan Sullivan of *Falcon Crest*
January 9 Emma Samms of *Dynasty*
January 16 Sharon Gless and Tyne Daly of *Cagney & Lacey*
January 23 "How We Feel About TV's Role in Campaign '88"
January 30 Priscilla Beaulieu Presley and Elvis Presley
February 6 Jaclyn Smith and Robert Wagner in *Windmills of the Gods*
February 13 The Olympics
February 20 Pierce Brosnan and Deborah Raffin in *Noble House*
February 27 Cheryl Ladd in *Bluegrass*
March 5 Oprah Winfrey of *The Oprah Winfrey Show*
March 12 "Is TV Getting Better–Or Worse?": Desi Arnaz and Lucille Ball of *I Love Lucy*; David Ogden Stiers, Harry Morgan, Mike Farrell, Jamie Farr, William Christopher, Alan Alda and Loretta Swit of *M*A*S*H*; ALF, Max Wright, Anne Schedeen and Benji Gregory of *ALF*; and Ted Danson and Kirstie Alley of *Cheers*
March 19 Philip Michael Thomas and Don Johnson of *Miami Vice*
March 26 Sheree J. Wilson of *Dallas*
April 2 Kirk Cameron and Tracey Gold of *Growing Pains*
April 9 Harry Hamlin of *L.A. Law*
April 16 Tim Reid and Daphne Maxwell Reid of *Frank's Place*
April 23 Jason Bateman of *Valerie's Family*
April 30 "Dr. Ruth to the *Golden Girls*: How to Keep That Spice and Sparkle in Your Lives": Betty White, Rue McClanahan, Bea Arthur, Ruth Westheimer and Estelle Getty
May 7 Richard Chamberlain and Jaclyn Smith in *The Bourne Identity*
May 14 "Beat the Press": Lesley Stahl, Sam Donaldson and Chris Wallace
May 21 Princess Diana and Prince Charles
May 28 Brian Bonsall and Michael J. Fox of *Family Ties*
June 4 "Stars and Strife at ABC Sports": Carl Lewis, Donna de Verona, Howard Cosell and Al Michaels
June 11 Mel Harris, Brittany Craven and Ken Olin of *thirtysomething*
June 18 "The 1988 Network News All-Star Team": Peter Jennings, Tom Brokaw, Bruce Morton, John McWethy and Rita Braver
June 25 "The Best and Worst": Brian Boitano and Katarina Witt; Kirstie Alley and Ted Danson of *Cheers*; Oliver North; and Tom Selleck of *Magnum, P.I.*
July 2 Delta Burke, Annie Potts, Dixie Carter and Jean Smart of *Designing Women*
July 9 Brian Robbins, Khrystyne Haje, Howard Hesseman, Robin Givens, Dan Frischman and Daniel J. Schneider of *Head of the Class*
July 16 "The Six Most Beautiful Women on TV": Kim Alexis and Nicollette Sheridan
July 23 "How TV Is Shaking Up the American Family"
July 30 Leann Hunley of *Dynasty*
August 6 "Daytime Soaps: The Best and the Brightest": Susan Lucci of *All My Children*, Peter Barton and Lauralee Bell of *The Young and the Restless*, Tristan Rogers of *General Hospital* and Drake Hogestyn of *Days of Our Lives*
August 13 ALF of *ALF*
August 20 Johnny Depp and Holly Robinson of *21 Jump Street*
August 27 Mariel Hemingway in *Steal the Sky*
September 3 "The Best You Can Do This Fall–a Survivor's Guide": Kaye Lani Rae Rafko; Charlie Sheen in *Platoon*; Charlie Brown, Linus Van Pelt and Snoopy in *This Is America, Charlie Brown*; and Phoebe Mills
September 10 Kaye Lani Rafko
September 17 The Olympics
September 24 Phylicia Rashad, Malcolm-Jamal Warner, Tempestt Bledsoe, Keshia Knight Pulliam and Bill Cosby of *The Cosby Show*
October 1 Fall Preview
October 8 "Watch the Master Strategist Plot to Stay No. 1": Brandon Tartikoff, Judd Hirsch of *Dear John*, Gary Cole of *Midnight Caller*, Kate Jackson of *Baby Boom* and Maryam d'Abo of *Something Is Out There*
October 15 World Series: Kevin Costner and Susan Sarandon
October 22 "The AIDS Scare–What It's Done to Hollywood...and the TV You See"
October 29 Linda Kozlowski and Harry Hamlin in *Favorite Son*
November 5 "Election Day: Which Network You Should Watch"
November 12 Hart Bochner, Victoria Tennant, Robert Mitchum, Rhett Creighton and Jane Seymour in *War and Remembrance*
November 19 John F. Kennedy Jr. , Jacqueline Kennedy, Caroline Kennedy and John F. Kennedy
November 26 "Q. What Does It Take to Get This Odd Mix of Stars Together? A. Barbara Walters": Muhammad Ali, Dudley Moore, Brooke Shields, Victoria Principal, Loretta Lynn, Jimmy Stewart and Walters
December 3 Holiday Preview: Hermey, Sam the Snowman, Rudolph, elf and Santa Claus in *Rudolph the Red-Nosed Reindeer*; LeVar Burton and Louis Gossett Jr. in *Roots: The Gift*; and Marlo Thomas, Donald Faison, Elizabeth Kandel and Michael Kim in *Free to Be...a Family*
December 10 Dinah Manoff, Kristy McNichol, Richard Mulligan and Dreyfuss of *Empty Nest*
December 17 "Shaping a Career: How Beauty Can Get in the Way": Stepfanie Kramer, Sheree J. Wilson and Shari Belafonte-Harper
December 24 Angela Lansbury of *Murder, She Wrote*
December 31 Sandy Duncan and Jason Bateman of *The Hogan Family*

1989

January 7 "Our 8th Annual J. Fred Muggs Awards": Bryant Gumbel, Jane Fonda and Geraldo Rivera
January 14 Cybill Shepherd and Bruce Willis of *Moonlighting*
January 21 "Rock Stars on TV...Elvis Is Still King!": Elvis Presley, Bruce Springsteen, Madonna and Michael Jackson
January 28 John Goodman and Roseanne Barr of *Roseanne*
February 4 Sweeps Preview: Catherine Oxenberg in *Swimsuit*; Burt Reynolds of *B.L. Stryker*; Lisa Hartman in *Full Exposure: The Sex Tapes Scandal*; Billy Crystal at the Grammys; and Robert Duvall and Diane Lane in *Lonesome Dove*
February 11 Larry Hagman of *Dallas*
February 18 "Parents' Guide: The Best Children's Shows on TV": Garfield of *Garfield and Friends*, Mighty Mouse of *Mighty Mouse: The New Adventures*, ALF of *ALF*, Bill Cosby and Keshia Knight Pulliam of *The Cosby Show*, Big Bird of *Sesame Street* and Pee-wee Herman of *Pee-wee's Playhouse*
February 25 Victoria Principal in *Naked Lie*
March 4 Vanna White of *Wheel of Fortune*
March 11 "One-Upmanship Guide": Ken Olin and Mel Harris of *thirtysomething*, Candice Bergen of *Murphy Brown* and Corbin Bernsen of *L.A. Law*
March 18 Oprah Winfrey, Jackee and Robin Givens in *The Women of Brewster Place*
March 25 The Oscars: Jodie Foster, Melanie Griffith, Gene Hackman and Dustin Hoffman
April 1 Susan Ruttan, Susan Dey, Michele Greene and Jill Eikenberry of *L.A. Law*
April 8 "A Busy Person's Guide to TV": Bruce Willis and Cybill Shepherd of *Moonlighting*; Alex Trebek of *Jeopardy!*; Dan Rather of *60 Minutes*; and Olivia d'Abo, Alley Mills, Dan Lauria, Fred Savage and Jason Hervey of *The Wonder Years*
April 15 Joan Collins and John Forsythe of *Dynasty*
April 22 "What It's Like Being a TV Heartthrob": Kirk Cameron of *Growing Pains* and Jason Bateman of *The Hogan Family*
April 29 Sweeps Preview: Robert Mitchum and Victoria Tennant in *War and Remembrance*; Brigitte Nielsen in *Murder by Moonlight*; Holly Hunter and Ali Grant in *Roe vs. Wade*; and David Keith in *Guts & Glory*
May 6 "TV Is 50: Happy Birthday!": John F. Kennedy Jr.; Bill Cosby and Keshia Knight Pulliam of *The Cosby Show*; Edwin "Buzz" Aldrin; Carroll O'Connor of *All in the Family*; Harry Morgan, Mike Farrell and Alan Alda of *M*A*S*H*; Desi Arnaz and Lucille Ball of *I Love Lucy*; and Georgia Engel, Valerie Harper and Mary Tyler Moore of *The Mary Tyler Moore Show*
May 13 Tracy Scoggins of *Dynasty*
May 20 Roseanne Barr of *Roseanne*
May 27 Ted Danson and Kirstie Alley of *Cheers*
June 3 Oprah Winfrey of *The Oprah Winfrey Show*
June 10 Fred Savage and Danica McKellar of *The Wonder Years*
June 17 Donna Mills of *Knots Landing*
June 24 "The Joys of Summer": Tristan Rogers and Edie Lehmann of *General Hospital* and James DePaiva and Jessica Tuck of *One Life to Live*
July 1 "TV Favorites Go for It in Movies": Virginia Madsen, Tom Selleck, Michael J. Fox and Don Harvey
July 8 "The Best and Worst": Bryant Gumbel and Willard Scott of *Today*; Greg Louganis; Chelsea Field, Roxann Biggs, Kristy Swanson and Susan Walters of *Nightingales*; Robert Duvall in *Lonesome Dove*; John Goodman and Roseanne Barr of *Roseanne*; Harry Hamlin and Linda Kozlowski in *Favorite Son*; Geraldo Rivera of *Geraldo*; Morton Downey Jr. of *The Morton Downey Jr. Show*; and Oprah Winfrey of *The Oprah Winfrey Show*
July 15 "The 1989 Network News All-Star Team": Tom Brokaw, Peter Jennings, Andrea Mitchell and Lesley Stahl
July 22 "TV Stars to Watch–and Ignore–If You Want to Look Sharp": Roseanne Barr of *Roseanne* and Nicollette Sheridan of *Knots Landing*
July 29 David Faustino, Christina Applegate, Buck, Ed O'Neill and Katey Sagal of *Married...With Children*
August 5 "In Defense of Tabloid TV": Phil Donahue, Geraldo Rivera, Maury Povich and Oprah Winfrey
August 12 "TV's News Queens": Maria Shriver, Diane Sawyer, Connie Chung and Mary Alice Williams
August 19 Loretta Lynn and Crystal Gayle
August 26 Oprah Winfrey of *The Oprah Winfrey Show*
September 2 "Two Fall Classics": Gretchen Carlson of Miss America and Lawrence Taylor, Mark Rypien and Eric Dorsey of *Monday Night Football*
September 9 Fall Preview
September 16 "*Roseanne*'s Plan to Bump *Cosby* as America's No. 1 Series": Roseanne Barr of *Roseanne* and Bill Cosby of *The Cosby Show*
September 23 "The 11 Stars You'd Better Keep an Eye On": Kimberly Foster of *Dallas*, Khrystyne Haje of *Head of the Class* and Richard Tyson of *Hardball*
September 30 Elizabeth Taylor and Mark Harmon in *Sweet Bird of Youth*
October 7 "The Ultimate Prime-Time Love Story": Delta Burke of *Designing Women* and Gerald McRaney of *Major Dad*
October 14 "Hot Choices This Week": World Series; Perry King and Chynna Phillips in *Roxanne: The Prize Pulitzer*; and Faye Dunaway in *Cold Sassy Tree*
October 21 Jamie Lee Curtis of *Anything But Love*
October 28 Lane Smith in *The Final Days*
November 4 Sweeps Preview: Farrah Fawcett in *Small Sacrifices*, Valerie Bertinelli in *Taken Away* and Michael Keaton in *Batman*
November 11 Richard Chamberlain of *Island Son*
November 18 Courteney Cox and Barry Bostwick in *Till We Meet Again*
November 25 Victoria Principal in *Blind Witness*
December 2 Holiday Preview: Bob Hope; Natalie Wood and Edmund Gwenn in *Miracle on 34th Street*; "Peanuts"; Julie Andrews and Carol Burnett in *Julie and Carol Together Again*; and Kenny Rogers and Kenny Rogers Jr. in *Christmas in America: A Love Story*
December 9 "The '80s": Vanna White, Don Johnson, Oprah Winfrey, Ted Koppel, Hulk Hogan, David Letterman, Bill Cosby, Joan Collins, ALF, Sam Donaldson, Ronald Reagan, Tom Selleck, Larry Hagman, Michael J. Fox, Dan Rather and Roseanne Barr
December 16 Neil Patrick Harris of *Doogie Howser, M.D.*
December 23 Candice Bergen of *Murphy Brown*
December 30 "New Year's Special": Julia Duffy of *Newhart*, Jean Smart of *Designing Women*, Seib Blake and Kayla Reece

1990

January 6 Rock Hudson
January 13 "Can *Roseanne* Lift *Coach* to Victory?": Roseanne Barr of *Roseanne* and Craig T. Nelson of *Coach*
January 20 "Dynamite Dozen" : Catherine Crier of *The World Today*, Arsenio Hall of *The Arsenio Hall Show* and Dana Delany of *China Beach*
January 27 Super Bowl; Harrison Ford in *Indiana Jones and the Last Crusade*
February 3 "Oh, What a Week!": Lesley Ann Warren in *Family of Spies: The Walker Spy Ring*; Anna Maria Horsford and Clifton Davis of *Amen*; Jennifer Grey in *Murder in Mississippi*; and Sammy Davis Jr., Goldie Hawn, Frank Sinatra, Steve Lawrence and Eydie Gorme
February 10 "A Valentine Guide to TV Romance": Maury Povich and Connie Chung;

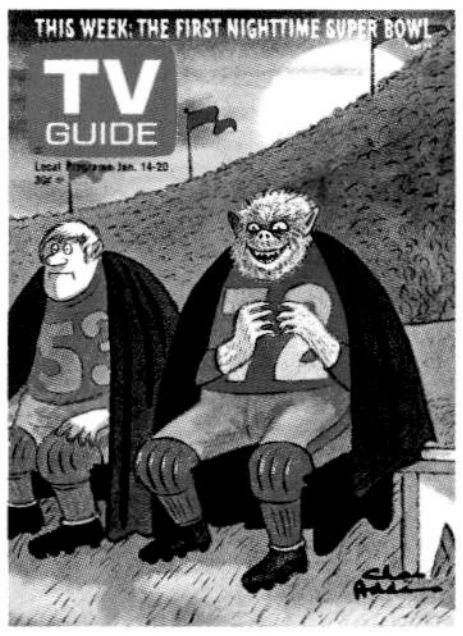

January 14, 1978
BY CHARLES ADDAMS

It was only right that master of the dark Charles Addams commemorate the Super Bowl's first nighttime game. With 102 million viewers, it was the largest audience for a sporting event to date.

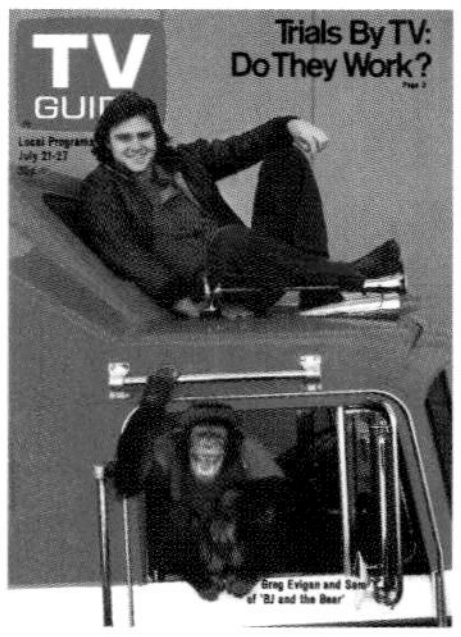

July 21, 1979
BY PETE TURNER

The '70s had its share of silly comedies, and *B.J. and the Bear* was one of them. Greg Evigan (Danny in the original production of *Grease*) was a trucker teamed with a chimpanzee. Hilarious high jinks ensued.

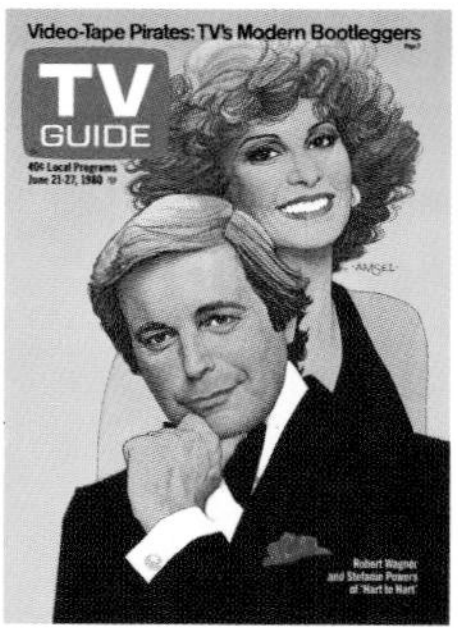

June 21, 1980
BY RICHARD AMSEL

Inspired by the *Thin Man* films of the '30s, *Hart to Hart* showed Robert Wagner and Stefanie Powers outsmart the criminal world in high style. As their manservant, Max, said, "When they met, it was 'moider.' "

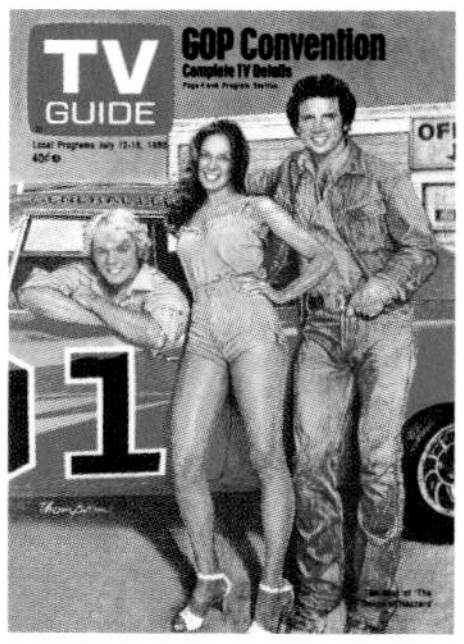

July 12, 1980
BY JOHN THOMPSON

Not since *The Beverly Hillbillies* did a family of country folk capture attention like this. *The Dukes of Hazzard* even entered the vernacular with "Daisy Dukes," a term for short-shorts of the denim variety.

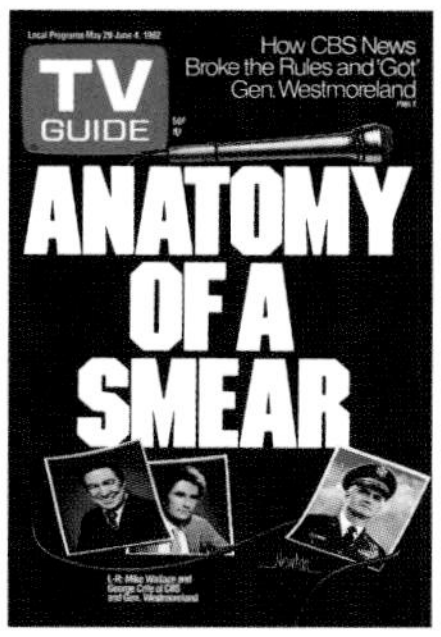

May 29, 1982
BY RICHARD NEWTON

CBS found itself on the defensive when Gen. William C. Westmoreland sued for libel over the documentary *The Uncounted Enemy: A Vietnam Deception*. After 18 weeks of testimony, the suit was settled out of court.

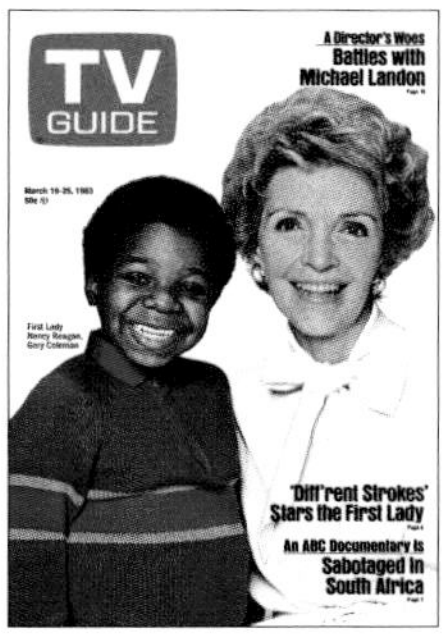

March 19, 1983
BY ROBERT PHILLIPS

Nancy Reagan took time out from her first-lady duties to guest-star in an episode of *Diff'rent Strokes*. In a very special antidrug episode, Arnold (Gary Coleman) learned to "Just say no."

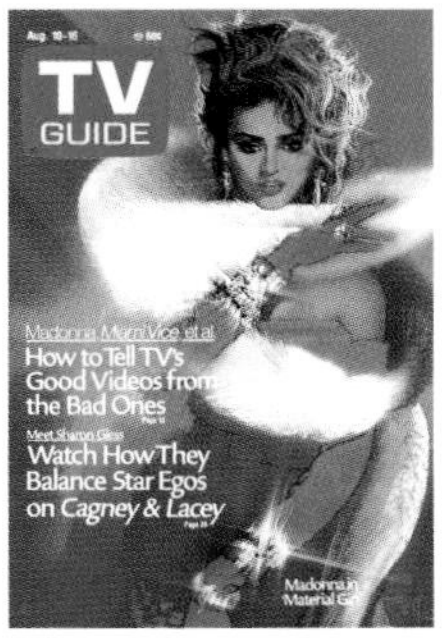

August 10, 1985
BY BOB PEAK

The '80s will be remembered as the decade that gave birth to music videos and Madonna, icon of the new genre. In a world that goes through its pop stars quickly, she has endured.

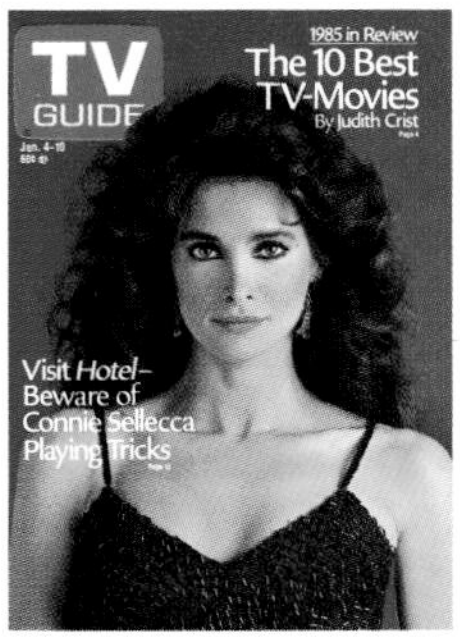

January 4, 1986
BY PETER KREDENSER

Next to the Fall Preview issue, this was the top-selling TV GUIDE of '86. Connie Sellecca and the future Mr. Barbra Streisand, James Brolin, hosted rotating guests—including Liberace!—on *Hotel*.

Michael Tucker and Jill Eikenberry of *L.A. Law*; and Patricia Wettig and Ken Olin of *thirtysomething*
February 17 Michael St. Gerard in *Elvis* and Elvis Presley
February 24 Brian Kerwin, Joe Morton, Julie Fulton, Richard Jenkins, Barry Bostwick, Karen Allen and Keone Young in *Challenger*
March 3 "Parents' Guide to Children's Television": Fred Savage of *The Wonder Years*, *Muppet Babies*, Babar, Winnie the Pooh, Fred Rogers of *Mister Rogers' Neighborhood* and Pee-wee Herman of *Pee-wee's Playhouse*
March 10 Larry Drake, Susan Ruttan, Corbin Bernsen, Alan Rachins, Jimmy Smits, Richard Dysart, Michele Greene, Michael Tucker, Susan Dey, Blair Underwood, Harry Hamlin and Jill Eikenberry of *L.A. Law*
March 17 Bart Simpson, Lisa Simpson, Maggie Simpson, Marge Simpson and Homer Simpson of *The Simpsons*
March 24 The Oscars: Billy Crystal
March 31 Bob Saget of *America's Funniest Home Videos*
April 7 Spring Preview: Valerie Bertinelli of *Sydney*; Michael Woods, Lloyd Bridges and Helen Slater of *Capital News*; and Carol Burnett of *Carol & Company*
April 14 "America's Top TV Critics Tell What's In, What's Out"
April 21 Arnold Schwarzenegger of *Tales From the Crypt*
April 28 Sweeps Preview: Robin Williams, Whoopi Goldberg and Billy Crystal in *Comic Relief '90*; Flying Continental in the Kentucky Derby; Greg Kean, Casey Sander, Bo Foxworth, Andrew Myler and Bruce Greenwood in *Summer Dreams: The Story of the Beach Boys*; and Ariel in *The Little Mermaid*
May 5 Oprah Winfrey in *Brewster Place*
May 12 Barbara Cameron, Kirk Cameron and Joanna Kerns of *Growing Pains*
May 19 Carol Burnett of *Carol & Company*
May 26 "TV Goes to the Movies": Madonna in *Dick Tracy*; Michael J. Fox and Christopher Lloyd in the *Back to the Future* trilogy; and James Woods and Melanie Griffith in *Women and Men*
June 2 "Summer Shape-Up Special": Steve Bond of *Santa Barbara* and Barbara Crampton of *The Young and the Restless*
June 9 "America's New Love Affair With Cartoons": Bart Simpson, the Teenage Mutant Ninja Turtles and the Little Mermaid
June 16 Dana Delaney of *China Beach*
June 23 Arsenio Hall of *The Arsenio Hall Show*
June 30 Summer Preview: Jose Canseco; Carey Lowell and Timothy Dalton in *Licence to Kill*; and Isabella Rossellini and John Lithgow in *The Last Elephant*
July 7 "The Best and the Worst": Suzanne Pleshette and Bob Newhart of *Newhart*; Energizer Bunny; Sherilyn Fenn and Kyle MacLachlan of *Twin Peaks*; Andrew "Dice" Clay; Erika Eleniak, Shawn Weatherly and David Hasselhoff of *Baywatch*; Lynn Redgrave and Jackie Mason of *Chicken Soup*; and Sam Donaldson and Diane Sawyer of *PrimeTime Live*
July 14 Sinbad, Dawnn Lewis, Jasmine Guy and Kadeem Hardison of *A Different World*
July 21 "TV's Top Teen Superstars": Malcolm-Jamal Warner of *The Cosby Show*, David Faustino of *Married...With Children*, Neil Patrick Harris of *Doogie Howser, M.D.* and Alyssa Milano of *Who's the Boss?*
July 28 "Guide to Home Video's High Flying New Season": Peter Pan
August 4 "Dressed to Thrill": Candice Bergen of *Murphy Brown*, Nicollette Sheridan of *Knots Landing* and Kirstie Alley of *Cheers*
August 11 "TV, Sports and Money": Joe Montana, Michael Jordan and Bo Jackson
August 18 Annie Potts, Delta Burke, Dixie Carter and Jean Smart of *Designing Women*
August 25 "Is One of These Women the Most Beautiful on TV?": Nicollette Sheridan, Dana Delany and Jaclyn Smith
September 1 "Why Women Now Rule Rock": Janet Jackson, Paula Abdul and Madonna
September 8 Sheryl Lee, Lara Flynn Boyle and Peggy Lipton of *Twin Peaks*
September 15 Fall Preview
September 22 Fall Preview II: Bart Simpson of *The Simpsons* and Bill Cosby of *The Cosby Show*
September 29 Fall Preview III: Lenny Clarke of *Lenny*, Will Smith of *The Fresh Prince of Bel Air* and Laila Robbins of *Gabriel's Fire*
October 6 Fall Preview IV: "What's Best...and What's Waiting in the Wings"
October 13 "A High School Report Card on the New Teen Shows": Corin Nemec of *Parker Lewis Can't Lose*, Will Smith of *The Fresh Prince of Bel Air* and Charlie Schlatter of *Ferris Bueller*
October 20 "The Best and Worst Dressed on TV": Marge Simpson of *The Simpsons*, Oprah Winfrey of *The Oprah Winfrey Show* and Delta Burke of *Designing Women*
October 27 "Why We Go Batty for Horror on TV": Ari Lehman in *Friday the 13th*, the Crypt Keeper of *Tales from the Crypt*, Ben Cross of *Dark Shadows* and Robert Englund of *Freddy's Nightmares*
November 3 Woody Harrelson, Ted Danson, Roger Rees, Kirstie Alley, George Wendt, Kelsey Grammer, Bebe Neuwirth, Rhea Perlman and John Ratzenberger of *Cheers*
November 10 Susan Lucci of *All My Children*
November 17 Bert and Ernie of *Sesame Street*, Miss Piggy and Kermit the Frog of *The Muppets* and Jim Henson
November 24 Linda Evans
December 1 Holiday Preview: Jasmine Guy, Patti LaBelle and Kadeem Hardison of *A Different World*; the Grinch in *How the Grinch Stole Christmas*; Dolly Parton in *Home for Christmas*; and Chevy Chase in *National Lampoon's Christmas Vacation*
December 8 David Coulier, Ashley Olsen and Mary-Kate Olsen of *Full House*
December 15 Dixie Carter of *Designing Women*
December 22 "How Hollywood Brings Our Comic-Book Heroes to Life": Warren Beatty in *Dick Tracy*, Michael Keaton in *Batman* and Jon Wesley Shipp of *The Flash*
December 29 Charles Kimbrough, Candice Bergen, Joe Regalbuto, Robert Pastorelli, Faith Ford, Grant Shaud and Pat Corley of *Murphy Brown*

1991
January 5 Jane Pauley of *Real Life*
January 12 Farrah Fawcett and Ryan O'Neal of *Good Sports*
January 19 Mike Wallace, Morley Safer, Harry Reasoner and Ed Bradley of *60 Minutes*
January 26 Cybill Shepherd in *Which Way Home*
February 2 Sweeps Preview: Julia Roberts in a Barbara Walters special, M.C. Hammer at the Grammys and Gary Cole in *Son of the Morning Star*
February 9 Lucille Ball and Desi Arnaz
February 16 "Watching the War: How TV Has Stirred Our Patriotism, Pride, Anger and Fear"
February 23 Roseanne Barr of *Roseanne*; "TV's War Stars": Christiane Amanpour, Arthur Kent and Peter Arnett; and Fred Rogers
March 2 "Parents' Guide to Children's Television": Jaleel White of *Family Matters*, Captain Planet, Bart Simpson, Big Bird, the Teenage Mutant Ninja Turtles and Tiny Toons
March 9 Dreyfuss of *Empty Nest*
March 16 "Cartoons Grow Up": Barbara Walters with the Teenage Mutant Ninja Turtles
March 23 The Oscars: Whoopi Goldberg, Julia Roberts and Kevin Costner
March 30 Cheryl Ladd in *Changes*
April 6 Bo Jackson, Nolan Ryan, Roger Clemens and Jose Canseco
April 13 Delta Burke of *Designing Women*
April 20 Burt Reynolds, Marilu Henner and Caroline Rhymer of *Evening Shade*
April 27 Sweeps Preview: Earl Sinclair of *Dinosaurs*, Magic Johnson and Patrick Bergin in *Robin Hood*
May 4 Larry Hagman of *Dallas*
May 11 Jimmy Smits, Harry Hamlin, Susan Dey, John Spencer, Cecil Hoffmann and Amanda Donohoe of *L.A. Law*
May 18 Robin Thomas, Candice Bergen and Jay Thomas of *Murphy Brown*
May 25 Summer Movie Preview: Arnold Schwarzenegger, *101 Dalmatians* and Julia Roberts
June 1 Jasmine Guy of *A Different World*
June 8 Michael Landon
June 15 "The Best 50 Videos to Watch Over and Over Again": Ray Bolger, Jack Haley, Judy Garland and Bert Lahr in *The Wizard of Oz*; Julie Andrews in *Mary Poppins*; Dustin Hoffman and Jessica Lange in *Tootsie*; Humphrey Bogart and Ingrid Bergman in *Casablanca*; and R2-D2 and C-3PO in *Star Wars*
June 22 Gerald McRaney of *Major Dad* and Delta Burke of *Designing Women*
June 29 "The Battle for Carson's Crown": Arsenio Hall of *The Arsenio Hall Show*, Johnny Carson of *The Tonight Show*, David Letterman of *Late Night With David Letterman* and Jay Leno
July 6 "The Best and the Worst": Baby Sinclair of *Dinosaurs*, Abraham Lincoln, Katie Couric of *Today*, Frances Fisher and Maurice Benard in *Lucy and Desi: Before the Laughter* and Roseanne Barr of *Roseanne*
July 13 Michael Landon
July 20 Michael Landon
July 27 "The 2,000th Issue of TV GUIDE"
August 3 Madonna
August 10 "TV's Most Beautiful Women": Jaclyn Smith, Candice Bergen and Vanna White
August 17 "Viewers' Guide to Home Video's Hottest Season": Kevin Costner and Macaulay Culkin
August 24 Shannen Doherty of *Beverly Hills, 90210*
August 31 Patrick Stewart of *Star Trek: The Next Generation* and William Shatner of *Star Trek*
September 7 Janine Turner of *Northern Exposure*
September 14 Fall Preview
September 21 Julia Duffy and Jan Hooks of *Designing Women*
September 28 "Parents' Guide to the New Kids' Shows": Wilma and Waldo of *Where's Waldo?*, Duck Dawking of *Duck Dawking*, Hammerman of *Hammerman*, Doug and Porkchop of *Doug* and Macaulay Culkin
October 5 "The Best and Worst Dressed on TV": Sharon Gless and Arsenio Hall
October 12 Jacqueline Kennedy Onassis
October 19 Linda Evans and Joan Collins in *Dynasty: The Reunion*
October 26 Joan Rivers
November 2 Michael Jackson
November 9 "Is Network News Crumbling?": Tom Brokaw of *NBC Nightly News*, Peter Jennings of *World News Tonight* and Dan Rather of *The CBS Evening News*
November 16 Valerie Bertinelli in *In a Child's Name*
November 23 Madonna
November 30 Naomi Judd and Wynonna Judd
December 7 Holiday Preview: Babar; Winnie the Pooh; Opus; Bob Hope; Richard Thomas and Katharine Isabel; and Andy Rooney, Mickey Mouse and Goofy
December 14 Luke Perry and Jason Priestley of *Beverly Hills, 90210*
December 21 John Corbett of *Northern Exposure*
December 28 John Goodman of *Roseanne*

1992
January 4 Roseanne Arnold of *Roseanne*
January 11 Jane Fonda in *Fonda on Fonda*
January 18 Dreyfuss of *Empty Nest*
January 25 Super Bowl
February 1 Jessica Lange in *O Pioneers!*
February 8 The Olympics
February 15 Regis Philbin and Kathie Lee Gifford of *Live With Regis and Kathie Lee*
February 22 "Fake News: A Special Report"
February 29 Corey Carrier of *The Young Indiana Jones Chronicles*
March 7 Macaulay Culkin
March 14 Jane Pauley of *Dateline NBC*
March 21 Magic Johnson
March 28 The Oscars: The Beast of *Beauty and the Beast*
April 4 Ronn Moss and Katherine Kelly Lang of *The Bold and the Beautiful*
April 11 "S.O.S.: Save Our Shows"
April 18 Patricia Richardson and Tim Allen of *Home Improvement*
April 25 Burt Reynolds of *Evening Shade*
May 2 Woody Harrelson and Jackie Swanson of *Cheers*
May 9 Johnny Carson of *The Tonight Show*
May 16 Oprah Winfrey of *The Oprah Winfrey Show*
May 23 Jerry Seinfeld of *Seinfeld*
May 30 Dan Lauria, Alley Mills, Jason Hervey and Fred Savage of *The Wonder Years*
June 6 Grant Show of *Melrose Place*
June 13 Bob Saget of *Full House*
June 20 "The Year's Best and Worst": Ross Perot, Burt Reynolds and Michael Jeter of *Evening Shade*, Candice Bergen of *Murphy Brown*, Bette Midler and Johnny Carson of *The Tonight Show* and Anita Hill
June 27 Phil Donahue of *Donahue*
July 4 Delta Burke of *Delta*
July 11 Luke Perry and Shannen Doherty of *Beverly Hills, 90210*
July 18 "TV's Top Turn-Ons": Patrick Stewart of *Star Trek: The Next Generation* and Cindy Crawford
July 25 The Olympics: Kim Zmeskal
August 1 Dana Carvey and David Letterman
August 8 Princess Diana and Prince Charles
August 15 "America Zaps! The All-Powerful Remote Control": Whoopi Goldberg, Roseanne Arnold, Homer Simpson, Ted Koppel and Michele Pfeiffer
August 22 "Is TV Violence Battering Our Kids?"
August 29 Roseanne Arnold of *Roseanne*
September 5 Joan Lunden of *Good Morning America*
September 12 Fall Preview
September 19 Candice Bergen of *Murphy Brown*
September 26 The Country Music Awards: Billy Ray Cyrus and Reba McEntire
October 3 Bob Newhart of *Bob*
October 10 "Would You Take $1,000,000 to Give Up TV Forever?"
October 17 "TV's Best Dressed": Leeza Gibbons of *Entertainment Tonight* and Jay Leno of *The Tonight Show*
October 24 Goofy and Max of *Goof Troop*
October 31 Sweeps Preview: Julia Roberts, Peter Falk, Jaclyn Smith and E.T.
November 7 Frank Sinatra and Philip Casnoff in *Sinatra*
November 14 Michael Jackson
November 21 Diane Sawyer of *PrimeTime Live*
November 28 John Ritter and Markie Post of *Hearts Afire*
December 5 John Stamos, Blake Tuomy-Wilhoit and Dylan Tuomy-Wilhoit of *Full House*
December 12 Katey Sagal of *Married...With Children*
December 19 *Tiny Toon Adventures*
December 26 "Year in Cheers and Jeers": Angela Lansbury of *Murder, She Wrote*, Ted Danson of *Cheers*, Michael Jordan and Madonna

1993
January 2 Avery Brooks of *Star Trek: Deep Space Nine* and Patrick Stewart of *Star Trek: The Next Generation*
January 9 Bill Clinton and Hillary Clinton
January 16 "How to Be a Funny President": Dana Carvey and Phil Hartman
January 23 Will Smith of *The Fresh Prince of Bel Air*
January 30 Craig T. Nelson of *Coach*
February 6 Katie Couric of *Today*
February 13 The Grammys: Billy Ray Cyrus
February 20 Jane Seymour of *Dr. Quinn, Medicine Woman*
February 27 "Parents' Guide to Kids' TV": Jane Pauley and Barney of *Barney & Friends*
March 6 Regis Philbin of *Live With Regis and Kathie Lee*
March 13 Mary Tyler Moore
March 20 "Soaps' Sexiest Stars": Antonio Sabato Jr. of *General Hospital* and Hunter Tylo of *The Bold and the Beautiful*
March 27 The Oscars: Billy Crystal
April 3 Heather Locklear of *Melrose Place*
April 10 Ted Danson and Shelley Long of *Cheers*
April 17 "40th Anniversary Issue"
April 24 Patricia Richardson and Tim Allen of *Home Improvement*
May 1 Michele Lee, Joan Van Ark, Nicollette Sheridan and Donna Mills of *Knots Landing*
May 8 Arsenio Hall of *The Arsenio Hall Show*
May 15 Kirstie Alley, Ted Danson, Woody Harrelson, Rhea Perlman, Kelsey Grammer, John Ratzenberger and George Wendt of *Cheers*
May 22 Linda Ellerbee
May 29 Richard Simmons
June 5 Connie Chung of *Eye to Eye With Connie Chung*
June 12 Joey Lawrence of *Blossom*
June 19 A Martinez of *L.A. Law* and Cody Martinez
June 26 "Supermodels Take on TV": Cindy Crawford, Lauren Hutton, Naomi Campbell and Beverly Johnson
July 3 Vanna White of *Wheel of Fortune*

July 10 Larry Hagman
July 17 "Hot-Blooded Hollywood": Julia Roberts and Lyle Lovett
July 24 Armin Shimerman of *Star Trek: Deep Space Nine*
July 31 Patrick Stewart of *Star Trek: The Next Generation*
August 7 Mary-Kate and Ashley Olsen of *Full House*
August 14 "The Furor Over R-Rated Network TV"
August 21 Loni Anderson of *Nurses*
August 28 "Late-Night Star Wars": Jay Leno of *The Tonight Show*, Chevy Chase of *The Chevy Chase Show*, David Letterman of *The Late Show With David Letterman*, Ted Koppel of *ABC News Nightline*, Conan O'Brien of *Late Night With Conan O'Brien* and Arsenio Hall of *The Arsenio Hall Show*
September 4 William Shatner of *Star Trek*
September 11 Kelsey Grammer of *Frasier*
September 18 Fall Preview
September 25 Raymond Burr
October 2 Victoria Principal
October 9 "The *Night Court* Boys Are Back!": Harry Anderson of *Dave's World* and John Larroquette of *The John Larroquette Show*
October 16 Anthony Geary and Genie Francis of *General Hospital*
October 23 "Who's Right and Who's a Fright": Kelly Rutherford of *The Adventures of Brisco County Jr.*, Paula Poundstone of *The Paula Poundstone Show*, Jason Alexander of *Seinfeld* and Faye Dunaway of *It Had to Be You*
October 30 Ernie and Bert of *Sesame Street*
November 6 Mike Wallace of *60 Minutes*
November 13 Hillary Clinton with Big Bird of *Sesame Street*
November 20 Richard Thomas, Ralph Waite and Michael Learned of *The Waltons*
November 27 Dolly Parton
December 4 Holiday Preview: the Grinch in *How the Grinch Stole Christmas*, Donna Reed and Jimmy Stewart in *It's a Wonderful Life*, Will Smith of *The Fresh Prince of Bel Air* and Jennie Garth of *Beverly Hills, 90210*
December 11 Bette Midler in *Gypsy*
December 18 "Our 40th Anniversary Show": Heather Locklear, Robert Wagner, Lindsay Wagner, Adam West, Candice Bergen, Jackie Gleason, Jean Stapleton, Carroll O'Connor, Mary Tyler Moore, Dick Van Dyke, Leonard Nimoy, Kate Jackson, Farrah Fawcett, Jaclyn Smith, Carol Burnett, Jerry Seinfeld, Don Johnson, Johnny Carson, Larry Hagman, Sonny Bono, Cher, Lucille Ball, Don Adams and Barbara Feldon
December 25 Johnny Carson in *The Kennedy Center Honors*

1994
January 1 Tim Allen of *Home Improvement*
January 8 David Caruso of *NYPD Blue*
January 15 Avery Brooks of *Star Trek: Deep Space Nine*
January 22 Winter Preview: Henry Winkler of *Monty*, Dan Cortese of *Traps*, Ellen DeGeneres of *These Friends of Mine*, Ed Begley Jr. of *Winnetka Road* and Tim Reid, Tamara Mowrey, Tia Mowrey and Jackee Harry of *Sister, Sister*
January 29 The Super Bowl: Valerie Bertinelli
February 5 Courtney Thorne-Smith and Heather Locklear of *Melrose Place*
February 12 The Olympics: Nancy Kerrigan
February 19 The Olympics: Jayne Torville and Christopher Dean
February 26 The Grammys: Whitney Houston
March 5 Dennis Franz and Caesar of *NYPD Blue*
March 12 Erin Davis of *The Sinbad Show*
March 19 The Oscars: Barbara Walters and Whoopi Goldberg
March 26 Diane Sawyer
April 2 Loni Anderson
April 9 Kirstie Alley in *David's Mother*
April 16 Nicollette Sheridan in *A Time to Heal*
April 23 Jason Alexander of *Seinfeld*
April 30 Garth Brooks
May 7 Rob Lowe and Laura San Giacomo in *The Stand*
May 14 Patrick Stewart, Jonathan Frakes, Gates McFadden, Michael Dorn, LeVar Burton, Marina Sirtis and Brent Spiner of *Star Trek: The Next Generation*
May 21 Farrah Fawcett in *The Substitute Wife*
May 28 Andrew Shue of *Melrose Place*
June 4 Elizabeth Taylor
June 11 "The Best and Worst of the Year in TV": Brett Butler of *Grace Under Fire*, David Caruso of *NYPD Blue*, Laura Leighton of *Melrose Place* and Madonna
June 18 "TV's Top Dogs": Moose of *Frasier* and Maui of *Mad About You*
June 25 "Who Are Hollywood's Best Loved Stars?": Jane Seymour of *Dr. Quinn, Medicine Woman*, Tim Allen of *Home Improvement* and Jay Leno of *The Tonight Show*
July 2 Gillian Anderson and David Duchovny of *The X-Files*
July 2 Reba McEntire in *Is There Life Out There?*
July 9 Red Ranger of *Mighty Morphin Power Rangers*
July 16 Cindy Crawford of *House of Style*
July 23 Oprah Winfrey of *The Oprah Winfrey Show*
July 30 O.J. Simpson and Nicole Brown Simpson
August 6 Paul Reiser of *Mad About You*
August 13 Alexandra Paul, David Hasselhoff, Yasmine Bleeth and Pamela Anderson of *Baywatch*
August 20 Barbra Streisand
August 27 David Letterman of *The Late Show With David Letterman*
September 3 Red Ranger of *Mighty Morphin Power Rangers*
September 3 NFL Preview (seven covers):
John Madden
John Elway
Dan Marino
Joe Montana
Troy Aikman
Barry Sanders
Thurman Thomas
September 10 The Emmys: Tim Allen of *Home Improvement* and David Caruso of *NYPD Blue*
September 17 Fall Preview
September 24 John Mahoney, David Hyde Pierce, Kelsey Grammer and Moose of *Frasier*
October 1 Christie Brinkley in *Ford's Supermodels of the World 1994*
October 8 Kate Mulgrew of *Star Trek: Voyager*
October 15 Melissa Gilbert in *Cries From the Heart*
October 22 Suzanne Somers of *Step by Step*
October 29 *Mighty Morphin Power Rangers*
November 5 Shannen Doherty in *The Margaret Mitchell Story*
November 12 Joanne Whalley-Kilmer and Timothy Dalton in *Scarlett*
November 19 Sherry Stringfield, Anthony Edwards and Noah Wyle of *ER*
November 26 Ellen DeGeneres of *Ellen*
December 3 Crystal Bernard of *Wings*
December 10 Jane Pauley of *Dateline NBC*
December 17 Kathie Lee Gifford
December 24 "The Year in Cheers & Jeers": Roseanne of *Roseanne*, Burt Reynolds and Dorothy Letterman
December 31 "Viewers' Guide to College Bowls" (12 covers):
Joe Paterno
Kerry Collins
Lawrence Phillips
Danny O'Neil
Danny Wuerffel
Danny Kanell
Jay Barker
Joey Galloway
Lou Holtz
Ron Powlus
Rashaan Salaam
Frank Costa

1995
January 7 Oprah Winfrey of *The Oprah Winfrey Show*
January 14 Kate Mulgrew, Tim Russ and Robert Beltran of *Star Trek: Voyager*
January 21 Winter Preview: Shawn Wayans and Marlon Wayans of *The Wayans Brothers*, Delta Burke of *Women of the House*, Julia Campbell of *A Whole New Ballgame*, John Leguizamo of *House of Buggin'* and Richard Grieco of *Marker*
January 28 Super Bowl
February 4 Jerry Seinfeld of *Seinfeld*
February 11 Heather Locklear of *Melrose Place*
February 18 Sally Field in *A Woman of Independent Means*
February 25 George Clooney of *ER*
March 4 "Parents' Guide to Kids' TV": Genie of *Aladdin*, Blue Ranger of *Mighty Morphin Power Rangers* and Beast of *The X-Men*
March 11 David Duchovny and Gillian Anderson of *The X-Files*
March 18 "TV's 10 Most Powerful Stars": Roseanne of *Roseanne*, Tim Allen of *Home Improvement*, Oprah Winfrey of *The Oprah Winfrey Show* and Jerry Seinfeld of *Seinfeld*
March 25 The Oscars: David Letterman
April 1 "Are Talk Shows Out of Control?": Jenny Jones, Jerry Springer, Ricki Lake and Montel Williams
April 8 Jennie Garth of *Beverly Hills, 90210*
April 15 Fran Drescher of *The Nanny*
April 22 Susan Lucci in *Seduced and Betrayed*
April 29 "Boss Ladies": Kate Mulgrew of *Star Trek: Voyager*, Courtney Thorne-Smith of *Melrose Place* and Roxanne Hart of *Chicago Hope*
May 6 Jane Seymour and Joe Lando of *Dr. Quinn, Medicine Woman*
May 13 Naomi Judd, Wynonna Judd and Ashley Judd
May 20 Gail O'Grady and Sharon Lawrence of *NYPD Blue*
May 27 Pamela Anderson of *Baywatch*
June 3 Larry King of *Larry King Live*
June 10 Summer Preview: George Clooney, *Pocahontas*, Barry White, Lisa Marie Presley and Michael Jackson, David Charvet and Barbara Mandrell
June 17 Brett Butler of *Grace Under Fire*
June 24 Jason David Frank of *Mighty Morphin Power Rangers*
July 1 Victoria Principal in *Dancing in the Dark*
July 8 Cal Ripken Jr.
July 15 Jennifer Lien and Ethan Phillips of *Star Trek: Voyager*
July 22 Dean Cain of *Lois & Clark: The New Adventures of Superman*
July 29 Josie Bissett of *Melrose Place*
August 5 Tom Selleck in *Broken Trust*
August 12 "Best Dressed Stars": Jimmy Smits of *NYPD Blue* and Cybill Shepherd of *Cybill*
August 19 Regis Philbin of *Live With Regis and Kathie Lee*
August 26 Tiffani-Amber Thiessen and Brian Austin Green of *Beverly Hills, 90210*
August 26 "A Complete Guide to the SEC's Must-See Season" (four covers):
Peyton Manning
Danny Wuerffel
Shannon Brown and Stephen Davis
Peyton Manning, Stephen Davis, Steve Taneyhill and Moe Williams
September 2 NFL Preview (24 covers):
Steve Young
Brett Favre
Cris Carter
Frank Reich
Dan Marino
Jeff George
Trent Dilfer
Steve Beuerlein
Chris Zorich
Jeff Hostetler and Steve Young
Rick Mirer
Haywood Jeffries
Chris Miller
Steve Bono
John Elway
Troy Aikman
Vinny Testaverde and Jeff Blake
Jim Kelly
Barry Sanders
Ricky Watters
Drew Bledsoe
Rod Woodson
Heath Shuler
Boomer Esiason and Dave Brown
September 9 The Emmys: Kelsey Grammer of *Frasier*, Paul Reiser of *Mad About You* and Garry Shandling of *The Larry Sanders Show*
September 16 Fall Preview
September 23 Lisa Kudrow, David Schwimmer, Jennifer Aniston, Matt LeBlanc, Courteney Cox and Matthew Perry of *Friends*
September 30 Mary McCormack, Daniel Benzali and Jason Gedrick of *Murder One*
October 7 Avery Brooks and Michael Dorn of *Star Trek: Deep Space Nine*
October 14 George Clooney and Julianna Margulies of *ER*
October 21 Andrew Lawrence, Matthew Lawrence and Joey Lawrence of *Brotherly Love*
October 28 Sarah Ferguson, Duchess of York
November 4 Brooke Shields in *Nothing Lasts Forever*
November 11 Oprah Winfrey of *The Oprah Winfrey Show*
November 11 College Basketball Preview (nine covers):
Tony Delk, Rick Pitino and Antoine Walker
Moochie Norris and Eric Washington
Mike Krzyewski, Tim Duncan and Dante Calabria
Porter Roberts and Bobby Knight
Ron Riley and Joseph Blair
Ryan Minor and Chianti Roberts
Raef LaFrentz and Tyrone Davis
John Wallace, Kerry Kittles and Ray Allen
Quinton Brooks and Maurice Taylor
November 18 John Lennon, Paul McCartney, George Harrison and Ringo Starr
November 25 Jane Seymour of *Dr. Quinn, Medicine Woman*
December 2 Tea Leoni of *The Naked Truth*
December 9 Scott Wolf, Neve Campbell and Matthew Fox of *Party of Five*
December 16 Kathie Lee Gifford, Cody Gifford and Cassidy Gifford
December 23 "The Big Hair Issue": Lisa Kudrow, Jennifer Aniston, Lorenzo Lamas, Heather Locklear and Daniel Benzali
December 30 "Viewers' Guide to College Bowls" (eight covers):
Danny Wuerffel and Tommie Frazier
James Brown
Tony Graziani and Herschel Troutman
Stephen Davis and Bobby Engram
Gary Barnett and Darnell Autry
Danny Kanell and Danny Wuerffel
Eddie George and Peyton Manning
Joe Paterno and Bobby Engram

1996
January 6 "The Best (and the Worst) of '95": Jerry Seinfeld of *Seinfeld*, Oprah Winfrey of *The Oprah Winfrey Show*, David Schwimmer of *Friends* and Cybill Shepherd of *Cybill*
January 13 Morgan Fairchild of *The City*
January 20 "Sci-Fi & Fantasy Issue": Lucy Lawless of *Xena: Warrior Princess*; Kevin Sorbo of *Hercules: The Legendary Journeys*; William Shatner; and Morgan Weisser, Rodney Rowland and Kristen Cloke of *Space: Above and Beyond*
January 27 Super Bowl: Troy Aikman and Neil O'Donnell
February 3 Ted Danson and Mary Steenburgen
February 10 David Schwimmer and Jennifer Aniston of *Friends*
February 17 John de Lancie and Kate Mulgrew of *Star Trek: Voyager*
February 24 Tori Spelling of *Beverly Hills, 90210*
March 2 Jimmy Smits and Dennis Franz of *NYPD Blue*
March 9 "50 Great Things About Television Now"
March 16 "Parents' Guide to Kids' TV": Billy Crystal and Animal, Kermit the Frog and Gonzo of *Muppets Tonight*
March 23 The Oscars: Mel Gibson, Babe, Sharon Stone and Brad Pitt
March 30 Joan Lunden of *Good Morning, America*

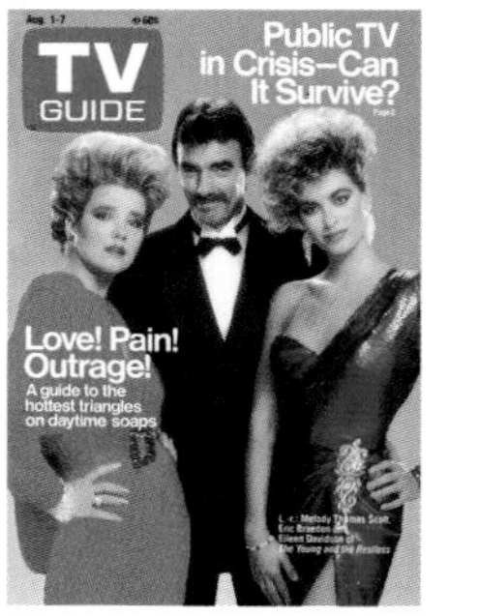

August 1, 1987
BY BERNARD BOUDREAU

The No. 1 soap opera for 12 consecutive years, *The Young and the Restless* opens with the haunting piano melody "Nadia's Theme"—originally from the movie *Bless the Beasts and the Children*.

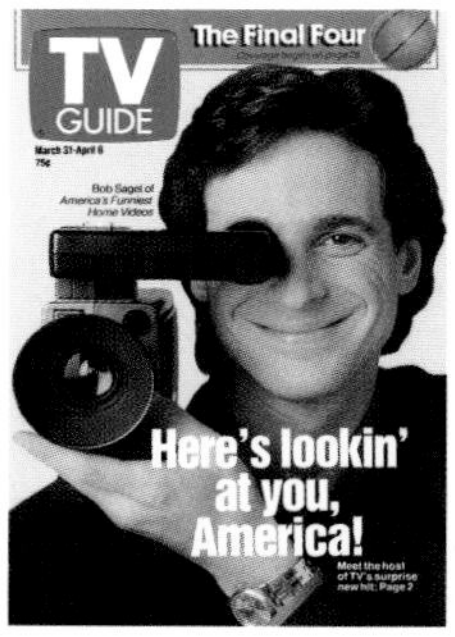

March 31, 1990
BY TONY COSTA

America's Funniest Home Videos featured real-life submissions from viewers who didn't mind showing the world how thick-skulled or clumsy they could be.

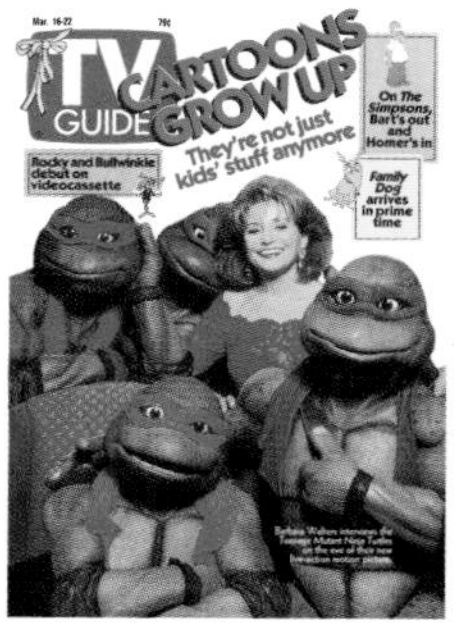

March 16, 1991
BY STEVE FENN

One of TV GUIDE's more surreal covers featured Barbara Walters with the Teenage Mutant Ninja Turtles. During the interview, she made all but Michelangelo cry.

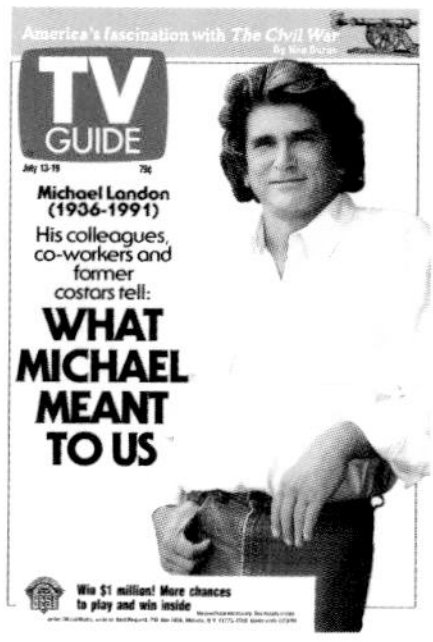

July 13, 1991
BY NBC/GLOBE PHOTOS

Michael Landon is the No. 2 champ for most TV GUIDE covers ever (26). No wonder—he starred in three of TV's most beloved shows: *Bonanza*, *Little House on the Prairie* and *Highway to Heaven*.

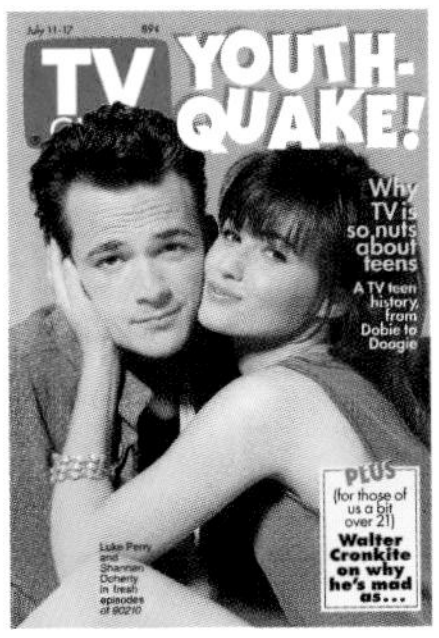

July 11, 1992
BY JEFF KATZ

Aaron Spelling's *Beverly Hills, 90210*, a high school soap opera full of romance, betrayal and Clearasil, made stars out of Luke Perry and Shannen Doherty.

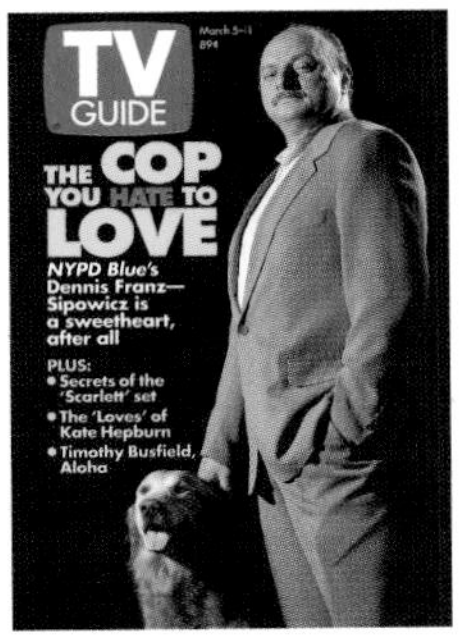

March 5, 1994
BY TIMOTHY WHITE

It could have been called "blue" because of all the skin and swearing, but viewers tuned in to *NYPD Blue* for its quality. The show switched leading men four times, but Dennis Franz stood tall as the irascible cop's cop, Andy Sipowicz.

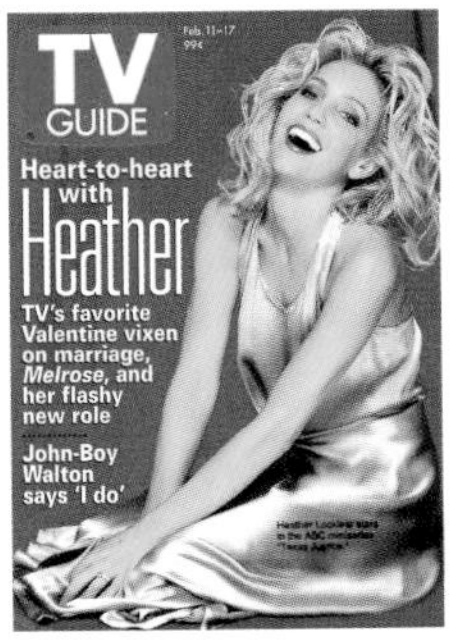

February 11, 1995
BY DAVIS FACTOR

The multigenerational shenanigans of *Dallas* were replaced in the '90s with fare like *Melrose Place*, filled with pretty, if un-emotive, faces. Heather Locklear's, however, was worth watching.

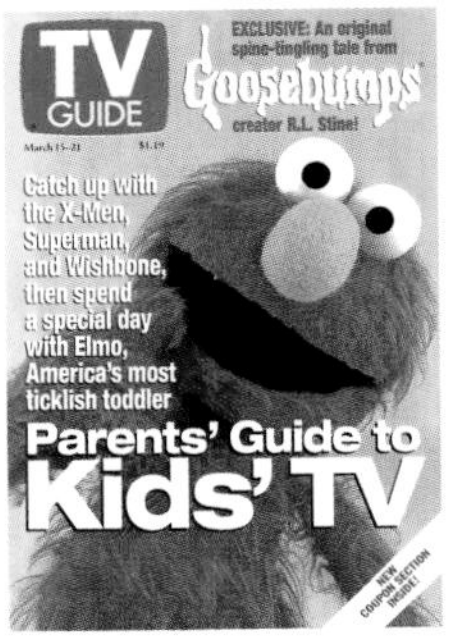

March 15, 1997
BY JOHN E. BARRETT (©1997 CTW, ©JIM HENSON PRODUCTIONS, INC.)

Sesame Street boasted a neighborhood full of famous characters, but in the '90s, it introduced a giggly, red-furred young muppet named Elmo whom everyone wanted to tickle.

April 6 Gillian Anderson and David Duchovny of *The X-Files*
April 13 Anthony Edwards of *ER*
April 13 Hockey Playoffs Preview (four covers):
Eric Lindros
Mario Lemieux
Wayne Gretzky
Steve Yzerman
April 20 Cybill Shepherd of *Cybill*
April 27 Andy Rooney, Morley Safer, Ed Bradley, Mike Wallace, Lesley Stahl and Steve Kroft of *60 Minutes*
May 4 Whitney Houston
May 11 Courteney Cox and Tom Selleck of *Friends*
May 18 Candice Bergen of *Murphy Brown*
May 25 Heather Locklear of *Melrose Place*
June 1 Jerry Seinfeld of *Seinfeld*
June 8 Jenny McCarthy of *Singled Out*
June 15 Teri Hatcher of *Lois & Clark: The New Adventures of Superman*
June 22 Conan O'Brien of *Late Night With Conan O'Brien*
June 29 "100 Most Memorable Moments in TV History": Ringo Starr, George Harrison, Paul McCartney and John Lennon on *The Ed Sullivan Show*; George Foreman and Muhammad Ali; Richard M. Nixon; Pernell Roberts, Michael Landon, Dan Blocker and Lorne Greene of *Bonanza*; and Anthony Geary and Genie Francis of *General Hospital*
July 6 Gillian Anderson of *The X-Files*
July 13 "What Happened to Family TV?": Jerry Mathers and Barbara Billingsley of *Leave It to Beaver*
July 20 The Olympics: Janet Evans
July 27 "The Other Dream Team": Lisa Leslie, Rebecca Lobo and Dawn Staley
August 3 "TV's Best (and Worst) Dressed": Dean Cain of *Lois & Clark: The New Adventures of Superman* and Jennie Garth of *Beverly Hills, 90210*
August 10 "Stars We Still Love": Maureen McCormick, Barbara Feldon and Chad Everett
August 17 Matthew Perry of *Friends*
August 24 "*Star Trek* Turns 30!" (four covers):
William Shatner
Patrick Stewart
Kate Mulgrew
Avery Brooks
August 31 NFL Preview
September 7 Helen Hunt and Paul Reiser of *Mad About You*
September 14 Fall Preview
September 21 Returning Favorites: Cybill Shepherd of *Cybill*; Matthew Perry, David Schwimmer, Lisa Kudrow, Courteney Cox, Jennifer Aniston and Matt LeBlanc of *Friends*; Brandy of *Moesha*; Gillian Anderson and David Duchovny of *The X-Files*; Teri Hatcher of *Lois & Clark: The New Adventures of Superman*; and Jerry Seinfeld of *Seinfeld*
September 28 Michael J. Fox of *Spin City*
October 5 Jay Leno of *The Tonight Show*
October 12 Robyn Lively, Shannon Sturges and Jamie Luner of *Savannah*
October 19 Brooke Shields of *Suddenly Susan*
October 26 Tommy Pickles, Angelica Pickles, Phil DeVille, Chuckie Finster, Lil DeVille and Spike of *Rugrats*
November 2 Michael Jordan
November 9 Robert Urich
November 16 Lance Henriksen of *Millennium*
November 23 "Who's Hot...": Carey Lowell of *Law & Order* and Kyle Chandler of *Early Edition*
November 30 Roma Downey of *Touched by an Angel*
December 7 Drew Carey and Kathy Kinney of *The Drew Carey Show*
December 14 "50 Greatest TV Stars of All Time": Michael Landon, Rosanne, Carroll O'Connor, Bill Cosby, Mary Tyler Moore, Lassie and Jackie Gleason
December 21 David Duchovny of *The X-Files*
December 28 Michelle Forbes, Andre Braugher and Kyle Secor of *Homicide*

1997
January 4 Oprah Winfrey of *The Oprah Winfrey Show*
January 11 Dilbert
January 18 Winter Preview
January 25 Super Bowl
February 1 Kevin Sorbo of *Hercules–the Legendary Journeys*
February 8 Neve Campbell of *Party of Five*
February 15 David Letterman of *The Late Show With David Letterman*
February 22 Chuck Norris of *Walker, Texas Ranger*
March 1 John Lithgow, Kristen Johnston and French Stewart of *3rd Rock From the Sun*
March 8 Howard Stern
March 15 Elmo of *Sesame Street*
March 22 The Oscars: Tom Cruise, Kristin Scott Thomas, Barbara Hershey and Woody Harrelson
March 29 "God and Television"
April 5 Rosie O'Donnell of *The Rosie O'Donnell Show*
April 12 Michael Jordan, Hakeem Olajuwon and Grant Hill
April 19 Jenny McCarthy
April 26 Tom Hanks
April 26 *The Shining*
May 3 Lucy Lawless of *Xena: Warrior Princess*
May 10 Kate Mulgrew of *Star Trek: Voyager*
May 10 Adam Arkin, Christine Lahti and Mark Harmon of *Chicago Hope*
May 17 Gillian Anderson, David Duchovny and Nicholas Lea of *The X-Files*
May 24 "20 Great Faces": Kim Delaney of *NYPD Blue*
May 31 Michael Richards of *Seinfeld*
June 7 Farrah Fawcett
June 7 Summer Preview: Leann Rimes
June 14 Lea Thompson of *Caroline in the City*
June 21 Joan Lunden
June 28 "100 Greatest Episodes of All Time"
July 5 Claudia Christian, Bruce Boxleitner and Jerry Doyle of *Babylon 5*
July 12 "Animation's New Wave": Hank Hill of *King of the Hill*, Daria of *Daria* and Dr. Katz of *Dr. Katz: Professional Therapist*
July 19 Kathie Lee Gifford of *Live With Regis and Kathie Lee*
July 26 Jennifer Aniston of *Friends*
August 2 Sarah Michelle Gellar of *Buffy the Vampire Slayer*
August 2 Jeff Gordon
August 9 "TV's Best (and Worst) Dressed Stars": Jennifer Love Hewitt of *Party of Five* and French Stewart of *3rd Rock From the Sun*
August 16 Elvis Presley (four covers)
August 23 "Look What They've Done to Miss America": Madison Michele
August 23 "The Past Is Now": Neil Armstrong, Martin Luther King Jr. , Marilyn Monroe, Eleanor Roosevelt, Abraham Lincoln and John F. Kennedy Jr.
August 30 NFL Preview (33 covers):
Brett Favre
Steve Young and Steve Mariucci
Steve Young and Jeff George
Raymond Harris and Rashaan Salaam
Jeff Blake and Carl Pickens
Thurman Thomas and Marv Levy
Neil Smith and Terrell Davis
Derrick Brooks and Trent Dilfer
Simeon Rice and Kent Graham
Tony Martin and Stan Humphries
Kimble Anders and Elvis Grbac
Marshall Faulk and Tony Bennett
Daryl Johnston and Darren Woodson
O.J. McDuffie and Karim Abdul-Jabbar
Irving Fryar and Ty Detmer
Jamal Anderson, Dan Reeves and Chris Chandler
Rodney Hampton and Jim Fassel
Keenan McCardell and Jimmy Smith
Hugh Douglas and Wayne Chrebet
Rodney Hampton and Wayne Chrebet
Herman Moore and Scott Mitchell
Eddie George and Steve McNair
Brett Favre and Mike Holmgren
Sam Mills and Lamar Lathon
Drew Bledsoe
Desmond Howard and Jeff George
Isaac Bruce and Dick Vermeil
Michael Jackson and Vinny Testaverde
Terry Allen and Gus Frerotte
Heath Shuler and Mike Ditka
Joey Galloway
Jerome Bettis and Kordell Stewart
Cris Carter and Brad Johnson
September 6 Returning Favorites: Gillian Anderson and David Duchovny of *The X-Files*, Candice Bergen of *Murphy Brown*, Eriq LaSalle and Noah Wyle of *ER*, Julia Louis-Dreyfus of *Seinfeld* and Michael J. Fox of *Spin City*
September 13 Fall Preview
September 20 Princess Diana
September 27 Drew Carey of *The Drew Carey Show*
September 27 Baseball Playoffs Preview (four covers):
Moises Alou
Mike Mussina
Rafael Palmeiro
Craig Biggio and Jeff Bagwell
October 4 Gregory Hines of *The Gregory Hines Show*
October 11 Ellen DeGeneres of *Ellen*
October 18 Melissa Joan Hart of *Sabrina the Teenage Witch*
October 25 "Parents' Guide to Kids' TV": Larisa Oleynik of *The Secret World of Alex Mack* and Irene Ng of *The Mystery Files of Shelby Woo*
November 1 Whitney Houston and Brandy in *Cinderella*
November 8 "The Women of *Star Trek*" (two covers):
Jeri Ryan of *Star Trek: Voyager*
Terry Farrell of *Star Trek: Deep Space Nine*
November 15 Gillian Anderson, Chris Carter and David Duchovny of *The X-Files*
November 22 "TV's Top 20 Sexy Stars": Jenna Elfman of *Dharma & Greg*
November 29 Brooke Shields of *Suddenly Susan*
December 6 Roma Downey of *Touched by an Angel*
December 13 Peri Gilpin of *Frasier*
December 20 Matt Lauer and Katie Couric of *Today*
December 27 College Bowl Preview

1998
January 3 *The Simpsons* (four covers):
Bart Simpson and Santa's Little Helper
Grampa Simpson, Homer Simpson and Selma Bouvier
Patty Bouvier and Lisa Simpson
Marge Simpson and Maggie Simpson
January 10 Winter Preview: Tom Selleck of *The Closer*; Vivica A. Fox of *Getting Personal*; Peta Wilson of *La Femme Nikita*; and Joshua Jackson, Katie Holmes, James Van Der Beek and Michelle Williams of *Dawson's Creek*
January 17 Steve Harris, Dylan McDermott and Lara Flynn Boyle of *The Practice*
January 24 Sonny Bono
January 24 Super Bowl (five covers):
Brett Favre
John Elway
Dorsey Levins
Antonio Freeman
Mark Chmura
January 31 Yasmine Bleeth in *The Lake*
February 7 The Olympics (four covers):
Michelle Kwan
Tara Lipinski
Tommy Moe
Keith Tkachuk
February 14 Jenna Elfman and Thomas Gibson of *Dharma & Greg*
February 14 NASCAR (three covers):
Richard Petty and Dale Earnhardt
Dale Jarrett and Cale Yarborough
Mark Martin and Bobby Allison
February 21 Kelsey Grammer and David Hyde Pierce of *Frasier*
February 28 Calista Flockhart, Gil Bellows and Courtney Thorne-Smith of *Ally McBeal*
March 7 *Dawson's Creek* (four covers):
James Van Der Beek
Katie Holmes
Michelle Williams
Joshua Jackson
March 7 Harry Caray
March 7 Patrick Stewart in *Moby Dick*
March 14 D.W. and Arthur of *Arthur*
March 21 The Oscars: Helen Hunt, Leonardo DiCaprio and Kate Winslet, Matt Damon and Burt Reynolds
March 28 Cartman, Stan, Kyle and Kenny of *South Park*
March 28 Benjamin Bratt, Carey Lowell, Sam Waterston and Jerry Orbach of *Law & Order*
April 4 "45th Anniversary Celebration"
April 11 Madonna
April 18 "Before They Were Movie Stars!": Leonardo DiCaprio, Brad Pitt and Jodie Foster
April 25 Peta Wilson of *La Femme Nikita*
May 2 Matthew Perry of *Friends*
May 9 *Seinfeld* (four covers):
Jerry Seinfeld
Michael Richards
Jason Alexander
Julia Louis-Dreyfus
May 16 Julia Roberts in *Murphy Brown*
May 23 Summer Movie Preview: Godzilla, Tom Hanks, Jim Carrey, Drew Barrymore and Ben Affleck
May 30 Frank Sinatra
June 6 Magic Johnson
June 13 Summer Soaps Preview: Jensen Ackles of *Days of Our Lives*, Laura Wright of *Guiding Light* and Ingo Rademacher of *General Hospital*
June 20 The *X-Files* movie (two covers):
David Duchovny
Gillian Anderson
June 27 Hanson: Taylor, Zac and Isaac Hanson
July 4 Matt Lauer of *Today*
July 11 "TV's 50 Greatest Sports Moments"
July 18 Brandy of *Moesha*
July 25 "TV Confidential": Jerry Mathers, Johnny Carson, Ted Nugent and Soupy Sales
August 1 Drew Carey of *The Drew Carey Show*
August 8 "The 50 Greatest Movies on TV and Video": Bette Davis in *All About Eve*, John Travolta in *Saturday Night Fever*, Darth Vader in *Star Wars*, Margaret Hamilton and Judy Garland in *The Wizard of Oz* and *The Lion King*
August 15 Princess Diana
August 22 "TV's 10 Best Dressed": Vivica A. Fox of *Getting Personal* and Thomas Gibson of *Dharma & Greg*
August 29 NFL Preview (30 covers):
John Elway
Jamal Anderson
Jake Plummer
Bruce Smith
Michael Jackson
Kerry Collins
Erik Kramer
Carl Pickens
Troy Aikman
Barry Sanders

Brett Favre
Kimble Anders
Brad Johnson
Peyton Manning
Mark Brunell
Dan Marino
Drew Bledsoe
Billy Joe Hobert
Bobby Hoying
Jerome Bettis
Ryan Leaf
Joey Galloway
Isaac Bruce
Trent Dilfer
Steve McNair
Gus Frerotte
Steve Young
Danny Kanell
Glenn Foley and Danny Kanell
Jeff George and Steve Young

September 5   Returning Favorites: Calista Flockhart of *Ally McBeal*, Kelsey Grammer of *Frasier*, Bill Cosby of *Cosby*, Dylan McDermott of *The Practice*, Sarah Michelle Gellar of *Buffy the Vampire Slayer* and Anthony Edwards of *ER*

September 12   Fall Preview

September 19   Tim Allen of *Home Improvement*

September 26   Lisa Nicole Carson, Calista Flockhart and Jane Krakowski of *Ally McBeal*

October 3   David Hyde Pierce, Kelsey Grammer, Jane Leeves, Dan Butler, Peri Gilpin, John Mahoney and Eddie of *Frasier*

October 10   Oprah Winfrey of *The Oprah Winfrey Show*

October 17   Homer Simpson, Marge Simpson, Lisa Simpson, Bart Simpson and Maggie Simpson of *The Simpsons*

October 24   "A Time for Heroes": Walter Cronkite and John Glenn

October 31   Steve Burns and Blue of *Blue's Clues*

November 7   "Young Hollywood": David Boreanaz of *Buffy the Vampire Slayer* and Keri Russell of *Felicity*

November 14   Robin Williams

November 21   Christopher Reeve in *Rear Window*

November 28   Kristen Johnston of *3rd Rock From the Sun*

December 5   Wrestling (four covers):
The Undertaker
Goldberg
Stone Cold Steve Austin
Hollywood Hogan

December 12   Shannen Doherty, Alyssa Milano and Holly Marie Combs of *Charmed*

December 19   Darrell Hammond and Molly Shannon of *Saturday Night Live*

December 26   "1998 Tribute": Robert Young, Flip Wilson, Tammy Wynette, Esther Rolle, Roy Rogers, Shari Lewis and Phil Hartman

1999

January 2   "Talk Scoop": Diane Sawyer and Barbara Walters

January 9   Winter Preview: Eddie Murphy of *The PJs*, Dilbert of *Dilbert*, Jennifer Grey of *It's Like, You Know* and John Larroquette of *Payne*

January 16   Rick Schroder of *NYPD Blue*

January 23   "The 50 Funniest TV Moments of All Time": Carol Burnett, Lucille Ball and Jerry Seinfeld

January 30   The TV GUIDE Awards: Jenna Elfman, Bill Cosby, Calista Flockhart, Michael J. Fox, Christina Applegate, Jimmy Smits, Roma Downey and Tim Allen

January 30   "Super Broncos": John Elway

January 30   "Super Falcons": Chris Chandler

February 6   George Clooney of *ER*

February 13   Stephen King's *Storm of the Century*

February 13   NASCAR (four covers):
Dale Jarrett
Jeff Gordon
Mark Martin
Rusty Wallace

February 20   Patricia Heaton, Ray Romano and Brad Garrett of *Everybody Loves Raymond*

February 27   Tina Majorino and Martin Short in *Alice in Wonderland*

March 6   Catherine Hicks, Stephen Collins, Jessica Biel, Mackenzie Rosman, Beverley Mitchell and Barry Watson of *7th Heaven*

March 13   Jenna Elfman and Matthew McConaughey in *Ed TV*

March 20   The Oscars: Gwyneth Paltrow, Tom Hanks, Nick Nolte and Meryl Streep

March 27   Peter Krause, Robert Guillaume, Felicity Huffman and Josh Charles of *Sports Night*

March 27   Wrestling (four covers):
Stone Cold Steve Austin
The Rock
Sable
Mankind

April 3   Bender of *Futurama*

April 10   "Cosmic Encounter": Lucy Lawless of *Xena: Warrior Princess* and Jeri Ryan of *Star Trek: Voyager*

April 17   David Duchovny of *The X-Files*

April 24   Sweeps Preview: Brandy and Diana Ross, Heather Locklear and Garth Brooks

April 24   "Go Flyers!" (four covers):
John LeClair
Rod Brind'Amour
Eric Lindros
Mark Recchi

May 1   Calista Flockhart of *Ally McBeal*

May 8   Camryn Manheim of *The Practice*

May 15   *Star Wars–Episode I: The Phantom Menace* (four covers):
Anakin Skywalker, C-3PO and R2-D2
Qui-Gon Jinn and Darth Maul
Darth Maul and Obi-Wan Kenobi
Queen Padme Amidala

May 22   Patricia Richardson and Tim Allen of *Home Improvement*

May 29   *Star Trek: Deep Space Nine* (four covers):
Avery Brooks
Nana Visitor and René Auberjonois
Michael Dorn, Armin Shimerman and Nicole deBoer
Alexander Siddig, Colm Meaney and Cirroc Lofton

May 29   David Spade, Laura San Giacomo, George Segal, Enrico Colantoni and Wendie Malick of *Just Shoot Me*

June 5   Ricky Martin (two covers)

June 12   *Star Wars–Episode I: The Phantom Menace* (four covers):
Jabba the Hutt
Jar Jar Binks
Watto
Boss Nass

June 19   Sable

June 26   Pamela Anderson Lee of *V.I.P.*

July 3   "The 50 Greatest Commercials of All Time"

July 10   Chris Rock in *Bigger & Blacker*

July 17   Dennis Franz of *NYPD Blue*

July 17   NASCAR (four covers):
Bobby Labonte
Tony Stewart
Jeremy Mayfield
Jeff Burton

July 24   "TV Confidential 2": Madonna, Scott Baio, Bob Eubanks and Susan Olsen

July 31   John F. Kennedy Jr.

August 7   "TV's 16 Sexiest Stars" (two covers):
Alyssa Milano of *Charmed*
David James Elliot of *JAG*

August 14   Wrestling (four covers):

Kimberly Page
Kevin Nash
Randy Savage
Sting

August 14   "Action!...TV's Macho Men": Sammo Hung of *Martial Law*, Kevin Sorbo of *Hercules–the Legendary Journeys* and Chuck Norris of *Walker, Texas Ranger*

August 21   Cher

August 28   NFL Preview

September 4   Returning Favorites: David Duchovny of *The X-Files*, Jennifer Aniston of *Friends*, Ray Romano of *Everybody Loves Raymond*, Roma Downey of *Touched by an Angel*, D.L. Hughley of *The Hughleys* and Katie Holmes of *Dawson's Creek*

September 11   Fall Preview

September 18   Faith Hill

September 25   "The Best New Shows": Shiri Appleby of *Roswell*, Jay Mohr of *Action*, Linda Cardellini of *Freaks and Geeks*, David Boreanaz of *Angel*, Sela Ward of *Once and Again* and Rob Lowe of *The West Wing*

September 25   "Mets Mania" (four covers):
Mike Piazza
Edgardo Alfonzo
Al Lecter
Robin Ventura

October 2   Melissa Joan Hart of *Sabrina the Teenage Witch*

October 9   Katie Couric of *Today*

October 16   "TV's 50 Greatest Characters Ever!"

October 23   Billy Campbell and Sela Ward of *Once and Again*

October 30   *Pokémon* (four covers):
Pikachu
Psyduck
Togepi
Charmander

November 6   Regis Philbin of *Who Wants to Be a Millionaire*

November 6   "Spurs Rule!": Tim Duncan

November 6   "Tough T-Wolves!": Kevin Garnett

November 13   Pierce Brosnan

November 20   Celine Dion

November 20   Walter Payton

November 27   Rosie O'Donnell of *The Rosie O'Donnell Show*

December 4   Michael Jackson

December 11   Amy Brenneman of *Judging Amy*

December 18   Calista Flockhart, Lucy Liu, Peter MacNicol, Greg Germann and Portia de Rossi of *Ally McBeal*

December 25   Dennis Haysbert, Eric Close and Margaret Colin of *Now and Again*

2000

January 1   Elvis Presley (two covers)

January 8   James Gandolfini, Edie Falco, Robert Iler, Michael Imperioli, Jamie-Lynn Sigler and Dominic Chianese of *The Sopranos*

January 15   John Carpenter, Jane Oviatt, Regis Philbin and Andres Rivera of *Who Wants to Be a Millionaire*

January 22   Barbra Streisand

January 29   Wrestling (four covers):
Triple H
Mankind and Socko
The Rock
Chyna

February 5   Mary Tyler Moore and Valerie Harper in *Mary and Rhoda*

February 12   Debra Messing, Eric McCormack, Megan Mullally and Sean Hayes of *Will & Grace*

February 19   Sarah Michelle Gellar of *Buffy the Vampire Slayer*

February 26   Dylan McDermott of *The Practice*

March 4   The TV GUIDE Awards: Lisa Kudrow, Sam Waterston, Sela Ward, Ray Romano, David Hyde Pierce, Phylicia Rashad, Amy Brenneman and David Duchovny

March 11   Josh Charles, Felicity Huffman and Peter Krause of *Sports Night*

March 18   Frankie Muniz, Jane Kaczmarek and Bryan Cranston of *Malcolm in the Middle*

March 25   Cybill Shepherd

April 1   'N Sync (five covers):
Chris Kirkpatrick
JC Chasez
Joey Fatone
Lance Bass
Justin Timberlake

April 8   George Clooney in *Fail Safe*

April 15   The Three Stooges (four covers):
Curly
Larry
Moe
Evan Handler, John Kassir, Paul Ben-Victor and Michael Chiklis in *The Three Stooges*

April 22   The Dixie Chicks

April 29   Bryant Gumbel of *The Early Show*

April 29   Cal Ripken

May 6   *Jesus* (two covers)

May 6   Kentucky Derby

May 13   Michael J. Fox of *Spin City*

May 20   Donny and Marie Osmond

May 27   *Survivor*

June 3   Britney Spears (two covers)

June 10   "Where Are They Now?": Mr. T, Butch Patrick, Lisa Whelchel and Larry Storch

June 17   *Sex and the City* (four covers):
Kim Cattrall
Kristin Davis
Cynthia Nixon
Sarah Jessica Parker

June 24   Jamie, Kelley, Danny, Julie, David, Melissa and Matt of *The Real World*

June 24   "Dynasty Two: The Lakers" (four covers):
Kobe Bryant
Rick Fox
Shaquille O'Neal
Glen Rice

July 1   *The Wizard of Oz* (four covers):
Judy Garland
Bert Lahr
Ray Bolger
Jack Haley

July 8   Rudy Boesch, Kelly Wiglesworth, Jenna Lewis and Sue Hawk of *Survivor*

July 15   *X-Men* (six covers):
James Marsden
Famke Janssen
Patrick Stewart
Anna Paquin
Halle Berry
Hugh Jackman

July 22   Martin Sheen of *The West Wing*

July 29   "The Sexiest Stars in the Universe" (eight covers):
Jeri Ryan of *Star Trek: Voyager*
Renee O'Connor of *Xena: Warrior Princess*
Claudia Black of *Farscape*
Virginia Hey of *Farscape*
Xenia Seebert of *Lexx*
Roxann Dawson of *Star Trek: Voyager*
Gigi Edgley of *Farscape*
Katherine Heigl of *Roswell*

August 5   Clint Eastwood

August 12   NASCAR (four covers):
Dale Earnhardt
Bill Elliot

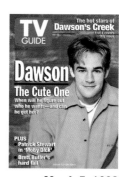

March 7, 1998
BY FERGUS GREER

Dawson's Creek brought more fresh-faced kids (such as James Van Der Beek) with continuing problems, but this time the teens had snappier dialogue and were more self-aware than their adult prime-time peers.

December 18, 1999
BY AL HIRSCHFELD

This love-it or hate-it "dramedy" *Ally McBeal* made ample use of musical numbers, stunt casting and digital dancing babies. The neurotic Ally seemed to spend more time on the couch than in her law office.

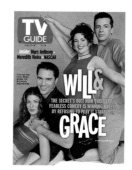

February 12, 2000
BY CHALLENGE RODDIE

Ellen may have opened the closet door, but *Will & Grace* came out dancing. Appealing leads, a madcap supporting cast and sharp scripts made everyone a little gayer–happier, that is.

July 22, 2000
BY DAVID BURNETT

This drama about a U.S. president (Martin Sheen) and his staff was a hit from the start. *The West Wing* also set a new record for most Emmys won by a series in a single season (nine).

January 13, 2001
BY NBC/GLOBE PHOTOS

With the reissue of a classic Presley documentary, *That's the Way It Is*, and by adorning the cover of the year's best-selling issue, Elvis proved he was still the King in 2001.

December 8, 2001
BY ALEX ROSS

As seen in *Smallville*, Superman's 21st-century incarnation (Tom Welling) didn't wear the traditional tights. Instead, Clark Kent's salad days were portrayed in a contemporary hybrid of teen-angst soap opera and sci-fi spectacle.

December 22, 2001
BY JAMIE WYETH

With terrorist attacks against the United States, the fall of 2001 saw much heartache and patriotism. TV GUIDE ended the year with a five-cover issue—this one by Jamie Wyeth—featuring the American flag by different artists.

February 23, 2002
BY KATE GARNER

The cop genre took its darkest turn yet with *CSI*, a smart and graphic depiction of criminal forensics starring William Petersen and Marg Helgenberger. Viewers might have winced, but they didn't change the channel.

Ricky Rudd
Rusty Wallace

August 19 Wrestling (four covers):
Kurt Angle
Chris Jericho
The Kat
Rikishi

August 26 MTV Video Music Awards (five covers):
Christina Aguilera
Metallica
'N Sync
Sisqo
Marlon and Shawn Wayans

September 2 NFL Preview (two covers):
Levon Kirkland
Randy Moss

September 9 Returning Favorites: Leslie Bibb and Carly Pope of *Popular*, Frankie Muniz of *Malcolm in the Middle*, Eric McCormack and Debra Messing of *Will & Grace*, Drew Carey of *The Drew Carey Show* and Mo'Nique of *The Parkers*

September 16 The Olympics (six covers):
Julie Foudy
Maurice Greene
Chamique Holdsclaw
Marion Jones
Lenny Krayzelburg
Jenny Thompson

September 23 Tim McGraw

September 30 Fall Preview: Geena Davis, Michael Richardson, John Goodman and Bette Midler

October 7 Katie Couric and Matt Lauer of *Today*

October 14 Melina Kanakaredes of *Providence*

October 21 *The Simpsons* (24 covers):
Groundskeeper Willie
Chief Clancy Wiggum
Waylon Smithers
Principal Seymour Skinner
Sideshow Bob
Selma Bouvier
Santa's Little Helper
Ralph Wiggum
Professor John Frink
C. Montgomery Burns
Moe Szyslak
Millhouse Van Houten
Sea Captain McCallister
Krusty the Clown
Mrs. Edna Krabappel
Kang
Itchy and Scratchy
Grampa Abe Simpson
Ned Flanders
Dr. Julius Hibbert
Comic Book Guy
Bumblebee Man
Barney Gumble
Apu Nahasapeemapetilon

October 28 Lucy Liu, Drew Barrymore and Cameron Diaz in *Charlie's Angels* (two covers)

November 4 *The X-Files* (three covers):
David Duchovny
Gillian Anderson
Robert Patrick

November 11 "The Beatles 2000" (four covers):
George Harrison
John Lennon
Paul McCartney
Ringo Starr

November 18 Jim Carrey in *The Grinch*

November 25 Jessica Alba of *Dark Angel*

December 2 Barbara Walters, Joy Behar, Meredith Viera, Lisa Ling and Starr Jones of *The View*

December 9 "We've Got Game! The Latest in Video and Computer Games" (six covers):
Tony Hawk of *Tony Hawk's Pro Skater 2*
Lara Croft of *Tomb Raider Chronicles*
The Titans' Eddie George of *John Madden Football*
Pikachu of *Pokemon*
Firionavie of *Everquest*
Ryo and Ling Sha of *Shenmue*

December 16 Benjamin Bratt of *Law & Order*

December 23 *Gone With the Wind* (five covers):
Vivian Leigh (three covers)
Clark Gable
Clark Gable and Vivian Leigh

December 30 Orange Bowl

2001

January 6 "The Year in Jeers!"

January 13 Elvis Presley (four covers)

January 20 *Survivor 2* (two covers):
Debb Eaton, Kimmi Kappenberg, Rodger Bingham, Nick Brown, Alicia Calaway, Michael Skupin, Jeff Varner and Elisabeth Filarski
Keith Famie, Amber Brkich, Jerri Manthey, Colby Donaldson, Maralyn Hershey, Mitchell Olson, Kel Gleason and Tina Wesson

January 27 "The 50 Greatest Game Shows of All Time"

February 3 Anthony Hopkins in *Hannibal*

February 10 "TV's MVPs" (three covers):
Megan Mullally of *Will & Grace*, John Spencer of *The West Wing* and Amy Brenneman of *Judging Amy*
Edie Falco of *The Sopranos*, Conan O'Brien of *Late Night With Conan O'Brien* and Carson Daly of *Last Call With Carson Daly*
Jane Kaczmarek of *Malcolm in the Middle*, Matt LeBlanc of *Friends* and Steve Harris of *The Practice*

February 17 Kyle Petty

February 24 Judy Davis in *Life With Judy Garland*

March 3 The TV GUIDE Awards: Marg Helgenberger, Oprah Winfrey, Jessica Alba, David James Elliott, Eric McCormack, Sela Ward and Tom Cavanagh

March 10 Janet Jackson (two covers)

March 17 Edie Falco and James Gandolfini of *The Sopranos*

March 24 "The 50 Greatest Movie Moments of All Time"

March 31 Rachael Leigh Cook, Tara Reid and Rosario Dawson in *Josie and the Pussycats*

April 7 Ioan Gruffudd in *Horatio Hornblower*

April 7 Mario Lemieux

April 14 David Letterman of *Late Show With David Letterman*

April 21 Sela Ward, Billy Campbell, Shane West, Julia Whelan, Meredith Deane and Evan Rachel Wood of *Once and Again*

April 28 Lara Flynn Boyle of *The Practice*

April 28 Kentucky Derby

May 5 Paul McCartney

May 12 Marilyn Monroe (five covers)

May 19 *Star Trek: Voyager* (four covers):
Kate Mulgrew
Jeri Ryan
Jeri Ryan, Alice Krige and Kate Mulgrew
Robert Beltran, Kate Mulgrew and Tim Russ

May 26 Backstreet Boys (six covers):
Kevin Richardson
Nick Carter
Howie Dorough
A.J. McLean

Brian Littrell
Backstreet Boys

June 2 Laila Ali and Jacquelyn Frazier-Lyde

June 9 Tiger Woods (four covers)

June 16 Bill O'Reilly of *The O'Reilly Factor*

June 23 Ming-Na, Michael Michele, Alex Kingston, Maura Tierney and Laura Innes of *ER*

June 30 Jerry Seinfeld

July 7 *Passions* (two covers):
Juliet Mills, Galen Gering and McKenzie Westmore
McKenzie Westmore, Galen Gering and Juliet Mills

July 14 Julianna Margulies in *The Mists of Avalon*

July 21 *Rugrats* (four covers):
Angelica
Chuckie
Lil and Phil
Tommy

July 28 *Planet of the Apes* (three covers):
Tim Roth
Mark Wahlberg
Estella Warren

August 4 *That '70s Show* (five covers):
Danny Masterson
Ashton Kutcher
Mila Kunis
Topher Grace
Laura Prepon

August 11 "Young Hollywood in Love": Justin Timberlake and Britney Spears, Sarah Michelle Gellar and Freddie Prinze Jr., Jessica Alba and Michael Weatherly and Katie Holmes and Chris Klein

August 18 Kelly Ripa of *Live With Regis and Kelly* and *All My Children*

August 25 *Enterprise* (three covers):
Jolene Blalock and Scott Bakula
Scott Bakula
Jolene Blalock

September 1 NFL Preview

September 8 Returning Favorites: Calista Flockhart of *Ally McBeal*, Rob Lowe of *The West Wing*, Sarah Michelle Gellar of *Buffy the Vampire Slayer*, Billy Campbell of *Once and Again*, Chi McBride of *Boston Public* and Amy Brenneman of *Judging Amy*

September 15 Fall Preview: Jill Hennessy of *Crossing Jordan*, Kim Delaney of *Philly* and Jennifer Garner of *Alias*

September 22 Tom Hanks and Frank John Hughes, Damian Lewis, Ron Livingston and Scott Grimes in *Band of Brothers*

September 29 "Terror Hits Home"

October 6 *Survivor: Africa* (18 covers):
Carl Bilancione
Clarence Black
Diane Ogden
Ethan Zohn
Frank Garrison
Jessie Camacho
Kelly Goldsmith
Kim Johnson
Kim Powers
Lex Van den Berghe
Linda Spencer
Lindsey Richter
Silas Gaither
Teresa Cooper
Tom Buchanan
Brandon Quinton
Samburu Tribe
Boran Tribe

October 13 *I Love Lucy* (eight covers)

October 20 Jessica Alba and Michael Weatherly of *Dark Angel*

October 27 *Harry Potter and the Sorcerer's Stone* (four covers):
Daniel Radcliffe
Emma Watson
Rupert Grint
Robbie Coltrane

November 3 Elisha Cuthbert, Kiefer Sutherland and Dennis Haysbert of *24*

November 10 Michael Jackson (two covers)

November 17 Jennifer Aniston and David Schwimmer of *Friends*

November 24 R2-D2

December 1 The Rock

December 8 *Smallville* (four covers):
Superman
Tom Welling
Kristin Kreuk
Michael Rosenbaum

December 15 *The Lord of the Rings* (four covers):
Orlando Bloom and Cate Blanchett
Liv Tyler and Viggo Mortensen
Ian McKellan
Sean Astin, Elijah Woods, Billy Boyd and Dominic Monaghan

December 22 "The American Spirit" (five covers):
American flag by Al Hirschfeld
American flag by Peter Max
American flag by R.A. Miller
American flag by Beata Rubin, age 7
American flag by Jamie Wyeth

December 29 "Tribute 2001": George Harrison, Jack Lemmon and Dale Evans

2002

January 5 Carol Burnett, Tim Conway, Harvey Korman and Vicki Lawrence of *The Carol Burnett Show*

January 12 *Today* (three covers):
Dave Garroway
Hugh Downs and Barbara Walters
Katie Couric and Matt Lauer

January 19 Harrison Ford

January 26 Stephen King's *Rose Red*

February 2 Bernie Mac of *The Bernie Mac Show*

February 9 The Olympics: Michelle Kwan

February 16 NASCAR (two covers):
Dale Earnhardt
Dale Earnhardt Jr.

February 23 William Petersen and Marg Helgenberger of *CSI: Crime Scene Investigation*

March 2 Charlie Sheen of *Spin City* and Martin Sheen of *The West Wing*

March 9 "2002 TV's MVPs" (four covers):
Tina Fey of *Saturday Night Live*, Cynthia Nixon of *Sex and the City* and Esai Morales of *NYPD Blue*
Allison Janney of *The West Wing*, Peter Krause of *Six Feet Under* and Patricia Heaton of *Everybody Loves Raymond*
Chi McBride of *Boston Public*, Maura Tierney of *ER* and Bryan Cranston of *Malcolm in the Middle*
Dan Rather of the *The CBS Evening News*, Tom Brokaw of *NBC Nightly News* and Peter Jennings of *ABC's World News Tonight*

March 16 Christopher Masterson, Justin Berfield, Erik Per Sullivan and Frankie Muniz of *Malcolm in the Middle*

March 23 The Oscars: Russell Crowe, Halle Berry, Marisa Tomei and Ethan Hawke

March 30 Celine Dion

April 6 "TV GUIDE's 50th Anniversary: TV We'll Always Remember": Ed Sullivan with the Beatles; Kermit the Frog; Carol Burnett; Danny Thomas; Michael Landon, Dan Blocker, Lorne Greene and Pernell Roberts of *Bonanza*; Neil Armstrong; Elvis Presley; John F. Kennedy; Howdy Doody; Jerry Seinfeld; Jackie Gleason; Valerie Harper; and Jean Stapleton and Carroll O'Connor of *All in the Family*

PHOTOGRAPHY CREDITS

Pages 12-13, WARNER BROS. CARTOONS (both): "What's Opera, Doc?", Looney Tunes characters, names and all related indicia are trademarks of Warner Bros. © 2002; Page 17, LASSIE: Zinn Arthur; Page 20, MARY TYLER MOORE: MTM; Page 21, MARY TYLER MOORE (top left): CBS Photo Archive; Page 23, BOB NEWHART: CBS Photo Archive; Page 25, AMERICAN BANDSTAND (top): ABC Photography Archives; (bottom): Curt Gunther; Page 26, LORETTA YOUNG: Elmer W. Holloway/NBC; Page 27, JACK BENNY: George E. Joseph; Pages 28-29, YOUR SHOW OF SHOWS: NBC; Page 30, FANTASY ISLAND: ABC Photography Archives; LOVE BOAT (both): Jim McHugh; Page 31, SATURDAY NIGHT LIVE (top left and bottom left): NBC; (top right): Al Levine/NBC; (bottom right and bottom center): Edie Baskin Studios; Page 33, SATURDAY NIGHT LIVE: Edie Baskin Studios; Page 35, NFL: Walter Iooss Jr./SI; Page 36, NASCAR (top): AP/Wide World; (bottom): Robert Laberge/Getty Images; Page 37, WIDE WORLD OF SPORTS: ABC Photography Archives; Page 42, SIMPSONS: TM and © 20th Century Fox Film Corp. All rights reserved; Page 44, BULLWINKLE SHOW: TM & © Ward Productions Inc.; Page 46, MASTERPIECE THEATRE (left): Eric Roth for WGBH Boston; (right): BBC Picture Archives; Page 47, MASTERPIECE THEATRE (left): BBC Picture Archives; (right): Granada; Page 49, GUNSMOKE: Zinn Arthur; Page 50, BONANZA: NBC; Page 51, DINAH SHORE: NBC; Pages 52-53, ED SULLIVAN (all): CBS Photo Archive; Pages 54-55, SOPRANOS (both): Photographs from "The Sopranos®" courtesy of HBO®; Page 58, TODAY: NBC; Page 59, TODAY (top): Sarah Friedman/Corbis Outline; (middle right): NBC/Media Village; (bottom): Lisa Berg/NBC News Today; Page 61, MISTER ROGERS: Family Communication TV; Page 63, PRICE IS RIGHT (top): ABC Photography Archives; (bottom): CBS Photo Archive; Page 64, JEOPARDY!: Jeopardy! Productions, Inc./Steve Crise; Page 68, FRENCH CHEF: A La Carte Communications; Page 69, MARTHA STEWART: Victoria Pearson/Martha Stewart Living Omnimedia; Page 70, GONG SHOW: Gene Trindl; Page 71, TABLOID TV: Todd Buchanan/Newsmakers; Page 72, OPRAH WINFREY (top): © 1996 Harpo Productions, Inc./George Burns; (bottom): © 1997 Harpo Productions, Inc./George Burns; Page 73, OPRAH WINFREY: © 2000 Harpo Productions, Inc./George Burns; Page 76, MTV: C. Taylor Crothers; Page 77, MICKEY MOUSE CLUB: Walt Disney Television/ABC Photography Archive; Page 79, AFTERSCHOOL SPECIALS: ABC Photography Archive; Page 80, GENERAL HOSPITAL: Erik Hein/ABC Photography Archive; Page 81, PRINCE CHARLES AND LADY DIANA: Wally McNamee/Corbis; Page 82, ALL MY CHILDREN: ABC Photography Archive; Page 84, JOHN F. KENNEDY: Bob Jackson/Library of Congress; Page 85, JOHN F. KENNEDY (top): Library of Congress; (bottom): Cecil Stoughton/Library of Congress; Page 86, O.J. SIMPSON: 1994 Branimir Kvartuc/ZUMA Press; Page 87, CHALLENGER: Corbis; Page 88, SEPTEMBER 11: AP/Wide World; Page 92, EDWARD R. MURROW (both): CBS Photo Archive; Page 93, WALTER CRONKITE (both): CBS Photo Archive; Page 94, CNN/GULF WAR: AP/Wide World; Page 97, KENNEDY-NIXON (bottom): Corbis; (top left and right): Bettmann/Corbis; Page 102, LUCILLE BALL: John Engstead/MPTV; Page 103, LUCILLE BALL (all): CBS Photo Archive; Page 104, HAPPY DAYS: Carl Furuta; Page 107, BRADY BUNCH: Gene Trindl; Page 108, SURVIVOR: Monty Brinton/CBS Photo Archive; Page 109, GILLIGAN'S ISLAND: Gene Stein; Page 110, TWENTY ONE: NBC; Page 113, WHO WANTS TO BE A MILLIONAIRE: Maria Melin/ABC Photography Archive; Page 114, ADDAMS FAMILY: ABC Photography Archive; BRADY BUNCH: Bud Gray/MPTV; FAMILY TIES: Ken Whitmore/MPTV; COSBY SHOW: Mario Casilli/MPTV; Page 115, LEAVE IT TO BEAVER: 1991 Universal Studios Inc.; BEVERLY HILLBILLIES: CBS Photo Archive; SIMPSONS: TM & © 20th Century Fox Film Corp. All rights reserved; Page 118, FLINTSTONES: Hanna Barbera; Page 119, EVERYBODY LOVES RAYMOND: Darryl Tooley; Page 123, PERRY MASON: Gene Trindl; Page 124, FUGITIVE: ABC Photography Archive; Page 126, DRAGNET: NBC; Page 130, WALTONS: Albert Watson; Page 131, LITTLE HOUSE ON THE PRAIRIE: NBC; Page 132, BRIAN'S SONG (both): ABC Photography Archive; Page 133, PLAYHOUSE 90: CBS Photo Archive; Page 135, BRIDESHEAD REVISITED: Granada; Page 136,

HALLMARK HALL OF FAME: Bob Greene/CBS Photo Archive; Pages 136-137, ROOTS: ABC Photography Archives; Page 140, ELVIS: NBC; Page 142, CHARLIE'S ANGELS: ABC Photography Archive; Page 143, BAYWATCH: All American TV; Page 144, DALLAS: Warner Bros.; Page 145, DYNASTY: ABC Photography Archive; Page 147, TWIN PEAKS: ABC Photography Archive; Page 148, BEWITCHED: ABC Photography Archive; Page 149, BUFFY THE VAMPIRE SLAYER: Warner Bros.; Page 150, TWILIGHT ZONE (left): Julian Wasser/Getty Images; Page 153, STAR TREK/NEXT GENERATION: Paramount; Page 154, LONE RANGER, ADVENTURES OF RIN TIN TIN, LANCELOT LINK and BARETTA: ABC Photography Archive; FLIPPER: NBC; Page 155, PEOPLE'S CHOICE: NBC; MY THREE SONS: Long Photography, Inc.; JETSONS: Hanna Barbera; DAKTARI: Gunther/MPTV; GENTLE BEN: Allan Gould; CROCODILE HUNTER: Discovery; Page 156, AMERICAN FAMILY: Courtesy Thirteen/WNET New York; Page 157, OSBOURNES: Stewart Volland; Page 159, ADDAMS FAMILY: ABC Photography Archive; Page 162, ODD COUPLE: ABC Photography Archive; Page 163, BEAVIS AND BUTT-HEAD: Used with permission by MTV: Music Television; Page 164, SOUTH PARK: Comedy Central; Page 166, CANNON: Marv Newton/MPTV; Page 167, STARSKY AND HUTCH: ABC Photography Archive; MACGYVER: ABC Photography Archive; QUINCY: Gene Trindl/MPTV; POLICE SQUAD: ABC Photography Archive; WISEGUY: CBS Photo Archive; POIROT: LWT; PRIME SUSPECT: John Timbers Studio London; Page 171, SONNY AND CHER: CBS Photo Archive; Page 172, ERNIE KOVACS: CBS Photo Archive; Page 174, LAUGH-IN (top): Ed Thrasher/MPTV; (middle and bottom): Douglas Jones/Look Magazine Collection, Library of Congress; Page 175, IN LIVING COLOR (top left and bottom right): Nicola Goode/20th Century Fox Film Corp.; (top right and bottom left): 20th Century Fox Film Corp.; Page 176, MILTON BERLE: NBC; Page 177, CAROL BURNETT: Ken Whitmore/MPTV; Page 180, ROLLER DERBY: ABC Photography Archive; Page 181, MONDAY NIGHT FOOTBALL: Ben Weaver; Page 183, WRESTLING: Globe Photos; Page 184, A-TEAM: Gene Trindl/MPTV; Page 187, ADVENTURES OF SUPERMAN: ABC Photography Archive; Page 188, NBA: Fernando Medina/NBAE/Getty Images; Page 189, MAJOR LEAGUE BASEBALL: AP/Wide World; Page 190, HILL STREET BLUES: Paramount; Page 192, LAW & ORDER: Al Levine/MPTV, Page 193, ER: Warner Bros., Page 194, ST. ELSEWHERE: Gene Trindl/MPTV; Page 195, M*A*S*H: 20th Century Fox Film Corp.; Page 202, PATTY DUKE: ABC Photography Archive; Page 203, MY SO-CALLED LIFE: ABC Photography Archive; Page 204, CHEERS: Paramount; Page 205, FRIENDS: Dann Feld/Warner Bros.; Page 208, 77 SUNSET STRIP: ABC Photography Archive; CAR 54, WHERE ARE YOU?: NBC; ADAM-12: NBC; SCOOBY-DOO: ABC Photography Archive; PARTRIDGE FAMILY: ABC Photography Archive; Page 209, GIDGET: ABC Photography Archive; DUKES OF HAZZARD: CBS Photo Archive; Page 211, BARNEY MILLER: ABC Photography Archive; Page 212, LARRY SANDERS: Darryl Estrine; Page 213, FRASIER: Paramount; Page 215, BOB HOPE: Jack Albin; Page 217, MARRIED...WITH CHILDREN: Tony Costa; Page 221, THIRTY-SOMETHING: ABC Photography Archive; Page 223, COPS: Brian Davis/20th Century Fox Film Corp.; Page 225, COLUMBO: ABC Photography Archives; Page 231, ROSEANNE: ABC Photography Archive; Page 232, HONEYMOONERS (left): Arthur Rothstein/Look Magazine Collection, Library of Congress; (top right and bottom right): CBS Photo Archive; Page 233, HONEYMOONERS: Lester Glassner/CBS Photo Archive; Page 234, SEX AND THE CITY: Photograph from "Sex and the City®" courtesy of HBO®; Page 235, SEINFELD: Gino Mifsud/Castle Rock; Page 238, STAR TREK: Paramount; Page 239, APOLLO 11: NASA; Page 242, TONIGHT SHOW/JOHNNY CARSON: NBC; Page 243, TONIGHT SHOW/JOHNNY CARSON (top left, top right and bottom right): NBC; (bottom left): Gene Arias/NBC; Page 244, TONIGHT SHOW/STEVE ALLEN: NBC; TONIGHT SHOW/JACK PAAR: NBC; Page 247, DICK CAVETT: Christopher Little; Page 248, NIGHTLINE: ABC Photography Archive; Page 249, SPORTSCENTER: Danny Clinch; Page 250, DAVID LETTERMAN (middle left): R.M. Lewis Jr./NBC; (top right and bottom right): Alan Singer/CBS Photo Archive; (bottom left): Patrick Pagnano/CBS Photo Archive; Page 251, DAVID LETTERMAN: Alan Singer/CBS Photo Archive; Page 252, AFTERWORD: Paramount

THIS BOOK WAS PRODUCED BY
MELCHER MEDIA, INC.
55 VANDAM STREET, NEW YORK, NY 10013

PUBLISHER
Charles Melcher

EDITOR-IN-CHIEF
Duncan Bock

ASSOCIATE PUBLISHER
Jessica Marshall

PROJECT EDITOR
April P. Bernard

DESIGN
Helicopter

PHOTOGRAPHY EDITOR
Gwen Smith

TV GUIDE SENIOR EDITOR
Beth Arky

EDITOR-AT-LARGE
David S. Cashion

TEXT EDITOR
Tim Moss

DIRECTOR OF PRODUCTION
Carolyn Clark

EDITORIAL ASSISTANTS
Andrew Ackermann,
Anne Gardiner and Max Levine

MELCHER MEDIA WOULD LIKE TO THANK
Jenny Frost, Kristin Kiser and Steve Ross at Crown; Helene Curley,
Michael Fell, Jay Gissen, Hazel Hammond, Amanda Kelley, Lori Bishop Murphy,
Steven Reddicliffe and Nancy Schwartz at TV GUIDE; Gerana Barbosa,
Mike Blaxill, Laura Ciechanowski, Kevin Ford, David Georgi, Sue Hostetler,
Bruce Kluger; Marcy Lovitch, John Meils, Allison Murray, Anne Newgarden,
Amy Pastan, Lia Ronnen, Brooke Showell, Patti Wilson, Megan Worman
and Giulia Zarr.

TV GUIDE WOULD LIKE TO THANK
Max Alexander, Diane Clehane, Hilary de Vries, Frank DeCaro, Robin Honig, Ted Johnson,
Shawna Malcom, Mark Nollinger, Joe Rhodes, Ileane Rudolph, Janet Weeks and Tim Williams.

ABOUT THE CONTRIBUTORS
MARK LASSWELL is a writer and editor who lives in New York City. His articles have
appeared in publications including *New York* magazine, the *Wall Street Journal*
and TV GUIDE, where he is a frequent contributor.

HELICOPTER is partners Ethan Trask and Joshua Liberson,
a design studio based in New York City.

MELCHER MEDIA is an award-winning book producer, based in New York City.

Look for the new TV GUIDE compact disc,
TV GUIDE'S 50 Greatest TV Themes.
From *I Love Lucy* to *Cheers* to *Friends,*
this is a celebration of the top TV
theme songs from each of the last 50 years.
AVAILABLE EVERYWHERE FROM TVT RECORDS

OR ONLINE AT SHOP.TVGUIDE.COM.

Published by Crown Publishers, New York, New York.
Member of the Crown Publishing Group, a division of Random House, Inc.
www.randomhouse.com

CROWN is a trademark and the Crown colophon is a registered
trademark of Random House, Inc.

TV GUIDE and design are trademarks of TV GUIDE Magazine Group,
Inc. in the United States. In Canada TV GUIDE and the TV GUIDE logo are
trademarks of Transcontinental Media Inc. and used under license.

Produced by Melcher Media, Inc.

Printed in China

Library of Congress Cataloging-in-Publication Data is available on request.

ISBN 1-4000-4685-8

10 9 8 7 6 5 4 3 2 1

First Edition